B000936

RENEWALS 458-4574
DATE DUE

PARTY/POLITICS

TRANSGRESSING BOUNDARIES
Studies in Black Politics and Black Communities
Cathy Cohen and Fredrick Harris, Series Editors

The Politics of Public Housing: Black Women's Struggles against Urban Inequality
RHONDA Y. WILLIAMS

Keepin' It Real: School Success beyond Black and White
PRUDENCE L. CARTER

Double Trouble: Black Mayors, Black Communities, and the Call for a Deep Democracy
J. PHILLIP THOMPSON, III

Party/Politics: Horizons in Black Political Thought
MICHAEL HANCHARD

PARTY/POLITICS
Horizons in Black Political Thought
MICHAEL HANCHARD

2006

OXFORD
UNIVERSITY PRESS

Oxford   New York
Auckland   Bangkok   Buenos Aires   Cape Town   Chennai
Dar es Salaam   Delhi   Hong Kong   Istanbul   Karachi   Kolkata
Kuala Lumpur   Madrid   Melbourne   Mexico City   Mumbai   Nairobi
São Paulo   Shanghai   Taipei   Tokyo   Toronto

Copyright © 2006 by Oxford University Press, Inc.

Published by Oxford University Press, Inc.
198 Madison Avenue, New York, New York 10016

www.oup.com

Oxford is a registered trademark of Oxford University Press

All rights reserved. No part of this publication may be reproduced,
stored in a retrieval system, or transmitted, in any form or by any means,
electronic, mechanical, photocopying, recording, or otherwise,
without the prior permission of Oxford University Press.

Library of Congress Cataloging-in-Publication Data
Hanchard, Michael George.
Party/politics: new horizons in black political thought / Michael Hanchard.
p. cm.—(Transgressing boundaries)
ISBN-13 978-0-19-517624-7
ISBN 0-19-517624-3
1. Blacks—Politics and government.   I. Title.   II. Series
DT16.5.H36 2006
306.2089'96081—dc22   2005027724

9 8 7 6 5 4 3 2 1
Printed in the United States of America
on acid-free paper

In Memoriam
Hamilton Cardoso, Vanderlei José María, Lelia González,
purveyors of Afromodern politics, and, in the Orwellian sense
of the term, true patriots

ACKNOWLEDGMENTS

Sometimes detours prove so interesting and satisfying that it matters not whether one arrives at the originally intended destination. I hope that readers will find aspects of this particular detour interesting and satisfying on its own terms. While waiting for state archival materials from various former governments so that I might complete a comparative book project on the relationship between transnational black politics and modernity, Michael Dawson and Danny Dawson (no relation) encouraged me to write a shorter book based on concepts, theoretical propositions, and themes that emerged in several conversations I had had with each of them over the past ten years. Those discussions—which took place in New York, Cambridge, Massachusetts, and Chicago in the United States; Rio de Janeiro, Brazil; and Naples and Bellagio, Italy—concerned matters of cultural and political agency in practices ranging from the Haitian Revolution; black nationalisms and feminisms; all-black political parties; the Nation of Islam; black Marxism; the role of black athletes and artists, ranging from *capoeiristas*, boxers, and basketball players to singers, sculptors, musicians, and novelists; Western imperium; and the discourses of modernity.

The fact that Michael Dawson is a political scientist, and Danny Dawson a cultural historian, certainly influenced the contours, substance, and objects of our discussions. Those conversations served as a rough-hewn template for the theoretical and conceptual aims of *Party/Politics*. The choice of which topics to write about—and how to write about them—was entirely my own. I would first like to thank both of them for their steady encouragement and nourishment of my intellectual life over the past ten years, and for their continued friendship.

Other conversations and excursions along the way also helped me develop the concepts and led to several objects of analysis I chose for some purpose in this book. As I waited for the usual admittances and denials of requests for governmental information, Nancy Randall, then my research assistant and a Northwestern University undergraduate, began developing a reference list, transcribing my lecture notes and other musings in the earliest stages of this project's development. Peter Fenves, of the German Department of Northwestern University, first introduced me to the writings of Heinrich Von Kleist, and encouraged me to undertake the comparison with E. L. Doctorow's *Ragtime*. His periodic query, "Have you finished your short book yet?" over the past two years spurred me on in ways that would not be immediately apparent to him, but for which I am very grateful.

Linda Zerilli, a dear colleague in my department, helped guide me through the vast literature in political theory on notions and concepts of politics, the political, and political community, that helped expand and complicate my own understanding of not just black politics, but all forms and distinctions of politics. For her insights, friendship, and encouragement, I am also extremely grateful. Robert Gooding-Williams, Richard Iton, and Barnor Hesse each provided critical engagement with my ideas, if not the manuscript itself, at the crucial early and final stages of the manuscript's development.

The Rockefeller Foundation residential fellowship program for scholars on Lake Como in Lombardy, Italy, provided an ideal setting for undisturbed reading, writing, and reflection. The staff of the Bellagio Conference Center, particularly Gianna Celli, the former managing director, and Elena Ongania, receptionist, were spontaneously resourceful and generous with their time and resources to make my stay at Bellagio a pleasant and productive one. Students of my 2003 graduate course on black political thought probed my lectures and assigned readings in ways that helped illuminate the conceptual and theoretical issues of black politics. Class discussions provided the rare opportunity to explore black politics not as a set of empirical problems or isolated cases, but as links to specific phenomena and texts to wider debates in the humanities and the social sciences about modernity, identity and identification, nationalism, fascism, democracy and, ultimately, politics itself.

Readers such as Lisa Weeden provided the most careful, critical reading of an earlier draft of the entire manuscript, which led to significant improvements. Mark Sawyer, Charles Hale Jr., and Michael Dawson read and offered useful suggestions about several chapters. Shannan Mattiace, Emma Cervone, Peter Fenves, Jan French, Irene Kacandes, David Schoenbrun, Amalia Pallares, Eddie Telles, Miguel Vatter, and Linda Zerilli provided helpful comments on individual chapters, and Doug McAdam gave useful insights about my conceptualization of the ethics of aversion in chapter 3. Tejumola Olaniyan provided me with an opportunity to present an earlier version of chapter 2, a theory of quotidian politics, to his workshop at the University of Wisconsin, Madison. I am grateful for his spirited engagement with my work. Alice Furomoto Dawson helped transform crude drawings into intelligible models and charts, particularly the continuum of quotidian politics in chapter 2 and the black critical perspectives chart in chapter 3. Graduate student Kendra Koivu transformed a rough outline of the model in chapter 8 into a coherent model.

Ella Myers, a graduate student in the political theory program of my department, provided invaluable editorial assistance, a critical eye for rough spots in the chapter-by-chapter argumentation, as well as detailed engagement with the overall statement I seek to make with this book. Like many superb graduate students, she also served as a key interlocutor. Although I paid her handsomely for her work (no kidding), her careful, competent attention to my manuscript, in addition to her wit and laughter, was incalculable in monetary terms. Rupal Vora, another Northwestern University undergraduate, helped in the execution of the model in chapters 4 and 8, tracked down missing and incomplete references, and helped with most of the final touches that transform a manuscript into a book. Thanks to both.

Dedi Felman and Laura Lewis were first-rate editors, providing tough love when necessary. Thanks also to Cathy Cohen and Fred Harris for encouraging me to publish in their "Transcending Boundaries" series.

Then there are those whose presence in my life at times buoyed, perplexed, humbled, and inspired me. Jenna, my teenage daughter, provided the energy and sense of conviction that only a teenager can bring, and a daughter's love that makes a middle-aged father feel special, if only for a moment. Nancy Tartt has been an excellent co-parent, helping me navigate the wilderness of our daughter's adolescence.

My son Mattias has already revolutionized my life, providing many moments of joy during sleepless nights and exhausting days. My companion Emma Cervone has been a constant source of strength, insight, love, and support, and is a soldier in the best sense of the term. Gregory Walker Sr. has taught me the art of relaxation, for which I am forever grateful. Eddie Davis and my Brazilian brother Julio Cesar Tavares constantly remind me through their respective arts and conversations that nimbleness and agility are states of mind and spirit. The Three Degrees Global crew, particularly Felix Cuevas (DJ FLX), Pritti Ghandi, and Julius Spates (The Mad Thinker) are to be lauded for generously sharing their Wednesday and Sunday night spaces with me, enabling their house music to become my home as well.

CONTENTS

1 Introduction 3

Part I **Politics and Form**

2 A Theory of Quotidian Politics 25

3 Ideology and Political Culture in Black
 Michael Hanchard and Michael Dawson 68

4 Between Confrontation and Acquiescence:
 An Ethics of Aversion 103

Part II **Politics in Fact and Fiction**

5 Black Public Intellectuals and Civil Society
 in Comparative Perspective 133

6 Kohlhaas/Coalhouse
 Race, Foreigners, and States of Exception 154

Part III **Hemispheric Perspectives/Black Internationalism**

7 Garnet's Dictum, the Color Line, and Mixed Race:
 Notes on Hybridity and Miscegenation 183

8 Conclusion: Which Community? 223

Notes 265

References 297

Index 319

PARTY/POLITICS

CHAPTER 1

Introduction

The romantic cult of the self is a form of complacency, an idolatry; the reintroduction of the subject is the reinsertion of subjectivity . . . and of liberty into politics.[1]

Aims

The impetus for this book and its conceptual core emerged from a series of conversations with the late Vanderlei José Mariá, a member of the Workers' Party (PT) in Brazil and one of the founding members of its black nucleus (Nucleo Negro), in 1988. Vanderlei was one of my first contacts in São Paulo during the early stages of research for my dissertation and subsequent book on black social movements in Rio de Janeiro and São Paulo. Vanderlei was considered one of the Workers' Party's most promising young intellectuals during the mid-1980s. As the Brazilian military slowly, reluctantly moved Brazilian society toward popular, democratic governance, the Workers' Party had become a significant political force in Brazilian politics and political culture, led by the eventual president of the republic, Luis Ignacio Lula da Silva.

During our third or fourth conversation, Vanderlei expressed an unusual hope and vision for a melding of the interests of the black movement with those of the PT, helping to transform the PT into a party in both senses of the term—party as an expression of festivity and party as a form of political mobilization, organization, and discipline. "Since the black community's religion, culture, dance and energy have been used for everything else in this country, it might as well be utilized for its own, and the country's transformation," I recall him saying. He then made a vague reference to Lenin's advocacy of the dual sense of party in the Russian Revolution as the inspiration for his idea. Party's dual meaning, as both festivity and hedonism, replete with rituals of play and insubordination, as well as discipline, regimentation, and a quest for political power, would be contained within a singular political and cultural formation.

The idea jarred me on several levels. Vanderlei often discussed the disjuncture between Afro-Brazilian representation in popular culture (in religion, dance, sports, and as symbols of national eros) and their relative lack of representation in the "commanding heights" of the economy and polity. He was one of several black and brown members of the Workers' Party nucleus who combined an experiential knowledge of Afro-Brazilian practices—often defined as cultural—with an understanding of Marxism, Leninism, and anticolonial literatures during the period of African independence, to create a distinct vision of black-left internationalism from the vantage point of Brazilian politics.

When I inquired as to why he believed in the need for such a party to attract black and brown Brazilians specifically, particularly when race and racial identification had rarely been mentioned in Brazilian politics until the 1980s, Vanderlei replied, "Because that's how black and brown Brazilians conceive most expressions of politics, that's where they believe politics are. And the Workers' Party has to become more relevant to this population and its economic and social needs if it is ever going to win national elections."

The more I thought about the implications of Vanderlei's assertion, the more I grew convinced that his perspectives of Afro-Brazilian politics for *a comunidade negra* had wider implications for black politics and life-worlds in various nation-states. Like U.S. African Americans, Jamaicans, Black British, or Afro-Colombians, Afro-Brazilians were political actors as well as descendants of slaves, participating in forms of modern politics that were not of their own creation. Could a single political party represent the political and normative interests of black and brown Brazilians across the divides of class, religion, gender, ideology, as well as many other possible points of community and distinction within a group of people defined in "racial" terms? Could such a political party address national as well as black community concerns simultaneously?

Vanderlei, felled by AIDS in 1989, never got the opportunity to fully appreciate the prescience of his deceptively simple assertion. The Workers' Party leader did finally gain the presidency, in no small part through the efforts of a coalition of black militants, environmentalists, unions, intellectuals, and large segments of Brazilian society, to alter the direction and discourse of a party that often took its primary political and ideological cues from the European left. Even before the victory of the Workers' Party, however, black militants and professional politicians in the cabinets of Fernando Henrique Cardoso were instrumental in placing issues of racial discrimination and affirmative action on the national political agenda.

Vanderlei's insight encapsulates at least one key problem in thinking about the tensions between political and cultural articulation within transnational black politics, not only in Brazil. His fusion of the duality of party was motivated by a cluster of ideas, norms, and beliefs that constituted a politics, and that politics informed his call for a political organization that could house both Afro-Brazilian cultural expression and a program and policy of societal transformation and maintenance. This perspective, like virtually all political ideologies, harbors normative assumptions about how the world *should* look. Like most political actors in social movements that undergo transformation into a political party, Vanderlei's normative assumptions also contained a certain amount of what could be characterized as necessary utopianism. Yet this perspective also encompassed a vision of how the world works, and not only a vision of black suffering, the trap of a fixed (and fixated) identity with readily identifiable coordinates. Vanderlei's dream also contained a distinction between a party of and a party for black and brown Brazilians.

For several years I tried to track down Vanderlei's Lenin reference, but couldn't locate its source. The idea, nonetheless, fascinated me, not only for thinking about the relationship between the Workers' Party and Afro-Brazilians, but more generally about the tensions and antinomies between politics and culture in black politics, as well as the operative definitions of politics in black politics and political thought. As I thought more over the years about the conceptual, comparative, and theoretical issues implicit in his vision, my ethnographic observation was transformed into a statement about the tensions between the practices of racial and political solidarity, between concepts of politics and culture, and most important, between competing understandings of politics itself in black political thought. Over time, I came to consider Vanderlei a theorist of politics in some sense, because of his urge to outline and implement a vision of politics and community that merged political and cultural practice. Vanderlei's distinction between politics and culture as separate categories—if not practices—is one of the core preoccupations of this book.

The quest for political community, like politics itself, often entails the imagining of texts, institutions, societies, even people that exist only in the headquarters of the imagination (socialism's "new man" is just one example). As an extension of politics, political communities provide a network of actual affiliations and circumstances that bring together people into circles of commonality, however fleeting. Political community is defined not only by its circle of commonality, by those who express their willing membership, but implicitly by the negation of another community. Imagination, organization, and will, more than rational choice and deliberation, are the foundational, nonprocedural bases of politics.

Political and social theory are not usually brought to bear on the examination of matters of political identity and community involving black subjects.[2] *Party/Politics* is an elaboration on the idea of political community, though not in ways that might be immediately apparent to a student of political theory or philosophy. It is a contribution to social and political theory through the identification and probing of neglected and varied forms of black political thought and agency. A systematic, cross-national project on the history of black political parties and political thinkers is an important and necessary project, but I am less interested in outlining the history of political parties in the black world or a history of black thinkers and intellectual tendencies. The core concern of this book is the sources of political imagination, the disparate sets of ideological forms, norms, and beliefs that inform various modalities of black politics. It is my belief that the sources of black political imagination and the forms of political practice and expression that emerge in part from such imagination are distinctly modern forms, rather than phenomena easily attributed to a postmodern condition.

A few points about terminology here. I use the term "black political thought" as a framing device to enable myself, and readers, to consider how certain political and cultural phenomena, and the theories utilized to explain them, can be applied, revised, or discarded through the consideration of black political and cultural forms. I use the term "black politics" to characterize behaviors, ideals, and ideologies in societies where self-described African-descended populations participate and deliberate over the distribution of resources, modes of inequality, racial identity and identification, and matters of power, justice, and equality.[3] Black politics also involves deliberation over matters of self-representation, citizenship, notions of racial pride and self-hatred, gender and sexuality, and the antinomies of individual and collective action.

The term "black life-worlds" takes its meaning from the work of phenomenologists such as Alfred Schutz[4] and, in an anticipatory and corrective mode, is meant to convey the vast array of identities and identifications associated with black subjectivity that are not reducible to nationality, gender, race, or region. Black life-worlds are constituted by experiential knowledge and the lessons learned from such knowledge, acted out in daily life. Individuals and groups who refer to themselves as Black Peruvian, Black British, Malagasy, or even U.S. African American do not—and could not—have identical cultural or national experiences that make them "black" in the same way. Blackness and black life-worlds encompass two aspects of identity formation: self-ascription and identification, and societal/state definition.[5]

When combined with national and personal affiliations, black life-worlds necessarily contain texts, debates, and cultural and material forms that neither emanate from nor are reducible to those communities. Musical forms, ranging from cumbia to hip-hop, reggae to samba, are some obvious examples of such bricolage. Often neglected in the examination of black life-worlds, however, are the forms of politics in thought and action that display similar combinations of endogenous and exogenous factors. Thus, even the Black Power social movements and ideologies in Jamaica, Mali, Guinea, the United States, or Canada by the late 1960s and early 1970s were not solely "black" undertakings, even if some Black Power advocates have spent a lifetime arguing otherwise. Matters of polity, economy, materialism, community, and culture invariably cropped up in debates, polemics, and community initiatives that forced many Black Power advocates to acknowledge that Black Power could not simply be a matter of being black.

By extending Vanderlei's ideas and ideals into black life-worlds outside of Brazil, *Party/Politics* is also an attempt to better understand the tensions between politics and culture in what is often referred to as the African diaspora, by reminding students of African diaspora and African American studies of the importance of power—as both concept and presence—in the constitution of black communities as well as in their examination. The encounter between literatures of black-life worlds and the theoretical preoccupations of modern and postmodern political theory will enable readers to consider matters of black internationalism, collective action, and agency in a more comparative and global perspective than normally accorded by students outside the fields of African American and African diaspora studies. As an interpretive enterprise, my intentions are to help promote a series of conversations among students of the aforementioned fields and disciplines.

Finally, that which distinguishes the best of black political thought from other modes of critical inquiry is the context in which theory is situated. In contrast with a standpoint-based perspective, which assumes that there is some ontological means by which inquiries into black politics, sociology, and culture are automatically distinguished by the race, gender, or class status of the inquirer, I use the term "situated" as shorthand for the following question: What does contemporary political and social theory look like when viewed from a vantage point of a black life-world? My response to this question, this book, is an entirely personal one, even as it is informed by the history, politics, and culture of several black-life worlds. While my interpretations are situated in a series of experiences, they are also constituted by concerns, texts, and ruminations shared by members of other so-called racial groups and political and cultural communities outside the realm of my immediate experience and reflection.

Like most other modes of political and social thought, the literature of black political thought contains judgments, perspectives and debates about black politics that are not fully encompassed in survey data or clusters of questions concerning a particular topic, candidate or phenomenon of daily life. There is a diversity and complexity to black life in the United States and elsewhere that is often overlooked. The best work in black political thought goes beyond the preoccupation with contemporary attitudes and past histories and attempts to forecast the possible range of dispositions and attitudes, hopes and aspirations for black communities in the future.

Du Bois's now well-worn phrase concerning the "century of the color line" in the *Souls of Black Folk* provides one example of such a projection into the future and its impact upon both social and political thought and daily life. Theorization and speculation about the future is not some obscurantist exercise, but the imperative of the chronicler and charter of ideas in circulation. Neither the survey researcher nor the theorist is a fortune-teller, but theoretical speculation at least enables us to project a range of political possibilities, choices, and consequences arising from shifts in political, economic, and cultural circumstances. Neither the theorist nor the survey researcher has any critical methodological advantage at this juncture. It might be the theorist, through the identification and expression of visions of a better future, who is best prepared to sift through the historical, normative, structural, and ideological factors that congeal in a particular epoch and to understand the causes and motivations of acquiescence, protest, rebellion, and collective action. It is not just the dominant ideas and political practices, but the marginal, the implausible, and the unpopular ideas that also define an age.

The chasm between the "is" and the "ought" that informs much social and political theory also undergirds black political thought. In this sense, prospects for theory exist in the chasm between political roads and avenues not (yet) taken and "reality." One could not have predicted the accelerated urgency of the civil rights movement in the late 1950s, for example, by identifying prevailing attitudes in black and white public opinion, but only by examining the ideas, tactics, and strategies of a group of people whose opinions about the direction of the black liberation struggle were not popularly held.

Some of the major themes shaping black political attitudes and behaviors welled up from political ideals and dispositions in the past that had only a marginal hold on black popular consciousness. The Southern Christian Leadership Conference's philosophy of civil disobedience had few adherents among black church hierarchy in the late 1950s. Marcus Garvey's brand of Pan-Africanism, with its advocacy of self-help and entrepreneurship, was sneered at by many Jamaican, African, and U.S. African American notables in the first half of the twentieth century. The Black Consciousness movement in South Africa, eclipsed in some ways by the African National Congress's nonracialism during the anti-apartheid and immediate post-apartheid era, has returned in the post-Mandela era as many black South Africans find the language of nonracialism politically limiting for asserting collective grievances against ongoing practices and patterns of institutional and noninstitutional racisms.

These three examples suggest that black political thought, like most forms of political thought, often presents a vision of political community or of the world at large that generates little or no support at the moment of its initial presentation. Survey research can track popular opinion to some extent, and track shifts and change in contours of popular opinion over historical time, but it cannot necessarily anticipate or forecast change in popular opinion. Questions, for example, concerning how black political agency in both formal institutional politics and in popular culture might look twenty years from now are as much theoretical matters as challenges for empirical research.

The relationship between politics and culture has long preoccupied political scientists as well as anthropologists. Within political science, the tensions between cultural and political articulation in black public spheres has garnered much less sustained attention. Undergirding any examination of the relationship between politics and culture requires that we consider the questions, "What is politics? What is culture?" For black politics, we must also begin with these questions. Although most of the theoretical discussion in *Party/Politics* is directed toward understanding the boundaries between cultural and political articulation, considerations of theory are also designed to demonstrate that some—though not all—advocates of "hard" model-driven social science scholarship, in deriving definitions of politics through the structure and process of method, neglect certain black political phenomena. Methodological habits affect not only the deliberations and decisions concerning how phenomena should be studied but also whether certain phenomena are studied at all.

The third implication of the debates over methods in relation to black political thought is epistemological, insofar as the neglect or dismissal of certain topics lessens the prospect of studying related, linked topics with which those who specialize in methods may be entirely unfamiliar.[6] We should remember that the rhetoric and practice of politics are rarely if ever in the form of mathematical equations, but in speeches, social conflicts, policies, edicts, and constitutions. The linguist, philosopher, and historian, no less than the political scientist, are also students of politics. As quiet as its kept in certain fields of the discipline, particularly in contemporary "American" politics, the political scientist has always borrowed her or his methods from other disciplines, sometimes within the social sciences, but also from the humanities. Increasingly, the methodological and interpretive "loans" or appropriations from mathematics and economics are considered more legitimate than others.

In much of the black world, the realm of culture provides opportunities and sites for the exercise of politics. As a result, politics often takes on distinct connotations and meanings. Definitions of what constitutes the political are often challenged, reconceptualized, and in some instances, distorted. In the discipline of political science, politics is often reduced to observable behavior and behavior-related phenomena, enabling political scientists to draw generalizable conclusions about the likelihood of particular political behaviors and outcomes in contestations over power and influence, usually in the form of electoral competition. Survey research and game theoretic approaches operate with this assumption. Although more scientific approaches to identifying and analyzing political behavior have their merits, particularly in large N, cross-spatial analyses, what often gets crowded out of the lens of quantitative methodological approaches are matters of ethno-history, context, epistemology, and political imagination.

This book operates with a more expansive definition of the political while simultaneously attempting to demarcate political and nonpolitical boundaries. The examples from literature, social movements, formal politics, and daily life analyzed in *Party/Politics* illustrate forms of identity formation, social and political mobilization, and cultural production across space and time that cannot be wholly accessed by or encompassed in nation-centered, survey-based, or institutional approaches to political phenomena. For this reason, this book has been developed and organized conceptually and theoretically, rather than by "cases," as a means of illuminating the similarities and differences that characterize politics and the political across black life-worlds. Antinomies of cultural and political articulation in black politics nationally and transnationally will enable readers to further delineate types of politics, the distinctions between micro- and macropolitical phenomena, and the conflation of the two in many scholarly accounts of politics and culture in various black life-worlds.

Party/Politics can also be read as an effort to identify and carve out a place for social and political theory in the study of black politics and, conversely, a place for the examination of racial politics in dialogue with now common themes and texts of social and political theory. There are theoretical implications for the practices detailed and described in this book that have not been defined as specifically political, which should have relevance for political and social theorists. There are also empirical implications in the theoretical dimensions of this project, since the analysis here might enable more empirically driven scholars to identify, name, and differentiate forms and types of politics as well as power dynamics, and the distinctions between politics and culture, not only in black politics but in virtually any form of politics.

My approach here is situated between two very different interpretations of the role of cultural practices within political life, not only in methodological terms, but in ideational and conceptual terms as well. Throughout the black world, cultural practices and production have been viewed in terms of and created with the intention of intervening in political discourse and practice, at the level of family, society, state, economy, and polity. Politics, in both its formal and informal modes, creates its own set of structural limitations, related to yet distinct from economic and material constraints. As my assessment of several cross-national debates and phenomena will demonstrate, cultural practice, performance, and production are often presented within and outside black public spheres as intrinsic, even natural to black politics. I seek to interrogate the presumed connection between politics and culture in black politics and culture, and the implications of this presumption for differentiating between forms of politics.

Many positivist understandings of the relationship between politics and culture in the social sciences claim that cultural explanations are limited in their ability to account for how culture affects political, social, or economic change, or, put in positivist terms, are characterized by culture's lack of independent variability.[7] Yet even the more positivist approaches to the study of politics have to acknowledge the empirical fact of dominant political parties or organizations utilizing a range of cultural practices (song, dance, religion, and literature) for the purposes of obtaining, maintaining, or transforming political allegiances—in short, mobilizing and obtaining votes. Positivist understandings of political phenomena and probability notwithstanding, cultural practices and contexts are indispensable to political articulation.

What I hope to demonstrate in *Party/Politics* are the ways in which the study of black politics can provide a window onto considerations of politics, culture, and political community more broadly. The employment of cultural practices in political life offers insights into a larger series of interactions and relationships between the individual and the state, between collective and individuated modes of political identification, and between material conditions and political agency (the "is" and the "ought").

The implications of the politics/culture conundrum extend well beyond the historical and interpretive demarcations of transnational black politics and thought, however, and have comparative implications for many political and cultural phenomena not specific to African and African-descended peoples. The range of scholars involved in epistemological and methodological exploration of the implications of culture for politics includes Raymond Williams in sociology, Marvin Harris's work on cultural materialism, and Aaron Wildavsky and Lloyd Rudolph and Susanne Rudolph in political science.[8] These explorations across ideological and disciplinary divides involve a conception of political culture that largely focuses on (and assumes) a causal relationship between norms and values and political life, mostly in observable political behavior and the mobilization of bias in political institutions. Comprehending the nexus of cultural and political articulation in black transnational, national, and local public spheres requires more analytically rigorous delineation between forms, arenas, and avenues for politics. Understanding the intersections of political and cultural articulation in these spheres, and their enmeshment in the economy and polity requires more nuanced treatment than normally offered by the generic distinctions made between politics and culture.

Each chapter explores the theoretical and conceptual implications of exclusion and discrimination for black politics. In various national societies and black public spheres in various parts of the world, black politics first emerged in the spheres of society not categorized as political. Apartheid and colonialism circumscribed or prohibited outright the full participation of slaves, colonial subjects, and second-class citizens in the polities of Western and Western-dominated societies. Yet these same-excluded people found ways to intervene in or disrupt the formal spheres of the political. Movements such as labor strikes, slave rebellions, marronage, boycotts, clandestine activities, and even forms of violence force us to employ more expansive definitions of the political and of politics.

The history of black protest and resistance outside the formal spheres of Western politics help underscore the manner in which the very distinctions made between the political and the nonpolitical are themselves political constructs. In classical theories of political science and philosophy, however, politics is equated with matters of state and civil society, a restrictive understanding of politics and its presence in human interaction.[9]

The separation of the political from other dimensions of public—and private—life, according to Carl Schmitt, is a consequence of eighteenth and nineteenth century "antitheses and divisions pertaining to the state-society (political against social) contrast"[10] that automatically position religious, cultural, economic, legal, and scientific matters as antitheses of the political. Schmitt's distinction between politics (produced by the state) and the political (the implications of the political emanating from the state) is contestable. Schmitt's key contribution to comprehending the politics/culture conundrum, however, is in identifying the twentieth-century state's increasing incursions into daily life with the rise of liberal individualism and bourgeois democratization in Western nation-states. Once Western European forms of the modern state began to encroach upon the affairs of civil society, the distinction between state and civil society became blurred. Unlike the idealized Hegelian model of the nineteenth-century German state, above and apart from civil society, Schmitt's understanding of the relationship between the state and civil society is more dynamic and intertwined.

Although the state, in Schmitt's view, presupposes politics, its presence in civil society subsequently introduces the political into previously nonpolitical spheres. Schmitt writes, "The substance of the political is contained in the context of a concrete antagonism . . . expressed in everyday language, even where the awareness of the extreme case has been entirely lost."[11] He writes earlier of this transformation: "What had been up to that point affairs of state become thereby social matters, and vice versa, what had been purely social matters become affairs of state—as must necessarily occur in a democratically organized unit. Heretofore ostensibly neutral domains—religion, culture, education, the economy—then cease to be neutral in the sense that they do not pertain to state and politics. In such a state, therefore, everything is at least potentially political, and in referring to that state it is no longer possible to assert for it a specifically political characteristic."[12]

In theorizing a distinct role for politics in the modern world, Schmitt considers illogical the equation of politics with other spheres of life. In other words, if politics is *already* insinuated in all forms of public life in societies where the state is the predominant political unit, then the separation and seeming isolation of cultural, religious, and other dimensions of human existence (as outlined and applauded by several prominent liberal theorists of his day) are undermined and begin to erode:

> The political can derive its energy from the most varied human endeavors, from the religious, economic, moral and other antitheses. It does not describe its own substance, but only the intensity of an association or dissociation of human beings whose motives can be religious, national (in the ethnic or cultural sense) economic, or of another kind, and can effect at different times different coalitions and separations.[13]

Thus, Schmitt rejects such equations as the political = party politics, considering them applicable only in societies where the depoliticization of public life has occurred alongside the erosion of the distinction between state and civil society.[14] Politics is reduced to the dirty, the vulgar and deceitful, pertaining to "deals" shady and otherwise, and is not a constitutive feature of human existence. Politics is ignored in the other dimensions of public life, becoming a phenomenon people can *choose* to avoid. The now shopworn but nonetheless effective rhetorical device employed by many politicians in U.S. political culture—the claim that they are "outsiders" who don't "play politics"—is an example of the object of Schmitt's disdain for the politics = party politics equation. Schmitt's configuration of politics at the core of modern human existence requires a reconceptualization of the culture concept, as noted by Strauss.[15] Schmitt's critique calls into question the notion of culture as a separate realm from politics proper, a view that has permeated even the most seemingly radical and oppositional forms of black cultural politics.

A key theme throughout this book is the role of politics, political communities, and power in the infusion of political intentions into cultural forms. It is my contention that one of the analytic errors often made in studies examining the relationship between politics and culture is to treat culture as a separate sphere from the political, rather than as a separate sphere from the state. As a consequence, a more fundamental understanding of the relationship between politics and culture is often overlooked: politics, power dynamics, and political communities determine, in the first instance, how "culture" first becomes political.

To put this somewhat comically, there are very clear ideological reasons, implicit and explicit, for the absence of song lyrics extolling the virtues of so-called miscegenation in the Third Reich's propaganda archives; for why Al Qaeda's announcements have so far been devoid of hymns encouraging intermarriage between Muslims and U.S. citizens; for why Strom Thurmond or Thomas Jefferson never publicly (though perhaps privately) sang songs or recited poetry praising the virtues of black women; and for why Clarence Thomas, in his critique of U.S. African Americans' alleged dependency on the welfare state, did not note the existence of whites on welfare. The realm commonly referred to as culture, specifically the arts and aesthetic practices as broadly defined in Western societies, is already suffused with the workings of the political. Political perspectives invariably determine how cultural forms are deployed in macropolitics: macropolitics structures the range of possibilities for cultural production in instances where politics, not simply performance and entertainment, is the aim of the mediator. Within the domain of formal politics, particularly the politics of state, the *content* (not the form) of cultural production and performance is determined by political intentions.[16]

Schmitt's mention of "extreme antagonism" refers to the friend/enemy distinction that, for Schmitt, is at the root of all politics. The friend/enemy distinction is useful for thinking about ethnic and racial antagonisms, and the manner in which racial politics operate in a society, often functioning relatively independent (or at least nonderivatively) from state power and authority and from political processes in civil society and public spheres. Given the global phenomena of anti-black racisms, Schmitt's broader claim concerning the friend-enemy distinction as the core characteristic "to which political actions and motives can be reduced"[17] has some applicability to the study of black politics and cultures. Friend/enemy distinctions are often drawn first in society, in conflict and conquest, before being drawn by the state. There is ample statistical evidence and quantitative data on incidents of racist violence toward these populations in places as disparate as Russia, China, Brazil, the United States, the Netherlands, and the European Union, which suggests a much broader theater of anti-black racisms than the stage of the state apparatus. My earlier work on Brazilian racial politics and Afro-Brazilian social movements convinced me of the decreasing analytic utility of racial slavery as an explanatory variable for more contemporary forms of anti-black racism. It is one thing to be a slave, another to be an enemy. Comparative analyses of slave institutions have demonstrated that racial enmity is not a necessary condition of enslavement. Nor is enslavement a prerequisite for racial hatreds. Politics constantly makes and reshapes one of the central antagonisms of the modern era: racial chauvinism.

Book Organization

The chapters are organized in accordance with the three thematic objectives noted above, moving from the most seemingly isolated and individuated modes of political expression in the second chapter to themes and topics of black internationalism in the final chapter. Along the way, the book has a tripartite coherence. The chapters of each section are written and organized in response to a separate theme.

The first section, entitled "Politics and Form" provides a theorization of politics that attempts to account for the full range of possibilities for politics in human interaction, ranging from individuated acts to large-scale collective action. Chapter 2 emphasizes what I have termed "quotidian politics," taking more than a few cues from Henri Lefebvre, C. L. R. James, and Antonio Gramsci, to review and synthesize contemporary readings and debates in the study of black politics on the presence and force of popular culture and what James Scott refers to as "Brechtian" acts of resistance.

Chapter 2 introduces the concepts of micro- and macropolitics, appropriate examples to illuminate their presence and operation, and the concept of *coagulation,* a practice devised and employed to forge circumstantial, incidental alliances between members of subordinate groups, without an overarching theory of resistance to daily acts of domination. The distinction between macro- and micropolitics, and the practice of coagulation are part of a theory of quotidian politics that is partially a response to James Scott's innovative theories of quotidian resistance developed in the books *The Moral Economy of the Peasant* and *Domination and the Arts of Resistance,* in Robin Kelley's application of these theorems in his historiographic accounts of black working-class resistance in the United States, as well as in several other accounts of power and domination.

My theorization of quotidian politics identifies the borders of culture and politics, yet also offers two distinct forms of politics within a broader definition of politics. If matters of cultural and political articulation are distinct and separate, where does culture end and politics begin? How do we distinguish the impact of cultural practices at different levels—community (whether spatially or otherwise defined), nation, region, or state? How do we distinguish types of politics in relation to cultural practices? In what ways are cultural practices, artifacts, and ideational systems inherently political, and political in what ways?

The first type of politics to be defined is macropolitics, the dimension of political life where the powerful are most dominant, and where the expression of politics in its institutional forms is most prevalent. Instruments of formal political contestation such as political parties are one example of a macropolitical form. The second type is the politics of the weak, which is less formal and more, in the words of Antonio Gramsci, "fragmented and episodic," forged in conditions of denial, repression, prohibition, and negative sanction. Macropolitics characterizes politics at the societal level, wherein the distribution of goods, services, resources, and the management and maintenance of specific social units and categories (such as racial classification and distinction) involves the state and its related institutions, and dominant modes of production not only within the state but also within the economy. Most social science scholarship examining African American, African, and other African-descendent populations has focused on the macropolitical implications of race and racism upon the daily lives of these populations, whether within the institutional and bureaucratic processes of apartheid (United States, South Africa, Zimbabwe), colonialism, or multiracial and plural societies. This is politics at its most obvious, conforming to most conventional social science definitions of political life, political movements, and even political apathy.

"Micropolitics" are forms of politics involving more direct, interpersonal modes of interaction. States, institutions, and bureaucracies are abstractions, after all, even as they exact specific structural effects on groups and individuals. Individuated responses to structural constraints of movement (whether in the economy, polity, or civil society) can have macropolitical consequences even if the political behavior does not assume collective form. Protracted conflict between groups can increase the propensity of quasi-collective action. Thus, the behavior of Palestinian youths in the occupied territories or black and Latino youths in major urban areas in the United States responding to incessant police surveillance and violence represent highly personal, idiosyncratic responses to constrictions of Israel and the United States, respectively, and can be viewed as disparate battles at analytic border between micro- and macropolitics.[18] One of my aims in this chapter is to continue to expand dialogue about power dynamics, dominance, subordination, and the now dreaded term, resistance, beyond characterizations of subordinate groups as either complete dupes or recalcitrants par excellence in relation to processes of domination.

Chapter 3, "Ideology and Political Culture in Black," explores the connections and dissonances between political science literature on public opinion and ideology on the one hand, and black ideological forms, social criticism, and social movements on the other, to identify the ways in which the discipline of political science, in its contemporary biases toward positivist methods, restricts and limits our understandings of the contours of black politics and black political cultures. What are some of the ideas, ideals, and norms that motivate people to identify themselves as black subjects and to name something known as white supremacy and concomitantly, Afro-centrism? How might ethnographic, intersubjective, and hermeneutic approaches enable us to better apprehend black political phenomena and perspectives in the polity and public spheres, not just in the United States, but in other national contexts as well? Written with Michael Dawson, this chapter treats ideology as a cluster of ideas, ethics, experiential knowledge, and normatively driven practices that come to constitute a vision of the world that is not only political (engaged with themes and processes of power) but perspectival (how one engages, produces, and acknowledges power). This more multidimensional sense of ideologies has been largely obscured or ignored in contemporary sociology and political science. Despite its neglect, black ideologies continue to inform certain facets of black public opinion. The chapter concludes with one possible alternative method for examining black ideologies in historical, ideational, and social context.

Chapter 4, "Between Confrontation and Acquiescence: An Ethics of Aversion" seeks to chart part of the "middle-range" forms of political articulation theorized in chapter 2 that often go unaccounted for in scholarly accounts of domination, resistance, and acquiescence. The theory of aversion offered in this chapter can be read as an elaboration upon some of the idea-elements, norms, and fully fledged ideological forms identified in chapter 3. The disparate examples of individuals who respond to conditions of racial discrimination with avoidance and aversion provide the most isolated examples of political community and collective consciousness imaginable. This chapter is a theoretical and intuitive statement about the consequences of long-standing patterns of social interaction between dominant and subordinate group members and the possibilities of individual political responses to those patterns by individuals. Subordinate group members, in this case U.S. African Americans of varying class and status backgrounds, engage in strategies and tactics of avoidance regarding dominant group members, reinforcing conditions of extant spatial segregation, but by ethical means. These tactics and strategies also evidence political community even under the most isolated conditions of circumstantial, individual encounters. As alluded to in the first section of this chapter, political communities are defined not only by the expressed allegiances of individual members and collectives, but by what they detest, confront, remain indifferent to—or avoid.

Chapters 5 and 6 constitute section 2 of the book, "Politics in Fact and Fiction." This section explores another dimension of the culture/politics conundrum: the 1990s debates about black public intellectuals in the United States, and in the comparison of two stories. Chapter 5, "Black Public Intellectuals and Civil Society in Comparative Perspective," had a previous incarnation as "Cultural Politics and Black Public Intellectuals." This more recent version places the mid-1990s debates about black public intellectuals within a hemispheric perspective, expanding the contours of its polemics beyond the borders of the United States to make the Americas part of the discussion of what it means to be a public intellectual, black or otherwise. The term "public" is the least examined component of the term "public intellectual." The conflation of "public" with "celebrity" in the polemics about black public intellectuals may tell us more about contemporary politics in the United States than it does about public intellectuals, regardless of their race or color.

Chapter 6, "Kohlhaas/Coalhouse: Race, Foreigners, and States of Exception" charts the space between micro- and macropolitics in literary form, though the comparison of a short story and a novel. There are obvious characterological and political parallels between the Coalhouse Walker character in *Ragtime* and the figure Kohlhaas in Heinrich Von Kleist's short story about a man who ignites a rebellion in the German countryside after a nobleman steals two of his most prized horses. Coalhouse Walker in E. L. Doctorow's *Ragtime* is a prototypical figure of black middle-class politics—a politics of resentment and agitation over the limitations of a bourgeois public sphere of representation, status, and consumption, rather than a vision of a macropolitics revolution that would transform an inherently feudal system of economic relations into a more egalitarian one. Doctorow's ability to make a believable black character out of a sixteenth-century pre-German middle-class trader is not only a feat of novelistic imagination and depiction but also suggestive of the possibilities and analytic advantages of cross-spatial and cross-temporal comparison organized through a concept: the state of exception.

For discussions of power and resistance, the comparison of the two characters also provides an opportunity to revisit concepts of social banditry, primitive rebels as expressions of political imagination, and their transformative practices in socially unjust societies. Both fictional tales provide an opportunity to consider the virtues and limitations of rebellion and resistance steeped in revenge tales and individual notions of justice. Chapter 6 leads the reader toward a broader, cross-national, and transnational view of black politics outlined in chapters 7 and 8.

Chapters 7 and 8 comprise the third and final section of the book, "Hemispheric Perspectives/Black Internationalism." This section threads several strands of black political thought and agency within the fabric of black internationalism. With a few notable exceptions, the global dimensions of black politics are often ignored by scholars of social movements and students of racial politics and nationalism. Transnational black political thought and activism has existed since at least the nineteenth century, allowing for the possibilities of comparison with other movements, political actors, and intellectuals from other causes or parts of the world.

Chapter 7, "Garnet's Dictum, the Color Line, and Mixed Race: Notes on Hybridity and Miscegenation" uses part of a speech by the famous orator and abolitionist, Henry Highland Garnet, to examine some of the similarities between late nineteenth- and early twentieth-century ideologies of racial egalitarianism in the New World and contemporary advocacy of hybridity, or what one scholar refers to as the "amalgamation thesis." In both eras, the culture concept is used as a trump card for the race concept, but, as I shall explain in this chapter, the culture concept is often wrongly identified and utilized in several contemporary, normatively based antidotes for quelling racism through cultural mixture. This chapter uses Garnet's declaration that the Western world is destined to become a "mongrel race" to pose a counterfactual for students of African-American studies, black politics, and African diaspora studies: What if Garnet's dictum, rather than Du Bois's declaration in *The Souls of Black Folk* concerning "the color line," were the dominant trope for the probing of racial identification, categorization, and consciousness? Much of the comparative literature on racial and chromatic categorization in the New World focuses on the seemingly national distinctions and preoccupations with race—as in the United States—as opposed to color in Brazil, Venezuela, or Haiti. What is often neglected in much of the comparative literature is the role of what I have termed "racial valuation" at the normative core of both chromatic and putatively racial categorization.

Chapter 8 concludes the book with an overview of race-first politics throughout the black world, utilizing examples of political parties and cultural organizations on the African continent, Europe, and the New World. As I have formulated elsewhere, black politics in various nation-states of the Caribbean, Africa, and Europe exhibit networks of affiliation linking various black life-worlds and political actors. These networks are often not the result of state-generated activity (particularly in instances where blacks constitute racial minorities), but of independent, nonstate, transnational organization and mobilization. Students of feminism, international labor organizations, and social movements have traced the history and contours of international feminisms, labor movements, as well as forms of international environmentalism, such as the Green Party and anti-nuclear movements. The interactions between these movements and world historical events shifts in the international political economy, and the technological advances of the late twentieth century have fundamentally transformed how macropolitics are conducted in the twenty-first century.

The fall of the last formal apartheid regime, the *herrenvolk* republic of South Africa, was the black world's equivalent of the Berlin wall and the fall of the Eastern bloc. As in the case of cold war politics, transnational black political actors and organizations had to shift their focus away from the political objectives of a previous era—apartheid and civil rights—toward matters of human rights, authoritarianism, AIDS, and a host of other problems disproportionately affecting African and African-derived populations. What does this shift signal for black politics and black political thought? The wholesale collapse of the Soviet experiment motivated reassessments of Marxism from opponents and supporters alike. This chapter explores the unfulfilled dreams and wishes of black internationalism as a means of not only assessing black internationalism's past but also its possible contours in the future. Rather than privilege collective action as the most efficacious means to alter conditions of inequality, this chapter highlights the pitfalls of race and culturally based collective action projects by drawing parallels with twentieth-century Marxist global mobilization.

Chapter 8 is the chapter that most explicitly addresses political community as an underexplored dimension of black transnationalism, synthesizing issues of ideology, micro- and macropolitics, and ethics as discussed in chapters 2 through 6 to argue for more politically sophisticated understandings of black solidarity that can have salience not only for adherents to solidarity-based movements and organizations but also their detractors. Political communities express and convey *sensibilities,* reacting to opposing viewpoints and threatening policies the way most human beings respond to the smell of rancid meat. Politics produces gut-level reactions to conflicts and differences in ways that distinguish human beings from other species. Only humans create and respond to politics the way that other animals respond to vagaries of the flesh, life, and death.

I self-consciously began this introductory chapter with an excerpt of an interview with the late Octavio Paz as a means of distinguishing the individual self from social and political subjectivity. I have utilized personal incidents at the outset of several chapters as inductive devices to map a larger set of issues concerning power, identity, and identification, not for the purpose of autobiography. Ludwig Wittgenstein arrived at the vocation of philosophy through self-reflection about his own lying. W. E. B. Du Bois innovated upon the concept of the veil to understand that most twentieth-century dilemma—the color line—after experiencing personal rejection. Franz Fanon began to interrogate the realities of everyday racism and the derogation of blackness through his encounter with a French child.[19] Although I certainly am not claiming to match the accomplishments of these three individuals, it is this tradition of self-reflection I follow, and, I hope, contribute to the examination of phenomena well beyond my individual self.

The following chapter provides further development of the concepts of micro- and macropolitics, situating them in a continuum of politics, and developing a broader theory of quotidian politics, the politics of daily life. Such politics requires its own theorization because it is often underappreciated and, thus, neglected in accounts of power dynamics and struggles that focus on large-scale revolt, rebellion, and revolution. The themes, concepts, and theoretical account provided in chapter 2 will recur throughout the book as part of my account of black politics and black life-worlds.

PART I
Politics and Form

CHAPTER 2

A Theory of Quotidian Politics

We live in familiar terms with people in our own family, our own milieu, our own class. This constant impression of familiarity makes us think that we know them, that their outlines are defined for us, and that they see themselves as having those same outlines. We define them . . . and we judge them. We can identify with them or exclude them from our world. But the familiar is not necessarily the known.[1]

You don't know me.[2]

Introduction: Another Theory of Power?

By the first two decades of the twentieth century, the emergence of the modern state and its related bureaucratic, administrative, and coercive forms prompted social scientists, practicing politicians, economists, and intellectuals within Marxist traditions in the West to call for the development of a science of politics, a discipline for the examination of political phenomena and the interrelated theories, histories, and philosophical perspectives. The rise of the state as the dominant unit of political recognition and sovereignty in the West and its increasing role in the organization, production, and reproduction of political life also led to the seeming coincidence of all politics with the state, since the object of most political actors, with the exception of anarchists, was to seize state power, whether through legal or illegal means.

Interpretations of the importance of the state in modern societies were as varied as its observers. Much conservative and liberal theory and philosophy attributed most if not all of politics to the state, not only for the constitution of the individual subject, but for the participation of the individual subject in political society. The libertarian view of the state as an encumbrance upon capital and human freedom was advanced most forcefully by Friedrich Hayek, though the history of states' roles in the preservation and maintenance of capitalist enterprise and political economy, particularly in nation-states such as Germany after World War I, the United States after the Great Depression, and Great Britain after World War II, discredits, in my view, the Hayekean assertion.

Marxists rejected the notion of the state as necessary for the production, maintenance, and reproduction of material and political life, attributing the Western states' seeming indispensability to the need for capitalist administration. This is why, other than Marx's brief analysis in *The Eighteenth Brumaire of Louis Napoleon Bonaparte,* there is very little writing by Marxists on the role of the state until the post–World War II period. Marxists were quick to point out that politics, when reduced to matters of state, ultimately became the politics of capitalist enterprise, at the expense of laboring classes, specifically the proletariat. In the Marxist (rather than Leninist) view of the state, the state would become obsolete in the advent of a proletarian order.

Marxists, Frankfurt School thinkers, as well as postwar French, British, and Italian theorists ranging from (in no particular order) Louis Althusser, Hannah Arendt, and Norberto Bobbio, to Georges Bataille, Cornelius Castoriadis, Stuart Hall, and Raymond Williams, sought to broaden our understanding of politics to a process that was not reducible to the economy or state as abstract entities. Instead, by focusing on the interactions and dynamics between social groups and classes, on the one hand, and state and economic policy on the other, these and other theorists sought, among other things, to analyze politics as an embedded process critical to daily life. Taken together, these efforts can be read as a response, not only to the limitations of Marxist views of the state but also in response to conservative theories that reduced all politics to the politics of state, specifically, electoral competition and its resultant elected officials. Thus, the politics of daily life, and the appearance of a broader, popular, potentially more egalitarian politics, a politics of non-elites, became the core focus of two generations of social and political theorists of Western societies, as well as comparativists such as Charles Lindblom. Theorists such as Henri Lefebvre (who is referenced at the top of this chapter) and Georges Bataille also theorized about the possibilities of an insurgent, nonbourgeois form of political participation in daily life in capitalist societies. More recently, the work of Phillip Pettit on republicanism has signaled a revival of a concept of politics not restricted to the institutional, representational forms in Euro-U.S. polities.

From the vantage point of twenty-first-century political science, it would appear as if the view of politics as the politics of electoral competition and the corresponding political actors preoccupy the majority of mainstream journals in political science, at least in Europe, the United States, and much of Latin America. The broader dimensions of politics, and the political, have been largely obscured. The mainstream journals of U.S. political science are a testament to the more restrictive definition of politics. This more restrictive application of an already restrictive definition of politics has also had specific consequences for the study and examination of black politics.

As described in chapters 1, 5, and 8, most black struggles for civil rights and cultural recognition first emerged outside the formal spheres of political disputation, bourgeois or otherwise (colonial), outside the realm of politics proper—the state in its administrative-legislative dimensions. This assertion is not limited to the empirical examples and cases of U.S. African Americans, black South Africans, or black and brown Brazilians, but can be applied to Afro-Colombian, Afro-Nicaraguan, Afro-Peruvian, Afro-German instances of mobilization for civil rights, cultural recognition, or remediation of past injustices ranging from land expropriation and rights claims to state-mandated sterilization. The disjuncture between modes and objects of analysis has had two repercussions for the critical examination of black politics, cross-nationally as well as intra-nationally. With few exceptions, within the discipline of political science, black politics—its political cultures and actors—is rarely examined outside formal spheres of politics, and the critical means to discern their impact upon the more formal spheres of political disputation remain underdeveloped.

As indicated in chapter 1, a more expansive definition of politics should encompass conflicts over the distribution of goods, services, and resources, civil rights, and cultural recognition and materialism that are not limited to the formal spheres of political disputation. At the same time, a more expansive definition of politics should also be conceptualized to avoid reducing all forms of conflict to political conflict. A theory of politics, then, must also distinguish between political and nonpolitical phenomena, as well as between formal and informal modes of political articulation.

I am attempting to develop what sociologists and political theorists conventionally refer to as a "middle range" theory of subordinate group power relations, political agency, and identification, encompassing the grey area in theories of power, domination, and resistance that lurks somewhere between the analytic boundaries and definitions of outright acquiescence and social mobilization, between total repression and total revolution. This exploration of the political in the quotidian also represents an attempt to provide an analytic guard against the tendency, displayed in certain trends in cultural studies and the analysis of popular culture in the humanities, to treat every instance of sociocultural tension and conflict as "political" without actually defining what constitutes the political or its opposite, the nonpolitical.

My principal concern in the explication of a theory of quotidian politics is to identify and uncover the normative and behavioral responses to structural and material conditions of racial politics and to distinguish micropolitics from macropolitics. Most attempts to characterize forms of political behavior in everyday life as broadly political compress micro- and macropolitical forms. Further still, the inability to distinguish between political and nonpolitical forms also leads to analytic confusion over what constitutes a political act, an action or behavior that helps beget a political community.

Nonpolitical acts are behaviors that are not generative of political community. An example of postfacto rationalizations of various acts, often destructive, as "political" would be Eldridge Cleaver's claim early on in his book *Soul on Ice* that his serial rapes of white women were political acts in the name of the black community (see chapter 3). Cleaver himself, later on in the book, disavows this claim. Yet the claim, though quite horrific, allows us to distinguish the political act from the nonpolitical, or even antipolitical act. If a political community is to be understood as the coalescence of disparate sets of interests, peoples, ideologies, and principles, what political community could emerge out of the rape of *any* woman that could be the basis for collective deliberation about the conditions that the African-descended—or any other population—find themselves in a national society? Though claims such as Cleaver's have been made by soldiers in instances of war, such claims, and the acts that precede or follow them, give indication of a breakdown of political community not its affirmation or creation. The creation and maintenance of political community requires more than isolated, individuated acts.

The reason for my juxtaposition of references from Henri Lefevbre and Ray Charles is to underscore from the very outset of this chapter the unknown aspects of black politics and to remind readers that the exploration of the unknown is first of all an epistemic enterprise, not an empirical one, that can apply equally to racial politics as it can to the examination of any political phenomena. Following Lefebvre in his *Critique of Everyday Life* as well as

C. L. R. James's examination of U.S. popular culture in *American Civilization*, there are knowns and unknowns in the practice and production of politics, as individuals and groups attempt to come up with new and creative ways to address old problems of equality of distribution, the access to goods and services, in response to their denial or repression by state and economic interests. To take a well-known example from Rio de Janeiro, several *favelas* (poor urban communities) on the vertical periphery of Rio de Janeiro have "liberated" electricity from the municipal power lines, a practice defined as illegal by both energy and municipal authorities. This practice occurs outside the bounds of commodified, market-driven power usage and pay-rate schemes and highlights the broader issue of unequal distribution of resources. This practice requires individuals and groups who are willing, out of a sense of necessity and right, but also equipped with the technical skill, to extract these energy resources for their own use. This practice, therefore, combines the social, the economic, the normative, and the macropolitical, even though it does not occur in the sphere of civil society designed by Brazilian elite political culture as the sphere of the political.

At the same time, my explication of quotidian politics serves as a corrective to political and cultural analysis that reduces all politics to the state or macroeconomic factors. Many classic definitions of politics attribute politics to the modern state because of the state's capacity for violence, decision making, and setting the boundaries for social relations. More economistic accounts of politics reduce politics to consequences of prior material determinations and constraints, thereby limiting the role of political actors and parties, treating mayors of large urban cities and the presidents of less economically and militarily powerful nation-states as mere prey for the appetites of more powerful economic actors. The political will and discretion of these less powerful actors are dictated by the aims and desires of more powerful actors, whether in national society or in the international political economy. Coincidentally, many Marxist and neoliberal (or more properly understood, economically liberal) perspectives share certain similarities in their view of the state's role as generator and arbiter of politics.

What my theorization of quotidian politics shares with critiques of libertarian and reductionist Marxist accounts of politics, however, is that individuals who are faced with conditions of inequality, whether as isolates or as parts of larger groups, institutions, and organizations, invariably must respond to the following questions: Do I accept the conditions of inequality in which I am enmeshed? If I do not accept those conditions, how might I respond? If I respond to the conditions of inequality before me, what might be the consequences—as well as limits—of my actions? These three questions, at least, must be posed in any expansive account of politics involving dominant and subordinate actors and institutions.

The concept of politics at work here involves individuals and groups with a disparate set of interests and subject positions, dominant and subordinate, who are in conflict and competition over goods, services, and resources. To the extent that their responses to these three questions are not foretold, we have politics, not only in theory but in practice. Responses to these three questions (as well as other questions) ultimately determine what a student of politics can study. If we already knew the answers to such questions, then there would be no such thing as politics, and as a consequence, no political phenomena to study. My understanding of politics thus remains consistent with the rather prosaic but nonetheless accurate definition of politics as the art of the possible, for opportunities and the lack of opportunities in a given situation or dynamic are what makes politics unpredictable, highly unstable and contingent, and in need of explanation.

For reasons that could be broadly construed as cultural in the conventional way in which the term is employed, this more open view of politics also has greater applicability to situations of political process, conflict, and inequality that are not directly or even indirectly attributable to interventions of state or capital among nations and peoples who do not have permanent seats on the United Nations Security Council, membership in the G8 group of nations, or nuclear and other forms of advanced technological industries. As Kamal Sadiq and other students of South Asian politics have demonstrated through careful examination of national and cross-national migration patterns within the region, the focus on the state as the locus of granting citizenship status, voting privileges, and civic authority to individuals living in several societies such as Malaysia, India, Sri Lanka, and Bangladesh is largely a Western preoccupation, misplaced in societies where noncitizens in many cases have the ability to vote in national elections and participate in other ways in the life of a national polity.[3] Historically, political actors and organizations in colonial societies organized politically and made demands on colonial and ultimately imperial liberal-democratic regimes such as Britain and France even though they were legally defined as colonial subjects and noncitizens of the metropolitan polity.

Thus, a more expansive understanding of politics is intrinsic to a theory of quotidian politics in general, and black politics in particular. Daily life provides its own normative, ethical, and moral contours that infuse the category of the political in daily life with substantive content. Quotidian politics, the sort of political phenomena that straddle the boundaries of micro- and macropolitics, do not always manifest themselves in collective action.

Two examples provide the analytic framing necessary to help readers identify the theoretical and empirical implications of an approach to the study of politics that does not begin and end with macropolitical economy, or at the other end of the categorical continuum, the allegedly separate sphere of culture. First, the owner of a professional football team in a midsize town in the United States decides to move his team to another city and state, based on better tax abatements, loans, and space allotted for the construction of a larger stadium to accommodate the team's fan base. This decision was the result of a breakdown in negotiations between the local city government and the team owner. Local fans are outraged. Some fans feel helpless, and assume that nothing can be done to halt the team's departure. Other fans turn their anger toward the owner, and begin a campaign to boycott all other products, investments, and financial concerns held by the owner, as an expression of their contempt. Still another cohort blames city officials for allowing the negotiations to break down and organizes into a voting bloc during the subsequent mayoral election in an effort to oust not only the mayor, but the entire party ticket. All three responses are to the same action and process, but each response, though related to the initial announcement of the team's departure, is distinct.

My next example comes from actual circumstances and conditions of racial politics in comparative perspective. The responses to South African, U.S., and Rhodesian apartheid ranged from civil disobedience and armed struggle to cultural politics and protest literature. Some of those responses were coordinated, to be sure, and often undertaken by the same political actors in different phases of a struggle. The shift that the African National Congress (ANC) made from violent resistance to nonviolent resistance is just one example. Yet the variety of responses to inequitable and racist conditions within national societies also suggests that individuals and groups perceive politics differently, and as a result, build distinct, often conflicting (if not conflictual) political communities. Returning to the South African case, the ANC and the Black Consciousness movement are examples of political communities of distinction, just as Unknown Slaves (US) and the Black Panthers are for the United States, or the black nuclei of contending political parties such as the Brazilian Social Deomocracy Party (PSDB) or the Worker's Party (PT). As I will explore in chapter 8, the lack of sameness is a condition of—not an obstacle for—politics.

I seek to avoid several pitfalls found in various historiographic and social science literatures about resistance, rebellion, revolution, and power relations in general. First, populist-oriented accounts of working-class resistance tend to equate individuated responses to unequal relations of power with macropolitical resistance on a grand scale, thereby blurring analytic clarity concerning types of resistance, scale, and individual versus collective resistance. An offhand comment by C. L. R. James criticizing Herbert Aptheker's "very bad" historiography of slave systems is an implicit critique of a tendency to indiscriminately assign the term "revolutionary" to any act that counters the interests of dominant groups. James provided the following commentary on Aptheker's historiography of slave resistance: "When two workers get together in a tree he says 'You see, the blacks are revolutionary.'"[4] Scale of protest and the articulation of dissent are crucial components of a more discriminating view of the dynamics of domination that enable scholars to distinguish among categories and types of resistance.

Second, state and econocentric models of power dynamics reduce politics to machinations and consequences of the economy, with the state merely doing the bidding of elites and dominant classes to reproduce and maintain class hegemony. Under these models, individual acts of resistance to status quo machinations of power are the equivalent of flipping a middle finger to the hangman before a descent into the gallows at the end of a noose. Such accounts of power and dominance, state and economy consider primarily the vertical implications of power (state/economy's impact on society), not its horizontal implications (between/among/within groups).

A third related pitfall is the restrictive view of politics found in liberal and conservative political theory, wherein politics solely emanates from the state. This view was commonly held by several key figures of the late nineteenth- and early twentieth-century German sociological tradition, including Schmitt, Hegel, Mannheim, and Kant. This view of the state as the source of all politics has devolved in many liberal democratic societies (as well as in societies with similar formal aspirations) into the popular and elite view that politics is entirely coincident with the state, its representatives, and elite re-presentation of mass opinion and electoral choices. This is in part why, as Schmitt rightly points out, the average person in many representative, liberal polities views politics so disdainfully, as a practice one avoids whenever possible, rather than as a constitutive element of human interaction.

The fourth pitfall is a Foucauldian one in which power, viewed in terms of discursive practices with material and institutional implications, is reproduced and reconstituted in such a way as to preclude the possibility of more egalitarian social orders, allowing only for role reversals. The Foucauldian web neglects the possibility that a distinctive normative matrix upheld by some members of subordinate groups might lead some group members to behave differently, in a more egalitarian manner, than their power superordinates. At the same time, however, I want to avoid treatment of these normative possibilities as somehow "natural" or given to marginalized groups, who are also quite capable of atrocities and injustices in quests for power and authority.

In the case of black politics, the resolutions and strategies of black subjects in daily life are responses to conditions of inequality and are not state or macroeconomic choices. Rather, they are responses to the structuring of the polity and economy by the state and capital in societies that are themselves structured by racial politics and inequality. As I will develop below, part of this theorization of quotidian politics has been mapped out by scholars such as Jim Scott and Robin D. G. Kelley, who have their own distinctive response to the three questions I have posed, through Scott's formulations of infrapolitics and Brechtian modes of resistance.

The component parts of my theorization of quotidian politics are several key conceptual innovations, which will be elaborated below: coagulation as a midway point between micro- and macropolitics, parallelism, and displacement. These conceptual innovations will be utilized to make sense of several small-scale dynamics of power between racially coded subjects located in relations of dominance and subordination. The theoretical implications of these relations will then be elaborated before considering their relevance to several accounts of power, resistance, and domination not only for black politics but also for subaltern politics more broadly. Finally, themes of violence and individual and collective sovereignty, as they relate to a theory of quotidian politics in black, will be explored.

Coagulate Politics, Political Aggregation

The *Oxford English Dictionary* (Fourth Edition) categorizes the word *coagulate* as a transitive verb (v.t. and i) for which it provides the following definition: "Change from fluid to more or less solid state, clot, curdle, set, solidify." *Coagulation* is one of its cognates. In terms of politics, forms of political behavior on the continuum of individuated and aggregated politics can be characterized as coagulate when the following phenomena are involved: (1) previously disparate political actors operating randomly in an environment are linked through episodic circumstances; (2) linkage of disparate political actors under specific though episodic circumstances produce coalitions that within their immediate environment, to increase the likelihood of positive political outcomes for the actors involved; and (3) the implications and consequences of their actions are limited to the immediate circumstances of the political environment therein.

The advantage of the concept of coagulation is that it provides a means of explaining clumps or clusters of political interventions that are neither entirely individuated nor aggregate, though they are plural. Second, the situational and circumstantial character of coagulate/quotidian politics does not necessarily lead to or unfold into collective action. Actors engaged in coagulate politics minimize risk and loss by retreating into the hidden transcripts of their private sphere lives, without assuming that their activities should lead into public mobilization in the form of collective action. To extend the metaphor of coagulation and the body, coagulate politics stops the material "bleeding" of subalterns in conditions of unequal access and recompense. These activities are distinct from other forms of Brechtian resistance, ranging from the petit marronage of slave rebels to Michel De Certeau's poaching (see below), because of their more resolutely interstitial dimension. Coagulate politics take place within public spheres and work sites in full view of superordinates, but are largely contingent upon the encounters between subaltern members, divided by the conditions of labor (agent and consumer) but united by a perceived commonality of subordination.

Aggregate and coagulate politics incorporate responses to circumstantial violence and situations of perceived injustice and inequality. Instances of political coalition and articulation often appear as behaviors at the middle of a continuum with quiescence at one end and elite representation in the public sphere on the other. As the examples below indicate, racial, gendered, and classed subordinates often utilize experiential knowledge based on their own personal or collective archive of acts of injustice, and frame potential, imagined, and extant conflicts against that backdrop of injustice. A personal archive of experiences, when shared with other similarly situated individuals, becomes part of a broader archive of collective memory, part of a moral economy of black agency that, if my theory of aversion in chapter 3 has any validity, can be found across class and status roles of U.S. African American experience. As a result, individuals from various group clusters, not just racially coded ones, activate a sense of injustice or outrage against an imminent or ongoing process of selective discrimination to reform, in macropolitical terms, the process to increase the likelihood that the outcome will be more favorable to the less powerful participants.

The concept of political coagulation represents what could be characterized as the halfway point between micro- and macropolitics. Political coagulation occurs within micropolitical situations when individual political actors assume positions of ephemeral power that enable them to exert influence upon the outcome of a particular encounter, transaction, or exchange. Those actors are not invested with political power more generally, and may, in fact, occupy subordinate positions within an overall political economy. Yet they are coagulants in the sense that they infuse a relatively self-contained instance with their own notions of justice, equality, and redress to significantly affect micropolitical—and sometimes macropolitical—outcomes in daily life. What makes these coagulants instances of aggregate politics and not quite collective action in the more conventional social science definition is that the conditions in which they appear do not make a declarative public statement. They are the embodiment of a synergistic relationship between political opportunity and circumstance, a much more scaled down version of political opportunity structures as conceptualized by social movement scholars such as Doug McAdam and Sidney Tarrow.[5] In general, such individuals have few opportunities to express their political beliefs. They might not be revolutionaries, but they certainly provide the counterpoint to images of the backward, acquiescent, immobile wage-laborer. I will now recount two instances that graphically underscore the concept of political coagulation.

A. Incident One

Before the scandal unfolded in the 1990s that exposed its automotive repair division as a cheat of its customers' hard-earned money, there was a service-oriented, popular department store that advertised its own brand of fail-safe car batteries. Their television advertisements featured cars starting with these batteries in the climatic equivalent of the Alaskan tundra, under conditions seemingly so frigid that one could envision wolves and polar bears with chattering teeth off camera. In 1990, a car battery I purchased from this store and had installed in my car only weeks earlier went dead. Perhaps it was the sweltering Texas heat, not the Alaskan tundra, that transformed my die-hard battery into a die-soft one. I accompanied the tow truck and car to the shop. In keeping with its advertising at the time, I assumed I would immediately be given a new battery as a replacement. The manager, however, informed me that my old battery would have to be charged first before I could receive a replacement battery, just to ensure that the battery was not faulty. This was not quite in keeping with the stated and advertised policy, I explained, since the battery was obviously weak, as the store's own gauges attested, and had refused to start my car, which was sufficient evidence of the battery's limitations and my need for a new one. My old—though new—battery would have to be recharged first, the manager insisted. I would be given a new battery only if the old one did not retain the charge.

I decided to follow the procedure, resigned to a shift in the rules of the game. I assumed I had no other choice. What would I do, buy yet another battery? Ok, I said, take the battery out of the car. All the while another employee, a young, black man roughly my age at the time (midthirties), also stood behind the counter, several yards away. Out of the corner of my eye, I could see him watching our exchange even as he attended to another customer. After finishing with the customer, he walked toward us. After his raised eyebrows indicated to me to follow him, he approached his manager and shot me a quick look of indifference. "I'll take care of this," he said to the manager, before leaving the counter and heading toward the store parking lot, where my car had been towed. Once the glass door shut he muttered, "These white people are something else," out of the left side of his mouth. "Do you know how many people I have seen him give a new battery to?" he asked rhetorically as he lifted up the hood of my car and began the quick and grimy task of extricating the battery. "All a white person has to do is act like their battery isn't working, and he gives it to them. A brother like you comes in," he said, anger rising in his voice, "and you get the policy" and pausing for effect, "that really isn't the policy." Before pulling out the battery from the engine's side he said, "I tell you what I'm going to do. I'm going to act as if the battery is charged, but I'm not going to charge it. Then when you come to pick it up it won't be charged and he'll be forced to give you a new battery!" With that he closed the hood, hoisted the battery into the crook of his right arm, and led me back to the reception area where I filled out the requisite paperwork. I returned several days later. The battery I originally purchased, I was told by same white manager I first encountered, did not charge. I would be given a new battery. After the new battery was installed, I spotted the young man in one of the garage pits, and gave him some money encased in a handshake. We wished each other luck and went our separate ways.

B. Second Incident

The second incident occurred in a now-defunct department store in New York City, a store noted for offering value instead of high prices. I made several purchases there over the years, and returned disgruntled only once, to return a wool blazer that, after one trip to the dry cleaner, was transformed into a fabric that more resembled seersucker, with countless wrinkles and folds. When I returned to the men's suit department with the jacket, I was greeted by a friendly but noncooperative department manager, who informed me he could neither return my money nor exchange the jacket. He even told me that he had similar problems with a jacket he bought from the store—his employer—and he had not bothered to return his jacket, so why should I, notwithstanding the fact that the store did have a return policy with the customary temporal constraints and proof of purchase requirements.

Watching alongside was a young, black male stock clerk loading garments onto displays. As soon as the manager walked away he confidently walked up to me and said, "Come with me," relieving me of jacket and receipt. I followed him to another part of the store, where he searched in vain for someone. "Not here," he muttered, and headed for another destination unknown to me. We went into the women's department where a glint of recognition flashed across his face as a black woman in her late thirties, a department assistant manager, approached him. He walked up to her with my coat and receipt in hand, with me walking dutifully behind, as he explained to her that I needed a refund for a defective jacket. When the woman asked him if I had gone to the men's department first, he replied with a yes and a look that generated an equally scornful gaze in return. She quickly extricated a pen from her jacket pocket, wrote an authorization for the refund, and sent us on our way. Finally, he led me to the refund desk in the basement, where the authorization slip, jacket, and receipt were hand delivered to the refund clerk (who was also black). Within minutes she refunded my money. I thanked the first clerk profusely, shook his hand, and left the store.

The incidents recounted above are just two of many I experienced over several years involving black women and men in service and service-related positions. These incidents triggered a series of ruminations about the relationship between black labor and resistance in relations of service, and encouraged me to revisit some of the literature and debates of the 1990s about the synergies between injustice and collective action. They provide partial evidence of how antagonisms premised upon racial hierarchy serve to trigger and offset a series of practices and procedures that would be considered, under other circumstances, "reducible" to dynamics of class inequality. Of course, some might read the above examples and argue quite forcefully that they are mere anecdotes of class warfare that working-class peoples have engaged in across races, genders, and cultures. There is the distinct possibility that in both instances the initial motivation for the interventions of these young men was largely gendered.[6]

To continue the metaphor of coagulation, these clerks' activities limited the hemorrhaging and loss of my investment in two separate commodities.

Their interventions rendered their hidden transcripts public, based on some combination of intuition, experiential knowledge, and Gramscian/Kantian "good sense" (a sense of how they believe the environment in which they live and/or work should function). Yet their activities provide little indication of how they operate politically in other circumstances. Neither actor provided a partial much less comprehensive political ideology, perspective, or project, even though one or both actors might have a partially or fully developed political perspective on redistributive justice more generally (reparations or socialized medicine, for example).[7]

The randomness of the interaction at the point of service in both incidents is underscored by three presumptions: (1) under identical circumstances not all black employees would have engaged in "Brechtian" behavior; (2) the actors themselves may not have engaged in such behavior with other customers, perhaps not even with black ones at other times; and (3) these two actors do not influence the outcome of sales or return transactions all the time, nor are they necessarily motivated to do so. The two individuals of both incidents engaged in a politics that straddled the border between micro- and macropolitics without fully inhabiting either category. Their responses to each instance could be characterized as fully voluntarist but also structuring, insofar as their interventions subtly but significantly altered the material consequences of decisions rendered by their superiors, without their supervisor's awareness of their activities. What I shall call aggregate politics is a form of political articulation and coalition that is neither entirely individuated nor entirely collective. Rather than view this kind of politics as "unorganized," it might be better characterized as self-mobilization—literally, a mobilization of the self, in order to address situations of inequality. This form of political behavior could be read as the enactment of the concept of self-sovereignty, regardless whether the individual was in fact a sovereign subject in civil society. Aggregation is the step toward coagulation, when an individual operating under circumstances that could not be characterized as collective action initiates the political work of building a political community, however brief and ephemeral.

Incidents like these underscore how members of subordinate groups might sometimes act amongst themselves, across class and other boundaries, not in the name of some vague "racial solidarity," but in specific response to a perceived injustice against a member of their own "race" under conditions that, in theory, should not only be democratic but should be the most banal and procedural (purchasing or returning goods, customer relations, and service). The memories of the racially subordinate are both common and uncommon, insofar as their experiences are at once distinctly personal and collective. Since racial domination at the level of the individual is experienced idiosyncratically, meanings attached to individual experiences can be sutured, in the sense in which Ernesto Laclau uses the term, to other individual experiences.

Working-class blacks who provide the kind of assistance described above are engaging in forms of coagulate, aggregate politics. In anticipation of those who might accuse such individuals of undermining the ethos of public good, I would simply suggest that they learned such behaviors from their bosses and coworkers. In a society such as that of the United States, the working classes, more than any other class, learn firsthand how to travel the distance between the rhetoric of meritocracy and the realpolitik of nepotism and comparative disadvantage. There is full irony in the fact that the clerks had to flout the store's practices and treatment of some of its customers in order to ultimately provide good customer service. This is no surplus, no gratuitous feat, but a necessity, a mechanism of subsistence. Such responses acknowledge that a gap exists and persists between rules and norms; both written and unwritten rules are applied differently. Whites often receive surplus satisfaction when returning an item or product; blacks rarely receive even the minimum service whites do. What if I could not afford another battery and needed it to drive my car to a meager-paying job? What if that suit jacket were the difference between my appearance or the postponement of a job interview?

As brilliantly outlined by de Certeau in the concept of poaching,[8] there are popular though highly selective practices developed by working people within the process of production that are designed to extract commodities or valuable labor time from that process. Whether it is a pieceworker in one of the various garment industries of the world who takes odd fabrics to make a dress for independent sale or exchange outside the system of production, a dockworker who "discovers" a broken crate of frozen steaks from Argentina, or the mechanic who decides to repair a friend's car for free on his break from work at the local gas station or car dealership, such activities lend credence to poaching as one of the modular forms of "weapons of the weak." Such activities, however, do not actually lead the dress manufacturer, commercial port, car dealership, or gas station to financial ruin, or to a fundamental reordering of relations of production. This is why such industries have insurance for graft (though in most instances the wage workers are the least egregious perpetrators). Ultimately, it is the workers who must pull additional human and material resources (more labor) from their production and production site to introduce their labor or products of their labor into other circuits of economy (bartering or "boosted" sales).

Although the relations of production are largely predetermined by the forms of labor people engage in, the type of service accorded to consumers varies widely in a given marketplace, dependent upon company policy as well as individual discretion. In other words, though working-class people might not be in a position to alter the conditions under which they labor, they can affect the extension and mediation of their labor and production in the marketplace. It is individual discretion that I want to focus on here, as exemplified in those cases when I was the beneficiary of an often momentary discretionary authority, in which a black person in a service position decided to provide me with a refund, discount, or repair within a broader logic of equity, rather than racial equality. Rather than view these interactions as symptomatic of the class character of race relations, I would argue that they illustrate the materiality of racial logics and consciousness, as some members of racially subordinate groups within service-oriented enterprises view the market of profit and deficit, recompense and loss, along racial parameters.

These circuitous routes to consumer satisfaction suggest, among many things, that when given the opportunity, some black working-class people in service sectors of the economy interpret the mistreatment meted out to black consumers as a double inequality or, put another way, the transactional dimension of racial inequality articulated in the circulation of production. Not only do blacks receive unequal treatment but unequal recompense. Workers' interventions ensure that at the very least, black consumers receive service and satisfaction in accordance with the verbal or written policies of their employers. Ironically, they have to circumvent hierarchies and procedures to ensure that those very policies are met. Here we return to the radical potential of black transgression in daily U.S. life. Like those who sat at whites-only lunch counters during the U.S. civil rights movement, blacks (and their similarly committed compatriots in struggle of all colors) must circumvent tacit and written laws in order to receive equal treatment.

Behavior like that displayed by the young man at the automotive repair shop might appear in a variety of places and circumstances, so that one could plausibly argue that, taken as a whole, such acts are collective. Yet the critical difference here is that these acts were not undertaken collectively, but individually. Due to the distinct nature of their job tasks, the two young men had distinct responses to the similar structures of racial domination, but their respective laboring functions dictated the terms under which each rebelled. Their "on-the-job training" prepared and socialized them to engage in modes of resistance suitable to their realm of discretionary influence. The clerk in the automotive repair shop could not exchange my jacket; nor could the young man at the department store provide me with a new car battery. Only under circumstances wherein these young men could be identified as part of a group of men and women engaged in similar service-oriented occupations who have decided, amongst themselves, to engage in such activities could it be plausibly argued that their activities be conceived of as collective action.

There are black people (as among any group of people) who would not engage in the activities I described under any circumstances, and would, in fact, oppose "poaching" altogether in an almost Kantian, categorical fashion. How would the young black man in the automotive repair section of the department store provide me with a new battery, in keeping with company policy (and his own) if he were relegated to another area of the store? What if the young man in the department store happened not to be walking by the men's suit department on that particular day, at that moment? What if one of them were caught and reprimanded for such actions afterward? Such is the phenomenological nature of presumably racial solidarity.

I offer the chart below to enable readers to visualize a continuum of micro- and macropolitics, distinctions between individuated and aggregated modes of resistance. The chart outlines the continuum of resistance from absolute compliance (largely nonexistent), coagulation and aggregate politics, outright rebellion, revolt, and revolution. It is designed to trace the dynamics of reaction and response involving dominant and subordinate groups and individuals, not to valorize collective action (aggregated politics) at the expense of individual volition (individuated politics).

A key operative assumption of the chart is that individuated and aggregated politics often occur simultaneously, and may indeed operate in relation to one another. James Scott's "weapons of the weak" is characterized within my model as a form of contextual micropolitics with macropolitical implications. One of Scott's key assertions, which I believe is correct, concerns the emergence of covert/Brechtian political actors at moments of revolt/rebellion and revolution who engage in outward, direct manifestations of protest at propitious moments, mostly when elites and status quo institutions are in disarray.[9] The second key assumption is that few subordinate political actors resemble the "fatalistic peasants" who made a brief, convenient appearance in the behavioralist-based modernization literatures in the 1950s and 1960s, in the work of scholars like Edward Banfield. Though such actors exist in a variety of political and economic circumstances, we should not assume the complete absence of what Scott calls "the hidden transcript." Social movements and rebellions are extraquotidian modes of resistance because of their relative infrequency and spectacular character. They produce spectacle and spectators in the form of mass mobilization and mass audiences. We know from Elias Canetti that crowds involved in either spectatorship or mass mobilization generate their own modes of power,[10] a power distinct from individual protest. Spectacular and macropolitics can be distinguished from micropolitics by the dynamics they generate that are distinct from individuated action.

There are, nonetheless, longitudinal as well as more immediate analytic implications of the distinction between micropolitics, coagulation, and macropolitics. The key distinguishing feature of macropolitical, collective response to inequality is that states and economies, in their response to direct action and protest, define the limits of their capacities to either incorporate or quell protest. With coagulate politics, the person employing "weapons of the weak" is not necessarily challenging the state, its economic machinations, or even an employer. That person's resistance operates within the realm of that which is rarely observed or acknowledged.

Table 2.1
Political Continuum: From the Barely Noticed to the Spectacular

I. Acquiescence	II. Micropolitics	III. Coagulation	
Absolute domination, fatalism, compliance, extreme anomie	Social activities that do not culminate in the formation of political community, a community of norms and interests that exceed the boundaries of individual concern and interest	Parallelism, displacement	
Total lack of micro or macropolitical activity	actors often use macropolitical phenomena, institutions, or actors for personal, idiosyncratic gain	Weapons of the weak, covert (Brechtian) resistance, Petit Marronage	
Status quo/disparate modes of dissent. No agglutination	Individual expression or gain; social banditry, antisocial behavior that can have reactionary or countervailing importance	Neglect, isolation, repression of individual or narrowly coalitional dissent	
Least Resistance		Continuum of Resistance	

Brechtian actors may be no more reliable than other, more passive social actors in times of open revolt. To return to the two examples I have provided, if the young man in the automotive repair department and the one in the now defunct department store were to be transferred to another department of their respective places of employment, they would have to engage in other types of coagulate politics, if they were able to do so at all. They would certainly not announce to their supervisors or managers that they engaged in the sort of aggregate politics of redistribution in their prior departments. Nor would such a declaration be appropriate or useful, for example, under circumstances in which black workers decide to make demands upon the general manager or store ownership to institute an examination of the implementation of policies when dealing with black customers. Such a declaration would undermine collective initiatives and reduce their moral claims to the claims of criminals. What I am suggesting here is that the "Brechtian" political actors

IV. Macropolitics: The Observable and the Spectacular		
Conventional political competition, social protest	Revolt/Rebellion	Revolution
Organized dissent against a particular regime, policy, or practice of state or economy that leads to collective action and possible extension of social and political networks to political and social actors outside of immediate network/matrix. States, elites, and labor interests perceive threat to overall stability.		
Reform, isolation of conflict, localized, resolution of conflict, state/elite/capital collusion	Potential for nationalization/ expansion of conflict	Regime change, repression, negotiation, cooptation of local and/ or national leaders

▶ Most Resistance

A Theory of Quotidian Politics

would have to develop and engage in a different type of politics. Just as the macropolitics of revolt, rebellion, and revolution are not translatable to the politics of everyday life, coagulate politics are not easily grafted onto open, social protest, except, perhaps, in instances of violence. They are two distinct modes of political articulation and protest. The former is necessary for dreamers and politicians, the latter for the survival of common people. Dreamers and survivors often trade places, however.

III Violence, the Final Frontier

Racist violence is one of the continuing legacies of racial slavery, which is inextricably bound up with histories of imperialism and colonialism (see chapter 6). As Timothy Mitchell has suggested in a recent book on Egypt, violence in both its coercive and symbolic forms often engenders a culture of fear in colonial and postcolonial societies. I believe similarly symbolic forms of violence, the cultural legacy of specific histories of racist violence, have also been operative in black life-worlds of several national societies. Like Mitchell, I believe that a culture of fear "cannot be revealed by a survey of attitudes" yet I do wonder about his attendant claim that "the essence of symbolic violence is that it is never recognized as such, but is experienced as a system of morality."[11]

As will be made evident below, the literatures on popular responses to racist violence in many former slaveholding societies give some indication that slaves and former slaves well understood the culture of fear and symbolic violence in the daily life of slave and apartheid societies. Part of the power of racist violence lies not only within racist states but also in people in societies that were once premised upon *herrenvolk* notions of polity and democracy who are emboldened by the state's racist behaviors and ideological practices to generate their own forms of racist violence. Such forms of statist and nonstatist violence were central to the colonial and apartheid experiences, as historians such as Thom Holt, Steve Hahn, Robin D. G. Kelley, and George Fredrickson have chronicled in the cases of black populations in South Africa, the United States, and Jamaica. More contemporary examples of antiblack racisms include vigilante squads in the peripheral areas of major urban centers such as Rio de Janeiro and São Paulo, Brazil, neo-Nazi and so-called New Right groups in various European Union (EU) countries,[12] and to long-standing problems in the United States revolving around statist and nonstatist forms of violence against U.S. African American and other black and brown populations. These and other historiographic examinations of racist violence and the responses they have engendered can be read alongside the writings of Hannah Arendt, Michel Foucault, and Franz Fanon to consider more generally the role, importance, and limitations of violence as an act or process of politics.

Since violence has been so central to the maintenance of apartheid and white supremacist logics, theories of violence should be brought to bear on situations of inequality involving subordinate populations in these societies, not only to better identify and comprehend gratuitous expressions of power or policing mechanisms of state and capitalist control but also to understand popular responses to state and individual racist violence. Racist violence also provides an opportunity to identify acts of political coagulation in black quotidian politics, within the historiography of daily life and popular culture, and in testimonial narratives about violence and self-defense by black political actors. Writings in political theory, U.S. African American studies, and black studies, more broadly defined, will be combined in this section as they help enrich a theory of quotidian politics in black.

I begin with Arendt, because of her concern with the tendency to attribute meaning to violence independent of politics and without first coming to terms with the intentions undergirding violent acts, intentions mediated by socioeconomic structures, institutions, organizations, and individuals. Arendt, in her magisterial, though deeply flawed[13] account of violence as politics in the black struggle in the United States, writes that "violence is by nature instrumental; like all means, it always stands in need of guidance and justification through the end it pursues. And what needs justification by something else cannot be the essence of anything."[14] Fanon's belief that violence produced by the earth's wretched could bring about the catharsis necessary to transform subjugated populations and, ultimately, the societies, peoples, and states that subordinate them, is precisely the sort of perspective Arendt critiques:

> For if the last shall be the first, this will only come to pass after a murderous and decisive struggle between the two protagonists. That affirmed intention to place the last at the head of things, and to make them climb at a pace . . . the well-known steps which characterize an organized society, can only triumph if we use all means to turn the scale, including, of course, that of violence.[15]

The violence-as-progress narrative is where Sartre and to a lesser extent Regis Debray, differs from Fanon, whose advocacy of violence, even under highly restrictive circumstances, was presented as a way out of the colony in both mind and body, an existential breakthrough. Arendt specifically charges Fanon and several other thinkers with projecting violent prophecies that "would not result in changing the world (or the system) but only its personnel."[16] Arendt's critique comes not from some evangelical ideal of a conflict- or violence-free world, but from a firm conviction of the intrinsically antimoral character of violence. As Anne McClintock has suggested, Fanon's advocacy of violence as progress is a decidedly masculinist posture, a posture that synthesizes manhood, freedom, and sovereignty with a language of nationalism.[17]

Nonetheless, Fanon's position has at least one critical advantage in relation to Arendt's account of the intrinsically instrumentalist character of violence. Unlike Arendt, Fanon does not treat violence as the antithesis of politics, but an oft-utilized instrument, a conditioning agent for politics as domination, as in colonial and racial rule. Separate but equal voting practices or Bantuslands and political representatives in South Africa are inconceivable without a prior legacy of institutionalized colonial violence. Perhaps this is one of the reasons why Arendt's critique of civil rights activists in Little Rock, Arkansas, and Black Power mobilization in New York City is devoid of the context of daily violence that these divergent forms of black struggle were up against.[18]

A more granular account of an individual's response to racist violence, both as symbol and as coercive practice, is found in the autobiography of Frederick Douglass. Douglass's account of his fateful encounter with Edward Covey, a notorious "negro-breaker" who specialized in taming recalcitrant slaves through excessive brutality, provides a narrative of existential transformation that in some restricted ways evokes Ho Chi Minh, Sartre, and Fanon. After a series of frightful beatings at the hands of Covey, Douglass decided to resist further punishment. After a struggle that, by Douglass's estimate, lasted two hours (which seems exaggerated), Covey's attitude toward Douglass, and Douglass's self-perception changed:

> This battle with Mr. Covey was the turning point in my career as a slave. It rekindled the few expiring embers of freedom, and revived within me a sense of my own manhood. It recalled the departed self-confidence, and inspired in me again with a determination to be free. The gratification afforded by the triumph was a full compensation for whatever else might follow, even death itself. . . . My long-crushed spirit rose, cowardice departed, bold defiance took its place; and I now resolved that, however long I might remain a slave in form, the day had passed forever when I could be a slave in fact.[19]

At stake for Douglass are self-constituting notions of manhood, dignity, and courage. Douglass's fight with Mr. Covey is represented as his liminal ritual phase, through which he is transformed into a free spirit, if not immediately a literal freeman. Douglass's equation of his manhood with the ability to successfully defend himself provides a heroic dimension to the narrative that Douglass—and the abolitionist movement—so desperately needed to project in order to convey that there were truly significant people being squeezed under slavery's thumb.

This part of the Douglass narrative, along with other accounts of individual acts of physical resistance to racial slavery and racist violence, has often been utilized as a rallying cry for black mobilization. As Arendt's critique of Fanon suggests, however, violence cannot be a strategy, only an instrument of strategy. When mistaken for a political project, violent struggle is symbolically represented as moral. Morality, however, does not fight. It is men, overwhelmingly, who have articulated the desire for violence as a political project, whether in the Black Power movement of the United States, or nineteenth- and twentieth-century nationalist movements around the world. As we have come to know, most violent expressions of masculinity and heroic nationalism have had disastrous consequences. Douglass's physical resistance spared him from Mr. Covey's clutches, but could never ensure the physical liberation of an entire group of people.

Neither acquiescent nor "activist" in the conventional sense, examples of everyday resistance to racist violence must be viewed as tactical, on-the-spot responses to apartheid domination. Although learned in social and communal circumstances, individual responses can be taught and secretly encouraged. Yet it is precisely for this reason that these responses to racist domination cannot be viewed as the building blocks for overthrowing a *system* of domination, but only as one or more individuals associated with such system. The contrary perspective entails the undigested belief that individual responses to an act of violence automatically undermine a system of domination, whether immediately or during the course of historical time. Vague and general descriptions of macro- and micropolitics among subaltern populations such as "human will," the "agency of the working-class," and "black working-class resistance" provide little insight into the actual formation, development, and deployment of micro- and macropolitical responses to actual, historical, or imminent practices of coercion.

Douglass's almost mythical battle with Mr. Covey forces us to revisit the concept of sovereignty, in addition to coagulation. Foucault's methodological precaution against viewing power as an artifact of sovereignty, and not the other way around, is useful here. Rather than focusing on systems of rights, juridical law, and the concept of sovereignty, Foucault decided to focus instead on power's "outer limits at the point where it becomes capillary: in other words, to understand power in its most regional forms and institutions, and especially at the points where this power transgresses the rules of right that organize and delineate it, oversteps those rules and is invested in institutions, is embodied in techniques and acquires the material means to intervene, sometimes in violent ways."[20]

Despite his rejection of the concept of sovereignty and a theory of rights as a means of framing power relations in modern nation-states, Foucualt's theory of domination, when fused with Hobbes's classic description of individual and state sovereignty, provides a means of explaining the actual practice of state racism in relation to matters of individual sovereignty. The key difference between state racisms, and racisms of all sorts without the support of strong states, or racism in societies where the state does not condone and will not support popular racism, lies in the corporal privilege state laws, practices, and policies provide to dominant group members.

In the case of U.S. African American resistance to violence, self-mobilization in response to racist violence is linked to matters of sovereignty, in the traditional sense of state and citizen, but also in terms of racial subjectivity. Hobbes wrote that "every Sovereign hath the same Right, in procuring the safety of his People, that any particular man can have, in procuring the safety of his own body."[21] Thus, each person is her or his own state, with capacities for both reason and violence. Hobbes's description of sovereignty, however, introduces a paradox for those outside the body politic of the nation-state, for "procuring the safety of his own body" may in fact lie outside the condition of sovereignty itself. Foucault recognizes this. There is no absolute guarantee that the state's imposition of sovereignty, or the racist individual's imposition of corporal sovereignty upon the unincorporated, marginalized subjects, will result in a "victory" of the superordinate state or citizen. Many acts of self-defense and violence against racially empowered individuals, such as the Zoot Suit Riots or confrontations on public buses and trolleys in Birmingham, Alabama, remind us of the limits of state power and racial supremacist logics in relation to subordinate subjects. The linkage between racist logics and concepts of sovereignty is evident in most masculinist accounts of black male agency, such as Frederick Douglass, Malcolm X, and Frantz Fanon, who at times equated the ability to exact violence as a mode of self-defense or revenge as an expression of sovereignty. It must be remembered that sovereignty is an essentially "public" concept. There is nothing hidden about it.

This also leads to more conceptual and at the same time comparative assessments of the relationship between violence and subjectivity explored, for example, in the work of anthropologist Veena Das. There are many cases in which the juridical systems of South Africa, Brazil, Germany, Australia, New Zealand, the United States, and the Netherlands, as well as many colonial regimes have secured and upheld convictions against members of racially and ethnically subordinated groups who dared to contest the violence visited upon them or members of their community. Such decisions have often acknowledged the death of subordinate group members by the hands of dominant group actors, while simultaneously, through decisions by jury or judge, absolving dominant group members from societal guilt or conviction of a crime. In such instances, racial supremacy and rule of law have an interlocking relationship, and the former has often been given priority by the juridical dimension of the state apparatus over the latter. Under these circumstances, law often follows rather than precedes violence, much in the way that Giorgio Agamben describes the interrelationship of law and violence under the state of exception in Nazi Germany (see chapter 6).

Self-mobilized racially subordinate subjects might not be able to overturn a state's application of the concept of racial right or racial sovereignty (nor sovereignty itself), but they can at times halt the march of the individual, group, or even institution invested with the dual power of racist supremacy and state power. Such instances are processes of displacement generated by the dynamic outcome of the "victory" of the subordinate group member. Although subordinate group members may be judged and convicted afterward for committing an act of violence against a white person, or for transgressing laws against violence of any sort against anyone, such judgment occurs after the racially empowered citizen has been immobilized or otherwise halted in the attempt to impose racist and statist authority. This is part of the reason why vengeance tales are an integral part of subaltern political culture, and almost invariably there is at least one popular folk tale (that later becomes part of a popular novel or film) about an individual or group who took on state or popular dominant group violence and won, even if the person (or persons) was ultimately punished by the state for his or her acts. From Australia there is *The Chant of Jimmy Blacksmith* and *The Tracker, Sweet Sweetback's Badasssss Song* in the United States, *The Harder They Come* in Jamaica, *Once Were Warriors* of New Zealand, *Serafina!* of South Africa, *Lampião* of northeastern Brazil, or to stretch beyond the phenotypic harmony, stories of the legendary Ned Kelly of Australia,[22] and Michael Kohlhaas (see chapter 6).

Working-class resistance to racial and class domination did not necessarily yield to the demands of either white supremacy, with its prerequisites of subservience and acquiescence, or to the dominant tactics of the civil rights movement, which required civil disobedience and a renunciation of violence that often cost people their lives. Working-class resistance to violent practices of racial domination did not automatically transform Birmingham's black consumers of public transportation into activists, intellectuals, and sloganeers reflexively advocating violent responses to state and individual racial domination, in the mode of a Robert Williams, H. Rap Brown, or Eldridge Cleaver, or in the tradition of black and third-world intellectuals ranging from Franz Fanon, Albert Memmi, Jomo Kenyatta, or Ho Chi Minh.

IV Displacement and Parallel Politics

Displacement and political parallelism are the two remaining conceptual components of a theory of quotidian politics and its resonance in black politics. I define parallel political communities as those that operate alongside or at the periphery of dominant macropolitical practices and communities. Protests, assemblies, and marches that seek to critique the substantive content as well as the processes of closed proceedings, such as the meetings of the so-called G8 nations in 2005, are examples of political parallelism. The attendant concept of displacement emphasizes the spatial and temporal components of political parallelism. In response to general conditions of subordination or specific acts of racist violence and oppression, subordinate actors respond in spheres of society and in cultural forms that are not the medium or spheres in which the acts of deliberation or violence first occur. Certain forms of rap music, graffiti, and other visual arts are perfect embodiments of displacement and parallel macropolitics. These expressions of parallel politics enter civic discourse and its symbolic systems as objects of consumption first, and only later—if at all—enter into formal political discourse.

Rather than asserting that popular culture *necessarily* involves macropolitics, or conversely dismissing the possibility that individual acts of defiance or the expression of displeasure with some aspect of a status quo constitutes macropolitics, I am interested in examining where and when forms of popular culture are utilized as vehicles for political expression. The examples of expressions of dissent in popular culture that I analyze below come from two distinct genres and parts of the New World—Terry Callier, a folk-blues practitioner originally from Chicago's South Side, and the Chilean poet Pablo Neruda. Both works highlight the tensions of the politics/popular culture nexus manifest in political parallelism. Both Callier's and Neruda's art asks us to imagine and exceed our capacities for empathy and understanding of the horrors of two disparate events.

Terry Callier's ode is to Amadou Diallo, the Guinean immigrant who, in Februrary 1999, was killed by four New York City police officers who shot at him forty-one times, pumping nineteen bullets into his body right in front of his apartment door, on the *suspicion* that he was armed. The police officers were acquitted of charges of murder and commended by Rudolph Guiliani, KBE[23] then mayor of New York, for protecting the city from potential violence. Callier's lament follows:

> Lament for the Late AD
>
> Yo Manhattan, There's a secret hidden just behind your smile
> Stopped my dreamin'
> And it really messed me up for quite awhile
> I wish I could express it, but i must confess i just don't have
>   a clue
> New york, New york
> I thought I could depend on you
>
> What's up harlem
> Child my heart goes out to you like no one else
> 'Trane is gone now so we'll have to find the answers for
>   ourselves
> Honey, don't you hear the thunder
> Makes me wonder what this world is comin' to
> New york, New york
> I thought I could depend on you
>
> Bronx is burnin'
> People stand and watch in silent rage
> Some folks care not
> Others dare not try to read the printed page
> Ah, but I have seen a message
> With a meaning that you just can't misconstrue
> New york, New york
> I thought I could depend on you[24]

Callier's indictment of the city of New York is subtle and indirect. Indirection as a rhetorical strategy is an integral part of U.S. African American and other black world popular and political cultures, employed particularly during the era of slavery.[25] The murder of Diallo is expressed as disappointment with the city, rather than as an outraged, detailed account of the actions that preceded, constituted, and followed the murder. The indirection gives a vague, diffuse quality to the lyrics, at the same time that it conveys a broader, more comprehensive indictment of the city itself. The refrain "New York, New York, I thought I could depend on you" suggests surprise either that such an incident could occur in New York, or that four police officers could be acquitted of so blatant (at least to this observer) a case of murder. The killing of an unarmed black male in the United States, given the national history, is not surprising. What seems to surprise Callier, however, is its occurrence in New York.

As a consequence, Callier is forced to view the city differently, to interpret the "secret hidden just behind your smile," an unanticipated malevolence in a city he thought he could depend on. Yet, just what precisely is that upon which Callier could depend? There are features of black urban life in the United States that are peculiar to the U.S. African American experience, while at the same time resonant with the experiences of other ethnically and racially marginalized groups in cities throughout the world that have undergone vast waves of immigration, expansion, and industrialization. The movements of such groups are often brought under surveillance as a consequence of the anxieties their presence induces. Thus, Algerians in Paris, Indo-Pakistanis in English cities like Bradford and London, Bantus in Pretoria or Capetown, or Palestinians in Israel move at times in accordance with, or at other moments in dialectical relation to, the state surveillance apparatus' preoccupation with them. In this way at least, several classic sociological studies of the city, as well as the poetry of the monumental Walt Whitman, which presuppose the city's provision of anonymity and "blended in-ness" quality, have to be modified when considering the relationship of the marginalized within urban spaces. As evidenced by anti-loitering laws specifically designed to discourage black congregation in cities like New York, Chicago, Buenos Aires, and São Paulo after the abolition of slavery, municipal regimes have historically implemented laws to adjust to the influx of pariah populations for the purposes of labor. Codified and de jure segregation with just the right dose of coercion serves to ensure that members of these populations labor in these cities and are able to do little else comfortably without the authoritative gaze of the state and civic leaders.[26] Callier's disappointment comes from the recognition that the island of Manhattan is not safe for him or those who look like him.

Pablo Neruda, in contrast, uses direct, violent language in response to Richard M. Nixon and the U.S. government's meddling in the internal affairs of the Chilean nation. He criticizes U.S. intervention into the democratic election of Salvador Allende to the presidency of the Republic of Chile, the coup d'état, and subsequent counterrevolution.

Pablo Neruda:
Comienzo Por Invocar A Walt Whitman

Es por accíon de amor a mi país
que te reclamo, hermano necesario,
viejo Walt Whitman de la mano gris,

para que con tu apoyo extraordinario
verso a verso matemos de raíz
a Nixon, Presidente sanguinario.

Sobre la tierra no hay hombre feliz,
nadie trabaja bien en el planeta
si en Washington respira su nariz.

Pidiendo al viejo Bardo que me invista,
asumo mis deberes de poeta
armado del soneto terrorista,

porque debo dictar sin pena alguna
la sentencia hasta ahora nunca vista
de fusilar a un criminal ardiente

que a pesar de sus viajes a la luna
ha matado en la tierra tanta gente,
que huye el papel y la pluma se arranca

al escribir el nombre del malvado,
del genocida de la Casa Blanca. [27]

I Begin by Invoking Walt Whitman
It is for the love of my country
That I invoke you, my necessary brother
old, grey hand Walt Whitman

so that with your extraordinary support
verse by verse we will kill at the root
Nixon, bloody president

There is no happy man on earth
No one works well on the planet
If in Washington his nostrils still breathe

> Asking the old Bard to invest me
> I assume my duties of a poet
> Armed with terrorist sonnet
>
> For I must dictate without any punishment
> The unprecedented sentence
> Of shooting an ardent criminal
>
> Who in spite of his journeys to the moon
> Has killed so many people on earth
> That the paper flees and the pen stops
>
> When writing the name of the genocidal,
> evil one of the White House.[28]

"Genocide," "murder," "killing," and "bloodiness" are vivid terms used to characterize the Nixon regime's role in the usurpation of the body politic of the Chilean people and the death of its head of state. Neruda is responding to an activity undertaken by a specific regime against another, democratically elected regime. Unlike most songs and poetry deemed to be "political" by virtue of a mere mention, indeed description, of an unjust practice, Neruda is actually calling for a reaction and collective response. That he evokes the name of the poet Walt Whitman complicates the often simplistic "the United States of America versus the rest of the Americas" politics undertaken by many opponents of U.S. state policies toward Latin America and other regions of the world.[29] Neruda suggests, instead, opposition to a regime and its advocates, rather than to an entire national population.

There are similarities between these two poetic expressions as modes of parallel political articulation. Both forms of art evoke, rather than intervene in, circumstances for which the authors are hopeful, but ultimately powerless, to change. Neruda can critique the U.S. government's role in Vietnam and Chile, but cannot intervene to alter the course of events. He can summon the poetry, politics, and memory of Walt Whitman to kill Richard Nixon, yet Augusto Pinochet exacted a heavy toll on his own people, nonetheless. The fact that these events occurred are certainly not the fault or the limitation of the poet or the songwriter. The displacement and parallelism of Neruda's politics are characterized by the fact that the place from which he articulates his dissent is distinct from the actual site and moment of contestation, even though the site and moment of contestation were the inspirations for his dissent. What makes the strongest of rebellions and revolutions significant are the ways in which popular revolt and seizure of state power actually *displace* the state and its attendant apparatuses as the principal sites of macropolitical competition. In moments of revolution, the temporal and spatial divisions between the macropolitics of status quo political actors and the macropolitics of state aspirants are compressed. Status quo actors must at least acknowledge not only the claims of the revolutionaries, they must also acknowledge in some way the prospect of their own demise as political actors associated with a particular regime or institution. As long as the principal, predesignated sites of political contestation remain, revolution and rebellion are held at bay. This holds true whether in the case of "democratic elections" during the waning years of authoritarian rule in Brazil, Alberto Fujimori's self-coup in Peru in the 1990s, or even Richard Nixon's resignation in 1974 in response to the Watergate scandal.

This speaks to the dilemma of political articulation in parallel politics more generally. If the troops are not behind the drum major, if they are already defeated before even joining the battle, or argue amongst themselves to the point of disintegration, we must acknowledge that the artist as drum major is perhaps better prepared for war than the would-be troops. Much like the helpful stockperson in the defunct department store, Neruda makes his claims against Nixon and his call to poetic armament from a site distinct from both Pinochet's presidential palace and the White House of the United States. In both cases, the dynamics of political parallelism and displacement are in place.

V. Hidden Transcripts, Infrapolitics, and Quotidian Politics

Of the scholarship in contemporary political science, the work of James Scott resonates most with the methodological and conceptual implications of my theory of quotidian politics. Scott's innovations on existing concepts such as "moral economy," and creation of new concepts such as "weapons of the weak," infrapolitics, and "Brechtian modes of resistance" enlivened debates within history and the social sciences about power, powerlessness, and modes of subaltern resistance.

I believe that there are several unexplored assumptions in the weapons of the weak argument that have great relevance for black political thought and questions of political agency, especially the implicit assumptions, correlations, and causal relationships concerning collective and individuated (so-called voluntarist) action. Some of the issues, conceptualizations, and interpretive schemes undertaken by Scott have been utilized by Robin D. G. Kelley, one of the most perceptive historians of black popular culture in the history of black studies and African American history. Taken together, Scott's and Kelley's work highlights the comparative implications of Scott's formulations for scholarship outside the domain of Southeast Asian studies, comparative politics, and political anthropology. Scott's combination of ethnography, history, and interpretive methods to identify and discern political behavior places him in the company of a qualitative methodological tradition that includes such diverse figures as Charles Taylor, Sheldon Wolin, and Clifford Geertz.

I share Scott's view that "structurally similar modes of domination will bear a family resemblance to one another"[30] and that "to the degree that structures of domination can be demonstrated to operate in comparable ways, they will, all other things being equal, elicit reactions and patterns of resistance that are broadly comparable."[31] If African American and other black political cultures in Western nation-states are still subaltern political cultures (and I believe they are), what are the relative strengths and weaknesses of Scott's approach for an understanding of their macro- and micropolitics? Second, how does an examination of these modes of politics in relation to Scott's approach help sophisticate our ideas about nonquantifiable but nonetheless observable articulations of power and powerlessness?

For Scott, everyday life is but a bubbling cauldron in which anger over injustice pours through a seemingly fastened lid of status quo norms, rules, regulations, and social graces. With little possibility of upending conditions of domination (turning over the pot, to continue the metaphor), the tactical rationale of the public transcript is to produce false trails of obedience at the end of which lies resentment, anger (some of it personalized), and an often clear-eyed view of the injustices before them. Scott's metaphor of the barrier reef provides the clearest, albeit figurative, declaration of his intention to portray infrapolitics as a form of political articulation: "Just as millions of anthozoan polyps create, willy-nilly, a coral reef, so do the multiple acts of peasant insubordination and evasion create political and economic barrier reefs of their own." [32]

Scott believes daily subversion has an incremental dimension, providing peasants, working classes, and members of ethnically or racially oppressed minorities with a basis for an even more radical resistance to domination. Scott argues, "If we think, in schematic terms, of the public transcript as comprising a domain of material appropriation . . . a domain of public mastery and subordination . . . then we may perhaps think of the hidden transcript as comprising the offstage responses and rejoinders to that public transcript. It is, if you will, the portion of an acrimonious dialogue that domination has driven off the center stage."[33]

Many of the key examples utilized in Scott's original formulation focus on relations of domination in nonwage and outright unfree labor (slavery, feudalism, serfdom). A key correlation in Scott's split-screen (public/private) model of peasant political behavior is that the higher the stakes involved in public articulation of discontent, the greater the importance of the hidden transcript. It is under such bleak and meager conditions that a peasant, subaltern politics of resistance focuses on reciprocity and off-stage acts of class retribution, rather than class and societal transformation, as when the nearly feudal prerogatives of landowners to peasants are increasingly ignored in the mechanization of agricultural production. Under such conditions, revolt is seen by peasants as highly unprofitable, with little prospect of overturning relations of domination, despite the claims of political organizers in the region who view the actual villages upon which Scott's Sedaka was based as ripe for proletarian or Maoist revolution.

Over the course of three books, *The Moral Economy of the Peasant: Rebellion and Subsistence in Southeast Asia, Weapons of the Weak: Everyday Forms of Peasant Resistance,* and *Domination and the Arts of Resistance: Hidden Transcripts,* Scott's perspective grew increasingly more sympathetic to what could be characterized as voluntarist, individuated responses to conditions of labor exploitation. One of Scott's ambitions was to provide a more general account of how individuals of less powerful socioeconomic and cultural groups responded to ongoing processes of material and communal domination. In these works Scott adeptly underscores the false polarity of resistance versus subsistence and highlights the dynamic, relational aspects of political contestation and conflict in arenas of society not framed by the rationalist logic of reasoned debate, upon which formal politics in liberal societies are premised, and in forms of subaltern struggle that escape strictly "proletarian" categorization.[34]

The logic of Scott's formulation is largely consistent throughout and across examples ranging from peasant struggles to the popular dismantling of the Berlin wall: *hidden transcript/private sphere—public transcript/public sphere—public utterance/collective sentiment—open contestation and unveiling of hidden transcripts—transformation of dynamics of power and powerlessness.*

As a concept, coagulation shares some normative attributes with Scott's application of E. P. Thompson's concept of moral economy, as well as Scott's own conceptualizations of infrapolitics, Brechtian acts of resistance, and "weapons of the weak." Within the broader theorization of quotidian politics, however, the concepts of displacement and parallelism, focused on the temporal and spatial aspects of power relations, emphasize the processual aspects of power dynamics. The examples I have assembled and analyzed provide an opportunity to examine three aspects of Scott's formulation: the distinction between the public and private spheres, crucial to his conceptualization of infrapolitics and hidden transcript; his resolutely modern teleology of politics that seeks to link infrapolitics and Brechtian acts of resistance to eventual collective action and the articulation of a public transcript; and his implicitly liberal view of political articulation, glimpsed in his preoccupation with speaking truth to power as evidence of a hidden transcript being made public.

Racist violence, whether meted out by the state or by racist individuals, explodes the public/private distinctions central to Scott's concept of infrapolitics. Scott's metaphor conveys an ecological sense of politics. His analogy assumes a cumulative, almost architectonic effect of Brechtian forms of resistance. Not only does the most recent incident rest upon the previous one, but knowledge of previous acts of resistance constitute the cumulative archive of conscious, collective recalcitrance. Are such barrier reefs to be understood as the accumulation of self-conscious acts, or merely acts that, in some coincidental way, occur naturally? The naturalism inherent in the metaphor could be read as positing a certain predetermination, a congenital predisposition toward the creation of such reefs, a survival instinct of subalterns. But human beings are not polyps, and thus the analogy elides a basic question regarding the distinction between collective and individuated resistance, insofar as we cannot be certain, in Scott's formulation, whether the construction of the barrier of resistance is a self-conscious act or if those who participated were aware of its construction.

The public-private split that Scott is so reliant upon cannot be sustained for two reasons. First, in the spatial and temporal aspects of power, the working-class men and women who decide to directly confront white citizens are not engaging in a politics of displacement or parallelism since they confront power directly in the here and now. Their direct confrontation with power and unity of thought and action further erodes the hidden-public transcript distinction. Like Scott, Kelley writes of the cumulative effect of U.S. African American infrapolitics without actually identifying or pinpointing their specific effects on power relations. Like Scott, Kelley's application of the concepts of infrapolitics and hidden transcripts to U.S. African-American experience neglects the temporal and spatial aspects of power dynamics identifiable in processes of displacement and parallelism.[35]

Scott's metaphor presumes the accumulated historical unity of a type of resistance, experienced as individual but when read over time, acknowledged as collective. Barrier reefs made up of polyps provide the sense of a structure created out of individual entities. The polyps are therefore more than just polyps. But in the case of actual human beings engaged in the politics of labor, their modes of resistance are more akin to individuated repertoires at different times and places, rather than stances undertaken collectively, and most important, simultaneously.

The "barrier reef" of black quotidian struggles is highly circumstantial and phenomenological, even if it presents itself with some regularity. Taking the two incidents of coagulation and aggregation in section two, quotidian resistance does not always emerge whenever two or more aggrieved black people, or members of any other subaltern group, appear. C. L. R. James's remonstrations about the work of Herbert Aptheker serves as a cautionary reminder against the tendency to read every gesture in the daily life of subaltern populations as signs or symbols of resistance.

The two examples of coagulation can be viewed as micropolitical responses to macropolitical structures of inequality. One can invoke macropolitical reasons for engaging in a particular act of rebellion or resistance without that act precipitating a larger collective action or public denunciation of conditions of inequality. None of the activities I have described and analyzed in this chapter, whether directly or parenthetically, could be properly understood as being incumbent upon a person occupying and performing a specific labor function. I'm certain that in the case of the young man in the automotive repair department "providing black people with new batteries if you believe they deserve them, even if your manager does not think so" was not part of his, or any other person's, job description.

I would like to turn, finally, to the role of language in Scott. My point not only concerns the limitations of the assumption that "speaking truth to power" constitutes successful collective action but also the problems entailed in upholding the liberal/rationalist presumption that discourse and the expression of opinion in the modern world is tantamount to political power, or at the very least, empowering. Freedom of speech and the articulation of dissent, once again, become the barometers for judging and accessing political power and resistance of state and economic authority. This idea is operative in the discourse-centered approach that is particularly evident in *Weapons of the Weak* and *Domination and the Arts of Resistance*.

If there is one cross-national lesson to be learned from the politics of subordinate groups even in liberal-democratic societies, successes or failures of popular protest have not hinged on the ability of, for example, indigenous groups in Australia, New Zealand, or the United States to publicly present a hidden transcript. Coercion, vast resettlement schemes, swindles, and mass slaughter have been visited upon these populations in spite of, not in the absence of, reasoned debate between elite representatives of subordinate and dominant groups. If, in fact, a theory of subordinate politics can emerge in relation to the transition from hidden to public transcripts, then the role of violence and state coercion needs to be foreground, rather than *parrhesia* or frank speech. Speaking truth to power may only serve to identify speakers of truth as candidates for "the disappeared." As the examples of state political repression in Chile, Nigeria, Argentina, and Brazil demonstrate all too well, speaking truth to power can get one killed.

How might we further make sense of Scott's concepts in light of black popular culture's modes of resistance to authority? In *Race Rebels: Culture, Politics and the Black Working Class,* Kelley applies Scott's understanding of subaltern resistance to U.S. African American quotidian politics that have largely remained unaccounted for in much of the history of the civil rights struggle in the United States. The motivating question for Kelley in *Race Rebels* is, "How do African-American working people struggle and survive outside of established organizations or organized social movements? What impact do these daily conflicts and hidden concerns have on movements that purport to speak for the dispossessed? Can we call this politics?"[36] This formulation and the historical examples of unorganized resistance presented and interpreted by Kelley provide an opportunity to evaluate the relative advantages and disadvantages of Scott's "hidden transcript" model, as well as the possible value of what I have called coagulate politics as an explanatory model for quotidian politics in U.S. African-American experience.

Though grounded in the historiography of comparative radical history and inspired by the work of historians such as E. P. Thompson, C. L. R. James, and W. E. B. Du Bois, Kelley takes his conceptual cues from James Scott's notion of "infrapolitics."[37] Though he does not diverge from Scott's framework, Kelley does acknowledge that the "hidden transcript" model of infrapolitics, which posits a progression from seemingly quiescent public accommodation and private contestation to public expression of the previously private/hidden transcript, does not encompass the entire range of open and spontaneous contestation of racial domination in the public sphere by working-class blacks.

Like Scott, Kelley's intention goes beyond finding historical and cultural evidence of resistance to class and racial domination among the vast segments of working poor, whether in Southeast Asia or the United States, who are not organized by union, syndicate, party, or social movement. More ambitiously, he wants to change the manner in which scholars interpret resistance and quiescence among black working-class subjects who do not engage in macropolitics. Kelley intuits the theoretical implications of his own experiences as a minimum-wage worker in McDonald's, and links his and other black workers' repertoire of rebelliousness and insubordination in relation to managers and owners to the social and cultural history of black resistance. Kelley is interested in how "power operates, and how seemingly innocuous, individualistic acts of survival and resistance shape politics, workplace struggles, and the social order generally."[38] Kelley's autobiographical account of his own labor experiences as a worker for the fast-food behemoth McDonald's help illuminate the more abstract themes and concepts of power and politics, domination and resistance:

> Like most working people throughout the world, my fellow employees at Mickey D's were neither total victims of routinization, sexism, and racism, nor were they "rational" economic beings driven by the most base utilitarian concerns.... If we are to make meaning of these kinds of actions rather than dismiss them as manifestations of immaturity, false consciousness, or primitive rebellion, we must begin to dig beneath the surface of trade union pronouncements, political institutions, and organized social movements... We have to step into the complicated maze of experience that renders "ordinary" folks so extraordinarily multifaceted, diverse and complicated. Most importantly, we need to break away from traditional notions of politics. We must not only redefine what is "political" but question a lot of common ideas about what are "authentic" movements and strategies of resistance.[39]

Like Scott, Kelley posits that infrapolitics "have a cumulative effect on power relations."[40] Kelley's examples, ranging from the Zoot Suit Riots of the 1940s, Malcolm X's normative and cultural transformation from hood rat to member of the Nation of Islam, to the role of the unorganized black poor in the civil rights movement, suggest that violence, whether mediated by the state or white citizens and economic interests in society, has been a far more commonplace factor in the daily life of the black poor than their black middle-class counterparts, and certainly more so than for whites of various socioeconomic backgrounds. Consequently, the quotidian politics of working-class blacks have necessarily entailed the negotiation of violence meted out by the state, racist organizations, individuals, and in labor relations. Responses to state and other modes of violence vary by gender, region, city, and personal disposition, but the frequency with which violent altercations involving black and white citizens occurred in segregated Birmingham, Alabama, for example, provides a sense of the role of violence in quotidian politics. As mentioned at the outset of this chapter, gratuitous acts of violence precipitated and practiced by dominant actors (in this instance whites) function to remind less powerful groups of their subordination in society.

Unlike a conventional definition of power such a Robert Dahl's classic formulation (A gets B to engage in behavior B would not otherwise do), wherein violence and coercion are utilized by dominant actors to force subordinate actors to modify their behavior, gratuitous expressions of power are characterized by modes of violence and coercion that do not seek to modify present or past behavior, but primarily to *punctuate*, adding an exclamation point to a condition of relative powerlessness among a subordinate population. In slave societies throughout the New World, and in the incompletely liberalized societies that emerged from these colonial societies in the aftermath of slavery, violence imposed on slave and freed populations was a means of not only inducing immediate coercion but also of producing terror and anxiety among the subordinate population. Of course, such violence also served to intimidate other members of slave and freed populations and limit the possibility of their resistance to racial domination.[41]

Kelley analyzes a combination of popular-coercive and state-coercive forms of power in the history of violent altercations in the Birmingham public bus system in the years leading up to the bus boycott. Public transportation is an apt choice for an analysis of quotidian politics among black or other working classes, because in most U.S. cities (New York and Boston being two exceptions), the preferred mode of transportation is privately owned automobiles. Class, age, infirmity, and income often determine who takes public transportation and who does not. Movement through society, whether by foot or by public transportation, increases the likelihood of encounters and interactions with various parts of the "public,"[42] which are, in fact, a diverse range of publics. Such movement also increases the likelihood of interactions with representatives of the state. Increased contact with both the state and with individuals increases the possibility of negative, indifferent, and positive encounters. In a society such as that of the United States, where racism has been a fact of life for several centuries, the public sphere is a site in which interactions with various publics in daily life increase the prospects for racist encounters. Not just in racial politics, but in macropolitics more generally, it is important to remember that voting, even for whites, was often fraught with violence at polling booths in many parts of the United States.[43]

Kelley writes that in 1941 alone, there were 176 reported incidents of racial conflict on Birmingham streetcars and buses. Many of these incidents involved black working-class women and were largely attributable to conflicts between white and black passengers, between black passengers and white conductors, and, more specifically, between black passengers and white conductors over passengers being shortchanged.[44] There were also altercations over seating and the racial compartmentalization of the bus or streetcar seating arrangements, a standard practice during the apartheid-era United States. Kelley rightly refers to these spaces as "small war zones" where class and racial conflict congealed.

As Kelley points out, daily acts of resistance to racial domination have often been neglected by scholars with more elite-driven accounts of the civil rights struggle. The work of Charles Payne and John Roemer provides rich examples of everyday resistance to white supremacy among black communities in rural Mississippi, the kind of resistance often neglected by more elite-driven accounts of the civil rights movements as a struggle for leadership, competing visions, and strategies for social mobilization. This kind of bottom-up historiography does not fit along current continua of integrationist and segregationist approaches to racial inequality, nor under the rubrics of liberal, conservative, nationalist, nonviolent, or violent protest. It also does not fit with the image of clean-cut, white and black middle-class college students engaged in lunch counter sit-ins and other forms of civil disobedience. Robert Williams, Joanne Chesimard, and Julian Mayfield provide counterexamples of U.S. African American instrumental use of violence as self-defense in response to state violence, as well as societal violence deployed by citizens and civic organizations empowered by white supremacy.[45] What made the U.S. civil rights movement uniquely successful was its advocacy of resistance *outside* the logic of racist violence. Those who refused to relinquish violence's instrumentality opted for other means to participate in the black struggle. Those who interest me (and I assume Kelley) most are individuals who do not fit in either obviously "political" category, but who deployed violence as a form of self-sovereignty in certain encounters with the state.

The larger question here is where to locate "weapons of the weak" in a theoretical account of a moral economy of resistance to unjust wages, material conditions, and overall life circumstances imposed upon poor populations. In several key respects, Scott's initial formulation and Kelley's application of infrapolitics and weapons of the weak concepts represent efforts to redefine phenomena as political that sociologists of the previous generation referred to as "pre-political." The weak may utilize overt as well as covert forms of resistance, but not necessarily in the same manner as those employing instruments of state power. In more abstract, analytic terms, "weapons of the weak" can be thought of as the employment of socially constituted implements by subordinate, relatively powerless agents to indirectly contest more powerful political actors and institutions. Instruments and/or behaviors of quotidian resistance are effective in cases where neither the state, dominant institutions, nor powerful individuals have a direct, immediate reaction or response. The consequences of weapons of the weak are more often than not indirect, disparate, and noncumulative.

Scott's theorization of infrapolitics and, to a lesser extent, Kelley's application of the concept, explicitly reject an oppositional juxtaposition of more formalized notions of institutional politics, political agency, and collective action with informal contestations of political domination. To the extent that Scott and Kelley reject the modern leftist trajectory and telos of collective mobilization, in which political agency and progress emanate solely from class struggle, their advocacy of infrapolitics is part of a critical methodology of nonformal political resistance that could be said to be postmodern. Yet their *trajectory* for infrapolitics, which involves building momentum and taking coherent form in an eventual public transcript, is decidedly modern. Though I share their desire to retain a modern rather than postmodern sense of political agency and collective action, I am more doubtful of their trajectory. Though my data base is limited, I believe I can safely posit that infrapolitics are certainly politics. If, as Linda Zerilli suggests, politics refers to something besides itself and is constituted in the relationship between two distinct entities, then coagulate politics is a form of politics.[46]

VI Conclusion

A theory of quotidian politics must consider the possibility that subordinate resistance to dominant actors can occur *within* the processes or instances of subordination and domination. If we accept the classic conceptualization of power dynamics as relational rather than absolute phenomena, subordinate actors necessarily have both a stake and role in the dynamics of dominance and subordination. Their resistance to dynamics of power and domination does not necessarily mean that they "win," either immediately, or ultimately. A theory of quotidian politics must be cautious not to indiscriminately characterize moments of resistance within processes of domination as resistance *outside* of relations of dominance and subordination. Otherwise, the spatial, temporal, and conceptual problems of formulations that do not distinguish between micro- and macropolitics, scale and type of resistance, and practices of subsistence versus practices of rebellion and revolution, will continue to frustrate attempts at more comprehensive theories of power relations and resistance. As Scott, Kelley, and my own examples illustrate, the response of subordinates to conditions of dominance are rarely if ever predetermined. The wildebeest does occasionally gore the attacking lion, as the bull does, on occasion, the matador. Yet in order to rid their species of the ongoing possibility of attack and consumption by their predators, wildebeests and bulls would need to curtail and limit the attacks of lions and matadors as a *group*. Successful individual encounters with predators have no cumulative effect on the safety of the group.

What *does* constitute collective action then? Is collective action the premeditated coalescence and formation of formerly discrete individual agents? Can collective action be the spontaneous response of disparate individuals to similar dynamics and circumstances of inequality? If so, what are the possible "cumulative effects" of Brechtian acts of resistance? Below, I sketch some possible hypotheses concerning cumulative effects:

1. Overturning conditions and mechanisms of domination due to the cumulative effects of coagulate politics (aggregate politics, poaching, Brechtian acts of resistance).
2. Partial amelioration of conditions of domination due to the cumulative effects of coagulate politics.
3. Contingent amelioration of certain conditions of domination, and not others, with the prospect of recidivism and reflux, or further erosion of conditions of domination.
4. Increased repression by the state, institutions of civil society, economy, and individuals in positions of power and dominance.

Of these four projected outcomes of aggregate politics, I believe the first is the most unlikely. It would be possible only under conditions in which a dominant group with superordinate positions in the state, civil society and/or society, military, and economy, is weakened to such an extent that increasing incursions and interventions by subordinate group members in coagulate politics leads to both mass mobilization and the collapse of a dominant group as a hegemonic, authoritarian, or totalitarian bloc. This outcome, then, is predicated not on quotidian politics solely, but a combination of factors and variables that would combine to weaken a dominant group's position in society as a whole, not just in their daily interactions with subordinate group members. The Portuguese in Lusophone Africa, or the fall of the Soviet state, are two rare examples of this form of quotidian political activity that resemble Scott and Kelley's notion of hidden transcripts becoming public with societal, national-popular, collective implications.

The overwhelming majority of subaltern politics cases, however, share some combination of attributes of outcomes 2, 3, and 4. Developments including the political recognition of Dalits in India, the U.S. African American and Native American civil rights movements, the formation of laws acknowledging distinct histories of injustice and denial, cultural practices such as religious observance and holidays, the nationalization of previously ethnic or racially specific heroes (Marcus Garvey in Jamaica, Zumbi in Brazil), and the creation of laws devised to combat ongoing practices of racism, such as affirmative action, and antiracist and defamation laws and organizations, are all examples of changes in plural societies brought about by a combination of quotidian and formal, organized resistance. These changes have not obliterated racial domination, but have helped lessen certain overt forms of racial domination in many societies, while making, ironically, the proponents of racial hierarchies practitioners of hidden transcripts as well. The theory of quotidian politics offered here can help remind students of politics that power dynamics are interactive, context-specific processes, where crises of authority and power can be induced not only by economic downturn or state fragility but by demands made around issues not entirely related or encompassed by the formal economy or state power. The obvious examples are nationalism and ethnic mobilization, which resist easy correlations between the degree of political competition and contestation and the health of a particular state or economy. As argued by Will Kymlicka and Charles Taylor concerning the case of Quebecois nationalism in Canada, by Joseph Carens in his assessment of ethnic conflict in Fiji, and by Mark Beissinger regarding nationalism's emergence and the Soviet state's demise in the former Soviet Union, state-based and economistic accounts of political crises in these three countries attempt, unsuccessfully, to reduce these cases of political transformation to a single variable or institution.

Another way of understanding quotidian politics is as an effort to make sense of the political implications of phenomena often excluded from the category and conceptualization of "the political" in state and materialist accounts of power and politics. In addition to some of the concepts, questions and themes I have raised in this chapter, there are also the ideational sources that people draw upon within quotidian politics and that motivate micro- and macropolitics. Chapter 3 explores further some of the contextual and methodological implications of my theory of quotidian politics, in the examination of black ideologies as forms of thought that motivate micro- and macropolitical practices.

CHAPTER 3

Ideology and Political Culture in Black

Michael Hanchard and Michael Dawson

The more aware one becomes of the presuppositions underlying his thinking, in the interests of truly empirical research, the more it is apparent that this empirical procedure (in the social sciences, at least), can be carried on only on the basis of certain meta-empirical, ontological and metaphysical judgments and the expectations and hypotheses that follow from them.[1]

If empirical knowledge were not preceded by an ontology it would be entirely inconceivable, for we can extract objectified meanings out of a given reality only to the extent that we are able to ask intelligent and revealing questions.[2]

Introduction

This chapter most centrally assesses the contemporary state of the study of U.S. African American politics by political scientists in the United States. Although relying heavily on the texts, contributions, and debates of this subfield within the discipline of political science, our development of a more ethnographic, context-sensitive approach to the study of black politics in this chapter can also help in the conceptualization and examination of political phenomena of black life-worlds in other parts of the globe. The above passage and footnote from Karl Mannheim's classic *Ideology and Utopia* helps illuminate the attenuated relationship between abstracted empirical knowledge and the larger social totalities in which such knowledge is situated. Mannheim's analytic framing of the relationship between empiricism and ontology, between presuppositions and observable behavior, provides an opportunity for the coauthors of this chapter to relate parts to wholes on the subject of black politics and topics of black political thought, and to identify the gaps within the literatures of black politics, in the United States and elsewhere. Part of the problem and process of identifying gaps in the study of black politics entails recognizing the role of methodology and epistemology in the determination of which phenomena will be defined as political and which people and institutions are identified and characterized as political actors.

Much of the debate within mainstream political science journals on black public opinion emphasizes three seeming truths: (1) black public opinion and black ideologies are one and the same, two descriptors for the same phenomena and therefore interchangeable terms; (2) black politics, namely, formal electoral politics and related public opinion, campaign and electoral processes, represent the entirety of black political behavior, not a subset or feature; (3) black public opinion is largely a distilled variation of black elite public opinion, in keeping with the verticality principle of ideological diffusion formulated by Philip Converse and innovated upon by scholars such as John Zaller.[3]

This chapter serves two purposes. First, we provide a brief overview of the evolution of scholarly literature on black public opinion in the United States in order to juxtapose several dominant interpretations of black politics and black public opinion with the larger discursive field of racial politics and U.S. African American political culture. An examination of key texts from black protest literature, social and political thought, as well as more ethnographic approaches to obtaining black perspectives on racial discrimination provides us with an opportunity to underscore that much of the survey-based literature on black public opinion provides only a glimpse of the ideals, norms, and outlooks of black political culture. Following Hanchard's theory of quotidian politics offered in chapter 2, this chapter will explore further the implications of quotidian politics in the U.S. black public sphere for the elaboration of various black ideologies.

The study of black ideologies, their origins and variations, has been largely absent from the discipline of political science. Black ideologies have been a topic of inquiry within the discipline only at moments of national crisis (the 1965 and 1968 riots, for example),[4] when students of American politics have stopped to consider the relationship between black politics, norms and values, and political behavior. Rarely have black ideologies been examined as a complex or cluster of ideas and perspectives in their own right, with principles, aims, and objectives that can only partially be viewed through the lens of race and racism, the aims and objectives of a white-majority population, or in campaign speeches, debates, and rhetoric. As a consequence, the metaphysical, meta-empirical, and ontological terrain upon which black public opinion rests has been curiously ignored by most students of black public opinion and politics.[5]

The evasion or neglect of the rich documentary and historical evidence of black ideologies and political thought has resulted in debates about black ideologies and public opinion that are narrowly skewed. Black ideologies, the landscape for much critical discourse classified by empiricists as "evidence" of a stated opinion or belief, constitute an important part of our joint endeavor here, to relate the parts of black public opinion to the larger context of black life-worlds. Black ideologies continue to inform black belief systems and political choices ranging from consumption patterns to voting preferences, yet are often missed by scholars whose methodological approaches leave little room for the interpretive paradoxes and complexities that black ideologies pose.

The neglect of ideologies in black politics, however, is symptomatic of a more general trend in U.S. political science over the past twenty years away from interpretive, qualitative investigations of political phenomena, in favor of less historically and ethnographically detailed scholarship. As political science has moved closer to approximating the "hard" sciences, there has been a move away from the study of ideology. Ideology, as an evaluative criteria of judgment, has come to be viewed as too flimsy a basis for scientific predictability.[6] This shift has had several self-limiting consequences for the study of black politics.

The overreliance on survey research, as opposed to the ethnographic, extended interview techniques utilized more often in sociology and anthropology, is one limitation. The second, which we will focus on in this chapter, is the limited use of literature on the topics of ideology and critical interpretive methods within the fields of political theory and political sociology. Ironically, political scientists regularly mine these two literatures in their work on topics pertaining to the welfare state, bureaucracy, status, class, union, and interest-group formation. Yet these literatures are rarely consulted by contemporary scholars of "racial attitudes" and behaviors in American politics, many of whom conduct survey opinion research with the operative methodological assumption that the study of ideology belongs to an earlier, less scientific stage of the discipline.

We believe that the subject of black ideologies is not an archaic area of investigation, but central to understanding much of contemporary black public opinion, political behavior, and political culture. The examination of ideological forms help to simultaneously distinguish the concepts of power, influence, and coercion and their effects on political behavior, and link political behavior to sources of memory, history, and personal and collective ethnography. Moreover, the origins of black ideologies, with their multiple, often competing class and status sources, help question some central assumptions about the evolution, deployment, and diffusion of ideologies in the modern world. Many survey researchers who ignore the relationship between black ideologies, political thought, and black public opinion attribute expressed attitudes and behaviors to the dominant political culture's norms, belief systems, and the foundational texts of American politics. As a consequence, they often miss what makes black ideologies, political thought, and public opinion distinctive in relation to the attitudes and political behaviors of other groups in the United States.

By highlighting some of the ideational and context-based features of black ideologies and political thought we will demonstrate how critical, interpretive methods, as opposed to quantitative approaches, bring into question several canonical and contemporarily prominent survey-based accounts of black public opinion. While certainly not dismissive of random survey approaches, we emphasize the need for a critical reexamination of black ideologies to more fully describe the interactive relationship between black public opinion, black ideologies, and black political thought.

Our preoccupation with epistemologies and methodologies deployed in the examination of black politics can be translated into the following question: What is black politics, and how do we know it when we see it? As outlined in chapters 1 and 2, a more expansive, context-sensitive definition and understanding of black politics requires attention to its transnational and cross-national dimensions and to forms of political life, perspectives, and outlooks not encapsulated in electoral competition. This is as true for black political mobilization in Brazil, Britain, Peru, and Germany as it is in the United States since, as elaborated in chapter 5, black participation in formal electoral politics—whether as voters or candidates—is a relatively recent phenomena in Western politics.[7] Unless we are prepared to suggest that black ideologies and perspectives on politics are entirely coincident with ideologies and perspectives on politics found in formal electoral competition, we believe it more prudent to employ a broader operative definition of the political, as offered in chapter 1, and deploy multiple research methods to make sense of them.

II What Is Ideology and What's "Black" about It?

Ideology as a keyword and research topic rarely appears in political science journals and debates within the United States today. Its disappearance was the consequence of a critical moment in the practice of political science in the United States roughly beginning in the 1970s, when two related events occurred. First, the behaviorist movement, armed with quantitative research methods culled from economics and mathematics, began to develop research methods that treated political phenomena in a manner reminiscent of—and informed by—the physical and mathematical sciences. The attempt to systematize the study of politics across temporal and spatial distinctions was—and is—viewed as a means to reduce analytic variability and inconsistency in the examination of political behavior, reducing what many contemporary political scientists refer to as "noise," and achieving harmony.[8]

Alvin Gouldner defines an ideology as a speech act, a form of critical discourse in daily life that names and provides meaning to a range of symbols.[9] While ideological forms are indeed fundamentally discursive, we find this definition incomplete. Ideology is not co-terminus with a speech act, since there are many speech acts in human communication that do not fall under the category of ideology. More specifically, since not all ideological forms and traces affect political behaviors and ideals, we are interested only in those speech acts that either explicitly express political ideals and objectives or bear traces of idea clusters that are part of more comprehensive ideological forms previously identified elsewhere.

What makes systematized ideals "ideological" are the ways in which people cohere and organize around a set of ideals or beliefs, which, in turn, inform political, cultural, social, and economic choices. For example, there are black nationalists and internationalists in the United States, Brazil, Jamaica, and Britain who consider Black/African Liberation Day a holiday for people of the black world, and often refuse to go to work or school, even though Black Liberation Day is not a nationally recognized holiday in any of these countries. An ideological form is more than what its adherents describe as their beliefs; it is also framed by what they reject, refuse to acknowledge, and, finally, assume as "natural" within their social and political order. Conversely, the celebration of Kwanzaa in these and now many other countries, has often come with the rejection or diminution of competing religiously based celebrations such as Christmas.

There are other examples as well. In reading, for example, Frederick Douglass's Fourth of July speech, we can identify the traces of the dominant ideologies prevalent in the U.S. republic in the nineteenth century, as well as core assumptions and passages from the U.S. Constitution, at the same time that we can identify Douglass's speech act as a severe critique of the discrepancy between the U.S. government and civil society's professed ideals of equality and its maintenance and defense of racial slavery. In the language of ideological debate, Douglass's speech can be read as a means for Douglass to point out the doctrinal rather than truth-based dimensions of U.S. rhetoric about democracy. This links particular forms of black ideologies to other ideological forms without being ultimately defined or determined by them. This example is but one of many indicators that suggest that the emergence and proliferation of black ideologies cannot be simply deduced from the battles between romanticism and rationalism in the history of Western thought, the left-right distinctions of the French Revolution, or the proclamations of the end of modernity and the dawn of postmodernity.

Black ideologies, for the most part, did not evolve from a dialectic of science and religion and certainly were not a consequence of secularization, although they were undoubtedly influenced by secularization. Secularization, which in the sociological and political science literatures is seen as one of the positive outcomes of the Enlightenment's emphasis on reason and scientific method, did not automatically lessen the advocacy of racial and ethnic hierarchies in Western political and social thought, or in state practices.

Many black ideologies from the eighteenth century onward combined religious belief with a scientific outlook to debunk racial hierarchies and appeal to spirituality as well as reason to evoke notions of racial and political community.[10] Noted black political activists and thinkers, including Robert Allen, Ida B. Wells Barnet, Malcolm X, and Martin Luther King, as well as more contemporary figures combined secularism and religiosity. Followers of Elijah Muhammad, the late potentate of the Nation of Islam, for example, employed faulty, pseudoscientific reasoning to proclaim innate white racial inferiority and cravenness. In these instances, there was no hard juxtaposition of the age of religion against the age of science. Since scientific and religious justifications for the enslavement of African-descended people were prevalent, black abolitionists did not rely exclusively on either to make their case when debunking religious and scientific racism. In the philosophy of religion and normative philosophy, scholars like Eddie Glaude and Cornel West consider many of the early black theologians as among the first postmodern thinkers.[11] According to several scholars of black theology, skepticism toward the use of reason to maintain rather than debunk the idea of a racial hierarchy made many black political thinkers and actors skeptical of the Enlightenment emphasis on science and rationality well before the advent of postmodern thought.

In addition to making claims for the existence of black ideologies and their continued relevance for comprehending black political cultures, we would also like to introduce the distinction between upper- and lowercase ideologies. Forms of ideology that we characterize as lowercase (small i) ideologies are far more diffuse than uppercase ideologies, but often, as in the case of black ideologies, more widespread. Lowercase ideologies, emerging from subaltern, marginalized and subordinate groups, often fuse secular, sacred, cosmological, and even futurist thinking in their more popular iterations.[12] Their adherents may not declare themselves Marxist, liberal, conservative, or Afro-Centrist, but fuse elements from a broad range of ideational sources in their critical deliberations concerning political events or circumstances in daily life. We will dissect the implications of uppercase and lowercase ideological forms for understanding black ideologies. But first, we will examine how the topic of ideology has been evaluated in political science and the implications of this evaluation for studying black ideological forms.

III Robert Lane, Philip Converse, and Black Public Opinion

Robert Lane and Philip E. Converse are the two scholars who have cast the largest shadow over the study of public opinion and have provided two central though competing understandings of the role of ideas, beliefs, and ideologies in U.S. political culture. Not only did their work contribute to the development of ethnographic and quantitative methods for the study of public opinion, it also led the way for a critique of ideology as a useful concept and area of study for American politics.

Race and public opinion is a relatively recent focus within the subfield of American politics. Even more recent is the attention given to the study of black attitudes about race relations and the republic more generally by political scientists. For years, the opinions of the black populace in the United States were considered inconsequential or marginal to the study of public opinion. Starting in the 1970s, the study of black attitudes and behavior underwent a process of topical desegregation. Black and white researchers examined black public opinion as a feature or component of the U.S. mass public, even as they approached the topic from distinct or competing methodological perspectives.

In most courses on American public opinion, Robert Lane is read as Philip Converse's eclipsed interlocutor. Lane wrote two widely read and substantively important books on ideology in U.S. politics, *Political Thinking and Consciousness*, and *Political Ideology*. Reading Lane's conceptualization of the importance of ideas and their diffusion for political attitudes, identity, and consciousness in the United States provides an interesting way to assess the shifting contours of the discipline of political science over the past forty years. Not only does his scholarship synthesize then prevalent topics in the disciplines of political science and psychology but Lane also borrowed liberally from social theory, sociology, and anthropology to underscore the importance of culture, temporality, and context in the evolution of distinctive political perspectives, attitudes and behaviors. In *Political Thinking and Consciousness*, Lane emphasizes what he characterizes as the inward, psychologically bound approach to understanding the "self-in-politics," or political identity. Familial relations serve as the basis for tracing the roots and routes of political attitudes of the men chosen in his study.

A pivotal familial relation in Lane's view is that of father and son. In reference to three men in the study who were particularly energized by discussions of injustice and inequality in the United States, Lane concludes in his chapter on "Political Consciousness and Citizen Self-Knowledge" that much of their anger against injustice and authority stemmed from relationships with abusive fathers. Only through self-knowledge can such men understand the source of their anger at inequities in society:

> What would happen if, discovering the sources of their anger in their personal lives (their quarrels with their fathers or with some more recent penalizing elite) they were to reflect on this and come to terms with their personal conflicts? Would their liberalism disappear, their causes fade? ... Actually, I think something else happens: they become aware of the roots of these views in family quarrels. And then, instead of changing their views, they change the grounds for their views.[13]

Thus, the terrain for the seeding of ideas and beliefs shifts from the private and personal to the public and political, reversing, according to Lane, Harold Lasswell's dictum. The process of genuinely "outward" political ideology and consciousness transforms individual preoccupations into worldviews, from insular, small horizons, to wider, more social concern for others.[14]

One way of thinking about Lane's psychosocial characterization of individual ideological dispositions is as a cartography of family psychology, resulting in national politics and ideology. This view of the family and of father-son relations is undoubtedly Freudian. Lane suggests that the dialectical relation between public and private can, in the case of the true political consciousness, lead to a deepening of political beliefs, because an individual's understanding of issues, concepts, and political phenomena is achieved independent of his or her personal experiences or psychology. Yet in attributing the source of political conflict to the family, Lane's clear separation between inward and outward forms of political education and development undermines the importance of context and culture, so heavily emphasized in other parts of his argument.

Although there were no blacks included in his study, this fact, in and of itself, should not be cause to dismiss the prospect of utilizing some of the qualitative facets of his inward approach for understanding black political identity and consciousness. Lane's ethnographic subjects often mention or discuss racial politics (under the topical headings of civil rights, Little Rock, white racial prejudice in the South, and social and sexual implications of desegregation). The politics of race in the United States, however, makes Lane's distinctions between inward (endogenous) and outward (exogenous) sources of political identity and identification tenuous at best. The ideological forms of racism problematize, if not collapse, outward and inward distinctions. Racist ideologies, as we will demonstrate, have both outward and inward dimensions, often operating simultaneously.

Lane's neglect of the racial and racist dimensions of individual ideological construction in the United States further undermines the applicability of his methods of ethnographic and interpretive inquiry. His treatment of the topic of evil provides the first instance of this neglect. The concept and practice of evil appears across societies, cultures, social classes, even so-called racial groups, and is at root an assessment of the character of an individual or group. Based on the interpretation of his interviews with fifteen men in the fictitious town of Eastport, Lane concluded that the common man of the United States had lost a sense of evil. Errors in judgment came to supplant characterizations of evil according to Lane.

Lane does not limit his findings to this particular cohort, however, but applies them to the United States writ large, and asserts that "the substitution of 'error' for 'evil' is apparent in many moral dilemmas."[15] The substitution of the word "error" for "evil" is perhaps another indication of American (U.S.)

pragmatism, the substitution of a rationalist, seemingly nonevaluative adjective for one that unambiguously declares not only moral wrong, but a nefarious, dastardly character. An error can be coincidental, without any intentionality on the part of an individual. Evil, however, suggests intentionality and motive, perhaps even Hadean sources for human misdeed.[16]

A quick review of abolitionist, emigrationist, and civil rights speeches, rhetoric and tracts that emphasize the moral dilemmas of racial inequality, slavery, and race-related violence, however, suggests a different conclusion about the substitution of "error" for "evil" in "American" public opinion. The pragmatic approach to basic moral questions that Lane finds in his interviews and ethnographies of white subjects could be contrasted with the emphasis on the moral failings of whites found in many accounts given by U.S. African Americans of the national moral character of their white counterparts. In fact, many blacks in various parts of the United States referred to whites as "devils" long before the use of "devil" as a racially pejorative term was popularized by Malcolm X and the then Nation of Islam. In the mid-nineteenth century, Henry Highland Garnet, among others, referred to racist whites and slaveowners in the following manner:

> "The diabolical injustice by which your liberties are cloven down, NEITHER GOD, NOR ANGELS, OR JUST MEN, COMMAND YOU TO SUFFER FOR A SINGLE MOMENT."[17] Later, Garnet made his charge more explicit even as he criticized black slaves' seeming turpitude in the face of gross injustice:

> You act as though you were made for the special use of these devils. . . . Awake, awake, millions of voices are calling you! Your dead fathers speak to you from their graves. Heaven, as with a voice of thunder, calls on you to arise from the dust.[18]

Heaven above, devils on earth, and voices from the grave are all a part of the evocative imagery Garnet summons in the effort to spark mobilization among the enslaved black masses to rise up against their oppressors. For these students, as well as the generations of U.S. African Americans socialized within various congregations and denominations of the black church, diatribes against white devils by adherents of the Nation of Islam are neither surprising nor unprecedented, but have roots in black Christianity. The diabolical nature of racial slavery transformed white slaveowners into devils who happened to be white.

Within the religious and philosophical traditions of the black church, the identification of whites as masters and purveyors of supremacist ideologies with the most immoral, rapacious, and sinful icon of Western Christianity—Satan—has a much longer history. Lane's omission of this thread within black political, social, and religious thought, which can be found in declarations of white moral turpitude ranging from Baptist ministers to the Nation of Islam, undercuts his larger claims about the pragmatic cast of political and social relations in the United States during the 1960s.

How do we make sense of Lane's omission? Could this be an example of the absence of moral outrage for which Martin Luther King and other members of the Southern Christian Leadership Conference chided whites in the 1960s?[19] Most students of U.S. public opinion now incorporate black public opinion into their research. Few would extrapolate from a sample pool of fifteen or twenty-four white men to offer general conclusions about U.S. racial attitudes and behavior. Some attention to black theology, not to mention mobilizing ideologies of the 1960s, might have led Lane to qualify some of his conclusions about the substitution of error for evil.

Even if one were to accept the public/private distinction so central to Lane's understanding of individual ideological development, one could still wonder whether arguments within families about macropolitics itself, rather than interpersonal dynamics within a family, could affect the transformation of consciousness. How have whites reconciled their memories of doting fathers, mothers, grandparents, and other relatives, with those same relatives' explicitly racist attitudes and behaviors? A person could, in both theory and fact, have limited internal tensions as a result of family dynamics and still come to question their political beliefs. Nazi SS officers, members of the Brazilian, Argentine, and Chilean authoritarian regimes, and Klansmen had loving families who were no more or less laden with conflict than their more liberal or radical counterparts.

IV Baldwin and Cleaver's Public and Private Selves

A close reading of two very different perspectives in black political and social thought helps expose the limitations of Lane's distinction between inward and outward forms of political identity.

The personal profiles and biographies of Eldridge Cleaver and James Baldwin, two very different social critics of the 1960s, fit squarely within Lane's psychologically oriented—as opposed to social-structural—approach to individual political behavior. Both men had complicated relations with their fathers and subsequently with other male authority figures in their lives, although with very different psychological responses. Sociologically, their subject positions are quite similar. Both men also traced the growing sophistication of their knowledge concerning racial discrimination to experiencing and witnessing a vast array of racial injustices that befell black communities and themselves. Their self-awareness enabled them to connect their own conditions to more general conditions of racism in U.S. society.

Their analyses were gendered as well. Both men highlighted the specific forms of discrimination and abuse that black men suffered in a white-dominated society, utilizing some of their deeply personal experiences to make larger claims. In his distinctive voice, Baldwin writes of his personal knowledge of "American masculinity which most men of my generation do not know because they have not been menaced by it the way that I have been. It is still true, alas, that to be an American Negro male is also to be a kind of walking phallic symbol; which means that one pays, in one's own personality, for the sexual insecurity of others."[20]

Earlier in the same collection of essays, Baldwin writes of his discovery during his first sojourn to Europe of the tensions between society and self that converged within his own social identity: "It turned out that the question of who I was was not solved because I had removed myself from the social forces which menaced me—anyway, these forces had become interior, and I had dragged them across the ocean with me. The question of who I was had at last become a personal question, and the answer was to be found in me."[21] Baldwin's self-reflections are instructive for analyzing black political identities because of his synthesis of psychological and social-structural factors. Though there is a distinction between outward and inward factors, Baldwin considers both in the assessment of his political, social, and cultural evolution. Societal racism was as much a part of his consciousness as were the relations with his father and brothers.

Baldwin writes very clear, poignant, and thinly veiled autobiographic descriptions of a father—his own—embittered and poisoned by experiences of racism. In *Tell Me How Long the Train's Been Gone* Baldwin offers the following description of the father of Leo Proudhammer, the novel's main character:

> For our father—how shall I describe my father?—was a ruined Barbados peasant exiled in a Harlem which he loathed . . . he brought with him from Barbados only black rum and a blacker pride, and magic incantations which neither healed nor saved. He did not understand the people among whom he found himself, for him they had no coherence, no stature and no pride. He came from a race which had

been flourishing at the very dawn of the world—a race greater and nobler than Rome or Judea, mightier than Egypt—he came from a race of kings, kings who had never been slaves. He spoke to us of tribes and empires, battles, victories, and monarchs of whom we had never heard—they were not mentioned in our schoolbooks—and invested us with glories in which we felt more awkward than in the secondhand shoes we wore.[22]

This passage provides a glimpse of many key themes in Baldwin's corpus, particularly the sense of displacement, alienation, and self-hatred brought about by a combination of poverty and racial discrimination. Baldwin returns to the theme of black history and pride many times in his writings, yet he certainly was no Afro-centrist, one who sought to depict a nostalgic, uncomplicated view of Africa and its histories. Proudhammer's father is a foreigner, a fact that enables Baldwin to introduce multinational and multicultural distinction and complexity into his images of U.S. African American communities, as well as the idea of competing historical narratives about Africa and its location in Euro-American historiography, an issue central to polemics surrounding Afro-centricity and Afro-centrism (see below). Proudhammer's father despises Harlem and its black people for their seeming lack of black pride and ignorance of their own African history. At the same time, Proudhammer is trapped alongside them in circumstances that are not of his own making. The ongoing tensions between father and son are set against the backdrop of a society with an ongoing legacy of racial discrimination combined with cultural alienation, poverty, and segregation.

The psychological concept common to both Cleaver and Baldwin is the concept of self-hatred, something that members of many marginalized groups identify with and also struggle against. In the Jewish case, self-hatred has alternatively been referred to as "Jewish self-hatred," "Jewish anti-Judaism," or "Jewish anti-Semitism,"[23] which Sander Gilman characterizes as a "specific mode of self-abnegation"[24] that "results from outsiders' acceptance of the mirage of themselves generated by their reference group—that group in society which they see as defining them—as a reality."[25] This concept can also be read as a description of an ideological form peculiar to societally marginal groups—the outsiders to which Gilman refers—who struggle with issues of self-identification and cultural assimilation, as well as residential and institutional segregation. Thus, Gilman's definition of self-hatred is applicable to African Americans in the United States, as well as other racially and ethnically demarcated groups in U.S. society.[26]

Eldridge Cleaver, author of the now legendary *Soul on Ice*, also wrote about self-hatred, the absence of historical memory and self-pride, and its impact on his development as a black adult male. As briefly noted in chapter 2, Eldridge Cleaver's career as a rapist—among other criminal activities—was influenced (according to the author) by the absence of self-pride, or perhaps more accurately, the presence of a distorted sense of pride. Of his career as a rapist he wrote:

> I started out by practicing on black girls in the ghetto—in the black ghetto where dark and vicious deeds appear not as aberrations or deviations from the norm, but as part of the sufficiency of the Evil of the day—and when I considered myself smooth enough, I crossed the tracks and sought out white prey. I did this consciously, deliberately, willfully, methodically—though looking back I see that I was in a frantic, wild, and completely abandoned frame of mind.... After I returned to prison, I took a long look at myself and, for the first time in my life, admitted that I was wrong, that I had gone astray—astray not so much from the white man's law as from being human, civilized—for I could not approve the act of rape.... My pride as a man dissolved and my whole fragile moral structure seemed to collapse, completely shattered. That is why I started to write. To save myself.[27]

This passage is emblematic of the process of cognitive self-transformation Lane identifies as crucial for increased self-knowledge, political consciousness, and rational decision making in politics. Again, the specter of evil in the form of white racism and black ghettos appears in ways unaccounted for by Lane's model of pragmatism in U.S. public opinion. Cleaver acknowledges his own hubris, the belief that white racism led him to rape first black women, then white women,[28] and the belief that the rape of white women was a politically insurrectionary act. Cleaver would have several other "transformations" in his public and private life, from fashion designer of men's pants that emphasized the penis to staunch Republican conservative. In contemporary parlance, the man clearly had issues.

The patriarchal and Freudian schema developed by Lane, however, gives us few clues as to why Baldwin and Cleaver diverge so radically in their responses to self-hatred and violence. For all of his indignation at the U.S. elite's refusal to acknowledge the evils of white racism, Baldwin was ultimately a Christian and preached forgiveness. Baldwin tied the fate of U.S. African Americans to whites and to a salvation that only religious love could provide, a love that could transcend personal sins and the collective evils of white supremacy.

Cleaver, on the other hand, detested what he termed Baldwin's "racial death-wish," which Cleaver concluded was the motivating force of Baldwin's writing. In *Soul on Ice*, Cleaver wrote that Baldwin's "hatred for blacks, even as he pleads what he conceives as their cause, makes him the apotheosis of the dilemma in the ethos of the black bourgeoisie who have completely rejected their African heritage, consider the loss irrevocable, and refuse to look again in that direction."[29] Those who have read *Soul on Ice* know that the aforementioned passage is Cleaver at his most tame in his critique of Baldwin.

Cleaver's critique of Baldwin can be plausibly attributed to Cleaver's desire for sexual and racial domination, and thus finds a curious harmony with Lane's analysis of the informant DeVita in *Political Thinking and Consciousness*[30] who uses intellectualism and ambition to dominate his social and intellectual subordinates. While we could identify some of the psychic origins of Baldwin's and Cleaver's public postures as political actors and critics in Lane's landscape, there is no historical or ethnographic space in which to situate them. We have little sense of the more contextual and ideological factors that led Cleaver to be attracted to the Nation of Islam, Marx and the Black Panthers, rather than to Baldwin's version of Christianity. Neither Baldwin nor Cleaver can be distinguished from other black males who have had difficult relations with their fathers or other family members, yet do not become writers, prison inmates, sexual predators, or social critics.

Lane's methodological reliance on psychological assessment shares the limitations of what Mannheim characterized as the particular conception of ideology:

> If we confine our observations to the mental processes which take place in the individual, and regard him as the only possible bearer of ideologies, we shall never grasp in its totality the structure of the intellectual world belonging to a social group in a given historical situation. Although this mental world as a whole could never come into existence without the experiences and productive responses of the different individuals, its inner structure is not to be found in a mere integration of these individual experiences.[31]

On the following page, Mannheim succinctly captures the methodological limitations of a critical method that emphasizes individual subjectivity in the assessment of the ideological disposition of the individual: "Analyses of ideology in the particular sense, making the content of individual thought largely dependent on the interests of the subject, can never achieve the basic reconstruction of the whole outlook of a social group."[32]

Missing from Lane's method are factors that mediate the relationship between subjectivity and ideological formation, such as social structure, individual volition, and agency.

Mannheim's distinctions between particular and total ideologies in *Ideology and Utopia* help to delineate between upper- and lowercase ideologies, between elite and mass, as well as between the psychological and social-structural. For Mannheim, particular ideologies are those that emanate first from a personal sense of skepticism toward another individual's professed opinion.[33] A more comprehensive or total conception of ideology refers to "the ideology of an age of a concrete socio-historical group."[34]

The more metaphysical and ontological dimensions of black ideological forms come to the forefront where they previously, often implicitly, lurked in the background. Baldwin's and Cleaver's view of an American heterotopia, dystopia, and in Baldwin's case, a possible utopia, can be gleaned.[35] The context of black politics and culture can help us both situate and distinguish the Eldridge Cleavers from the James Baldwins in black communities. In the case of Baldwin, we would need to have some sense of the eschatological, evangelical, revivalist, rhetoric of black Christianity, present in the churches Baldwin attended in Harlem as a child, in order to contemplate how black Christians could simultaneously condemn and attempt to love whites. In the case of Cleaver, students would have to read his text in relation to the jailhouse crucibles where most black men in the United States reside at some point in their lives, with their assortment of Five Percenters, Nation of Islam, Hebrew Israelites, Democrats, Republicans, the politically unaffiliated, the neophyte and hardened criminals, just to name several types of black people at different levels of political consciousness. There are dissertations waiting to be written analyzing the reception of various black literatures in federal and state penitentiaries, as a means of gauging what the future Malcolm Xes and Eldridge Cleavers are currently reading.

V Philip Converse, Black Ideologies, and Public Opinion

Converse's conceptualization of issue publics, applied by many subsequent students of black politics and public opinion, persists at the other end of the analytic spectrum of ideological analysis. For Converse and those who have subsequently employed and innovated upon his vertically oriented research methods, belief systems have supplanted ideology as an object of study. Consequently, beliefs and mass publics stand in place of ideological forms. Divorced from the study of either upper- or lowercase ideologies, however, mass publics emerge in a largely contextless fashion, devoid of the political, economic, and cultural factors that help shape belief systems. Thus, mass publics and belief systems operate in a self-contained discursive field. Second, mass publics and belief systems are invariably the result of elite dissemination and diffusion. The variability and recurrence of black ideologies across class and status distinctions, however, provide clues to the limitations of an elite-based approach to the study of black ideologies and their intertwined relationship to both black and white public opinion.

Converse's principle of verticality is the final distinction we would like to draw between the development and diffusion of black ideologies and the way in which ideological development and diffusion are chronicled in studies of Euro-American ideology. The overwhelming majority of studies of ideology assume that ideologies are first generated by elites and then diffused to masses and social groups. Whether in the work of Hegel, Gramsci, Mannheim, Marx, or Durkheim, there has been a tendency to assign ideological production and diffusion to elites of some sort—priests, intellectual vanguards, politicians, and industrialists, if not the state.

As in most other forms of modern politics with a broad array of political actors, there are a range of political actors within U.S. African American politics who could be characterized as elites. E. Franklin Frazier long ago suggested that the black bourgeoisie was one thing, the white bourgeoisie quite another.[36] Categorization of black political actors by class and status tells us little about the ideational content of black middle-class deliberation about issues of justice, fairness, and solidarity. The political sociology of the Black Panther Party provides another example. The origins of their leadership ranged from urban and rural poor with little formal education to individuals with multigenerational levels of high achievement and education. In other forms of black liberation struggle, Angela Davis and George Jackson had few formal sociological similarities (education, family background, occupation), yet participated in many of the same organizations.

Garveyism and Kwanzaa provide another set of observable, idea-related phenomena that belie the methodological limitations of elite-based approaches concerning black ideologies and issue publics. Both phenomena represent, in our view, examples of the *upward* circulation of some black ideologies. Garveyism, which had an enormous impact on U.S. African Americans in the 1930s and 1940s (so much so that many prominent middle-class U.S. African American leaders, including A. Phillip Randolph and W. E. B. Du Bois, railed against it),[37] had a decidedly working-class following, not only in urban areas such as New York City and Boston but also in parts of Kansas, Alabama, and Arkansas. Garvey's appeals to racial uplift and his mythical treatment of African civilizations met ready ears in many black communities, preparing the ground, in some respects, for subsequent Africa-centered ideologies in black political discourse. There is now a substantial literature by African American studies and Africana studies scholars on the impact of black domestic workers, wage laborers, and seaman and other naval personnel in the Caribbean who helped circulate and propagate Garveyism and Garveyite literature throughout the Western Hemisphere and upon the African continent itself.[38]

At the same time, Garveyism as a popular ideology would be unintelligible without an accompanying understanding of concepts such as fascism, authoritarianism, nationalism, as well as the practical importance of social networks and transnational black mobilization.[39] Kwaanza, created by Malauna Karenga, is increasingly being practiced in black middle-class families as an alternative to Christmas, not only in the United States but in England, Brazil, Jamaica and other locales. The kente cloth sold at African and African-diaspora markets throughout the United States circulated first within working-class communities before making its appearance in the vestments of college-educated blacks. These are just two examples of popular ideologies that first emanated from the vernacular and then recirculated among the middle classes. Many adherents to Garveyism and Kwanzaa are very committed to strict ascription to the foundational texts and practices of both ideological forms. There is ample evidence to suggest that working-class adherence to these ideologies, which are often used to guide adherents in many areas of life (where to shop, how to choose a love interest/partner, how to invest), is no more diffuse than adherence among the black middle classes who ascribe in whole or in part to these two ideological formations and related practices.

Black middle classes have often taken their normative and ideational cues from their working-class, less formally educated counterparts. Neither Lane, Converse, nor the bulk of mainstream accounts of ideology and public opinion can explain the upward diffusion of ideological forms and idea clusters in the circulatory system of black politics and political culture. The verticality principle cannot account for the upward trajectory of black ideological diffusion.

One reasonable objection to this critique of an elite-based approach to black ideologies could be crafted in the identification of Marcus Garvey and Malauna Karenga as elites themselves, regardless of the populist—and popular—cast of their exhortations, programs, and writings. Garvey, a printer by training, and Karenga, leader of a cultural nationalist organization in the 1960s known by the acronym US (Unknown Slaves), could certainly be distinguished within their eras from the bulk of the black populace by their respective levels of education and prominence. Yet both Karenga and Garvey were considered charlatans among much of the more educated black middle classes and national elite, as well as in more radically militant segments of black politics in their respective eras: the Black Panther Party and Asa Briggs's African Blood Brotherhood are their respective counterpoints.[40] In the case of Garvey, he was ridiculed by significant members of both the Jamaican colonial elite as well as the U.S. African American intelligentsia. Neither W. E. B. Du Bois, A. Phillip Randolph, nor Norman Manley (prime minister, prominent barrister, nationalist architect, and father of Michael Manley) considered Garvey as anything more than a crude rabble-rouser gifted in his ability to attract black masses with his message of racial uplift. [41] In Karenga's case, neither he nor his ideas were particularly popular among black elite, Marxist, or other black nationalist circles in the 1960s and 1970s. Garvey and Karenga's interstitial positions between black elite and mass may partially explain their popularity. Alternatively, both could be viewed as critical links between middle-class and working-class black mass publics, emphasizing forms of racial pride and solidarity across class lines. Their linkages, incidentally, are not unlike the roles of petit bourgeois leaders of nationalist and ethnic mobilization.[42]

The similarity between the processes of diffusion of elite and popularly generated ideologies in black public spheres lies in the fact that ideas first generated within limited-issue and social-movement networks often gain popularity and more widespread diffusion in subsequent generations, not necessarily in the era of their creation. The project of civil disobedience, for example, was initially unpopular among powerful black clergy in the United States. Without the support of individual ministers, entrepreneurs, and everyday folk within various black communities, many scholars have wondered whether the modern U.S. civil rights movement would have gathered the momentum that it did in the early 1960s.

There are other indicators to suggest that the line often drawn to distinguish between black middle and working classes is at best dotted, rather than continuous.[43] Data on residential segregation, for example, suggest that increasing numbers of black middle-class professionals are moving into predominantly black or black integrated neighborhoods with a high proportion of stable, working-class families and individuals due to greater comfort and the ability to move within their residential neighborhoods without generating undue suspicion by local police forces or neighbors. The innumerable cases of "mistaken identity" in which prominent and not-so prominent middle-class and elite blacks are arrested and/or harassed by police suggests that middle- and higher-status blacks are not just imagining prejudice among law enforcement officials and neighbors, but actually living and experiencing it.

There is at least one larger lesson for political scientists to take from this more contextual and interpretive account of the contours, complexities, and nuances of black ideological formation. The aforementioned ideological formations—popular and elite, sectarian and nonsectarian—were already saturated with ideas and beliefs of the larger society concerning notions of the public good, community, and proper and improper modes of conduct. It would be too crude to rely on a sociologically deterministic account that merely equates ideology with socioeconomic status, such as class, gender, or race.[44]

For example, the emergence of black conservatism as a topic in United States' political culture and debate has to be situated against the backdrop of the rise of the New Right in the 1980s, with its emphasis on a reduced role for government and an increased emphasis on morality and individual responsibility. Neither Afro-centrism, Kwaanza, nor black conservatism, can be fully analyzed as instances of "black" ideology, political thought, public opinion, or belief systems without first identifying their highly situated character within a wider field of political rhetoric, discourse, and ideology.

VI. Black Pride/Black Prejudice?

Even though survey researchers readily acknowledge the importance of perspectives on race in the formation of political attitudes and in the enactment of political behavior, context-specific, ideational and ideological sources of black public opinion remain largely underexplored by students of U.S. politics. One example of the ongoing neglect is a recent work by Paul Sniderman and Thomas Piazza, *Black Pride and Black Prejudice*. Published in 2002, this book is already being considered a classic work on black public opinion by many scholars on racial attitudes. Our focus here is not on the econometric and quantitative methods and measures in their scholarship, but their interpretive and qualitative ones.[45] If, however, Mannheim's assertion cited atop this chapter still has some validity (and we believe it does), then the political and cultural contexts of black ideological forms are critical to understanding the component parts of black public opinion as empirical evidence. The near total absence of a context-specific approach that incorporates black ideologies renders several of their key correlations and conclusions regarding black collective self-pride and racial chauvinism conceptually invalid.

The dimension of Sniderman and Piazza's argument most relevant for this chapter concerns their treatment of black racial solidarity, found in chapter 2 of their book. Their treatment of the phenomenon of racial solidarity can be considered alongside our explication of the specter of self-hatred in black critical discourse above and Hanchard's discussion of the ethics of aversion in chapter 4. Racial self-hatred, if there is such a thing, could be read as the opposite of racial solidarity, or perhaps more precisely as a paradoxical component of presumed racial solidarity, since a "race man" or "race woman" in the U.S. African American case would be able to identify and distinguish between the righteous and the traitorous. Rather than view racial self-hatred as the "flip side" of racial solidarity, then, it can be interpreted as a normative judgment that implies the existence of solidarity at the same time.[46] Sniderman and Piazza have little to say explicitly about the topic of self-hatred, other than to briefly consider the possibility that years of ongoing racial discrimination against U.S. African Americans and other blacks in the United States would leave certain psychological scars and wounds[47] to hamper self-esteem. They question (rightly, in our view) the idea that psychological scars caused by racial discrimination are something that can be effectively measured or correlated with black achievement or underachievement.

They focus much more attention on their definition of Afrocentrism as an indicator of black racial chauvinism and black racial solidarity. The definition of Afrocentrism, offered in two parts, focuses on both scholarly and popular iterations of the concept: "By Afrocentrism, we mean, roughly, a commitment to a point of view honoring the accomplishments of African civilizations."[48] The popular representation of Afro-centrism is their core preoccupation, however, and is defined as a two-part claim according to which "the primacy of European accomplishments have been grossly exaggerated" and "claims to genuine African accomplishments have been systematically slighted."[49]

Given the intricate, often arcane distinctions among scholars who ascribe to some form or component of Afrocentrism, Sniderman and Piazza took the more cautious route and provided a general description of Afro-centrism. Their description, however, is not based on what is considered the foundational text for the late modern variant of Afrocentricity, the 1980 book by Molefi Asante, or any other text by a self-avowed Afrocentrist. They base one of their key correlative axes for the assessment of black public opinion on a more generic description of Afrocentrism that they, not advocates of Afrocentrism, provide.[50] They rely heavily on the representation of Afrocentrism provided by some of its staunchest critics, Mary Lefkowitz and Stephen Howe, not on the now vast literature on Afrocentrism, Afrocentricity, Africology, and their many variants.[51] We raise this point not as a defense of Afrocentricity, but to point to a prerequisite for examining a particular ideological and ideational tendency. Without an engagement with the foundational texts of a belief system or ideology, how can one make distinctions not only between elite and mass beliefs and opinions, but between adherents and critics of a particular ideology or belief system?

The first interpretive consequence of this decision is that neither their scholarly (elite) nor popular definitions of Afrocentrism are derived from definitions of the term created by Afrocentrist scholars and ideologues or from popular black mass media sources. The two-part definition of Afrocentrism provided by Sniderman and Piazza must thus be distinguished from actual definitions of the term. What Sniderman and Piazza provide is a *concept* of Afrocentrism, which is then utilized as a definitional basis for assessments, correlations, and conclusions about the relationship among what they call "idea-elements" within black public opinion.[52] First, consider the potential interpretive dangers that can result from the divergence between respondents' understandings of Afrocentrism and the definition inserted by researchers into an already crowded field of definitions and distinctions about the term. Asante, incidentally, distinguishes Afrocentricity as a theoretical proposition from Afrocentrism and has maintained this distinction in several books responding to his critics. The actual philosophical aims and objectives of Afrocentricity and Africology have been subtly rendered and critiqued by philosopher Lucius Outlaw, among others. Thus while Sniderman and Piazza treat Afrocentrism as a single concept, most proponents of Afrocentric approaches to the study of Africa have multiple, sometimes competing, theoretical propositions about Afrocentrism itself.[53]

Sniderman and Piazza's decision to impose their own generic concept of Afrocentrism rather than rely on multiple theoretical positions does have the advantage of allowing for a wider array of beliefs and opinions about the relationship between European historiography and African histories among U.S. African Americans. Sniderman and Piazza's definition, as the point of entry into an exploration and examination of correlations between Afrocentric beliefs and other beliefs, is somewhat analogous to a commercial fishing net that, while designed to ensnare one species of fish, actually captures many others—not necessarily a bad thing for scholars engaged in public opinion as well as other forms of nonqualitative, ethnographic research. Continuing with this analogy, however, we should be able to distinguish one idea-element—or species—from another in the net provided by Sniderman and Piazza. The problem, as we will demonstrate below, is that much of what is ensnared in their net is not Afrocentrism.

A breakdown of their definition should help illuminate some of our concerns. They conclude that proponents of their definition of Afrocentrism who advocate "the minimization of European civilization and the valorization of African civilization, lend themselves to claims that violate ordinary standards of evidence and reasoning."[54] This claim could be interpreted in at least two ways. One could assume that "ordinary standards of evidence and reasoning" refers to a universally accepted standard of scholarly documentation and the expectation that honest identification and attribution of sources be upheld. This, by itself, we would concur with and is not the source of our concern. But should we assume that simply by questioning the interpretive conclusions of earlier generations of scholars about interactions between Greeks, Europeans, and Africans, contemporary scholars, Afrocentrist or not, are actively, knowingly, violating standards of first-rate scholarship?

Skepticism about European scholarship regarding Africa is not peculiar to Afrocentrists. How do we make sense of the following quotes, excerpted from the scholarship of two prominent Africanist scholars—both white—both first-rate historians of Africa, with a broad view of African continental history and its relation to the rest of the world? The first quote comes from Philip Curtin's "Recent Trends in African Historiography and Their Contribution to History in General" in *General History of Africa*:

> The colonial imprint on historical knowledge emerged in the nineteenth and twentieth centuries is a false perspective, a Eurocentric view of world history created at a time of European domination. It was then transmitted outward through the educational systems the Europeans had created in the colonial world. Even where Europeans never ruled, European knowledge was often accepted as modern knowledge, including aspects of the Eurocentric historiography.[55]

Curtin is not expressing an Afrocentric worldview or advocating an Afro-centered approach to the study of African history. Yet he explicitly critiques approaches to world history that automatically place Europe at the center of African histories. Without championing an Afrocentric view of African civilization's contribution to global and Western history, Curtin does call into question biased approaches to the study of Africa and Europe. Anyone familiar with the intense debates and polemics in the study of African history knows that Philip Curtin is no Afrocentrist, by any stretch of the imagination.[56]

Another historian of Africa, Basil Davidson, writes the following about European historiography of Africa well into the twentieth century:

> There are many anthologies of African exploration. With one or two exceptions, which I shall mention in a moment, they are all built to the same pattern. They are anthologies of the European discovery of Africa, conceived as companion books to a study of Africa which has regarded that subject as no more than an extension to the study of Europe or the new world. Keeping to sources, which are largely from the nineteenth century, they aim to show why and how it was that Europe "opened up" a continent, which was soon to become a European possession. . . . Yet much of West Africa has been "opened" to the outside world—or to a significant part of it—many hundreds of years earlier, and these earlier years are not without important records of their own.[57]

The interpretive possibilities opened up by Curtin's and Davidson's critiques suggest that there are ways to re-situate Europe's role in African development and underdevelopment, foregrounding African people and civilizations as agents in the making of their own histories, without adopting Afrocentric or Afrocentrist positions. By now, at least one problem with Sniderman and Piazza's definition of Afrocentrism should be apparent. Their definition of Afrocentrism is far too minimal. Their net traps the politically neutral Africanist as well as the anti-Afrocentrist Africanist, who both seek to provide a more balanced account of Africa's relation to the rest of the world. [58]

The interpretive quandary posed by Sniderman and Piazza's definition of Afrocentrism is a problem that is conceptual, epistemological, and historical in nature. First, how do we know Afrocentrism when we see it? If we base our definition of Afrocentrism on skepticism toward and contestation of traditional accounts of Africa's significance to Western civilization, then Curtin, Davidson, as well as several generations of Africanists, are Afrocentrists. Only when we move to an Egyptcentric account of African civilization and an emphasis on African contributions to Western civilization do we come remotely close to Afrocentricity or Afrocentrism as advocated and practiced by its adherents. Sniderman and Piazza's definition of Afrocentrism is not simply invalid because Phillip Curtin or Basil Davidson (or anyone else) are *not* Afrocentrists, but because the definition given to identify Afrocentrists renders their followers indistinguishable from their opponents. Second, if the definition is neither robust nor clearly delineated enough to distinguish adherents from opponents, how could it begin to distinguish *among* Afrocentrists or differentiate between those who are Afrocentrists and those who are merely skeptical about Western depictions of African civilizations and contributions to global history? Third, the quandary is also historical, and not only in relation to African civilizations' possible contributions to the Western world. Should scholars attribute the phenomena of anti-Semitism to Afrocentrism, when both anti-Semitism in general and anti-Semitism among blacks predates the emergence of Afrocentricity and its canon?

Africanists such as Curtin and Davidson seek not to valorize Africa, but to give a more objective and sophisticated account of Africa's internal dynamics, relations and contributions to the rest of the world, including Europe. While adherents to Afrocentrism believe that the cluster of ideas, beliefs, and texts of their theory provides the appropriate corrective to Eurocentric histories of Africa that diminish and neglect Africa's precolonial past, this may be the only common interpretive guideline shared with Davidson and Curtin.

Sniderman and Piazza's minimalist definition of Afrocentrism is not a problem that can be resolved by quantitative means (changing the scope of the survey data, increasing or decreasing the number of interviewees). Consulting the rich, interdisciplinary literature within African studies, African diaspora scholarship, comparative literatures, and comparative politics, as well as consulting the writings of scholars and polemicists on both sides of the Afrocentric divide, would have perhaps enabled Sniderman and Piazza to consider the possibility that Eurocentrism[59] has been a serious, rigorous scholarly preoccupation of many regional/area studies scholars working in the wake of colonial independence, as well as a factor in the critical examination, selection, and choice of reading for many African-descended and African people.

Although not the main focus of concern, the uppercase versions of Afrocentrism that Sniderman and Piazza first define can be understood as implicitly premised on a classic definition of ideology as doctrine or lie.[60] The idea-elements evidenced in the responses to Sniderman and Piazza's survey are actually bits and pieces of theory, folklore, apocryphal tales, and empirical fact, a melding of truisms, falsehoods, theoretical propositions, and generic assertions (such as anti-Eurocentrism) to be found in a range of black ideologies, even in some nonblack uppercase and lowercase ideological forms and theories.

Afrocentrist and Afrocentric views held by blacks may in fact share some ideational commonalities with ideologies that belong to other intellectual traditions. At least one adherent of Afrocentrism traces its genealogy to the writings of Aime Cesaire, one of the founders of Negritude, in 1939.[61] Commonalities, differences, and overlap among ideological and philosophical forms are not unique to Africa-centered scholarship, but can be identified wherever there are discourse communities worrying over shared texts with multiple audiences and, consequently, competing conclusions about their importance. What distinguishes Afrocentrism as a body of ideas from other ideological forms, philosophies and theories focused on African history is the manner in which certain interpretations, texts, and figures are given credence, while others are ignored or given less emphasis.

Up to now, we have focused on the uppercase (I) forms of Afrocentrism and their variants. What about the implications of the porous net cast by Sniderman and Piazza for lowercase (i) black ideologies, forms of Afrocentrism actually practiced or sedimented in daily life? The complex application of various ideological forms in individual or collective consciousness may vary. The distinction between the Kawaida principles of Malauna Karenga, upon which Kwaanza is based, and Afrocentricity is enough to motivate some to utilize (I) uppercase definitions in order to make decisions about holidays and family celebrations. The employment of less doctrinaire, less textually based forms of popular, lowercase (i) ideologies enables some middle-class and working-class blacks to celebrate Kwanzaa and Christmas, or combine Afrocentric, Pan-African socialist, and Kawaida principles depending upon the circumstances. While this is confusing and contradictory in some ways, to be sure, it is nonetheless instructive of how ideological forms actually work in daily life.[62] This might enable researchers of black political discourse in daily life to distinguish between blacks who believe that Africa has gotten short shrift in much of modern European historiography and philosophy and those who are seduced by what the Pan-Africanist George Padmore called "Black Zionism."[63]

One possible way to provide a more nuanced disentanglement of opponents, adherents, partial sympathizers, and empathizers of Afrocentrism is to treat the skepticism regarding depictions of Africa and Africans in European history as the first stage in a cognitive, dynamic process of critical thinking about Africa's relation to the West. There are at least three ways in which to situate this skepticism found in many students of Africa, regardless of their ideological affiliations. First, there is something called "Afrocentrism" itself, with competing ideologies (I) of the popular and sectarian sort. Next, there are those who could be called Africa-centered without being Afrocentric in any way. Scholars of Africa, out to rewrite various modes of African history, are one sort; Pan-Africanist and other anticolonials who were eager to "kick the Europeans out of Africa" are another type. People such as Kwame Nkrumah, George Padmore, and Sekou Toure come to mind as those in the latter group.

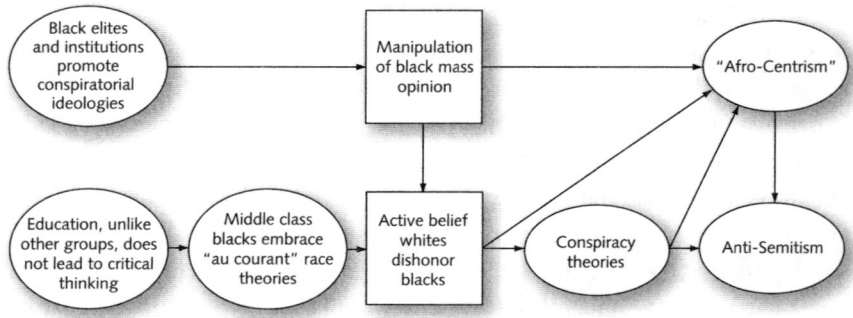

Figure 3.1
Sniderman-Piazza Explanation for Relationship between Belief in Conspiracy Theory, "Afro-Centrism" and Anti-Semitism

Third, African nationalists of the same era, as well as those whom they influenced throughout the world who emphasize the uniqueness of African culture and civilization, help constitute the third category of Africa-centered adherents. Leopold Senghor is one obvious example. Each of these categories contains perspectives that focus, in whole or in part, on Africa. Each could be said to highlight the ways in which African civilizations and peoples have been caricatured in much of modern Western, as well as, it must be noted, in many non-Western accounts of African peoples and civilizations. But this does not make them all Afrocentrists.

As a site of ideological conflict, Africa is like a train station where a huge number of trains share a common starting point, but then travel on widely distinct paths toward different destinations. It would be appropriate to posit that Molefe Asante, Philip Curtin, Basil Davidson, and St. Clair Drake produced Africa-centered scholarship. Their initial reaction to Western historiography is one of the few commonalities shared among Africa-centered, Afrocentric and Afroculturalist perspectives. Their subsequent responses to the slighting of Africa, however, could not be more varied. Only by elaborating the scholarly and political projects associated with each Africa-centered category can we fully appreciate the overlap and vast differences among Africa-centered approaches. Much of what follows in Sniderman and Piazza's account of black racial solidarity relies on similarly unpacked correlations with similar effects; negative opinions about the policies of the state of Israel are automatically correlated with anti-Semitism, for example. Now, there are blacks who detest Jews and the state of Israel equally, just as there are those among the white

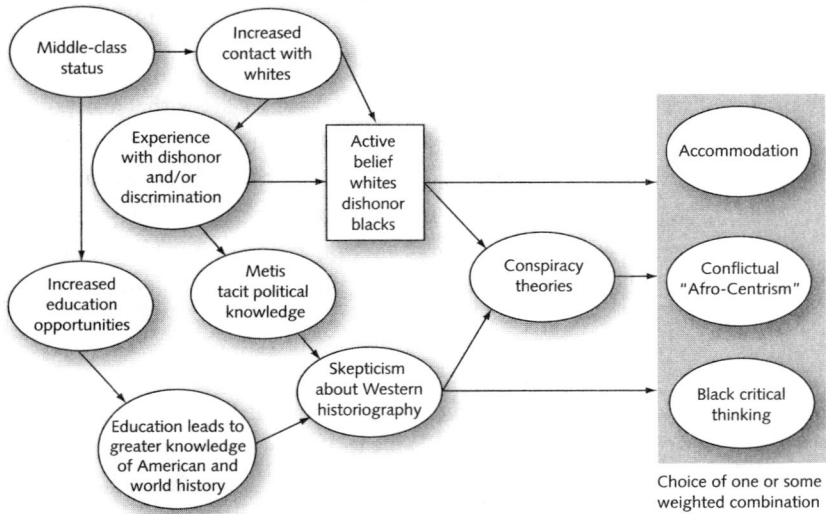

Figure 3.2
Dawson-Hanchard Nondeterministic Model of Black Perspectives on Racial Politics

population in U.S. society who feel this way. Sniderman and Piazza acknowledge discomfort in addressing the phenomena of "black anti-Semitism" as somehow distinct from white anti-Semitism.[64] Topics as contentious as racial solidarity, racial self-esteem, and anti-Semitism need far closer readings and sophisticated interpretive strategies. If scholars do not take the time and effort to examine the multiple, often conflicting and contradictory belief systems of black ideological forms and public opinion, who will?[65]

There is one final dimension of the interpretive strategies and normative assumptions concerning black racial solidarity in *Black Pride and Black Prejudice* that has implications beyond Sniderman and Piazza's book and its claims. Throughout their study, Sniderman and Piazza exhibit a certain incredulity toward the responses of black survey participants to questions concerning the possible contributions of "African civilization"[66] and conspiracy theories that depict U.S. African Americans as the target of destruction by the U.S. state, and its institutions and actors "at the very core of American society."[67] Conspiratorial thinking is positively correlated with Afrocentrism, across class categories, and is thus a feature of some forms of black pride. The nearly three-fourths positive response to the statement that "African wise men who lived hundreds of years ago do not get enough credit for their contributions to modern science,"[68] as well as assorted theories accusing the U.S. government of introducing AIDS to black communities, leads them to the following conclusion:

> however we have gotten to where we are, where we are is that a striking number of black Americans are ready to charge the government itself with directing a conspiracy against them. A glass half-filled with a potent liquor can have a considerable impact, and judged by any standard, a readiness to charge that officials responsible for law and order are engaged in what amounts almost to black genocide is a potent idea.[69]

The potent liquor in question is ideology. This conclusion is similar to a previous normative judgment in their section on Afrocentrism, where they attribute conspiratorial thinking among blacks to the "off-the-wall" and "off-the-cuff" statements of U.S. citizens, black and white. Richard Hofstadter[70] made the claim long ago that the U.S. populace was prone to paranoia, so Sniderman and Piazza may be reaffirming, armed with empirical data, a historically based argument made over forty years ago. We would like to suggest another possible interpretation of these responses, not to minimize the presence of conspiratorial thinking in black communities or any other group, but to point to other building blocks of conspiratorial thinking that actually may have far more objective roots.

While Sniderman and Piazza *do* acknowledge historical and contemporary forms of racial discrimination in the United States, there is no consideration of how specific processes of racial discrimination might affect critical deliberations among blacks of all classes about the collusive efforts, both real and imagined, of whites to maintain conditions of racial domination and to subordinate black aspirations. A more context-sensitive account of the formation of black ideologies, political perspectives, and public opinion should at least consider the possibility that even conspiratorial thinking may be steeped in part in an interpretation of an array of historical and personal experiences, organized into a worldview or outlook upon one's immediate environment. Given the range and degree of negative experiences[71] individuals may have had in relation to dominant institutions and peoples, these views might not be so far-fetched. We are assuming that readers of this chapter are at least partially familiar with the history of racial discrimination and segregation in the United States. We would need another book just of footnotes to reference all the literature written on the subject. What concerns us here is the utilization of historical knowledge in ideological and symbolic forms, or how blacks have used and interpreted objective historical knowledge, for better or worse.

Knowledge about actual instances of racial discrimination in the United States, ranging from the infamous Tuskegee experiment; the mutiny of black Navy seamen in response to being forced to handle live explosives while military officials refused to allow white soldiers to handle the same materials[72] to neighborhood "steering" by real estate representatives and observed and documented instances of racially discriminatory and economically arbitrary pricing of mortgages, and car and homeowner's insurance all form part of the historical knowledge base that leads many blacks to be skeptical about rhetoric of racial equality and claims of color-blindness in U.S. society, economy, and institutions.

People in positions of power and authority, such as judges, congressional representatives, and presidents drafted laws, the Constitution, and constitutional amendments that inscribed U.S. African Americans into positions of relative powerlessness, in civil society and in society at large. Should we really conclude that a black person with knowledge of the legal and juridical aspects of racial segregation and mandated inequality be considered the same categorical type as the person who claims to have seen a UFO?[73] If an elderly black person, for example, who is called by an interviewer on the telephone and asked to participate in a medical study, declines because of knowledge about the Tuskegee experiment, should we really assume that this person is paranoid? Or is this person making what most would call an educated guess based on actual histories of black mistreatment in medical experiments?

Sniderman and Piazza's methodology assumes that blacks' conspiratorial thinking must mirror the thought processes of their white counterparts. Shouldn't we at least entertain the possibility that the logics of subordinate groups, however "nonscientific," may in fact be more objectively and historically based than the paranoiac fantasies of their dominant-group counterparts?

VII A Context-Based Approach to Black Ideologies and Black Public Opinion

Our assessment of the scholarship in the preceding sections has emphasized the importance of context and history in the interpretation of black ideologies and public opinion. Conversely, Sniderman and Piazza and many other students of ideology and public opinion pay far less attention to context, displaying what Sheldon Wolin referred to as "Methodism," an attempt to use behavioral methods as a mode of investigation to supplant the need for theory.[74] Now that the behavioral revolution has been usurped by mathematical approaches to the study of politics, Wolin's definition of Methodism could be stretched to apply to mathematical models that emphasize reproducible, generalizable patterns at the expense of historical and contextual specificity and idiosyncrasy. Like Mannheim, Wolin attributes the narrowing of the range of research questions and approaches to the study of politics to the behavioral revolution's move away from epic theories toward partial theories. Frameworks of assumptions have replaced efforts to arrive at more comprehensive accounts of how people conceive of politics and community.

Their conclusions in this regard pay no attention to what Wolin has called tacit political knowledge,[75] political knowledge that is not formalized into a system. Tacit political knowledge is ambivalent and ambiguous, with contradictory meanings. For Wolin, tacit political knowledge is knowledge of the past, and is the basis of theoretical inquiry. One could add that historical knowledge can lead to skepticism about the present.

What follows is a formulation of *one* possible qualitative approach to the identification of ideas and ideologies within U.S. African American public spheres and their instrumental role in mediating the relationship between U.S. African Americans and four distinct but deeply integrated features of the U.S. polity: (1) the relationship between elites and mass within black public spheres; (2) U.S. African American and the multiple-ethnic and racial-mass publics; (3) the U.S. government and black political actors and organizations; and (4) interactions between U.S. African Americans and other black populations in the United States and abroad.

Traces and clusters of several overlapping as well as disparate and competing belief systems can be found within black public opinion and mass publics. Their identification, however, cannot be ascertained by formal methods, but through close readings of historical, political, and cultural contexts, and a familiarity with prevailing ideas and their resonance within black public spheres and mass publics. Identification of context is one thing; critical interpretation of those contexts is quite another.

Dawson's *Black Visions* represents the first systematic attempt to make sense of black ideologies in the context of black political culture, behavior, and thought, as well as in relation to the wider range of ideological forms in U.S. public discourse.[76] Whether Marxist, liberal, egalitarian, or conservative, black ideologies have veered slightly or radically from extant Euro-American ideological forms. Both authors of this chapter agree that *Black Visions* represents an initial, exploratory exercise in mapping black ideologies within a wider landscape of ideologies and ideas about justice, equality, community, and power, among other issues.

Subsequent scholarship on black ideologies could expand in two distinct but related directions. The first area would involve a more detailed examination of specific ideological forms in black political culture, to understand the nuances, often sectarian, *within* black conservatism, liberalism, Marxism, or radical egalitarianism. (Liberal philosophy as a descriptor does not enable us to differentiate between the liberal philosophical positions of John Stuart Mill and Adam Smith, for example.) The second area would entail engaging in more ethnographic and survey-based research to deepen and add greater complexity to our understandings of contemporary black ideologies in relation to black public opinion and observable political behavior.

Given the often acrimonious character of debates about methodological approaches to political phenomena, it is ironic to find one of the most prominent advocates of the development and application of scientific methods to the study of political phenomena declare that discussions of methodology belong to the early stage of a scientific discipline, "a stage which is concerned with the development of a largely 'empirical' concept system and with its use for description and for low-grade generalization."[77] Advocates on both sides of the analytic divide separating qualitative and quantitative approaches acknowledge that even the most resolutely formalistic models of rational-choice approaches to the study of political behavior necessarily entail some degree of ideational conceptualization, if not theorization, of what constitutes relevant and significant political behavior.

Charles Taylor's interpretive scheme emphasizes the role of hermeneutics, relating the parts of a narrative to a larger discursive formation. For Taylor, positivist social science's reliance on and isolation of brute data tends to ignore the larger contexts and realities that produce the "data" that empiricists pore over. Taylor instead advocates what he characterizes as the hermeneutic circle—the establishment of a certain reading of text or expressions, which itself is related to other readings and expressions. Within the hermeneutic circle, the interpretive capacities for understanding cultural and political practices are bound up with the site or "field" in which phenomena are observed. The understanding of phenomena is premised not on the isolation of facts, but on an understanding of those facts within the context of a larger symbolic field. Human beings are agents who are desirous of experiential meaning, which is necessarily hermeneutic. What Taylor calls intersubjective meanings provide people with a common language; common language becomes one of the bases for building community.

Taylor's nonpositivist account of critical interpretation, emphasizing wholeness and harmony, reveals the communitarian impulses of Taylor's normative theory, impulses that we do not fully share. Hermeneutic interpretation in a more restricted mode of critical engagement, however, can provide analytic cohesion to seemingly disparate pieces of information, context, and data, even if a student of political and cultural actors has no desire to engage a particular community or actors beyond the sphere of comprehension and understanding.[78]

Hermeneutics' normative and critical/analytical features are crucial for understanding one of the most influential modes of political and social thought within U.S. African American communities—U.S. African American churches and religious traditions. As is now amply documented, black religious traditions, cosmologies, and clergy have had a profound impact on multiple civil rights movements in the twentieth-century United States, as well in movements outside the United States. Communitarian and hermeneutic impulses abound in the black abolitionist and emigrationist traditions. The interpretive and political strategies of black religious leaders in many black churches, particularly those involved in clandestine activities such as the Underground Railroad and other modes of resistance to racial slavery, necessarily involved the use of hermeneutic strategies.

Hermeneutic reading strategies provided black orators a means of linking a specific incident or phenomenon (a slave uprising for example) to biblical examples of escape, vengeance, and redemption without mentioning the incident itself. By relating an isolated incident to a story that community members could identify with and, most important, share common meaning, preachers and other orators could provide guides to collective and individual action by underscoring the moral and ethical implications of the larger story *within* the smaller, seemingly nonrelated concern. Orators could utilize the book of Job, the story of Ham, the exodus of Jews from Palestine, and other biblical tales to provide either broad or specific parameters of critical interpretation for their audiences and constituencies. This dimension of critical engagement in black political thought has had secular and sacred implications, as evidenced in the oratory of Henry Highland Garnet, Sojourner Truth, and Frederick Douglass. Taylor calls these "intersubjective meanings."[79]

This particular employment of a hermeneutic tradition requires that users and receptors understand that the relation of parts to the whole involves the cognitive ability to bridge eras, peoples, and texts, producing a commonly held series of assumptions that would then motivate behavior. This ability, what the postmodernists would call bricolage, is critical to black hermeneutics and is not an unconscious or automatic shifting from one symbolic field to another.[80] Hermeneutic strategies employed in political practice, and not just in the retelling or suturing of different stories, represent another facet of the politics/culture and "weapons of the weak" conundrums examined in chapter 2. Secular hermeneutics from the period of slavery and abolitionist movements also served the purpose of making calls to collective action, justice, and freedom indirectly, without direct references to specific cultural and political actors. Thus, Nat Turner could be Gabriel, or in West African cosmologies, Shango. The more direct strategies utilized in confrontational modes of disputation of the status quo racial hierarchy, such as in the oratory of Frederick Douglass, David Walker, Henry Highland Garnet, and Ida B. Wells, exemplifies a more politically explicit and confrontational hermeneutics.

Hermeneutics are certainly not the sole interpretive strategy for deciphering black political ideologies and belief systems. There are a number of rich investigative possibilities for students of black politics interested in the ongoing role of hermeneutic strategies in U.S. African American political discourse and rhetoric. One option would be to consider the changes, over time, in the employment, number, and variation of hermeneutic strategies by black church leadership in electoral campaigns and other topical issues in local black communities. We assume that the more indirect hermeneutic strategies employed during the period of slavery or the brutality of apartheid after Reconstruction are less prevalent now, in the twenty-first century.

Finally, we would like to emphasize the importance of what we shall call experiential skepticism in the formation and development of black ideologies, political perspectives, and, ultimately, public opinion. Skepticism has a long and distinguished history in various fields of philosophy. It has attracted philosophers as distinct as Aristotle and Nietzsche, and characterized the age in which ideology as narrative and speech act first made its appearance in Western thought and publics. Popular skepticism, however, has received much less attention in the development of mass public opinion and ideologies that have evolved from nonelite sources. This form of skepticism often emerges first in lowercase ideological form, through the accumulation of experiences as a form of historical knowledge and interpretation. Prejudices, bigotry, and a seemingly endless mound of clichés often emerge from the relationship between self and experience among popular groups, yet knowledge of one's location in a neighborhood, society, nation, and world can emerge from this relation as well, forming the basis for a number of strategies employed in the behaviors of daily, public life. Aversion, developed in chapter 4, provides one possible example of a strategy of action emerging from experiential skepticism. Figure 3.2 outlines the presence of historically based skepticism in black critical thinking. We believe that skepticism is not the monopoly of philosophers. The practice of hermeneutics, tacit political knowledge, and what James Scott conceptualizes as *metis* are motivated at some point by experiential skepticism in the critical deliberations of daily life. Skepticism can influence how political, cultural, and social phenomena are *read* and interpreted in daily life, whether as truth, error, or even racism.

As several competing explanations of white and black racial attitudes indicate, meanings circulated within one micropublic sphere may be distinct from the significance attached to a similar or identical phenomenon in the larger, macrosocietal public sphere. The O. J. Simpson acquittal provides one example of such distinction, but there are and have been many others in the United States. The qualitative implications of these divergences lead us to two final questions: First, do ideas matter in the interpretation of public opinion? Second, is black public opinion informed, at least in part by texts, interpretations, and normative outlooks that can only be partially explained by Euro-American studies of ideology? In answering both questions affirmatively, we believe that the concept of ideology has continued relevance for the study of black politics and political thought. Chapter 4, motivated by an incident witnessed by the first author, becomes an opportunity to consider the possibilities for empirical observation provided by the interpretive scheme of quotidian politics, by means of an exploration of an ethical practice of aversion among subordinated groups, an example perhaps of black ideological forms operative in daily life.

CHAPTER 4

Between Confrontation and Acquiescence: An Ethics of Aversion

> *To say that the Negro question is an economic or that it is a political problem is at this stage of general political awareness in the United States not to say anything very important and something that may be, in fact often is, very misleading.*[1]

Introduction

To explore the ramifications of quotidian politics, one must mine the terrain of everyday life to uncover, as C. L. R. James did, that the "Negro question" must be understood as a phenomenon with several distinct yet interrelated constitutive elements before it can be understood as a discretely political or economic problem. I believe I stumbled upon one response to the quotidian forms of racism in daily black life in the United States at a dinner in downtown Manhattan, with a large group of friends and acquaintances at a restaurant between Chelsea and the Village. We were about an hour into our meal when a black gentleman came looking for someone in our party whom he was picking up. The hostess, a young white woman in her mid- to late-twenties engaged the man in a very friendly, professional manner and implored him to come back at some point to have dinner and enjoy the restaurant's wondrous food and hospitality. The man, courteous, poised, and well-dressed, was in his mid-twenties. Educated at one of the nation's best business schools and then employed by one of the world's top brokerage firms on Wall Street, he would be considered a statistical anomaly according to the oft-cited statistics about young black male underachievement in the United States. His response was slow but deliberate, with a curl of condescension at the right edge of his mouth.

"I'm sure, ma'am. The restaurant seems very nice and I'm sure the food is quite nice as well, but I do not normally associate with whites after hours, after work." The woman looked stunned, her mouth dropped, her eyes widened, and after a long pause, she asked feebly, in a plaintive voice, "Why?" To which he responded, "I simply don't. I get enough interactions with whites during my working hours and working days, which are quite long. No disrespect to you or to your restaurant, but the work day and work week is about as much from you people as I can stand." He picked up his companion and left, but not before wishing the woman a good night and best of luck. The woman looked to us for recognition and some solace. Most of the members of the table who were also black were equally surprised, though not stunned. After a pause, the conversation turned from job positions and the latest current events to interactions with whites in a professional environment. One by one, most people at the table partially concurred with the young man's sentiment, though not with his forthright expression. All agreed that while they had white friends with whom they interacted at work, their interactions with whites outside of work were far fewer. One person commented on the young man's honesty, his willingness to say what many blacks felt but dared not utter.

Was this incident another instance of black middle-class rage[2] or yet more evidence of the continued sense of alienation affecting whites and blacks when in each other's presence? There is far too much diversity of opinion and behavior across the humanities and social sciences concerning racial attitudes in the United States to impose a single explanation upon the partial agreements and disagreements evoked by the young man's utterance. Within sociology, there is a vast literature on the implications of racial discrimination for real-life encounters between racially and ethnically defined groups in the United States. A subset of this literature, has focused on some of the more emotional and normative implications of these interactions over generational time, in which long-standing patterns of interaction premised on prejudicial attitudes have produced varying degrees of anxiety, anger, frustration and mistrust, particularly among groups with a history of institutional and quotidian racisms imposed upon them by whites and white dominated institutions. Nicole Shelton has noted how social psychological experiments in the study of racial prejudice have focused mostly on white attitudes toward blacks and other minority groups. The methods employed for these studies focus on "intrapersonal as opposed to interpersonal procedures" primarily among members of the dominant group (whites).³

When focusing on blacks, the majority of studies outline the responses of blacks to long-standing patterns of discrimination. Largely restricted to specific behaviors and interactions, such studies, on the whole, rarely consider the possibility that the observed behaviors might be a subset of a more comprehensive strategy involving tactics and coping mechanisms designed to minimize the likelihood of experiencing racial prejudice and discrimination in public life. Even if we were to accept the proposition that subordinate groups automatically respond to conditions of inequality and discrimination (a dubious proposition), we would still not know why members of a politically subordinate group respond in one way and not another, or choose not to respond to certain modes of prejudicial treatment while responding to others. One thing we do know from the many studies on intergroup conflict, particularly in more ethnographic work, is that quotidian responses to racial inequality are as varied as the circumstances of racial and ethnic prejudice that prompt them. Politically and socially marginalized groups do not respond the same way in each instance of racial discrimination. Setting and context necessarily complicate the "response to oppression" claim, and point toward the need for a more comprehensive examination of how ethnically and racially stigmatized groups themselves situate acts of discrimination within an overall perspective on how to interact with members of a particular group.

Studies that provide evidence of prejudice and discrimination, while extraordinarily valuable, tell us surprisingly little about how members of stigmatized groups make sense of the varied, unpredictable but nonetheless corrosive and cumulative effects of racial and ethnic prejudice. The racial inequality experienced by marginalized groups ranges from interactions with coworkers and superiors and with parents in a carpool, to encounters with police officers and other members of state, to exchanges with bartenders, health club instructors, and many other people occupying the vast array of social roles that constitute a society such as that in the United States. Accordingly, no one tactic can suffice to manage and minimize the potentially negative impact of encounters with racially or ethnically prejudiced individuals who might occupy such positions in everyday life.

The incident described above led me to consider the possibility that this one particular tactic, employed at a restaurant, might be part of a broader strategy of aversion to a large segment of the white population—a multifaceted, varied, even contradictory strategy intended to minimize the negative impact of potentially prejudicial interactions. The behavior of the man I observed may have been informed by the cumulative effect of several overlapping but distinct legacies of racial domination, which have led him to minimize his encounters with whites, as well as to emotionally and affectively detach himself at moments where and when he must interact with them. The immediate responses of the cohort of blacks at the restaurant table indicated that at least some percentage of blacks would not have actually uttered this sentiment to a white person in a chance encounter.

What interests me, though, is whether a segment of the U.S. African American population condones or practices tactics of aversion and avoidance. If such a subgroup exists, how widespread is this attitude and behavioral predisposition? Could it be that this particular gentleman's behavior is the attitudinal consequence of a number of encounters over the course of years that led him to avoid encounters with whites? Is his form of self-segregation based on a matrix of norms developed within his personal, professional, and larger communal circle in response to a history and ongoing pattern of racial discrimination? How are its tactics and strategies manifest?

In interactions with members of a politically dominant group, subordinate group members often engage in an ethicopolitical practice that I have termed an ethics of aversion. An ethics of aversion is characterized by predispositions and attitudes that inform behavior that seeks to limit interactions with dominant-group members. I am interested in examining the more discretionary component of black daily life in a search for evidence of self-conscious modes of discrimination that are ethical and contextually—rather than racially—driven. As developed in the previous chapter on black ideologies, legacies of racial discrimination provide their own basis for critical deliberation among subordinate group members about their conditions in the present, and are not treated simply as events that occurred in the distant past. "Racial distinction" may be a marker for observation, but not a predictor of behaviors. The ability of practitioners to distinguish between "safe" and "unsafe" encounters with dominant-group members and, in turn, to distinguish between safe and unsafe members of the dominant group, suggests that these behaviors and tactics can be distinguished from racial discrimination, wherein an individual is unable to or refuses to distinguish traits and behaviors within another group and attributes those traits or behaviors to racial origin.

Such people ascribe neither to a "culture of subordination" nor to ideologies of assimilation, and may thrive in professional environments that require significant interactions with whites in positions of power. Their coping strategies and mechanisms acknowledge the formal, compulsory aspects of "racial" integration in workplace, educational, and even some associational venues.

They maintain, however, a form of *normative* segregation that overlaps but it not coincident with "racial" segregation in the workplace, neighborhood, and other facets of their sociocultural lives. This mode of ethical discrimination allows for the possibility of "safe" individuals within a larger discriminatory group. Discriminated-group members may develop critical, interpretive means to identify a particular subset of people within a discriminatory group, and can make nuanced observations of dominant-group members.

In this initial formulation based on a synthesis of extant literatures, concepts and theorizations, an ethics of aversion is informed by a process of critical deliberation that is quite distinct from processes of deliberation conventionally associated—and equated—with racist thought. Evasive tactics such as these are not passive, but could be more accurately characterized as active detachment from particular social and cultural encounters with members of the dominant group.

There are at least three broad explanatory categories for aversive strategies among subordinate group members. Minority group members may engage in avoidance strategies because they: (1) hate whites as a race (whites = aversion); (2) have a reductionist view of the race or culture concept and apply a bounded, static notion of racial identity to themselves and others (white behavior versus black behavior); or (3) find attractive and unattractive traits among all groups of people but find a particular group to exhibit unattractive behaviors with much higher frequency. The first two categories or types of rationalization rely heavily on presumed racial distinction and correlate phenotype with attitudes and behavior. These two rationalizations for aversive strategies reveal racialist, if not racist, logics, since a population is prejudged in its entirety based on an interpretation and observation of only certain members of the group. The third category, however, allows for the possibility of variation in attitudes and behavior among a potentially offensive group, thereby providing a critical barrier against absolutist racial reasoning by subordinate group members.

The third category of rationalization for aversive strategy interests me most. Not only is it the least explored rationalization among all the possible popular responses to ongoing patterns of racial prejudice and discrimination, but perhaps the most complicated to apprehend interpretively, since it is based on modes of discrimination that are not "racial." The third category of aversion implicitly rejects "assimilation" versus "integration" dichotomies, opting instead for partial acceptance and partial rejection of dominant norms and values in U.S. society, politics, and culture. It is a more fluid negotiation of institutional, civic, and voluntary discrimination, and is potentially the most complicated and certainly the least explored rationalization, since its judgments and conclusions are not premised on "racial" discrimination.

Groups that have experienced long-standing antagonistic relations with other groups, or a singularly traumatic experience with a group or nationality, may engage in behaviors similar to those witnessed among U.S. African Americans. Many Jews, as well as Allied soldiers refused to visit Germany after World War II. There were several generations of U.S. veterans, for example, who refused to buy German- and Japanese-manufactured automobiles, as well as North and South Koreans who refused to consume Japanese products as a consequence of the atrocities committed by Japanese occupation troops during World War II. Such behaviors can be distinguished from the more banal forms of jingoism found among most nationalities throughout the world arising during moments of competition or in various forms of nationalism, that preternaturally configure other nationalities as threats, predators, or inferiors.[4]

Viewed cross-nationally, the end of codified segregation and imperial rule throughout most of the world has also shifted terms of racialized discourses in both postcolonial and postimperial settings, making explicitly racist rhetoric less common. As both single-country and cross-national studies of racial attitudes and behavior in societies as distinct as EU nation-states, South Africa, and Brazil have demonstrated, many whites who hold prejudicial views toward nonwhites do not state their prejudices so bluntly, but rather utilize euphemisms, coded language, and other modes of rhetorical displacement. The long-standing tensions between white British and Asian neighborhoods in England, or among various immigrant and white French communities in France, provide some indication of the tensions between communities of people that, although not always ending in violence, harbor mistrust and patterns of avoidance.[5]

How do individuals come to develop an ethics of aversion? Is this ethics influenced by larger ethicopolitical concerns or does an ethics of aversion influence broader political, social, and cultural perspectives among U.S. African Americans, and perhaps other groups as well? How do blacks perceive white behaviors and attitudes in the relative absence of explicit racism? What are the cues "read" by blacks to discern the potentiality for prejudice, assumptions of privilege, and unveiling of bigotry in interactions with whites? In the "postracist" era where explicitly racist behavior is considered taboo, behaviors and attitudes previously viewed as "nonracial" require even greater scrutiny to better understand how putatively nonracial or antiracist attitudes and behaviors help transform and reiterate racist practices, norms, and prejudices. These are ethical rather than moral considerations, because the norms and values affecting social interactions are based on the limits of actually existing interactions and possibilities for conflict, the minimization of conflict through avoidance, or, alternatively, prospects for friendship, rather than consisting in the application of moral principles based on idealized versions of racial harmony or human nature.

In distinguishing morals from ethics, morality represents an ideal mode of judgment and action under circumstances in which a person can act relatively autonomously, based on his or her wishes. Ethical behavior, on the other hand, is the outcome of the encounter between one's best wishes and judgment and the external constraints imposed upon those wishes and judgment. Doctors caring for terminally ill patients in hospice settings are examples of ethical nuance. The infamous Nurse Rivers of the Tuskegee experiments, wherein black men diagnosed with syphilis were left untreated, could be characterized as engaging in both unethical and immoral behavior, though her behavior was no different from the doctors, administrators, and governmental officials who conducted and supervised the experiment. Perhaps the closest conceptualization in the sociological literature on race relations is "racial battle fatigue."[6] By merging political and social theory with more practically oriented approaches to empirical data, an ethics of aversion could have potential utility for studies in moral psychology, which fuses normative ethics with empirical psychology.

In detailing an ethics of aversion, what will be revealed is that behaviors often characterized as forms of black racism require far more complicated understandings of the relationship between behaviors and norms among members of subordinate groups in response to the behaviors and attitudes of dominant-group members. I believe an ethics of aversion can help scholars distinguish between responses to racism and racial prejudice. Racist ideologies are themselves framed by ethical and political deliberations, but they utilize an ethical compass distinct from those responding to racism. Several sociologists have argued for the abandonment of the use of the term "race relations" because of the misleading impression it conveys by using the categories of race, which do not exist.[7] In philosophy, David Theo Goldberg and K. Anthony Appiah have presented similar arguments, though Goldberg reminds us of the importance of distinguishing racism from race, since racism is an actually occurring phenomenon with real consequences.[8]

I share these author's sentiments concerning the race concept. As I elaborate in chapter 7 on Henry Highland Garnet and the concept of hybridity, and in an article coauthored with Erin Chung,[9] "races" do not relate to one another. Nonetheless, to the extent to which the race concept is utilized as a marker and factor in deliberations concerning the distribution of goods and services (an instrumentalist view), as well as in self-pronouncements of community membership and affiliation, the race concept could be said to be "alive" as a part of politics, though not as sociological dictum or biological essence. Instead, this chapter focuses on the norms, predilections, and interpretations of meaning that come to constitute the notion of race and the practice of racism in daily life.

What I aim to uncover is the ethical and political content or substratum of racism and its effects among existing populations and their dynamics. An ethics of aversion provides an opportunity to witness the "in-between" aspects of racial attitudes and behavior among U.S. African Americans, as evidenced in dispositions that contextualize integration and segregation within a normative, rather than an institutional, associational or consumptive environment.[10] If my theorization of an ethics of aversion is borne out by survey-based research, I will attempt to elaborate a cross-national research agenda to examine the prospect of an ethics of aversion among subordinate groups in societies such as those of France, Brazil,[11] New Zealand, Australia, and Japan. The ethics of aversion provides an opportunity to revisit, expand, and deepen our understanding of terms such as pluralism, discrimination, and assimilation, terms that have multiple, often competing meanings in different political and cultural contexts. "Pluralism," a term whose meaning has been significantly reduced and in some ways distorted in contemporary social science's treatment of race and liberal democracy in the United States, will be taken up in a more elaborate fashion in a subsequent article that engages the more comparative literature on ethnic and race relations in plural societies.

Aversion should not be construed to mean passive resignation under conditions of subordination, or outright rejection of members of the dominant group. Processes of aversion, in my view, are recognitions of the structural, affective, and voluntary limits of interaction with dominant-group members, an acknowledgment of the constraints that inform, rather than determine, the outcomes of interpersonal or personal-institutional interactions. The ethics of aversion is the normative response to either a singular, traumatic experience or an accumulation of negative experiences with a particular group, wherein nonengagement, as opposed to direct confrontation or submission, is utilized as a means to limit and reduce the range of interactions with members and institutions of the dominant group to only the most compulsory activities of the public sphere.[12] There are exceptions and qualifications made to exempt individuals from dominant groups who are considered friends or trustworthy, but such exceptions serve to prove, rather than disprove, the conclusions that first prompted the development of aversive strategies toward the larger group. Racism, rather than race, is the terrain upon which an ethics of aversion travels. The individuals from the dominant group who do not exhibit the pervasive attitudes and behaviors of that group are considered anomalies.

Like much of the political science literature on black political thought and ideology that treats black political thought as a microcosmic, paradigmatic subset or component of "American ideas,"[13] many sociological and ethnographic studies of black political and social behaviors treat black responses to racism as absolute manifestations of black prejudice, the dynamic or dialectical response to various modes of white racism. Here my concern is not restricted to matters of "race"; I am interested in a more general problem concerning power-laden social encounters between groups marked by some form of difference (somatic, religious, ethnic, or phenotypic). As in most theorizations of power, theories of "race relations" tend to emphasize the polarities on continua of power and powerlessness. I am more interested in how actual human interactions, as opposed to the clash of ideal-types, provide innumerable combinations of alienation, estrangement, intimacy, and proximity. There are a variety of evaluative assessments made by social groups—regardless of phenotype—subject to dynamics of inequality. Minority group members reach certain conclusions about dominant groups after a deliberative process of critical differentiation. Although this process may entail the primary categorization of groups by phenotype (race), a second-stage categorization—the identification of a more ethically sympathetic subgroup within the larger group—is the basis for the development of a differentiating principle that helps distinguish "good" white people from "bad."

Unlike first-order racial discrimination, wherein dominant-group members rarely differentiate among minority-group members (since an entire group supposedly shares the same characteristics and behaviors), the entire history of "race relations" in the United States suggests that U.S. African Americans have *had to* distinguish among members of the dominant group, if only for their own safety. To give just one example, John Brown and John Calhoun were both defined in racial terms as white. Opponents and advocates of slavery, however, could distinguish between the two white men, the former a rabid foe of slavery, the latter a rabid advocate and practitioner of white supremacy. It would have been a serious lack of critical judgment for any black person, much less an antislavery advocate, to assume that Brown's classification as white would have placed him in the same affinity group as that of John Calhoun. This example demonstrates how phenotype is an unreliable predictor of behavior. In interactions that are not organized by the state, values and outlook, not race, can influence "racial" segregation.

The nuance and complexity of cognitive and behavioral dimensions of black responses to racial prejudice are often neglected in survey-based approaches that draw correlations between racial solidarity and attitudes among U.S. African Americans. There is a tendency to sort black attitudes and behaviors into binary categories, in two distinct but related ways. The first concerns the tendency to seek to prove or disprove black attitudinal congruence, or even acceptance of core American values and myths, in toto. The second tendency is to construct binary categorizations of their attitudes and ideologies, as if the entire range of black popular opinion and political thought can be accurately and comprehensively encompassed in such simple, neat categorizations as separatist or assimilationist. How do we make sense of attitudes and behaviors that combine elements of seemingly oppositional and contradictory strategies, which would be normally labeled as the opposite of each other, assimilationist and segregationist?

Several structural and historical factors are at work in an ethics of aversion. Many societies that were once structured according to de jure segregation and stratification (postcolonial, postimperial, former slaveholding societies) remain segregated (though with significant variation) along religious, racial, or ethnic lines. Although formal segregation has been rendered obsolete, the structure, pattern, and process of interactions between groups remain codified in ways that combine phenotypic, class-based distinctions to correlate the degrees of segregation by space with those of putatively racial or chromatic distinction. Nation-states with spatial and social segregation without state-mandated codification and regulation, such as France, New Zealand, Brazil, and Japan, are examples of nation-states with segregation patterns that cannot be attributed to strictures of contemporary formal segregation. This leads to a revised version of a time-honored question normally posed by comparative sociologists: Why do people, in the absence of institutional and legal strictures, maintain patterns of "racial" segregation and distinction?

Under these conditions, spaces or zones of interaction between individuals or segments of specific group populations develop in economic, residential, institutional, and civic spheres, wherein a range of affective (voluntary) and mandatory (state, governmental, employment) relationships occur. In both the affective and mandatory realms, however, members of subordinate groups often are required to make spontaneous, intuitive judgments concerning their potential or actual interactions with dominant-group members. Under these circumstances, there are instances in which subordinate-group members employ strategies to avoid or minimize interactions with dominant-group members: such strategies are employed not because of a racial, religious, or ethnic prejudice, but due to a belief that a large proportion of dominant-group members adhere to norms and behaviors that are incongruent with the subordinate group members' belief systems, such as notions of justice, fair play, and the modicum of social gestures and conventions needed to remain within the threshold of nonconflictual interactions between group members.

Propensity is a key concept for an ethics of aversion. Propensity does not preclude the possibility that some members of dominant groups neither ascribe to nor display more generic dominant-group behavioral patterns and attitudes toward the subordinate group. Instead, propensity provides an interpretive filter to gauge the behaviors and attitudes of individuals belonging to the dominant group, in order to assess the likelihood that dominant-group members may behave negatively toward subordinate group members. Returning to the John Brown/John Calhoun distinctions, the threshold in the United States may now be lower. There may be fewer individuals who could represent either end of a continuum on explicit empathy or aversion toward blacks. This, in turn, negatively affects subordinate-group members in both structural (employment, educational, residential, financial) and subjective (slights, affronts, dignity-affecting behaviors) ways. Based upon their collective notions of propensity, subordinate-group members then strive to minimize encounters with dominant group members because of the great likelihood of negative encounters. In qualitative terms, aversive strategies are to subordinate groups what probability is to a mathematician, economist, or blackjackplayer. Subordinate-group judgments, therefore, are not necessarily reductionist or chauvinistic, but part of an overall coping and subsistence strategy in relation to dominant groups.

The concept of propensity shares some similarities with the concept some economists call "statistical discrimination." Firms (and other dominant-group institutions/individuals) are said to employ this practice when they discriminate against members of groups based on the firms' greater than average "bad" experiences with members of that group in the past or on the basis of expectations concerning that group (accounts vary). This is said to be a "rational" decision-making rule since, as Ellis Cose argued, information is costly and it is cheaper in the long run to minimize hiring members from the "problematic" group even though you may lose out on the occasional exceptional individual. A major difference in my formulation hinges on the range of ongoing, documented instances of individual and institutional discrimination that members of subordinate groups are well aware of (employment discrimination, encounters with the police, bodily harm). From the reservoirs of memory, firsthand accounts, and the history of racial discrimination, members of subordinate groups look for a cluster of behavioral forms that signal that a particular person is acting in a way that requires aversive strategies. Their tacit political knowledge, as discussed in chapter 3, helps constitute part of the critical perspective undergirding an ethics of aversion.

One final factor in the theorization of an ethics of aversion concerns the interplay between the more perspectivally driven aspects of aversion and the broader, structural (socioeconomic, institutional, state-generated) factors of "plural" societies. An ethics of aversion is mindful of the larger realities of living as a political and/or socioeconomic subordinate member of a larger society, where the assessment of individual value and worth may be influenced by racial stereotypes and valuation (see chapter 7) in addition to an individual's behavior or traits. Members of subordinate groups are fully aware of the necessity of certain interactions with dominant institutions and group members. Primary and secondary revenue extraction (taxation), consumption, private and public educational institutions, even socializing institutions for which group members may have a secondary relationship (children's activities such as soccer and Little Leagues) increase the likelihood of interaction with dominant-group members and institutions. The inevitability of these encounters, however, does not determine their variability, or the degree of distance and disaffection within specific interactions. It is precisely because of this larger reality that the second form of discrimination becomes a critical evaluative device to enable subordinate group members to distinguish among the dominant-group population.[14]

Using the example of the United States to explore and ultimately "test" the utility of the theory of an ethics of aversion, I am suggesting that U.S. African Americans may engage in an ethics of aversion in response to the cumulative effects of interactions with whites. The contemporary legacy of racial domination and segregation in the United States has meant for many U.S. African Americans that interactions with whites are often characterized by misidentification, forms of coercion or negative reinforcement, attempts to reimpose relations of dominance, subordination, or at the social and personal level to limit one's interactions, choices, and spaces of sociality.

Part of what I want to explore is why different groups of blacks accept some features of assimilation and not others, in some domains and not others, and under certain conditions and not others. As part of this dynamic process, aversive strategies, employed for various modes of interaction with dominant-group members such as white Americans, represent the ethical underside of assimilation. I am primarily concerned with the following questions: What factors inform the decision-making processes of relative assimilation and aversion? What are the limits of assimilation? What are the limits of aversive strategies?

II. Revisiting Concepts of Assimilation and Discrimination

The seemingly straightforward idea of assimilation is the first conceptual emendation required to fully comprehend an ethics of aversion. Assimilation is invariably employed in much contemporary debate on black attitudes and political behaviors as an indicator of degrees of acceptance and incorporation of "the American Dream" within black mass publics and individual attitudes.[15] Assimilation is widely used as a descriptor for those who assume postures, behaviors, and outlooks associated with a dominant group or institution, in a process of political, cultural, and economic incorporation. The rather restrictive use of the concept of assimilation provides an ultimately arbitrary means of developing a more substantive and systematic account of group-oriented dynamics.

By itself, the application of the concept of assimilation does little to probe—let alone explain—the terms and conditions under which groups incorporate values, allegiances, and behaviors associated with other groups or society as a whole. Conversely, the term "assimilation" alone cannot convey what features of "group behavior" are condoned or discouraged by a dominant group, unless we actually examine group interactions and interpersonal relations. The process of U.S. African American assimilation has multiple dimensions and facets. Groups and individuals *do* assimilate attitudes and behavioral patterns of other groups (often unconsciously). At a very basic level, to be human in society necessarily involves the assimilation of behaviors and attitudes based upon the observation of and interaction with others. But people do not assimilate *all* the attitudes and behaviors of dominant groups and institutions. All members of a society, then, adopt assimilative behaviors to some degree. Some whites, for example, have assimilated black cultural and political behaviors, ranging from popular culture, language, and gestures, to modes of political and social protest historically associated with the civil rights movement. Assimilation, then, should not always be associated with accommodation or self-hatred. In most plural societies, members of different ethnic groups adopt the behaviors, norms, even cuisine of other groups without necessarily wanting to become members of politically and economically dominant groups.

In addition to assimilation, the second important conceptual innovation concerns the concept of discrimination. Within an ethically aversive strategy, subordinate-group members may simultaneously assimilate and reject features of dominant-group behavior. A deeper cognitive process of ethical discrimination enables groups and individuals employing aversive behaviors to make strategic choices concerning the depth and frequency of their interactions with members of a dominant group. A key question that the ethics of aversion seeks to answer is: how does a subordinate-group member gauge a dominant-group member's propensity towards discrimination and subsequently deploy a strategy of ethical discrimination? An understanding of competing notions of discrimination is critical for identifying and ascertaining the processes of ethical and political discernment within the dynamics of aversion.

III A Theory of Aversion

The term "aversion" appears most prominently in the discipline of applied psychology, pertaining to the employment of techniques and methods aimed at behavioral modification of individuals or groups within controlled environments. Controlled environments include prisons, schools, and residential institutions for the developmentally disabled and mentally impaired. "Timeout" employed by teachers, electric shock therapy, cold showers, and light manipulation used to alter antisocial or regressive behaviors in institutional settings are examples of aversive techniques.[16] Within this literature, the term "aversion" is most directly associated with punishment and negative reinforcement.

This literature has limited utility for the amplification of a theory of an ethics of aversion, for three reasons. The first limitation is the controlled, focused circumstances under which aversive techniques are initiated and employed. Second, aversive techniques are employed by those in a superordinate position in relation to a controlled subject population. Third, aversive techniques are invariably employed in institutions of socialization or, in the case of penal institutions, resocialization, where, unlike the broader society, movements and interactions of populations under control are highly regulated and rarely random.

In contrast, the ethics of aversion is evidenced in the process of interaction involving members of dominant and subordinate "racial groups," in circumstances determined by the more phenomenological aspects of daily life. Though formal and informal institutions and other variables can mediate interactions between group members, individual volition and an overall sense of agency figure much more prominently in noninstitutionalized settings. In civil society, individual norms and behaviors are not necessarily subordinate to institutional prerogatives. One possible commonality linking an ethics of aversion to more clinically defined aversive techniques is the effect of dominant-group behaviors and interventions upon the lives of subordinate members. The effects of interactions with dominant-group members may lead some members of the subordinate group to interpret their interactions with the former group as a class or type of punishment. Thus, a form of behavior modification is the consequence of noninstitutionally mediated relations between dominant and subordinate groups in the more open aspects of civil society, with modifications premised on the belief that minimal interactions will reduce the prospects of individual or collective punishment.

For these reasons, the social sciences provide some of the most appropriate tools of analysis for apprehending the phenomena of aversive strategies and practices of daily life. Anthropological and sociological scholarship provide some conceptual elements for the development of a theory that can explain some of the tactics of interaction employed by politically subordinate groups in their relations with dominant-group members and institutions.

There are some cues in political theory, particularly in considerations of multiculturalism and pluralism. Joseph Carens writes that U.S. African Americans may nurture a "culture of subordination"[17] and thus manage expectations and aspirations for success and socialization within dominant white society. "A group which has been consistently denied access to things which the dominant groups in society value may come to say it does not want these things anyway"[18] writes Carens, echoing and following Jon Elster's conceptualization of "adaptive preference formation."[19] Though this may hold true for certain segments of the U.S. African American population, as studies of disparities in black student achievement have suggested, neither Carens's nor Elster's formulations can account for the existence of high black achievement, whether in conventional liberal professions, particularly among the two generations of black middle-class professionals trained in the post-segregation era or in professions such as music, entertainment, and sports. These conclusions and rationalizations of relative or even objective underachievement among U.S. African Americans have two shortcomings, in my view. First, Elster's and Carens's conclusions do not acknowledge class diversity among U.S. African American and other black populations in the United States, or the possibility that more well-to-do blacks may engage in adaptive preference formation not because of fear of success or disappointment, but out of a more pragmatic response to existing patterns of segregation, desegregation, and resegregation in civic life. Although their conclusions may accurately characterize one aspect of black coping strategies, their conclusions do not encompass the entire range of adaptive strategies utilized by U.S. African Americans and other blacks socialized into U.S. racial politics.

The second shortcoming concerns how these accounts of possible aversive behavior among a particular subset of a subordinate population fits within a more comprehensive account of power relations amongst dominant and subordinate groups. American political debates in the 1980s focused on the multidimensionality of power[20] provided theoretical, often granular accounts of class conflict and subordination in daily life. With the exception of Robert Dahl's more harmonious view of liberalism's incorporation of dissent and black protest into New Haven politics, or Floyd Hunter's "second" dimension of power, which addressed the preemptive capacities of liberal institutional and electoral politics when faced with challenges by insurgent black political organizations and actors, these debates rarely addressed how blacks responded to practices of exclusion. Much subsequent scholarship on quotidian race relations has moved, first to more ethnographic research, then to more quantitative, data-driven assessment, with little new theorization about what individual preferences and group choices of blacks and whites tell us about how racial politics is structured—or not structured—by dynamics of power and powerlessness.

As the ethnographic, survey-based, and focus-group evidence below will reveal, aversive strategies can be found across the spectrum of black lifeworlds[21] and are given distinct form contingent, in part, on class, regional, gendered, generational, and situational factors. This variation suggests that we have to construct several possible scenarios for understanding the correlation between racial identification, racial solidarity, and aversive behaviors, more than what present scholarship on the topic of black solidarity has suggested. As analyzed in the previous chapter, Paul Sniderman and Thomas Piazza correlate black solidarity with black prejudice. As part of a countervailing interpretation that emphasizes the need to comprehend black ethicopolitical choices in context and their constitutive elements before characterizing the problems and crises of black politics, political culture, and public opinion, I want to first raise the theoretical possibility that black solidarity and black aversive strategies can assume myriad forms, along several different ethical poles that do not necessarily result in group prejudice.

In addition to the correlation between black solidarity and black antipathy toward whites, there are at least four other possible ways of interpreting black attitudes and behaviors in relation to whites. First, black solidarity could also entail an outright rejection of assimilation in the more conventional sense, in the manner suggested by many critics (white and black) of black nationalism and Afrocentrism. Another possibility could be what others have characterized as an "immersion" strategy of complete racialism coupled with advocacy of separation and vocal antipathy toward whites. A third possibility is a mixture of the two previous scenarios, wherein blacks operate in a racialist mode in some contexts and not others, such as the example this chapter begins with. Yet a fourth possibility, one that may be more broadly representative of black behaviors more generally, is a nondeterministic approach that enables members of an ethnonational or racialized minority to distinguish among the dominant-group population, while at the same time, based on experientially based ethical knowledge, limit their interactions with the group.

IV Evidence of Aversion: Personal Conduct

A second example of aversion involves a middle-aged black male, a successful barber and small entrepreneur in the New England area, who also owns several condominiums. After the successful sale of a condominium for which, as is common custom in such transactions, he was paid with a cashier's check, the man brought the check to his *own* bank to cash. He was told by a cashier that the check could not be cashed without first being held for seven to ten business days, not standard practice for a cashier's check of any amount. After pausing for a moment to collect himself, the man calmly requested to withdraw all of the funds from his bank account at that bank, which exceeded the amount of the check he sought to cash. After consultation with the bank manager, the man's check was cashed. Only with the recognition that the potential check casher was worth more to the bank than the check itself was the check cashed.

This example elucidates at least one way in which the process of discrimination or discernment entailed in an ethics of aversion helps identify the collision and ultimate convergence of public and private worlds. The man did not accuse the individual teller, or the bank itself, of racism, though he did recount this incident to several friends. He understood the formal rules that applied to this particular transaction, which should apply to *all* transactions that involve the use of a cashier's check, once the authenticity of the cashier's check has been determined. The presumed race of the individual presenting the check *should* have been irrelevant to the completion of the transaction (authorization, determination, payment). The fact that he had already identified himself as an account holder and had conducted business at that bank branch previously, *should* have provided the teller some assurance and comfort in the knowledge that even if the check was fraudulent, the loss would be held against the man's account.

The man was well aware of the highly discretionary, informal criteria utilized to *disqualify* blacks from objective participation in relations of consumption, use, and exchange. Had he made good on his request to withdraw all of his funds from the bank, his behavior could have been characterized as an aversive act. His decision to close his accounts at the bank was based on ethicopolitical rather than economic criteria. Had he switched banks, he might well have encountered similar treatment, or invested his money with a bank that may have provided better customer service but at noncompetitive rates. At least he would have been certain that he would not be mistreated by an employee at his previous bank.

Several classic studies of African American attitudes reveal similar ethicopolitical responses to racist behaviors that result not in the outward denunciation of racism but in the withdrawal from interaction. Several respondents interviewed in the widely read *Drylongso* provide glimpses of their evaluations of whites based upon an ethical assessment of a history of interactions, rather than built-in prejudice.[22] Ruth Shays, an elderly black woman, recounted several experiences with whites wherein their behaviors differed drastically from blacks she encountered and lived with. In the last example of her interview, she recalls an incident in which a black friend suffering from diabetes had too much insulin in her system and required an infusion of sugar in the form of a glass of orange juice. Her description of the encounter, and her conclusions, follow:

> The woman was going into shock, but this white man wouldn't part with a glass of his orange juice until he was sure he was going to get his thirty cents. Now, your average black person wouldn' behave that way to anybody, white or black. I don' know how many white people would do what that dog did, but I do know that I never saw a colored person do anything like that. Most of that man's trade was black people, but he'll never get another dime out of Ruth Shays! There is nothing a person like that can give me.[23]

What is most revealing here for an understanding of an ethics of aversion is not her description of the circumstances. The description itself identifies the behavior of one individual purveyor of orange juice, what could be an isolated instance of malice or in more entrepreneurial terms, bad business practice or, finally, the juice purveyor's response to the cumulative effect of dishonest transactions with a particular person or community. The interaction does not necessarily have to be perceived as a racist practice or behavior that could be attributed to whites as an entire group. Her response, however, to make sure that this particular purveyor of orange juice would "never get another dime out of Ruth Shays" provides us with a view into the ethical responses by blacks to behaviors deemed racist. Much like the Montgomery bus boycott, where blacks of various class and status positions refused to utilize the municipal bus company because of their operator's history of mistreatment of black passengers, Ms. Shays's decision to refuse to engage in a transactional relationship with this particular businessman sheds light on a larger web of critical equations of behavior and race in black critical thinking.

Continuing with *Drylongso*, elderly respondents, in particular, were quick to distinguish white attitudes from phenotype, or more precisely, carefully divorced phenotype from behavior. Early in Porter Millington's deposition, for example, he notes that "you got to understand that it is not in the color but the thinking, how you might say, the attitude. And it's not in *your* attitude, but in the attitudes of all the people that growed you and of the people that you seen and heard about."[24] Hattie Lanarck stated in her brief deposition that "I thank God that I don't need anything from the white man. Nothing he has will do us any good and if you take anything from him, then you will be as sorry as he is. White people were not always so, but they have made themselves so by living sorry lives and now they are making us the same way."[25] While the blanketing of "white people" may give the impression that we are reading the words of an outright, essentializing bigot, several points in the passage give an indication of a more nuanced, contextual, and historicized sensibility. The idea that whites in general could "have made themselves so" suggests a transformation in behaviors over time, not a static, timeless account of whites in general. Socialization that emphasizes the maximization of profit, even at others' expense, is learned rather than "racial" behavior.

What links these accounts with those elaborated above are the disparate, rather than coordinated character of these ethical responses to circumstances of perceived racial discrimination. The glimpse of these practices both during and after the era of formal legal segregation may indicate that the ethical and political responses to racial prejudice persist despite the dismantling of formal legal barriers to equal access for blacks. The responses persist amidst ever-changing, highly circumstantial modes of discrimination that also persist. Collective memory may be an experiential and reflective source for an aversive ethics. The work of Frederick Harris examines the relationship between collective memory and social mobilization.[26] Aversive strategies may suggest a relationship between collective memory and a subaltern politics of fragmented, episodic, and more individuated responses to ongoing practices of racial discrimination.

V Biopolitics and Aversion

What Foucault called biopolitics, a politics of the body, or corporality, is a key dimension of "race relations" and racial politics. Amelie Oksenberg Rorty and David Wong write of the role of somatic identity in the formation of self-image and self-conception, "Because there are social norms for many somatic qualities…, those who stress the somatic aspect of identity attempt to confirm to social ideals of body types."[27] Extending this analysis to matters of racial discrimination, wherein individuals engaged in first order discrimination attach what Adrian M. S. Piper refers to as a "primary disvalued attribute"[28] to specifically marked bodies, U.S. African Americans can be seen as engaging in a long-standing symbolic struggle over the meaning of their bodies in the public sphere, markets, and mass media. The stereotypes of "looseness"/licentiousness among U.S. African American women, and hypersexual, athletically adroit, and intellectually feeble U.S. African American men have been employed at different times in U.S. history.[29] These stereotypes resonate in various parts of the black world, as witnessed in the polemical exchanges between U.S. and Mexican politicians in July 2005 over the caricatured depiction of an African American (non-U.S.) boy on a Mexican postage stamp, coupled with comments by several Mexican journalists and politicians, which gave evidence of a certain naïveté about racist stereotypes.[30]

Rather than conforming, however, to social ideals of body types, U.S. African Americans have helped transform ideals for both men and women in the United States, through the emphasis of body movement, posture, and exertion that have created new somatic ideals that have become normative, particularly among youth. At the same time, however, black men and women have had to address racially discriminatory attributions about their respective bodies that are also gender specific.

One example of this particular practice I personally witnessed occurred during a chance encounter with a childhood friend in Chicago's O'Hare airport, someone I had not seen for nearly twenty years. An accomplished collegiate athlete who narrowly missed a career in the NBA, he enjoyed a professional career in basketball as a player in several European leagues. After retirement, he became a successful basketball coach at the college level, and currently is an assistant coach for an NCAA Division I men's basketball team that is perennially among the top ten in Division I basketball teams in the country. At approximately 6'6" and (now) close to three hundred pounds, he is an imposing but friendly figure in public life. He is often asked to give motivational speeches to high school basketball players, to provide them with a sense of professional life in basketball as a coach and former player.

Once in the Los Angeles airport after our flight, several passengers on the flight, as well as people in the airport, approached him and generated some of the following questions and statements: "You must have played football somewhere!" "Are you or were you an athlete?" and "You are awfully big!" In one sense, such questions and assumptions are often fielded by men with large athletic physiques in the United States, regardless of race or ethnicity. Although there were many blacks and nonwhites on the plane and in the airport itself, only white men approached him. At one point, he made a point to mention to me in between gracious smiles and deflections of more personal questions about his relationship to sports (both real and imagined), "I get this all the time. When I tell them I'm a coach, though, most of the time the discussion stops. They expect us to know how to play. They don't expect us to know x's and o's" (referring to diagrammatic iterations of team strategy on a court or playing field).

In three separate encounters, he deflected questions about his professional life history in sports, and, in one instance, stated to an insistent man, "I'm just like you, man, just trying to make it in this world. I don't play anything," rather than rattling off his collegiate and postcollegiate accomplishments. In one instance, however, a man who overheard our conversation on the airplane asked a very specific, friendly but not intrusive question about his team's prospects for the upcoming college basketball season. My friend responded, and in the ensuing conversation between the two, the man (who was white) revealed that he worked for a major cable sports network. The discussion then shifted to the coverage of basketball by various sports networks. There was a pronounced shift in my friend's repertoire of communication. He seemed to distinguish both the questioner and the questions, and allowed the conversation to flow in several directions. By placing his query at the level of shared knowledge, rather than at the level of a desire to know the history of my friend's body (in terms of athletic function), my friend seemed far less "on" and performative. All of the questioners, including the last one, were white. This provides one example of an ethics of aversion within the dynamics of biopolitics.

At least one possibly generalizable phenomenon culled from these interactions concerns the coach's account of the reactions generated by his role and status as a coach, rather than athlete. There are certain professions in U.S. society that, at the elite level, provide opportunities for status, publicity, and the acquisition of social capital for its practitioners due to the public acknowledgment and admiration of the display and exercise of competency. Many of the relatively few blacks in such positions, ranging from corporate lawyers, professional athletes, professors, realtors, and others, particularly in knowledge- and information-based professions, have experienced various forms of cognitive dissonance expressed by whites in contexts outside their primary profession.

The presumption of their lack of resources, relative ignorance, and paucity of experience outside the mythical ghetto, has been recounted in numerous autobiographies of athletes and celebrities as well as in journalistic and sociological accounts of everyday racism. Blacks engaged in high-status professions with relative anonymity outside their immediate work environments are more prone to be "mistaken" for a low-status black person, especially in contexts where blacks are normally associated with menial tasks or even criminal marginality. One means of avoiding the confusion, embarrassment, anger, and frustration generated by such dynamics is to avoid or minimize contact with individuals who might not only "mistake" these high achievers for social subordinates but also be surprised to discover a black person with more status than themselves. This stage in an interaction introduces a dilemma for blacks involved. Should they find some way to indicate that their status position falls outside the status location in which prejudicial whites have placed them? This provides one of the few opportunities for more elite or higher status members of minority groups to utilize their status position favorably, albeit defensively, as a means of distinguishing themselves from both lower-status segments of their immediate community, lower-status whites, and society as a whole. This is evidenced in the example of the barber and multiple-dwelling owner. This response has paradoxical implications, however: by resorting to status projection, do middle-class and elite blacks reinforce negative stereotyping of lower-status blacks, while simultaneously attenuating status and class antagonisms in society as a whole?

This leads to cognitive categorization, an area of psychological experimentation that has received increased attention in recent years. Studies have demonstrated a widespread human tendency toward categorization that transcends national, cultural, gender, and other distinctions. Categorization is a crucial cognitive dimension in the process of racial discrimination, as people from one group may tend to bracket or categorize members of another group based upon certain attributes. Roland Fryer and Matthew Jackson refer to this process of listing a set of attributes with a particular category a "prototype," which provides the modular basis for the inclusion of other group members within a particular category according to an ensemble of specific attributes, as well as the distinction of this particular group from other groups.[31] What distinguishes aversive strategies and places them at the level of politics, rather than individual psychological examination and assessment, is that observable behavior is distinct from attributes. Observable behavior allows for practitioners of aversive strategies to make fine—as opposed to coarse—distinctions among the dominant-group population. Racially discriminatory practices, on the other hand, generally do not allow—at least at the outset—for finer, more granular distinctions because, as prejudicial interpretations, they foreground the category and its attendant attributes at the expense of individual differentiation among the group discriminated against.

The accumulation of an archive of experiential knowledge among U.S. African Americans may lead many blacks to the same conclusions that scientific survey research has demonstrated: the majority of whites believe blacks to be less intelligent, inferior citizens and humans hardly worthy of occupying the same occupational, cultural, and social and residential space.[32] This practical knowledge provides the evidentiary base for at least some of the various aversive strategies that some blacks adopt toward some whites. This experiential knowledge can be deployed within tacit political knowledge, as described in chapter 3, as people share stories about their experiences, offering encouragement, advice, and warnings concerning appropriate conduct under these circumstances.

VI Theoretical Implications

While aversive strategies can be viewed as reactions against injustice and, indeed, a prototheory of justice, they all share the inherent limitations of individual responses to inequality. Aversive strategies cannot ensure, for example, that individual or group members will never be harmed by members of the averted group. What may distinguish the U.S. African American case, as well as other groups who could be examined for evidence of aversive strategies, are the ways in which these strategies are a response to past and present injus-

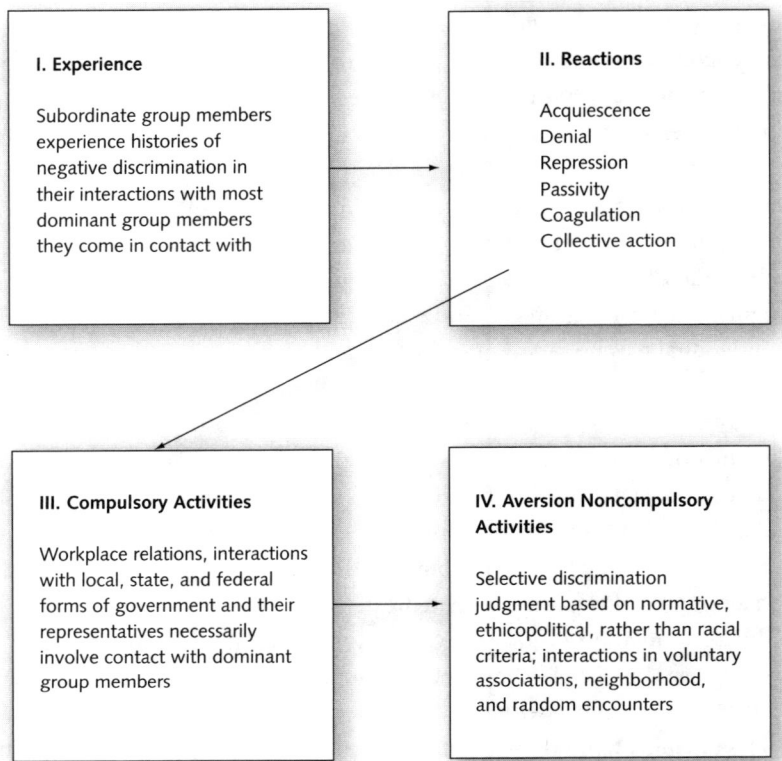

Figure 4.1
An Ethics of Aversion: A Dynamic Process

tice simultaneously. At the same time, future research might reveal generational differences in the use of aversive strategies. For example, U.S. African Americans and an increasing black immigrant population may have different enough collective memories, political experiences, and histories of racial discrimination and prejudice to make their responses to discrimination distinct from the responses of their predecessors.[33]

Aversive strategies among middle- and upper-class blacks are paradigmatic of the strategies of negotiation devised and employed by individuals who experience relative privilege coupled with deprivation and negation in society. This segment of the black population does not experience the outright and more objective forms of deprivation in the contemporary United States experienced by many white and nonwhite poor. Nor are they the sociological equivalent of their white counterparts across various high-profile professions, who move through the public sphere without the real or imagined slights, professional limitations, or conditions of actual danger to which quotidian racism makes them more susceptable. Those who employ aversive strategies are betwixt and between several vectors of status and anonymity, relative power and powerlessness, visibility and invisibility. Their responses are neither outright confrontation nor subjection, but a sidestepping of both absolute positions on the continuum of power and powerlessness.

Sources for an ethics of aversion are not restricted to collective memory. Other sources, such as religion, moral philosophy, and cosmology (systematic or heterodox–New Age) may inform the strategy. Neither race nor racism, by themselves or jointly, provides coping strategies. Most of the world's religions, ranging from Buddhism to Catholicism to Islam, as well as more cosmological forms such as Confucianism, Daoism, and Kikongo traditions of West Africa, emphasize the avoidance of conflict and aggressive personae as a feature of healthful living. Given that most social groups' and culturally based responses to conflict emphasize avoidance or indirection, it should come as no surprise (to some at least) that among U.S. African Americans one can find evidence of nonracial criteria for the assessment of human behavior. Although most religious and cosmological worldviews contain varying degrees and forms of chauvinism in their canonical texts and hermeneutics concerning other religions and peoples, modes of conduct aimed at the maximization of harmony and the minimization of conflict almost invariably emphasize avoidance of those whose views are not harmonious with the group (the Crusades, jihad, and stories of vengeance are obvious exceptions). So too for New Age composites of several cosmological and religious systems. Given this wider history of responses to potential and actual human conflict, should it come as a surprise that a segment of a national population, long accustomed to mistreatment by a significant portion of another group, should decide to avoid certain individuals, institutions, and public spaces where the norms, values, and behaviors associated with members of the dominant group may prevail?

Finally, a theory of aversion has implications for contemporary political theory on citizenship and multicultural recognition, which then have a second set of implications for the study of aversion in comparative perspective. After having struggled for and gained a formal set of rights, minority groups may no longer seek or desire recognition, in the sense in which Chales Taylor, James Tully, and Will Kymlicka, among others, utilize the notion of a politics of recognition to emphasize the distinctive set of challenges cultural, religious and ethnonational distinctions pose for the exercise of rights. With the exception of Tully and Taylor, most proponents of a politics of recognition in plural societies write of the need for the national state and dominant nationalities to acknowledge the presence of other groups in their society and civil society and to consider the possibility that the recognition of difference need not undermine democratic practice and citizenship rights, but may in fact enhance them. An ethics of aversion focuses on those minority-group members who, after several generations of living amongst a numerically and otherwise dominant population, not only experience the disjuncture between, on the one hand, a formal, constitutional commitment to cultural and other forms of equality in society and the public sphere and, on the other, the twists and turns of daily interactions with members of those groups. They also develop an evaluative system of judgment that, in their view, holds a greater priority for an ethical and pragmatic assessment of interactions within daily life than their recognition by members of the dominant group. Holders of this experientially based evaluative system of judgment may actually come to the conclusion that (1) in pragmatic terms, they are safer adhering to aversive strategies than holding onto a desire for recognition; and (2) ethically, their system of judgment is actually superior to the evaluative thresholds for social and individual conduct most often employed by dominant-group members.[34]

VII Conclusion

An ethics of aversion is not an essentializing or static interpretation of dominant-group behaviors, but a proactive, dynamic, and strategic response to ongoing practices of racial discrimination and cultural condescension. The evaluative and moral criteria of an ethics of aversion, premised on the moral interpretation of lived experiences, enable its adherents to identify and distinguish individuals from a collective, and thus qualify or limit the possibility of total condemnation of the group. Conversely, those individual members of a dominant group who do exhibit anomalous behaviors relative to their group, behaviors deemed more egalitarian and less invested in proclaiming, asserting, or maintaining a position of power, are accorded more familiar treatment. There is less likelihood that an ethics of aversion will be employed in interactions with such individuals. There is also less likelihood that an ethics of aversion will lead to collective action. Instead, there is a greater possibility of individual "boycotts" of certain individuals, transactions, and institutions.

In this sense, the strategy of aversion is perhaps one strain of a postmodern political outlook among U.S. African Americans. Though not leading to collective action of the more conventional sort of social movement activity, a theory of aversion thus questions one key assumption inherent in the sociological literatures that investigate race relations as well as immigration cycles and correlate greater tolerance and understanding with increased social contact.[35] On the contrary, those with constant contact with whites may adopt an ethics of aversion, since increased contact increases the likelihood of conflict or negative reinforcement, a greater chance of unequal and unpleasant interactions. This challenges the enlightenment, developmentalist argument about the role of education and interaction in ameliorating conditions of racial prejudice—the presumption that prejudice results from lack of contact, and that with an increase in social contact, prejudice and conflict between groups will subside.[36]

These distinct experiences and ethical judgments lead to another possibility: blacks may engage in aversive strategies in their private lives based on their interactions with whites in the public sphere, based upon an expanded definition of discrimination that includes ethical discrimination. If recent public opinion studies are any indication, the divergence between black and white attitudes about issues such as affirmative action, reparations, the war in Iraq, the moral status of those who protested the war, and evaluations of President Bush suggest that some of the chasm between blacks and whites is not due to race but simply to the fact that they may have less and less to talk about in a reasonable manner.[37] As the previously alluded to barber stated sadly and with some bitterness, he and many blacks find it is not *safe* to talk politics with whites.

When combined with substantive matters of the state of the union, racial attitudes of whites force many blacks to respond to the following question: How would it be possible to reasonably exchange ideas across a racial divide with people who don't even consider members of another group to be their human equivalent, capable of producing ideas and perspectives that are worth considering and debating in the public sphere? The increasing restrictiveness of public discourse is far removed from Jürgen Habermas's concept of ideal speech within a communicative ethos of a democratic public sphere.[38] For blacks and many others, communication presupposes community and reciprocity. Individuals, regardless of phenotypical categorization, are inclined to limit their interactions with those who would give little credence or positive reinforcement to their perspectives and views.

An ethics of aversion represents one possibility among many responses to first-order and second-order discrimination in a plural society, namely, a society marked by multiple categorizations and distinctions premised upon phenotype, ethnicity, religion, and national origin. Its forms are neither optimistic nor pessimistic, but sober, pragmatic responses to ongoing conditions of inequality. As part of a postconstructivist approach to understanding "race relations" (see chapter 8), optimistic and pessimistic views of race and immigration in plural societies are normative framing devices with neither predictive nor analytic capacity to determine or understand how groups interact and persist in the real world.

The next section of this book, part 2, examines forms of micro- and macropolitics in comparative literary analysis as well as in the assessment of a seemingly new black political actor, the black public intellectual. These forms represent the obverse of aversive strategies, insofar as they involve individuals and fictive characters who engage in either direct confrontation or coagulation to redress instances of injustice and inequality. Both direct and indirect practices of micro- and macropolitics, however, persist at the periphery of elite-dominated sites of political assembly and disputation. Although these actors, neither in fact nor fiction, overturn conditions of inequality, their perspectives and behaviors are instructive for those of us who are interested in identifying the borders between micro- and macropolitics, thought and action, and political community and racial community.

PART II

Politics in Fact and Fiction

CHAPTER 5

Black Public Intellectuals and Civil Society in Comparative Perspective

In the 1990s, the term "black public intellectual" was used with some regularity to define and characterize a handful of then forty-something black academics whose increasing ubiquity in the public sphere as commentators and pundits generated intense debate in elite public discourse and in the rarified corners of U.S. academy. The mere presence of figures such as Cornel West, Michael Eric Dyson, bell hooks, and others in mainstream television, radio, and newspapers in the United States seemed to signal a new, and in some ways unprecedented era of a black critical presence in public fora, beyond the more restricted circuits of black mass media outlets. The fact that these and other black public intellectuals were not entertainers or sports celebrities also provided some sense of an opening: perhaps whites in the United States were now ready to consider the possibility that U.S. African American intellectuals, might actually have some interesting things to say about the United States and its place in the world, and not just black communities. The heat and polemics surrounding these very public figures have now subsided, and it should be clear to almost anyone who paid attention to the debates about black public intellectuals that while a handful of emergent and now prominent figures appear regularly on talk show circuits, syndicated radio shows, and in newspaper columns, few actually inform or influence government political, economic, or social policy. It could be argued, quite persuasively, that contemporary black critical voices now have less influence in the U.S. body politic than at any other point in U.S. history. This is a consequence of at least three key factors: first, the perceptible shift in public discourse and political culture to the ideological right. Most black intellectuals and political actors remain to the left on a left-right continuum. Second, the vanishing presence of an actual left in public debate, with the proliferation of media conglomerates and monopolies that either accommodate or promote the nation's rightward shift, further contributes to the diminution of the black public intellectual. Third, as at least one commentator has suggested, the crisis of black politics is at least partly to blame. To suggest that black public intellectuals are nonetheless influencing critical debate and political culture in black communities is to imply, in a fundamental way, that not much has changed. Discursive segregation in the exchange of ideas and commentary can still be correlated with the larger processes of segregation in U.S. civil society.

The contours of the debate about black public intellectuals are instructive, however, in the manner in which they foreground certain themes and not others (celebrity rather than ideas for example). The overall level of rigor of these debates was disappointing, and not because of the lack of complexity of the subjects themselves (though some suggested that this was, in fact, part of the problem), but due to the manner in which black public intellectuals as a category or type of intellectual were read. Larger questions and issues at stake were, for the most part, ignored: the relationship between the intellectual and civil society, and some comparative perspective on how so-called black public intellectuals look when considered alongside public intellectuals of other times and places outside the United States[1] This chapter, which is a revised and expanded version of articles and essays I wrote on the topic of U.S. African American public intellectuals in the 1990s, can be read as an attempt to respond to two questions: what does it mean to be a black public intellectual in a society that has historically been quite suspicious of intellectuals of any sort (e.g., Adlai Stevenson, John Kerry)? What does it mean to be a public intellectual in a polity that values its intellectuals less than any other advanced industrialized country that proclaims itself a liberal democracy; less than even many not-so-liberal polities of what used to be referred to as the "Third World"? My response to these two questions can be read as an exploration of the third factor, what is often referred to as "the crisis of black politics," and the topic of how black public intellectuals as a category and concept obscures larger global, diasporic, and transnational themes of black politics.

While many of the articles compared the proliferation of black public intellectuals to the generation of emergent Jewish intellectuals in the post–World War II period, not one article attempted to compare black public intellectuals to their counterparts in the rest of the hemisphere, in Latin America, or the Caribbean. The U.S.-centric cast of this debate highlighted the manner in which the political imaginations and realities of our many, diverse neighbors of the Americas remain neglected, even though the formation of nation-states in Latin America and the Caribbean, legacies of racial slavery, and the severing of the colonial umbilical cord through anticolonial revolt provide greater symmetry for a comparative perspective on the sociological and political location of black public intellectuals in the contemporary United States.

As politics in the United States has increasingly been reduced to public opinion surveys, congressional debate, and electoral competition, rather than a more republican conception of politics as sophisticated, popular participation and engagement with the issues of the day, we would do well to consider that some of the most compelling black public intellectuals in U.S. history did not hold public office or appear regularly on TV and cable news networks. Figures such as Fannie Lou Hamer, Malcolm X, Martin Luther King, Marvel Cooke, Ella Baker, and even Al Sharpton developed constituencies without ever holding public office. We would do well to consider that contemporary U.S. political culture is further removed from world opinion than it has ever been on a range of issues from nuclear disarmament and the prosecution of war to nationalism and transnational cooperation (critiques from within this segment of the U.S. African American community often were in dialogue with critics outside the United States on U.S. foreign and domestic policies). One of the aspects of U.S. African American experience that distinguished the black population from its white counterparts was its paradoxical location as a marginalized group within a powerful nation-state. This paradoxical location remains, I believe, a key defining feature of U.S. African American political participation in deliberation and debate in society, civil society, and in more global, multinational public spheres.

The paradoxes of U.S. African Americans' marginal presence in the body politic of the United States helps us contextualize the contours of black politics in relation to formal, national macropolitics, cultural politics, and the world at large. The polemics about black public intellectuals were framed in entirely domestic and racial terms. Only when we consider black public intellectuals' relation to institutions of power and authority do we begin to broaden our perspective on the predicaments faced by any public intellectual, regardless of color or nationality, in a polity that is at once open and closed to them. Political actors from historically marginalized groups, and not just in the United States, have often spoken *to* civil society, but not *within* civil society, when formal channels for debate in civil and political society are barred to them.

The outsider status of most black public intellectuals in U.S. history can be tracked through the spaces from where their struggles for voice and civil equality have often been launched, vantage points that were not designed for direct political engagement—the concert hall or musical lyrics, the press conference following a major sporting event, and, indeed, the university lecture hall. Eartha Kitt's blacklisting in the 1960s for her negative comments about the Vietnam War, the withdrawal of Paul Robeson's passport in 1951, and Muhammad Ali's loss of his heavyweight championship in 1965 because of his refusal to be inducted into the U.S. army are just three examples of black public figures whose celebrity did not shield them from state sanctions against their livelihood when they voiced political opinions that were divergent from dominant norms.

Their impact and outreach were limited by their politics, not their vocations. The curtailing of their activities signaled their relative powerlessness and the uncomfortable distance between white political elites in institutions of power and black spokespeople for the race who, by and large, remained on the outskirts of dominant political institutions. The sanctions imposed upon these figures pinpoint the coordinates at which public discourse and state power intersect. The relative powerlessness of black public intellectuals and the larger crisis of black politics are themes that lurked behind debates concerning the role, virtues, and alleged decline of the black public intellectual in the United States. These themes went largely unacknowledged. Consequently, any consideration of what the characterization "black public intellectual" means for present-day black politics was largely absent. Instead, the celebrity status of certain individuals, with little attempt to place them in cultural contexts larger than their idiosyncrasies, flaws, and personalities, was a major preoccupation of most assessments of figures identified as black public intellectuals.

Black Intellectuals and the Limitations of the New York Left Paradigm

These accounts of the rise and emergence of black public intellectuals in the 1990s tended to focus on the three seemingly novel aspects of their formation and presence: their resemblance to an earlier generation of Jewish left intellectuals of the 1940s and 1950s, their relationship to postmodernism, and their celebrity status. The three most substantive articles about the state of black public intellectuals were Michael Berube's *New Yorker* piece,[2] Robert Boynton's ruminations on the new generation of black intellectuals under age forty-five in the *Atlantic Monthly*,[3] and Adolph Reed's sustained critique in the *Village Voice*.[4] Berube's and Boynton's articles utilize the New York, largely Jewish left of postwar New York as the comparative referent for their discussion of people like Michael Dyson, bell hooks, Cornel West, Henry Louis Gates Jr., as well as black ideological and cultural conservatives such as Thomas Sowell and Stanley Crouch, respectively. There are obvious, albeit superficial similarities. Both groups cut their political teeth upon a dominant ideological current within their respective communities (Marxism for Jewish intellectuals, cultural nationalism for blacks), only to discard or drastically qualify their ideological—often doctrinaire—positions.

Boynton emphasizes the role of racial difference as a line of demarcation separating black and Jewish intellectuals of these two very different time periods. Both Berube and Boynton note the societal transformations brought about by the civil rights movement and grudgingly administered by the U.S. government. Although both cadres had their respective shetls, crucibles of learning that combined experiential knowledge of the outsider with rarified academic training, they lived in different neighborhoods and in different times.

Most accounts of the New York left (not only Russell Jacoby's *The Last Intellectuals*) fail to mention that there were black public intellectuals, academic and otherwise, who were alive and well in New York from the 1930s through the 1950s. Only Reed's *Village Voice* article notes this fact.[5] Important figures like Ben Davis, a radical lawyer and Communist Party member in the 1940s; Marvel Cooke, the first woman to write regularly for a daily newspaper in the United States and a Communist as well; Paul Robeson, and others *were* in New York during this period. There are enough histories of strategic and substantive relations between the black and white left in New York City, beginning with the Popular Front and "Double V" campaigns against foreign fascism and domestic state and capitalist racism to forgo their reiteration here.[6] Amidst the genuine solidarity between figures like Herbert Aptheker, Paul Robeson, John Apt, and Doxie Wilkerson during this period, there were also uneasy relations between some white and black leftists due to the reductionist manner in which the former cadre—like many leftists then and now—treated racial oppression as mere flotsam upon capitalism's undulating surface.

As noted by George Fredrickson, Robin Kelley, and Nell Painter, Communists, black and white, had multiple, often conflicting motivations for fostering interracial alliances in response to white supremacist, paramilitary, as well as more liberal but nonetheless racist organizations. Fredrickson, Gerald Horne, Martha Biondi, and others have also provided useful correctives to the historiography of black left/Communist alliances, through their examination of movements and organizations of interracial alliance in response to local conditions of U.S. racism, rather than directives from the Comintern. In realpolitik terms, the economic determinists were no economic determinists. Nevertheless, certain segments of the white left have tended to prioritize class as an organizing principle for *all* forms of social struggle, eliding the obvious fact that in a society such as that of the United States, intraclass coalition between white and black workers was often frustrated or a complete fantasy due to the depth of white working-class bigotry toward their black working-class counterparts. Black leftists have struggled with white leftists over the importance of racism in maintaining capitalist dominance in the United States, formally and informally, from the much of the twentieth century.

The most relevant point here for an examination of black public intellectuals in some historical perspective is that with few exceptions, black public intellectuals in the United States, by virtue of the unique conditions of their formation, operated at the boundaries of society and civil society, of social movements and political parties and, of subjecthood and citizenship. Whether we are considering Sojourner Truth or Marvel Cooke, Frederick Douglass, or Martin Delaney, W. E. B. Du Bois or Marcus Garvey, or, more recently, Barack Obama or Jesse Jackson Sr., their alliances and the limitations of their power and influence were conditioned by their unique political/sociological location in U.S. society. Ultimately, it was their politics, and the politics of the domestic and international context surrounding them, that made them "public intellectuals." This is an important point to keep in mind as we consider the most contemporary generation of black public intellectuals.

Since the concept of a public intellectual is not, at least in its origin, "home grown," we can at least consider the ways in which the practice or performance of a public intellectual in the United States may differ from public intellectuals in other national societies. We could also consider how U.S. African Americans, given their minority status, may in fact share certain political and sociological characteristics with minority public intellectuals in other national societies, if not their own. The comparison between the white Jewish left, white left internationalists more generally, and black public intellectuals has its virtues as an initial means of understanding the formation of a vanguard of intellectuals and public activists among a historically marginalized group. Yet beyond this starting point, the comparison grows unwieldy. First, as Berube notes, U.S. racism has forestalled the transformation of the general U.S. African American population into just another ethnic group that, despite the lingering presence of anti-Semitism in the United States, Jewish U.S. citizens have ostensibly become. The New York, largely Jewish left, were emigrants from the Old World and operated within a

U.S. political culture of political parties, trade unions, social movements, and political ideologies that resembled their European predecessors and contemporaries in form, if not content. Jewish intellectuals and common folk could and did participate in civil society (voting, elected office, assembly, and other modes of formal political participation) long before U.S. African Americans as a group could, which amounts to another symbol of Jewish incorporation into the body politic of the United States, anti-Semitism notwithstanding.

If we consider not their putatively racial status, but focus instead on their political status, U.S. African Americans have been native-born foreigners, struggling over the course of three centuries for equal participation in the body politic. Thus, in two important respects, black public intellectuals, mostly nonacademic until the latter half of the twentieth century, had a very distinct relation to the formal public sphere of white society. This is true not only for black intellectuals in the United States but also for black and mulatto political and social activists throughout the New World. In this respect at least, the genealogy of black public intellectuals is quite distinct from Jewish or other white ethnic groups who came to dominate or at least have a presence in U.S. political culture. In the absence of an actual political sociology of the black intelligentsia in the United States of the sort that Martin Kilson has been working on for a number of years, what I am suggesting here is provocative but ultimately tentative. Nevertheless, it could be argued that U.S. African American intellectuals combined features of the political sociology of Caribbean and Latin American public intellectuals and political actors, regardless of phenotype. Black public intellectuals might share more commonalities with generations of public intellectuals operating under colonial and racial regimes than the public intellectuals of Euro-U.S. political culture.

▊▊▊▊▊▊▊▊ II ▊ Adolph Reed and the Crisis of Black Politics

Of the three commentators mentioned, only Adolph Reed, the political scientist and left activist, sought to situate the current crop of black public intellectuals within an analysis of black macropolitics. Tellingly, he does not rely upon the black/Jewish comparison and instead outlines a critical genealogy of black political debate, analyzing the parameters of black participation in national politics and criticism on their own historical and epochal terms. Reed provides insight into what could be characterized as a black public sphere over the course of the twentieth century, where informed individuals participated in reasoned debate about the condition of their communities.

While Reed does not utilize the concept of a public sphere, he discusses the impact of desegregation upon black journals and the demise of a racially specific audience for the black intelligentsia. Within the vise grip of McCarthyism, he explains, the black public sphere shrank even more. Subsequently, integration provided black thinkers with a larger theater, but fewer roles to play in media vehicles dominated by whites.

At this point, however, Reed's analysis takes a turn that unfortunately blunts his critique. He pays greater attention to the personal foibles of certain individuals and the cottage industry-like interactions between them, than the national political culture of the period in which contemporary black intellectuals were spawned. Ironically, Reed is deeply implicated within his own critique, in the sense that all intellectuals, whether anointed with the title of public intellectual or not, are public. As a regular contributor to *The Nation* and other left journals on matters of race, Reed himself is embedded in the national, popular tendency to treat the singular perspective of one black individual as the community perspective writ large, a quandary that has existed for black writers ever since they began writing with a white audience in mind, since the late eighteenth century (Phillis Wheatley) at least.

While Reed may dislike the manner in which certain black intellectuals relate to a white public, he (like the rest of us) is often placed in the role of racial translator, one of the consequences of the paucity of critical discourse in the public realm. Reception and consumption is a related though distinct dimension of black intellectual production. Neither the segment of the black public intellectual cohort who are the source of Reed's frustration, nor the larger community of intellectuals of which they are a part, have much control over how they are read. Reed's article does, however, raise a fundamental question about the relationship between black public intellectuals and black politics: to what *political* communities do black public intellectuals belong?

A 1992 article written by Rev. Eugene Rivers of Boston, entitled "Black Intellectuals in the Age of Crack," posed this question, but in so doing conflated racial community with political community, a concern I address in the concluding chapter to this book. The question embedded in the article and title was what relationship and responsibility do black public intellectuals of any sort have to poor black communities plagued by the social malaise of drug addiction? A 1994 conference inspired by Rivers's article brought together Glenn Loury, Cornel West, bell hooks, and other black public intellectuals. Both the conference and the article are emblematic of the various tightropes of relevance black public intellectuals have been required to tiptoe across. As pointed out by Robin Kelley, part of the problem with the framing of such a conference is the presumption that black public intellectuals have more ability to stem the then—and now—crack plague than white intellectuals.[7] Is it the black public intellectual's responsibility, as opposed to the welfare state, to provide social and healthcare services to black or any other crack addicts in U.S. society? If crack addiction is a clinically defined form of drug dependency, then it is not immediately apparent how intellectuals who are not drug counselors or medical doctors can alleviate or eradicate drug dependency. Black public intellectuals, like other black middle-class professionals, have had to provide defenses for their personal success amidst high black unemployment, urban violence, and whatever else has been deemed to be a "black problem," as if their successful dance with U.S. capitalism and racism required them to explain why they had become neither middle managers, athletes, nor crackheads. Perhaps Foucault's description of the demise of the general intellectual, and the emergence of the specific intellectual, is a useful way of considering the limitations of contemporary black public intellectuals to address *every* and *all* social problems black communities face.[8] One distinction between black public intellectuals of the late twentieth and twenty-first centuries in the United States and those of the eighteenth and nineteenth centuries is the increasing specialization of both intellectual and political labor. This is a consequence of the rise of literacy, mass media, and increased professional specialization in the United States, not just among U.S. African Americans.

Given the emergence and proliferation of specific intellectuals, it is a bit unrealistic and superficial to expect black public intellectuals to be all things to all people, whether in black communities or elsewhere. Leftists and conservatives have pointed to the materialistic aggrandizement of certain black public intellectuals as examples of co-optation. While certain individuals may have gotten much wealthier as a result of their punditry, we should also consider their success in light of the contradictions and antinomies of a class-based society, and the presumed role that black elites are supposed to play in the betterment of black communities. One of the unexplored presumptions of the conference's main themes was that black public intellectuals and their wealthy or middle-class counterparts in black communities are expected to provide for their more impoverished or drug-addicted brethren in ways that the state and other sectors of U.S. society and civil society presumably do not. I believe that such a presumption may give more insight into the expectations that black public intellectuals and celebrities can provide solutions to problems of social welfare that the state, private organizations and initiatives cannot. If so, then this tells us more about black expectations from civil society and society at large, than it does about black public intellectuals. In a society where the state has increasingly retreated from public life, private capital, foundations large and small, religious-based community organizations, and inviduals have sought to fill the gap created by the state's retreat from supporting and equitably distributing social services, access to medical care, housing, and solutions to a range of other societal ills. This larger context enables us to better situate the so-called crisis of the black public intellectual, as well as the precarious location of the black middle classes, who have been chastised in many circles for not doing enough for the black poor.

Never in the history of capitalism have the middle and upper classes of any ethnic group or national minority been expected to assist in the socioeconomic advancement of their working-class counterparts, yet there is the asumption that middle-class blacks —black public intellectuals among them— have a special role to play in helping communities that white elites, private businesses, public corporations, and the U.S. government have long abandoned. The left, in particular should be careful in joining this chorus, since this smacks of voluntarism of the worst kind, wherein individual will is meant to compensate for the absence of coherent state policies and practices of social welfare. Neither black intellectuals nor black middle classes more generally are in positions of power and authority to determine how tax revenues are spent, which businesses move in and out of neighborhoods, and what infrastructures should be in place to improve the lives of black poor. No mere assortment of intellectuals, white, black, or otherwise, can ever resolve these problems.

The absence of similar accusations and debates involving white ethnic communities, as well as Latinos and Hispanics, provides some clues to the peculiar set of demands and expectations heaped upon black public intellectuals. Could anyone imagine the late Daniel Patrick Moynihan, Jeanne Kirkpatrick, or Sean Penn participating in (much less attending) a conference entitled "Irish Intellectuals in the Age of Whiskey" in order to be chastised for not doing enough to address alcoholism in Irish-American communities? Class flight, not just white flight, is a core part of the U.S. success narrative.

Reed, however, is no conservative, and attempts to address a more substantive problem that has plagued left debate for at least thirty years. Reed's anxieties stem from a belief that the recent crop of cultural studies specialists and postmodernists are obsessed with the circulation of capitalist production—the marketing of goods, libidinal impulses, and music as the cultural artifacts of authentic blackness—while ignoring issues like electoral gerrymandering and disproportionate unemployment. Berube echoes a similar discomfort at the end of his article.

In his concluding ruminations on the current crisis, Reed asserts that blacks "should be in the forefront of the fight against ratification of the balanced budget amendment, crafting responses to the so-called tort reform, and finding ways to counter the assault on the Bill of Rights."[9] And so they should. Reed correctly assaults one of the lacunae in some (not all) forms of cultural analysis; the absence of sustained investigation of institutional forms of power, and the assumption that discourse is all. Both Reed's and Berube's worries, however, reflect an ongoing debate at cross-purposes not only between black social scientists and humanities scholars but also between structuralist and poststructuralist understandings of power.

Debates on tort reform, on the other hand, do not typically address issues of white supremacy, racial inequality, or black subordination, regardless of the race of debate participants. If racism has an enduring role in the structuring of social life in the United States, then its impact can be witnessed and experienced across a range of political, cultural, and economic phenomena, from redistricting to rap music. Rather than prioritize one form of analysis and political activism over another, as Reed does, there should (could?) be more synthetic and integrative analysis of the role of racism in national life.

Reed's dismissal of cultural studies and popular culture leads him to dismiss their subjects of analysis as well, including youth culture in general, and black youth culture in particular. Reed states near the end of his essay that black youth are "the least connected, the most alienated, and the least politically attentive cohort of the black population,"[10] which for Reed is proof of their political and scholarly irrelevance. It should be recalled that the Student Nonviolent Coordinating Committee (SNCC) of the 1960s was replete with alienated, disaffected youth who became the shock troops, key strategists, and thinkers of the civil rights and Black Power movements. Had scholars and activists of the civil rights movement considered the disaffection and alienation of black youth as grounds for dismissal of these young, aggressive uncouths, we would have had a very different type of civil rights movement and, consequently, a very different national history.

III The New World and the United States

How do U.S. black public intellectuals look when compared with their counterparts in other parts of the world? In class, racial, and status terms, many Latin American and Caribbean public intellectuals were marginal figures in relation to colonial administrators, white elite criollos or creoles, and Europeans from the metropolitan center. National intellectuals in places like Cuba, Guatemala, Argentina, Trinidad, Jamaica, and Brazil worried over the juxtaposition of Old World traditions and New World realities in ways that most New York or other white leftists never had to, beginning with the movements toward national independence in the early nineteenth century. While Latin American and Caribbean nations certainly had (and have) racial and ethnic inequalities, the mélange of cultural differences became ingredients for the constitution of national identity. Afro-inflected expressive cultures were constitutive cultural components of national identity in various New World nations (salsa, samba, tango, West African religions) by the 1940s (earlier in some places), in contrast to their largely regional and urban influences of jazz and blues in the United States by this time. In macropolitical terms, the independence wars in many Latin American nations were directly tied to the fate of Afro-Latin peoples, since the freedom of African and African-derived slaves was often directly tied to their participation in wars of national liberation. Afro-Latin participation in wars of national liberation helped usher in an era of abolition and emancipation, but not necessarily political and economic freedom. Afro-Latin populations have often fit uneasily in the national portraits of racial harmony depicted by intellectuals in Cuba, Brazil, Venezuela, and Ecuador. The pronounced cultural presences of Afro-Latin America in language, foodstuffs, music, and art, defined as national popular culture, can be contrasted with the economic and political marginalization of Afro-Latin peoples. On the other hand, U.S. African American culture has received belated recognition as an integral component of U.S. popular culture.

Common to the African-descended populations of Latin America and U.S. African Americans, however, are the disjuncture of cultural and macropolitical representation. The appropriation of African religious and musical expression, when combined with indigenous and European influences, would serve to erase distinctions between high and low cultures in many Latin American and Caribbean nations by the middle of the twentieth century. C. L. R. James's *Beyond a Boundary* exemplifies the kind of cultural analysis that has served as a prototype for forms of critical ethnography and theory subsequently advocated by students of cultural studies, poststructuralism, and postmodernism. His examination of the role of cricket as a conduit for disparate ethnic groups, an anchor for national identity, an expression of Afro-Trinidadian pride, as well as a transport toward his own political awakening is more akin to the writings of a Ralph Ellison, Alejo Carpentier, or Roque Dalton in at least one crucial respect. James's *Beyond a Boundary* was, if nothing else, a chronicle of national identity formation and the role of popular culture (the spectator sport of cricket) in producing a national imaginary and of Afro-Trinidadian intellectuals and sportsmen who would seek to transform the colony into an independent nation.

This is not to suggest that James anticipated postmodernism, but to suggest that James and many other black modern intellectuals who were also political activists had their own ideas about the relationship between racial slavery and capitalism, enough to question the universalizing presumptions in Hegel and Marx, the lofty idealism of a John Stuart Mill, the skepticism about civil society found in Rousseau, and the racism or ethnocentrism rampant in the writings of these and other Euromodern intellectuals. The skepticism about Western modernity found in the writings of Frantz Fanon and Richard Wright, two more black public intellectuals from different places and times, provides enough material to develop an archaeology of sorts of black public intellectuals whose suspicions about the West's sense of itself as a coherent, universalizing project appear well before postmodernism. This is merely to put forth the possibility that even for figures like bell hooks, Cornel West, and Michael Eric Dyson as contemporary black public intellectuals, their predecessors in the black world provided, at the very least, a more conflicted, ambivalent reading of the Age of Reason and Enlightenment than they have been given credit for. Black public intellectuals, therefore, both inside and outside the United States, have arrived at participation in public spheres of white-dominated civil societies and institutions on paths distinct from white ethnics, even if there has been a fellow-traveler quality to their sojourns into the public sphere.

James's work, though exemplary, is also paradigmatic of a black intelligentsia of the New World through most of the twentieth century who sought to self-consciously situate their writings, art, and activism in national and transnational terms. As Cedric Robinson's historical archaeology of the black radical tradition suggests to us, the black critical intelligentsia in the twentieth century, of which James is a part, had sources and motivating factors both identical to and distinct from their Euro-U.S. counterparts in the white radical traditions of the modern West. As I have analyzed in chapters 7 and 8, black transnational political actors—one type of public intellectual—have articulated substantive concerns about their politically marginal status in specific nation-states, as well as the more general condition of people of African descent globally, further distinguishing them as political actors from their national white counterparts.

One commonality among African American public intellectuals in the Americas is the documentation and conservation of black popular cultural traditions as sites of political and normative independence from white, elite-dominated national norms and popular culture. The importance of the popular—as a site for cultural fusion—emergent national solidarity, and the recognition of the role of African slaves and their descendents in the material and cultural development of a national society, have been a preoccupation of not only world historical figures like James, Du Bois, and Alain Locke but also less known African American figures such as Abdias do Nasicimento, Wilson Harris, Walter Rodney, Susannah Baca, and Nancy Morejon of Peru and Cuba respectively. Part of the reason for this is surprisingly easy to decipher. The realm of indigenous national popular culture, ranging from the steel drum and cricket teams in Trinidad and dread culture in Jamaica to Santeria in Cuba, provided the space for black intellectuals and artists to carve out their unique role in an evolving national cultural formation, amidst the racial formation of colonial and postcolonial society, at the same time that they, and other citizen-subjects, were treating and identifying their music, religion, sport, poetry, and prose as *national* culture throughout the New World. Negro spirituals were not quite the same thing as spirituals sung in white church congregations; the cricket played in Trinidad was not the same as that played in India or Britain; Santería is not quite Voudun, Candomblé is not quite Western Christianity, and so on. Within colonial, apartheid, and racially exceptionalist societies ranging from the United States to Brazil and Venezuela, there was a relative absence of a space *within* civil society for African Americans to not only engage with the issues of the day but also compete with their white, creole counterparts for formal positions in macropolitics and political representation. These African American intellectuals made the space and practice of culture resonate with macropolitical possibilities at a moment when the spheres of political society (the state) and civil society (the elite-driven public sphere) were largely denied them.

African descended cultural forms, their practitioners, and the spaces in which they operated and thrived would be considered popular rather than radical, as long as the cultural and macropolitical spheres remained discrete. This was unlike Jewish intellectuals in the United States, whose Judaism, whether practiced or not, was linked to a specific set of texts that constituted the "Jewish" in Jewish intellectual. Black public intellectuals had no such texts. Such texts had to be created and invented, often out of existing texts (such as the Bible or the Koran).

If, at any time, the cultural sphere was utilized by slaves and former slaves as a site for the articulation of dissent, mobilization, or rebellion (Boukman and St. Domingue, Paul Bogle's revolt in Jamaica), the cultural sphere was transformed into a space of danger to the interests of white elites. This is as true for the history of black cultural and political articulation in the United States as it is for Haiti or even Brazil. Hence, someone like Pelé in Brazil could be lauded by the Brazilian elite as an expression of *cultura brasileira* in the late 1970s while criticized at the same time by segments of the black movement in Brazil for not accurately representing the interests and concerns of black and brown Brazilians. What interests me here are the ways in which the application of the concept of representation is not an electoral one, while the expectations of a sort of racial or constituency representation remained, despite the fact that in the 1970s, Brazilians of any color could not vote for politicians or political parties of their choosing. Muhammad Ali, to provide another example from sport, was referred to as "the people's champion" after being stripped of his heavyweight title in 1965. In both examples, the issue of a popular, nonelectoral representation highlights the politics/culture division and its distinctive configuration in black public spheres.

This takes us further into more analytic and even philological territory concerning the very term "public." To what "public" do contemporary black public intellectuals belong? Ultimately, if being an intellectual is at least in part a social activity, isn't the "public" in the term "black public intellectual" redundant?

The public, the popular and the people, as we know from both political theory and the examination of the notion of the popular in the crafting of constitutional law, is plural, and not always ideologically radical or lowercase republican. What distinguishes black publics and, by implication, black public intellectuals, is that they have evolved and emerged first in the *social* spaces of white-dominated societies, rather than the *political* spaces of white dominated societies. What makes societies civil, in a Hobbesean sense, is the Euro-U.S. presumption that there could be institutions and places in a society where macropolitics could be conducted based on the rule of law, deliberation, and competition, rather than raw power, coercion, and violence. For abolitionists and civil rights activists, engagement with the issues of the day, with the political institutions and elites of civil society, was fraught with violence. The granting of suffrage and political independence in former colonial societies, and the extension of voting rights privileges to black populations without property or other conditional clauses in places like the United States or South Africa, represented the first instance of movement from the informally to the formally political for former slaves and colonials.

The granting of suffrage helped auger an era where the concept of politics in black public spheres would more closely resemble the concept of politics defined by white elites, namely, the politics of state. Prior to this moment, black political actors who engaged in public debate did not necessarily do so in civil society. Moreover, they experienced liberal democratic regimes and politics as resolutely authoritarian or even totalitarian polities in relation to matters of black equality. Thus, what would be considered extraordinary "exceptions" to liberal democratic, popular, representative political traditions in the ways normally framed and categorized by political scientists (fascism or authoritarianism, for example) in Western political traditions were more often than not the "normal" conditions under which black political actors engaged with the macropolitics of white civil society.

In the transition from informal to formal politics, black public intellectuals and political actors more generally were thus faced with the quandary of representation in a new form: should they continue to employ the techniques of politics associated with the era of formal political exclusion, or should they adopt the tactics and strategies of politics associated with formal politics of the elites of their national societies? It is no accident then that the first generation of black public intellectuals in colonial and apartheid societies became the elite in their own communities, and not in the elite sphere of white political and civil society. In terms of macropolitics, then, "crossover" should have a dual connotation, from black, colonial, and apartheid spaces to white ones; from black political rhetoric and repertoires to more "mainstream" ones. This is why, in some fundamental ways, Al Sharpton is both an anachronism and a nonelected "representative" of a small constituency of U.S. African Americans, for his political style represents another, earlier—though not necessarily worse off—era of black politics in the United States.

The routes, therefore, to representation as black public intellectuals are quite distinct from the paths of Euro-U.S intellectuals who have been defined as public intellectuals within civil societies defined by white elites. Therefore, when Berube explains the distinctive cultural features of black public intellectuals in terms of the encounter between black nationalism and postmodernism, I grow suspicious, because this form of intellectual and activist genealogy cuts off the prior context of black intellectual and political formation.

In macropolitical terms, it could be argued that New World academics and writers have had far greater impact upon public discourse in their own countries over the course of the twentieth century than their U.S. counterparts have had. In the process of national cultural development, Latin American and Caribbean intellectuals have long ago pulled back the transparent curtain separating "academia" from "real life," which is why, from a hemispheric perspective, the straddlings of a few black public intellectuals in the United States are nothing new. When one thinks of public intellectuals like Walter Rodney in Guyana, Octavio Paz in Mexico, Norman Girvan or George Beckford in Jamaica, and a slew of other intellectuals in other parts of the Americas, one is struck by how Latin American and Caribbean intellectuals have played a greater role in public discourse than their counterparts in the United States, regardless of their ideological positions.

The ambiguities of black public intellectuals in the United States resonate with the dilemmas of their New World counterparts in other ways as well. Rigoberta Menchú, the 1992 Nobel Laureate for Peace and a Quiche woman from Guatemala, has been criticized by fellow indigenous activists in her own country for becoming world famous and capitalizing upon the plight of her people in her testimonial *I Rigoberta Menchú*. According to her critics, she has assumed the role of "honorary indigena" at international conferences and heads-of-state dinners in foreign countries.[11] How different—or warranted— is this criticism from the accusations hurled at Cornel West, bell hooks, and Michael Dyson for their purported betrayal of a black public?

Like Rigoberta Menchú, black public intellectuals of the present day must leave the confines of their communities in order to make their plight more identifiable to a larger, presumably liberal audience. Menchú's testimonial exemplifies the contradictions between cultural revelation and cultural preservation that have plagued intellectuals of many minority and oppressed groups including, but not limited to, black, Jewish, and indigenous intellectuals. In order to give evidence of the slaughter and oppression her people have experienced at the hands of white landowners, she must write a book about her community's ways and values. She notes, however, at several times in the testimonial that her community's cultural practices must be kept secret and discussion of them is viewed as betrayal.

In this sense, Menchu's dilemma is quite similar to the paradoxes of her U.S. African American contemporaries and African American predecessors; in order to embody the travails of one's community, intellectuals belonging to marginalized ethnic or racial groups must travel some distance from them to make their concerns "public," which may place them at a distance from the people they claim to represent, or at least, identify with.

Common to all of the aforementioned public intellectuals in Latin America or the Caribbean is the history and risk of state sanction. Whether it is James's house arrest imposed by his former protégé Eric Williams in 1965, Roque Dalton or Walter Rodney's assassinations in Salvador and Guyana respectively, or the murders of Chico Mendes in Brazil or Cardinal Oscar Romero in El Salvador, the ability of public intellectuals to speak on the issues of the day without fear of state or paramilitary reprisal is a barometer of the safe vibrancy of a civil society. While no shortage of death threats and other kinds of threats have been directed at several of the contemporary black public intellectuals in the United States, their ability to participate in the major, mainstream media outlets without fear of sanction for their participation (as opposed to what they have to say) may signal something about U.S. liberal democracy at present: either the country has reached a political maturity regarding black participation in the public sphere or the country has reached a stage of consumerism and commodification of celebrity where the statements of a few black individuals in any public forum, in the end, are examples of largesse. This is not to suggest that black public intellectuals have nothing important to say, but to inject some comparative (temporal and spatial) perspective so that we might understand that the stakes for black public intellectuals in the United States are quite different now than they were twenty or thirty years ago. For public intellectuals operating in much more politically restrictive circumstances in other parts of the Americas and the world, the stakes for speaking out on the issues of the day continue to be more dangerous.

A comparative perspective on the dynamics of cultural and institutional politics and the dangers of ignoring cultural dimensions of political life is in order here. As Stuart Hall has argued, since the 1980s and the weakening of the welfare state in advanced industrialized nation-states like France, Britain, and the Netherlands, rightist social movements have been able to gain significant advantage over liberal-left coalitions by commandeering the terms of public debate over issues of social welfare and immigration. Objective facts of social policies aimed at helping the poor and minorities, as well as the changing nature of the international political economy, are obscured and discounted by a mountain of rhetoric and misinformation. Nationalist-xenophobic rhetoric has revolved around issues of family, racial purity, immigration, and biological and cultural justifications for the poor remaining poor. This is the outcome of political and cultural struggles in which center-right coalitions have gained the upper hand, beginning with the Thatcher and Reagan administrations of the 1980s. Such is the case with welfare and affirmative action debates in the United States.

In left academic circles, sectarian squabbles between structurally and culturally based approaches have been a recurrent theme in social theory and activism ever since people first quoted Marx. Again, a less U.S.-centered view on such matters is instructive. The inaugural debates in the British journal *The New Left Review,* founded in 1962, featured advocates of both sides of the economics versus culture debate. This debate resurfaced in exchanges involving Stuart Hall, Bob Jessop, and others over the relevance of qualitative analysis in general, and cultural studies in particular, the 1980s.[12] Such debates are not limited to *The New Left Review* or the left in Britain, but occurred in many postindustrial societies at the end of the twentieth century. The challenge to mobilize popular groups no longer socialized in traditionally understood working-class environments, labor and culture, amidst clamor about globalization, immigration, and multiculturalism, was and is the common crisis affecting the left in much of Europe as well as the United States. At stake is the continued relevance of left critique and discourse in public life.

IV Public Intellectuals of Various Hues

When considered more abstractly, the debates about black public intellectuals in the 1990s could have provided an opportunity to examine how public intellectuals from minority or emergent public spheres become barometers of the tensions and forms of interaction between regimes, dominant and subordinate groups, and national political cultures. The tensions between Rigoberta Menchú and other indigenous activists can, on one level, be attributed to jealousy, backbiting, the narcotics of fame and power, and other human failings. These tensions can also be viewed as the limitations of strategies for collective action and change that have not kept pace with the multimediated world that requires oppositional movements to be public relations specialists and political actors simultaneously. Strategies for collective action in a multimediated world require community activism that forces intellectuals to inhabit distinct, often contradictory positions for the purpose of macropolitical aims.

In *Representations of the Intellectual*, Edward Said writes that "there is no such thing as a private intellectual, since the moment you set down words and then publish them you have entered the public world."[13] This broadens the category of the public intellectual to include those who engage in debate and political action with fellow citizens, yet it also limits the category to those who write. Grassroots organizers, nurses, and grandmothers in communities across this country engage in sustained collective action against the burning of books, antiabortion guerrillas, paramilitary terrorists (homegrown and foreign), and teenage violence. They too are public intellectuals but operate within a distinctive public realm in which they are highly visible to some and invisible (for lack of celebrity) to others. They operate in what Nancy Fraser has called micropublic spheres, an idea that suggests multiple publics. Transnationally, groups as radically committed to societal transformation as the Irish Republican Army and the African National Congress housed mass media and intelligence experts within their organizations without contradiction.

How to mobilize? With different types of public intellectuals there is the possibility that some public intellectuals operate in different public realms, and that some intellectuals are more public than others. Perhaps a more appropriate reflection upon intellectual engagement in public life is Michael Walzer's *The Company of Critics,* rather than Russell Jacoby's *The Last Intellectuals.* Although there is only one female intellectual and no nonwhites in Walzer's book, he surveys intellectuals actively engaged in public debate in a variety of societies both inside and outside the West, not just in northwestern Europe or New York City. Walzer uses the term "social critic," rather than "public intellectual," to categorize those written about in his book. Their publicness is assumed, not lauded. By depriving the term "public intellectual" of its sexiness, we can recognize that public and organic intellectuals are not always one and the same.

For this reason, the category of the public intellectual needs to be broadened in public debate to include a class of committed people and their groups whose books (if they have them) and speeches may never reach the bookstores or your local video shop. Grassroots activists and organizations who fit into this latter category run the continuous danger of being ignored and neglected by an amorphous public whose intellectuals are already defined for them. What is at stake here are definitions of leadership (another category that overlaps with public intellectual but is not its coeval) and who comes to define them.

Part of the confusion about what constitutes a black public intellectual concerns a more general quandary about where and how to locate black politics. Previous generations of black public intellectuals could be identified with a mass movement, party, or particular tendency, inside or outside civil society. Much of the discussion about contemporary black public intellectuals has invariably focused on their relation to mass media and their audiences, mass publics rather than constituencies of either social movement or state politics. Guy Debord's prescient *Society of the Spectacle* characterized in social theory what we currently witness in U.S. mass culture and politics: political conflict is transformed into amoral spectacle. Protest, normally associated with group demands for justice, is translated into individual pleas for attention. As so beautifully characterized in the work of Michael Paul Rogin, macropolitics is transformed into national sessions of psychotherapy; calls for justice are replaced by calls for healing.

Yet the era of cheap psychologizing in U.S. politics may soon be over, replaced by the age of homeland security, where political positions and ideologies are assessed solely in relation to the U.S. state's war against terror. Will the current crop of highly visible, well-paid black public figures become enemies of the state and nation at war with "terrorists"? This is for the state, not black public intellectuals or their fans or critics to decide. The United States may yet return to an era when some of its best and brightest citizens, regardless of national or cultural origin, will be chastised, brought under surveillance, or incarcerated for being patriots, in the Orwellian sense, and not nationalists. Given this now very real possibility, the early twenty-first century could be an appropriate moment for black institutions, organizations, and common folk to distinguish between black public intellectuals and black political actors. The strengths and weaknesses of individual black public intellectuals are mostly irrelevant without any consideration of the larger political struggles they engage in, whether in the academy or in black communities. What is needed are prescriptive cultural analyses that could enable black progressives to begin discussions on how to suture the bits and pieces of coalitions together around common issues plaguing both black middle-class and working-class communities. The notoriety of a few black public intellectuals is symptomatic of the largesse of consumer capitalism in the United States, with its commodification of political marginality—not the deepening of participatory democracy—as market niche. The travails and celebrity of a few black public intellectuals are the least of our problems. It's time for discussions of black intellectuals to move beyond mere entertainment, for whites and nonwhites alike. A coherent political project awaits. Chapter 6 explores a more recognizable form of sociocultural protest, the rebellion, this time in fictive form, yet also in search of a coherent political project, a project of macropolitics.

CHAPTER 6

Kohlhaas/Coalhouse: Race, Foreigners, and States of Exception

> *The belief in the political and legal equality of the individual, which is an illusory belief for any proletarian who takes it at face value, becomes transformed into an admirable means of action as soon as he begins insisting that democracy stop being a legal and political fiction.*[1]

The relationship between politics and literature has multiple facets, wrinkles, and manifestations. Poets informed political and philosophical deliberations in ancient Greece and Rome. In the modern era, various genres of writing and particular writers have influenced matters of state in Europe, Latin America, Asia, and Africa. In nation-states where the role of the intellectual, particularly the public intellectual, is prominent, writers are taken quite seriously and, as a consequence (good or bad), are watched closely by citizenry and state alike. Their repression, whether in Nigeria, Cuba, or the former Soviet Union, provides an indication of regime anxiety, state anxiety, or both. Outside the realm of the state, the respect for (or lack thereof) and scrutiny of writers reveal the boundaries of tolerance, as in the case of Salman Rushdie in England. As part of an investigation into some tensions between political and cultural articulation in black public spheres, literature provides opportunities for the student of politics to examine tensions of power and authority, identity, and difference.

As in daily life, fiction helps illuminate some of the conceptual and analytic concerns I have first raised in chapters 1 and 2, the distinctions between micro- and macropolitics, instances of coagulation, aggregation, and parallel politics. In my attempt to add to our understanding of the breadth and complexity of black politics through a more expansive yet delineated conceptualization of the political, the practices and perspectives of fictional characters should matter no less than the assessment of political actors, social movements, and political institutions in daily life. In this chapter, neither "reality" nor the boundaries between the real or the imagined are at stake. What is at stake is an ability to use the critical methods developed in earlier parts of this book to identify and distinguish micro- and macropolitical forms and furthermore, to identify the antipolitical.

Independent of genre, there are at least three thematic means through which literary works have fictionally conveyed a preoccupation with politics. First, there are explicitly "political" novels, plays, and poetry that are crafted to depict a specific political era or regime (Carpentier's *Reasons of State*, Alexandr Solzhenitsyn's *Gulag Archipelago*, Boris Pasternak's *Doctor Zhivago*, and Graham Greene's *The Third Man* come to mind). Second, there are forms of literature that ferret out the political implications of a particular character or character type through allegory and metaphor (e.g., Franz Kafka's *The Trial* and Honore de Balzac's *A Passion in the Desert*). Finally, there are tales in which characters stumble upon modes of power and authority beyond the primary conventions, constraints, and discretions of their immediate lives, thereby moving from the personal and micropolitical to the macropolitical in one defining act, incident, or moment. Some characters are transformed by their encounters with individuals, institutions, and processes and develop a wider comprehension of their place in a fictive world of macropolitics. Others are so overwhelmed by their encounters that they retreat from this larger world altogether. Still other characters come to represent rage and rebellion against the status quo. When such characters are not imbued with an expanded, transformed vision of the world, they often end up as Hobsbawmean rebels, developing a politics of resentment and exclusion sure to awaken and frighten dominant groups and institutions from the half-slumber of privilege, but without actually transforming structures and relations of dominance.

Two seemingly unrelated examples of the politics and literature conjuncture belonging to the latter category are Heinrich von Kleist's novella *Kohlhaas: From an Old Chronicle* and the section of E. L. Doctorow's novel *Ragtime* that focuses on the character Coalhouse Walker. There are several clues in *Ragtime* that indicate Doctorow's admiration for Kleist's short story: the similarities of name, parallels in the structure of the narrative, and the shared themes of nepotism, corruption, jurisdiction, due process and the revolt of a member of an emergent social class. There are, of course, vast contextual differences between sixteenth-century Brandenburg and the twentieth-century United States. Emergent industrial capitalism in the United States helped invent a social class that was absent at the nation's founding, an aristocracy. Sixteenth-century Brandenburg and Saxony, the two states most preoccupied with Kohlhaas, were very much feudal societies, but the rise of unfettered trade created a commercial class not governed by the political economy of feudalism.

In their respective simulacrae, however, Michael Kohlhaas and Coalhouse Walker are representatives of an emergent class of individuals seeking to carve out a niche for themselves in professions premised upon expertise. Coalhouse Walker, the black male character in *Ragtime*, is a musician; his Brandenburgean counterpart is a trader and businessman. Both men represent threats to the existing political and economic order. Kohlhaas's demands for transparent authority and processes of state, for rules and regulations to replace the privileges of the well-born, constitute a challenge to the feudal order. Similarly, the uppity, educated, distant, and noningratiating Coalhouse Walker's demand to be treated as an adult citizen and his refusal to engage in the infantilizing, servile behaviors demanded of black folk is viewed by white characters in *Ragtime* as a threat to the white supremacist racial order of the United States.

A politics of resentment and scorn fuel their rages without being transformed into a more radical vision of the world that produces the inequities they encounter in their daily lives. The fact that both seek recompense for damaged property, rather than the more basic injustices of hunger or poverty, hints at the increasing importance of commodities in middle-class lives, as well as the increasing political importance of a category of people whose identities and social roles are intertwined with those commodities, as property owners with presumably individual rights.

This dimension of both stories leads us toward another facet of the literature and politics conjuncture, the encounter between individuals and the state and political economy.[2] I am interested in exploring these two characters and the stories in which they are enmeshed because of the opportunity comparative textual analysis provides in this instance to distinguish between the invocation and evocation of politics, between social rebellion and social movement, and between the spontaneous creation of a community of people with similar aims to overturn conditions of inequality, and a community of people organized to exact revenge and retribution. Although the objects of my analysis are literary, I believe the conclusions are generalizable in their potential application to various forms and objects of popular culture and consumption. Neither Coalhouse nor Kohlhaas has macropolitical purpose, even though their rage engenders states of siege in both fictitious societies. Their rage ultimately serves an antipolitical purpose, since their rebellions, and the people enlisted to express their rage, neither conceive of nor build a community of citizens or subjects larger than themselves. Both retreat from the prospect of generating forms of macropolitics that exceed their original intentions.

The routes of their exclusion and inevitable elimination, however, provide an opportunity to consider their respective plights in light of contemporary social and political theory. Renewed interest in theorists such as Ernst Kantorowicz and Carl Schmitt, as read by Giorgio Agamben in particular,[3] has led some contemporary students of political theory to deploy concepts such as *nomos* and sacred life and bare life as means of interpreting the status of refugees, foreigners, concentration-camp detainees, and other victims of genocide and mass slaughter in the modern era. The fate of these two characters, decided only after protracted debates between several forms and levels of state authority (federal, regional, city), illuminates the plight of individuals whose indeterminate status renders them powerless, without sanctuary or the protection of rule of law.

When considered jointly, these stories and their protagonists allow readers to consider the possibility that racial discrimination and inequality help engender a state of exception for subordinated subjects in daily life in societies with liberal polities, and not just in societies governed by fascist regimes. Racial alterity, implicit and ambiguous in the case of Kohlhaas, explicit and pervasive in *Ragtime*, makes the state of exception, to use Schmittean (and now Agamben's) language, plausible and practicable under "normal" conditions of everyday life. In the era of Coalhouse Walker's United States, the strenuous, vigilantly maintained limitations imposed upon U.S. African American and black political participation in the body politic are so amply documented as to make any further elaboration here redundant. For Coalhouse, who orchestrates a reign of terror in New York City and the state before ultimately being killed by police, racist and white supremacist logics expressed not only in ideologies and the isolated acts of individuals but also in governmental and state practices, made him the object of the state of exception by a liberal, not a fascist, regime. The implications of this particular form of the state of exception will be explored in the section preceding the conclusion to this chapter.

The manner in which states, bureaucracies, and elites respond to Kohlhaas and Coalhouse reveals the crucial linkage between biopower and political power in societies where political participation and power are premised on the ability of individuals to inhabit the body politic and an individual body simultaneously. The state ultimately emerges in both stories as not only the arbiter of power, authority, and class relations but also as the guarantor of inequity. State power not only provides the juridical and coercive underpinnings of the rule of law, but the state is also the site where nepotism, deeply entrenched political and economic interests, and the mistreatment of members of racially and ethnically subordinate groups are processed.

Distinctions between the corporal and the political body provide modern—and now postmodern—political theory with a critical means by which to distinguish premodern (largely feudal) and modern (republican and totalitarian) modes of governance. Racial, ethnonational and class categorization provides another vantage point from which to view the state-generated and monarchical distinctions of sacred, common, and profane bodies in relation to the body politic. Most accounts, including Agamben's, focus on the vertical and unilinear relationship between the modern state and classes of people who have been reduced to "bare life" (refugees, concentration-camp inhabitants, populations targeted for genocide). Kohlhaas and Coalhouse provide an opportunity to trace the activities and consequences of two fictive political actors who, while existing in a realm somewhere between political (sacred) and bare (profane) life, are reduced to bare life by state and society when they attempt to alter the direction and course of their relation to state and society. The "fact" of their political subordination is less interesting than the ensuing dynamics between state, society, and the individual when their subordinate status is put into question, and then reaffirmed and ultimately compounded by their erasure.

A Tale of Two Tales: Justice and Commodities

The epochs in which both tales are set are times of extreme tumult. The Kohlhaas character is based on the true story of a man whose horses were taken away by the Junker Wenzel von Troka, a local baron, and the castellan, as collateral for the requisite toll for passage over a bridge at the Elbe River in Saxon territory. Neither Brandenburg nor Saxony in the sixteenth century— the epochal setting for Kleist's novella—are republican polities. Yet Kohlhaas demands to be treated with the same respect accorded the nobility, in what could be either a revolutionary or a reactionary wish. In the case of sixteenth-century Brandenburg, competition between city-states and Polish, Saxon, and Austro-Hungarian empires was underscored by the jurisdictional dilemmas generated by Kohlhaas's reign of terror through several cities and towns. Kleist experts view the Kohlhaas novella as the author's way of foreshadowing the demise of Saxony as an independent state, and its reconstitution as a protectorate of Prussia.[4] The injustice meted out to Kohlhaas is symptomatic of the autocratic, highly corrupt nobility that dominated sixteenth-century Saxony. The death of Kohlhaas foreshadows a Saxony without citizenry or state, and as a consequence, without a reason to exist.

At first reading, the novella *Kohlhaas* and the story of Coalhouse Walker in the novel *Ragtime* appear as conventionally masculinist tales of vigilance, revenge, and honor. Both characters generate a wave of violence in response to personal slights. Both characters pursue legal means of redress before resorting to collective violence. Their responses to injustice could be viewed as quite feudal; in medieval times, duels and wars were fought over the loss of honor. What makes Kohlhaas and Coalhouse decidedly masculine, modern figures is that each considers violence only as a last resort.

These men conceive of themselves as Hobbesian microstates, capable of dispensing a righteous violence at the appropriate moment to effect, if not justice, then certainly retribution. Michael Kohlhaas, son of a schoolmaster, horse trader and, in the words of Kleist, "the very model of a good citizen"[5] of the state of Brandenburg, incites and leads a rebellion in response to the theft and mistreatment of his property (two stallions) by a well-connected local baron. The gentry, bureaucracy, and peasantry of several rural sixteenth-century towns are overwhelmed by his focused wrath and violence. Kleist writes that Kohlhaas's "sense of justice turned him into a brigand and a murderer."[6]

One distinguishing feature of his status as a trader is his dispassionate relation to the two stallions. Unlike a farmer, for example, whose investment in animals can be both emotional and material, Kohlhaas "cared nothing about the horses themselves—his pain would have been just as great if it had been a question of a pair of dogs."[7] Kleist's description of Kohlhaas's emotional detachment from the stallions suggests a remove from the agricultural origins of animal domesticity. The horses bear a commodity relation, rather than a domesticated, familial one, to the reproduction and maintenance of his life and living standard. At the same time, Kleist's reference to dogs to emphasize Kohlhaas's indifference to the actual lives of the stallions as stallions, foreshadows Kohlhaas's descent into political illegibility premised, in part, on his own devalued body. At one point, Kohlaas explains to his wife Lisbeth that he will resort to violent means because "I will not go on living in a country where they won't protect me in my rights. I'd rather be a dog, if people are going to kick me, than a man!"[8]

Kohlhaas suffers a double extortion; not only is he fooled/forced to leave his horses as collateral for a nonexistent tax, but his horses are ruthlessly exploited for the harvest until they are no longer recognizable as his horses. For Kohlhaas, integrity is built into bourgeois exchange, as evidenced in his contractual arrangements with the bailiff concerning the sale of his farm at Kohlhassenbruck. This exchange, an agreement between two reasonable beings premised on mutual benefit, differs from the usurious exchange between Kohlhaas and the castellan, corrupted by hierarchy and chicanery. Like horses and dogs, Kohlhaas will never enter the body politic as a political agent, only as a trespasser whose recalcitrance requires management, repression, and ultimately, erasure.

Kohlhaas's relation to commodities is crucial to an understanding of his multiple modes of alienation—from the state, society, his wife, property, and worldly existence more generally. The inability to garner redress for the theft and misuse of his property leads him to recognize his general inability to participate as a citizen of the state, and thus lawfully represent and protect himself, his wife, and property.

Transplanted to U.S. soil, Kohlhaas becomes Coalhouse Walker, a black man descended from slaves who makes his living as a musician. Like Kohlhaas, Coalhouse is a serious, purposeful individual. In an important moment in the text, he takes pains to distinguish his craft from minstrelsy and coon music in particular. When Father asks Coalhouse about coon music, the narrator references Father's lack of musical knowledge and his presumption that "Negro music had to have smiling and cakewalking."[9] Walker responds to Father's request for renditions of coon songs with "a tense shake of the head. 'Coon songs are made for minstrel shows,' he said. 'White men sing them in blackface.'"[10]

His profession is based on skill, not manual labor, which places him in a vocation that is neither elite nor proletariat, vaguely but decidedly middle class. Coalhouse was familiar with the so-called underside of black life: speakeasies, brothels, showgirls, murderers, numbers runners, pimps, all who would flock to the nightlife, yet his aspirations for marriage and family, his insistence on it through the relentless courtship of Sara at the New Rochelle home, suggest an acceptance of bourgeois norms of respectability—marriage, family, duty, and honor. He appears largely self-taught in music, manners, and language, yet he is no intellectual or political firebrand. His vocation prefigures an emergent social type and art form. Ragtime, after all, would eventually become "American music" with all the attendant ambivalences and silences befitting such a deceptive, cloaking characterization.[11]

Women Advocates for Men

Kohlhaas and Coalhouse decide to take a murderous path after their women die as a result of injuries sustained during attempts to gain public hearings for their men. Both women, symbols in their respective stories of potential (for Coalhouse) and actual (Kohlhaas) domesticity, are mortally beaten. Their mates are deprived of their status as heads of household, and as protectors of hearth and home. In the case of Coalhouse, Sarah also represents a rein on Coalhouse's nocturnal forays, an opportunity for the musician to "settle down" and abandon the life of a jazz musician, with all of its amoral connotations. Their deaths, therefore, represent the death of a certain familial and middle-class respectability attained through social mobility and conformity.

The death of these women while attempting to speak on behalf of their men dramatically foregrounds the centrality of violence in exercising and maintaining the boundaries between social and political privilege and privation, and citizen and subject. The violence imposed upon the two female characters at the exact instant they attempt to engage superordinates in direct, frank speech is testament to their politically subordinate status as women and as members of minority groups. These two women, members of the segment of the citizen and subject population considered—after children—to be the most vulnerable and least threatening, become the victims of coercive power the very moment they attempt to engage in free speech. Free speech is free only to those who are acknowledged by the state. The unfree, those denied the right to speak, whether through criteria of gender, class, race, or ethnicity, have no such freedom before the executors of the state.

Doctorow's account of Sarah's bludgeoning and death evokes the specter of exclusionary violence within the liberal polity. In both stories, the women are hopeful, even prayerful of a pacific, legalistic resolution to their mates' dilemmas. Lisbeth, not Kohlhaas, is initially optimistic about the possibility of obtaining recourse for the castellan's and the Junker's mistreatment of his two prized horses. Lisbeth and Sarah each seek informal, spontaneous audiences with powerful politicians and beseech their assistance on behalf of their men. Overhearing a conversation between Mother and Father about the impending visit of Republican Vice Presidential candidate James Sherman to a nearby hotel in New Rochelle, Sarah decides to seek out the candidate during one of his campaign stops there to plea for justice on Coalhouse's behalf. Excerpts from Doctorow's rendering of the tragic scene follows:

Knowing little of government, nor appreciating the degree of national unimportance of her Coalhouse's trials, Sarah conceived of petitioning the United States on his behalf.[12] When the Vice President's car, . . . rolled up to the curb and the man himself stepped out, a cheer went up. . . . Sarah broke through the line and ran toward him calling, in her confusion, President! President! Her arm was extended and her black hand reached toward him. He shrank from the contact. Perhaps in the dark windy evening of impending storm it seemed to Sherman's guards that Sarah's black hand was a weapon. A militiaman stepped forward and, with the deadly officiousness of armed men who protect the famous, brought the butt of his Springfield against Sarah's chest as hard as he could. She fell.[13]

Through the subtle depiction of the possibility that her black hand could have been perceived as a weapon, Doctorow links her phenotype to violence. More important than her phenotype, however, is the totality of her actions and their consequences for thinking about participatory democracy. Doctorow's Sarah is impulsive, impetuous, undisciplined, ignorant even, but nonetheless hopeful of the possibility of appealing to an authority more significant than the local fire chief, police, legal counsel, and mayor. She is characterized as childlike, an "impoverished uneducated black girl with such absolute conviction of the way human beings ought to conduct their lives."[14]

The juxtaposition between her lack of education, on the one hand, and her "absolute conviction of the way human beings ought to conduct their lives," on the other, signals a clash between a state that limits forms of political deliberation, participation, and protest, and individuals seeking to engage directly with representatives of state. What is not mentioned anywhere in the text, but must be assumed, is that the misdirected Sarah ("President! President!") could not use any other means to communicate an appeal for Coalhouse. White women in the United States, much less black women, could not vote at the dawn of the twentieth century. Participation in politics in a public sphere requires freedom of speech. To articulate the perspectives of a political community means to articulate a position larger than one's individual perspective. For both Sarah and Lisbeth, participation in politics was possible only in those spheres neither defined nor designed for political articulation. In pursuit of a peaceable means to justice, Sarah is also transformed into an outlaw. As my work in chapters 1, 2, and 5 suggests, Sarah's and Coalhouse's seemingly paradoxical locations as political actors in society, and nonpolitical subjects in relation to civil society, are emblematic of modern black political subjectivity. Their predicament is their exclusion from the formal spheres of politics. Every act, from the desecration of Coalhouse's car to his subsequent rampage, Sarah's appeal, and his incarceration and execution by an impromptu firing squad, operates outside the realm of jurisprudence, outside the realm of law. The implications of this portion of *Ragtime* are clear. The state and its privileged citizens of the body politic are capable of acting outside of the law. The theoretical and conceptual implications of this scenario of lawlessness will be detailed below.

III Due Process

Both characters produce texts that declare and justify their acts, identify their wrongdoers, and make initial claims on behalf of a larger group of rebels. Kohlhaas's written declaration, "Kohlhaas Manifesto," attracts the attention of the great reformer of formal Christianity, Martin Luther. Eventually, Kohlhaas seeks an audience with Martin Luther, and is visited by the reformer during his imprisonment. The exchange between Martin Luther and Kohlhaas begins the inquiry into Kohlhaas's relation to the state apparatus. Luther replies incredulously, "How could anyone cast you out of the community of the state in which you live? Where, indeed, as long as states have existed has there ever been a case of anybody, no matter who, being cast out of society?"[15] Kohlhaas replies, "I call that man an outcast . . . who is denied the protection of the laws! For I need this protection if my peaceful calling is to prosper; yes it is for the protection that its laws afford me and mine that I seek shelter in the community; and whoever denies me it thrusts me out among the beasts of the wilderness; he is the one—how can you deny it?—who puts into my hand the club that I defend myself with."[16] Kohlhaas's analogy of his plight with "the beasts of the wilderness" is telling. Beasts are not humans. The wilderness lies outside civil society. That he could exist within civil society but live as a beast in the wilderness, all the while obeying the laws, mores and norms of civil society means he is part of a class of people, of subjects, for whom civil society is nonexistent. Kohlhaas's response identifies a paradox for which Luther has no response other than a naïve optimism about the state and its functions.

Kohlhaas's understanding of his predicament compels us to consider the possibility of a class of people who reside within the spatial boundaries of state power but who are not protected by that power. Since he does not reside in a literal wilderness or even Hobbes's "state of nature" but among and alongside citizens who do have the state's protection, then it is the state that presides over the wilderness of civil society. Its citizens, then, are the predatory beasts from whom Kohlhaas must protect himself. Full of reason but without rights or the attendant ability to obtain an audience before a court of law, he can only resort to the club.

Luther's response suggests complete unfamiliarity with the possibility that the state differentiates among citizens and, as a consequence, treats distinct segments of the population differently. The exchange between Kohlhaas and Luther suggests more than just a difference of opinion concerning the appropriateness of social rebellion, mayhem, and murder as a consequence of two abused horses. Their differences also reveal for the first time in the story the possibility that the state has two faces or postures in relation to civil society. One face gazes at citizens, the second at subjects, who, not in spatial terms but in legal/bureaucratic terms, exist outside civil society. This sort of state is neither Kant's ethical fulcrum, nor Hegel's holistic, Christian manifestation of popular will, but an apparatus with at least three discriminating functions in relation to the population that inhabits the territorial realm over which the state presides: (1) the creation of both the category of the citizen and preconditions for the production of citizenship; (2) the creation of the distinction between citizens and subjects and their respective rights and considerations before the state; and (3) the creation and maintenance of a formal and informal set of laws, policies, and procedures that accord subjects and foreigners a distinct, invariably inferior set of political opportunities to participate in the body politic of the nation or city-state.

It is in this exchange that Kohlhaas makes a request that reveals his intention to obtain recognition as a citizen with rights, and thus protection from the state. Martin Luther's letter to the Elector of Saxony regarding Kohlhaas's proposal that his case be adjudicated advises that the Elector take up Kohlhaas's case as a matter of neglected justice, arguing that "the wrong done Kohlhaas had in a certain sense placed him outside the social union; and in short, . . . he should be regarded rather as a foreign power that had attacked the country (and since he was not a Saxon subject, he really might be in a way regarded as such) than as a rebel in revolt against the throne."[17] The most reasonable way for Kohlhaas's case to be treated is, in essence, to render him a foreigner, an invader into Saxon territory, rather than a citizen of another state who has been wronged by representatives of the state of Saxony. In order to be brought before the court of law that considers infractions and abrogations of Saxon authority, he has to be transformed into a non-Saxon, or more precisely, an anti-Saxon attacking the entirety of Saxony itself. Thus, the prosecution of his case, in Luther's argument, is predicated on national difference, not rule of law.[18] After much discussion, the Elector decides to follow Luther's suggestions.

Kleist's insertion of Martin Luther into the Kohlhaas story further complicates the relationship between political and literary form, since the real Martin Luther's resonance as a revolutionary reformer permeates the political culture of embryonic Germany. As the radical reformer of Christianity, Luther is most widely known for his scathing critique of the institutionalization of the Church and the consequent separation of the institutions of Catholicism from its popular adherents and practitioners. Luther's actions and motivations also help highlight the dynamic and relational character of political contestation. He can be viewed as revolutionary only in relation to the institutionalization of Catholicism that he railed against. His ultimate advocacy of obedience to authority both sacred and earthly makes Luther a reformer rather than a revolutionary. His aim is to make authorial power less corrupt, less mediated by bureaucratic inventions such as tithes, which enabled people to purchase salvation from their sins, at least from the institutional church. At the same time, the real Martin Luther was dead set against rebellion and revolution, evidenced in his opposition to peasant rebellion during the Great Peasant War of 1524–25. Moreover, his letter to the German people is a tract with explicitly anti-Jewish elements.[19]

Thus, if we juxtapose Martin Luther, the real-life radical reformer, with his namesake in Kleist's novella, we have some interesting paradoxes. Martin Luther's incredulity is, in part, premised on privilege and the presumption of inclusion. Luther's character cannot conceive of the possibility of a formal, juridical, legal, and practical disjuncture between individual and state or between society and individual. I would like to suggest here that this incredulity has its origins in the symmetries of race or ethnonationality and state. Although Kohlhaas never makes this explicit, there are enough clues in the story to suggest very distinct social origins for the characters of Luther and Kohlhaas, which lead, in turn, to very distinct modes of reasoning (consciousness) about the role and responsibilities of the state and the requirements of the individual citizen.

What I would like to highlight here is the political logic evolving from Kohlhaas's and Luther's respective subject positions. The key difference between their two subject positions is that Kohlhaas can imagine and witness Luther's political identity. Luther cannot imagine any political identity other than his own, not in the narrow sense of an individual, but as a citizen invested with the power of the state. As Rogers Brubaker reminds us, however, jus sanguinis laws were also part of the political legacy of German unification and immigration policy.[20] Blood became one of the criteria for citizenship. As will become clearer below, Luther takes his blood/citizenship privilege for granted, as a unilateral feature of membership in civil society. Kohlhaas only comes to understand the limitations of not being wellborn after twice filing claims against the junker and castellan, first in Brandenburg, later in Saxony. He only understands the folly of his attempts after discovering the blood relation that exists between his transgressors and potential adjudicators.

Coalhouse, on the other hand, holds no such hope. Coalhouse, unlike Kohlhaas, *never* assumes his case will be taken up in the manner in which it would be if he were white. For Coalhouse, the desecration of his car serves as both foreshadowing and foregrounding of how he and other blacks had been treated, and will be treated, for daring to share in the same consumption and celebration of commodities as whites. Thus, Coalhouse and Sarah understand in a way that Father and Mother (as well as Kohlhaas) do not, that Coalhouse's car *had* to be devalued, simply because of Coalhouse's relation to the car. Father, like Luther, cannot comprehend the enormity and comprehensiveness of Coalhouse's exclusion from civil society. Coalhouse, like Kohlhaas, lurks in the wilderness *created* by civil society.

The defaced car stood for Coalhouse himself and the aspirations of blacks as property owners. The coveted distinction between public and private, at issue in the damage to the car and in the pseudo-tax revenues that both the castellan and the fire chief want to extract, is shattered. The car distinguishes Coalhouse not only in the black communities through which he moved but also in white society. In the former, it as a sign of relative, perhaps brief or chimerical prosperity; in the latter, it further confirmed his pretentious aspirations. To have aspirations entails possessing knowledge of a disjuncture between an actual and a desired social and legal status, as well as knowledge of the means to attain higher legal and social status. Black aspirations toward upward mobility were considered dangerous.

IV. Booker T. Washington as Martin Luther

Booker T. Washington is Doctorow's answer to Martin Luther, although there are several notable contrasts. In contrast to Martin Luther, Washington was not a radical reformer but a resolutely pragmatic apologist for U.S. race relations and U.S. African American political underdevelopment. Washington plays the role of race man, admonishing Coalhouse much in the way Martin Luther admonished Kohlhaas, substituting the religion of racial solidarity and uplift for Christianity. Washington's diatribe against Coalhouse implicitly refers to the black race as a single organism, in which the misdeeds of one affect the entire body of the race: "Every negro in prison, every shiftless, no-good gambling and fornicating colored man has been my enemy, and every bit of faulted Negro character has cost me a piece of my life. What will your misguided criminal recklessness cost me!"[21] Washington continues in this vein, chastising Coalhouse for his actions that imperil the lives of the young men under his thrall, in addition to the innocents killed during the course of his public assaults. Self-interest and collective interest are thus conflated. Good Protestant behavior and Negro individual uplift are the presumptions inherent in Washington's prescription for black advancement, in the text as well as in his own political career. Yet the Wizard of Tuskegee's own career would plummet after being snared in a love triangle involving a white woman, prompting her infuriated husband to provide the Wizard with a fearful beating.[22]

From the standpoint of both liberal racism and white supremacist logics, Coalhouse displays an unsettling lack of pathological, ideal-typical behaviors associated with black male bodies. Unlike Washington, there is no hint of encounters with white women, or even a desire to ingratiate himself with a white world. He is neither Sambo nor Stagolee, neither Uncle Tom nor Uncle Remus, neither Jack Johnson nor Booker T., neither Malcolm X nor Martin Luther King. All the more reason why he might be viewed as potentially more dangerous, for there may be many more of him than any of the other aforementioned iconic figures. His character seems entirely unconcerned with making whites either comfortable *or* afraid in his presence. He neither runs from whites, nor attempts to appease them. As an iconic figure among an array of figures, female and male, Coalhouse complicates, confounds, and undermines long-standing black images in a field of racial representation. This potentiality is recognized even by whites, which is precisely why, in *Ragtime*, Coalhouse had to die. He is perhaps closer to being a radical character than Kohlhaas, as a consequence of his very *conventionality*.

Since the Negro or black is categorically coterminous with noncitizen, the state is obliged to demonstrate, through Coalhouse's assassination, that noncitizens do not require due process under the rule of law. Kohlhaas received court adjudication just before his head was severed. In his case, both judgments provided formal recognition of his presence in civil society. In contrast, Coalhouse's car was fully restored at the insistence of J. P. Morgan, a titan of capitalism to be sure, but not a judge.

V Gypsies and Blacks as Those without Value

The specter of racial alterity operates in both stories, though more implicit than explicit in the Kleist tale. In both stories, members of a dominant group seeking to track down a predatory, contestatory minority are unable to distinguish one racial subaltern from another. This would prove costly for the oppressors in both stories. In the Kohlhaas tale, the gypsy woman chosen for the task of impersonation is the very same woman who'd read the Elector's fate years previously in Justerbock. The Chamberlain, sent into town to find a "gypsy woman" who would resemble the actual fortuneteller of the previous spring, could not tell the difference, and assumed the woman he had employed for the task of impersonation of the gypsy woman could not have been the gypsy woman herself.[23] The inability of the chamberlain to distinguish one gypsy from another is a now classic interpretive dimension of racial stereotype, where actual physical characteristics are obliterated in favor of an indiscriminate, generic sameness—in this instance, gypsyness. The gypsy woman is formidable because she is herself while at the same time pretending to be just another "gypsy woman." The indiscriminate gaze of the chamberlain enables her to achieve an Ellisonian invisibility as a very visible invisible woman. Matters of propriety are informed by status. Status itself is informed by racial and ethnic distinction. Racial and ethnic distinctions made by the powerful serve to suppress the acknowledgment of differentiation within communities of racial and ethnic subordinates, which subordinates can then utilize to enter spaces of the dominant. Coalhouse and the gypsy take advantage of stereotype to move through society with a degree of imperceptibility, for their existence is relatively unintelligible. Thus, the boundaries are epistemic, masquerading as phenotype.

Upon meeting the gypsy woman during his imprisonment, Kohlhaas notices and suspects a family resemblance between her and his presumed dead wife, Lisbeth. "The horse dealer was so struck by the uncanny likeness he discovered between her and his dead wife that he was inclined to ask the old woman whether she was Lisbeth's grandmother; for not only did the features of her face, as well as her still well-shaped hands and the way she gestured with them as she spoke, remind him vividly of Lisbeth, but he even noticed a mole on her neck just like the one Lisbeth had had."[24] Is Lisbeth indeed a gypsy, and is Kohlhaas tainted by her alterity? So-called gypsies have been long depicted throughout Europe as the ultimate outcast, and in many instances, racially inferior. "Kohl" in German means "coal" in English. Kohlhaas is marked by blackness, even though he is not phenotypically and interpretively black.[25]

Thus, there is the possibility of a double, or what Marxists would refer to as an overdetermined racialization, of the Kohlhaas character.

This gypsy woman is a pivotal character complicating the horse trader's fate, linking him to the Elector in ways neither he nor the Elector are fully aware of. She holds a secret, fateful tale scrawled on a piece of paper that remains in Kohlhaas's possession, which he takes to his grave. The dramatic weight of the novella's conclusion rests not on Kohlhaas's fate, which to paraphrase Marquez, is a chronicle of a death foretold, but on the prospect of the revelation of the secret contained on a piece of scrap paper. That a gypsy woman could hold such power in relation to the Elector of Saxony serves to undermine the subaltern subjectivity of the gypsy woman as pre- or antimodern. It is not just her knowledge that the Elector seeks or fears, but what she has inscribed in text, and the possibility that through text, knowledge about his fate will be made known to others. The fact that a doomed man and a gypsy have knowledge about him that he, a wellborn man of high status, does not possess, induces several fainting spells, another indication of weakness.

Just before his execution, Kohlhaas swallows the tube containing the note. The Elector of Saxony is powerless before the knowledge possessed by the horse trader and the gypsy. The scrap of paper provides the Gutenberg moment of the text, as the gypsy's act of writing links her to a discourse community of gypsies and nongypsies alike, spelling the literal and figurative doom of aristocratic knowledge, insofar as knowledge about an aristocratic subject escaped the realm of the aristocracy. The mystical quality of this portion of the Kleist novella seems to further undercut the more radical political implications of the Kohlhaas character. The story oscillates between the social structural and the mystical, with little of the cynical, resolute, death wish pragmatism of Coalhouse Walker.

Similarly, the fire chief assumed that Coalhouse was any old nigger, not someone with knowledge of explosives, an educated, cultivated man in the bourgeois sense whose outlaw response to injustice might foretell not only his death, but the fire chief's demise as well. The fire chief's fate was thus linked to Coalhouse in the way that the Elector's fate was linked to Kohlhaas and the gypsy. The Coalhouse character is thus both Kohlhaas and the gypsy, as evidenced in his actions and in his relative invisibility before being willingly captured. Like the Chamberlain, the Fire Chief made the mistake of misidentifying Coalhouse who, like the gypsy, was thought to be a public nuisance, nothing more, who would ultimately disappear. But in *Ragtime*, the act of misrecognition is much deeper and more comprehensive than in *Kohlhaas*, because even one of Coalhouse's strategic allies, Father, the ever-ambivalent family patriarch, finds it extremely difficult to understand that Coalhouse actually believes he is someone, a liberal individual. Father can accept the notion of black freedom in theory but not in practice, for the actual inscription of a subject like Coalhouse Walker in the process of liberal adjudication (rule of law, due process, deliberation) opens the possibility of a judgment against a white person on behalf of a black person, thereby threatening the racial order undergirding, and ultimately superseding, the legal order. As a consequence, Coalhouse is literally and figuratively trapped; he can't be an individual because he is black, and the only way to be "American" in the larger, normative sense of the term, is to be an individual. He can't be black and assert his individuality at the same time. Both Father and the fire chief are unable to *conceive* of Coalhouse. For the white police, detectives, and common folk attempting to discern the identity of the man at the head of a literally explosive posse, Coalhouse poses a fundamentally epistemological problem. His very existence forces a reordering of their entire epistemology of racial domination. In order to imagine Coalhouse, they have to first reimagine themselves.

VI Knowledge, Power, and Commodification

The relation between writing, knowledge, power, and communication in *Ragtime* appears in the first encounter between Whitman, the New York City district attorney, and Coalhouse, when the New York City police determine that Coalhouse has occupied J. P. Morgan's library. Whitman communicates with Coalhouse by megaphone. In response to Whitman's opening call for dialogue,

> a cylindrical object came flying into the street. Whitman flinched and the men in the house behind him dropped to the floor. To everyone's astonishment there was no explosion. Whitman retreated to the brownstone and only after several minutes did someone using binoculars make the object out as a silver tankard with a lid.... The object, now dented, was a medieval drinking stein of silver with a hunting scene in relief. The curator asked to see it and advised that it was from the seventeenth century and it had belonged to Frederick, Elector of Saxony.... The curator then raised the lid and found inside a piece of paper with a telephone number that he recognized as his own.[26]

The district attorney is less impressed with the tankard's origin and previous owner than he is with the prospect of communicating with Coalhouse on the curator's own telephone number. There is a gap in time, between the tale of a sixteenth-century instance of revolt in response to an act of bourgeois (contractual, governmental, personal) bad faith, the bad faith of a dishonest transaction, and the seventeenth-century dating of the Saxon Elector's tankard. *Ragtime* provides no clues as to how J. P. Morgan came to acquire the tankard. We do know, however, that through the passage of time, once-coveted commodities become relics or museum artifacts, with little or no actual use in daily life. Their utility becomes secondary to their curatorial value, the only value later ascribed to them. A tankard becomes indistinguishable from a Tupperware cup in terms of its function, and its use value is actually lower than its plastic counterpart; a Model T's use and exchange value is diminished as new cars with more sophisticated features, faster speeds, and greater comfort appear. Like the tankard, Coalhouse's coveted possession would be reduced to a relic, independent of the fire chief's vandalism. Doctorow's assembly of J. P. Morgan, Frederick the Elector and Kohlhaas, Coalhouse Walker and Whitman, at the scene of negotiation over the fate of the library suggests a swirl of competing value systems, the relationship between the ephemeral and the historical, and between elite and popular notions of justice.

Father and Mother, Sarah's employers, are perplexed by Coalhouse's insistence on the repair of his car. Father thought it "ridiculous to allow a motor car to take over everyone's life as it now had."[27] If Coalhouse cannot be a property owner with the rights and privileges of other owners, he means nothing in a society whose legal-juridical premises link citizenship to property ownership, and freedom of commodity exchange with freedom of association, a society whose juridical and administrative dimensions intertwine the security of profit with the security of liberty. Father's observation concerning Coalhouse's obsession is from the vantage point of someone who can, and does, take commodities and liberties for granted. Viewed in this manner, Father's observation is accurate, but, like Luther, misses the point. Like Kohlhaas, Coalhouse recognizes that the inability to trade and consume freely means that the legal, political, and economic structures of the society are meaningless for entire classes and groups of people like them. This realization is not lost upon the Whitmans and Electors of the world, which is why both Kohlhaas and Coalhouse have to be destroyed.

J. P. Morgan's curt, brutal telegram, "GIVE HIM HIS AUTOMOBILE AND THEN HANG HIM,"[28] sent to Whitman during the speculative phase of negotiating strategy, provides the acknowledgment that Coalhouse desperately, stubbornly desires. Morgan's summary acknowledgment of the righteousness of Coalhouse's claim is evidenced in the suggestion that his car be repaired. Coalhouse, on the other hand, is irredeemable. Morgan could, in theory, be cheated in a transaction, or his goods damaged by another, but he could never be black. Race becomes a nontransferable commodity. The Castellan, Junker von Tronka, and their well-appointed relatives would never be horse traders or gypsies, but they could indeed be swindled. There is always the possibility of the swindle in the world of transaction. The destitute horses in *Michael Kohlhaas* and the dripping, mangled automobile are powerful images that help increase popular animosity toward the Junker and fire chief, respectively, for damaged goods in societies predicated on goods and their conveyance of nobility, propriety, and "hard work" are symbols everyone can recognize, regardless of ownership or race. One is reminded of the admonition to "beware of coveting those things which rust" as perhaps the overarching moral of these two tales.

Coalhouse, though harboring no such illusions, is nevertheless presented as coveting the very things the white bourgeoisie want. Kleist reminds us at various points in the text that Kohlhaas simply wanted to ply his trade in a reasonable manner without the capricious taxes and constraints imposed by greedy, exploitive nobility. Both during and after his rebellion, Kohlhaas is the character most preoccupied with the rule of law and the explicit purpose of his rebellion. Time and again, Kohlhaas is disappointed by the state's treatment and consideration of his case: "What he disliked most about the regime he had to deal with was the show of justice it put on, at the same time that it went ahead and broke the amnesty that he had been promised."[29] He too wants what the nobility has.

An interesting contrast between these two stories is found in the manner in which each act of rebellion is resolved. The electors of Saxony and Brandenburg provide two distinct judgments upon Kohlhaas's case. The first judgment, conferred by the Elector of Saxony, recognizes the injustice done to the horse trader. A second judgment, by the Elector of Brandenburg—Kohlhaas's home state—fixes a death sentence upon Kohlhaas for his reign of terror. Coalhouse's fate, on the other hand, is decided (though not the precise manner of death) by one of the greatest robber barons in the history of capitalism, sealed according to market norms and the improvised state and federal militia who pump bullets into him, without any legal precepts or pretense. The punishment exacted upon the fire chief who first damages Coalhouse's car also has an extrajuridical source. The law of the street, in class terms, and racism in more generic terms, further binds the fate of these two men.

Like his German characterological relative, Coalhouse recognizes the impossibility of overturning the institutions and people devoted to racial domination in the United States. Unlike his German counterpart, his death is the result of an abrogated agreement, the absence of due process. Perhaps the contextual distinction to be made between the two characters is that the former experienced justice in previous transactions between people of equal or superior status, as in the case of Kohlhaas's bailiff friend who purchases Kohlhaas's land at below market rate and who is responsible for the horse trader's children after his execution.

VII Race and the State of Exception

Here we have reached the point at which we can incorporate Agamben's elaboration on Schmitt's state of exception. In *Homo Sacer*, Giorgio Agamben asserts that the concentration camps are the paradigmatic example of the state of exception operative in the modern era. The state of exception is a condition in which a sovereign state decides to defend itself against a perceived internal threat in the same manner in which it would defend itself against an external one. A society has reached a state of exception when a state decides to exercise its right of sovereignty in response to a perceived internal threat. The threat "*ceases to be referred to as an external and provisional state of factual danger and comes to be confused with juridical rule itself.*"[30]

Agamben's concern with the spatiality of the concentration camp in Nazi Germany and his attempt to discern its unique yet distinctly modern character may conflate historical circumstances with more emblematic, epistemic, and conceptual features of the state of exception. In Nazi Germany, state violence often preceded state law. Law was often used as a post hoc justification for the deployment of state violence, and the deprivation, segregation, and systematic slaughter that characterized the concentration camps.

I would like to suggest here that what Kleist and Doctorow describe are states of exception that their fateful characters are attempting to escape, yet under very quotidian rather than extraordinary circumstances. It is not the concentration camp, but society itself, that is the space of exception for many racial and ethnic minorities. The state's two faces, as noted earlier, have distinct sets of expressions: one for subordinate subjects, the other for the dominant ones. In societies such as that of the United States, with its liberal polity, South Africa and Zimbabwe under apartheid, and Brazil (even with the ideology of racial democracy), African-descended populations experienced the state of exception as a normative feature of daily life. Could it be that the state of exception, as characterized by Schmitt and interpreted by Agamben, is exceptional insofar as the post hoc forms of repression, segregation, bare life, and extermination characterize a seemingly unique predicament in the history of Europe, but not a unique predicament for colonized and racialized subjects in Africa, Asia and the New World? What Foucault identifies as biopower (see chapter 4)—corporeality, not spatiality—triggers the state of exception for racial and ethnic minorities. For subjects excluded from the body politic, they are walking states of exception.

Rogers Brubaker, in his comparative examination of citizenship and immigration policies in France and Germany, reminds us that citizenship is an object of social closure. We can consider these racialized states of exception and the political ramifications of their existence for the political category of citizen. Agamben, following but also extending Schmitt, attributes these conditions of exception to fascist regimes, thereby making a qualitative distinction between fascism and liberalism. Yet all states, not just fascist ones, make and remake distinctions between citizens and foreigners. Foreign threats to the body politic of a liberal polity can and have been treated, by virtue of their foreignness, as categories of people to whom national-state law does not apply.

Kohlhaas's and Coalhouse's attempts to fuse their corporeal selves with the body politic of their localities led states, bureaucracies, and elites to unleash the coercive and administrative processes designed to separate the individual body from the body politic. The state used the two men as examples of the fates awaiting those who would challenge one of the central prerogatives of modern states, the identification and maintenance of the distinction between citizens and subjects. For the citizen, corporality and citizenship are coincident. For the subject, corporality and citizenship (in the sense of belonging to and participating in the body politic of the nation) are kept separate. Just because both characters inhabit nation-states with civil societies does not make them de facto citizens. Instead, they are the macropolitical equivalent of living ghosts who conjure terror in their societies until they are exorcised.

The brutality dispensed by the state and various individuals against Coalhouse and Sarah, and Kohlhaas and Lisbeth, supplants the need for laws condoning their execution. Violence, therefore, precedes the law and comes to supplant law itself. Juridical, bureaucratic justification for the exercise of violence occurs after the fact of violence. Violence—not law—instantiates political order. The history of racist violence in the United States provides evidence of the use of violence as a form of parallel law that often precedes or renders irrelevant formal law. The making of examples has invariably been part of the symbolic deployment of the artifacts of racial terror, as in lynchings, decapitated heads, eviscerated genitalia, charred bodies, or other public displays of violence that serve as warning to those who would trespass the precious, exclusionary terrain of white supremacy.

In the United States alone, examples such as the Dred Scott case, the Asian Exclusion Acts targeting Chinese, Japanese, and Korean immigrants, and the Anti-Alien Land Law of 1913 to limit Japanese settlement in California together demonstrate the ways in which municipal, state, and federal law become entangled with concepts of foreignness. In Germany, the circumscribed political status of Turkish residents before the amendment of immigration law in 2000 made Turkish residents, in effect, people subject to bare life and the state of exception. North African immigrants in France, particularly Algerians, have, for a variety of political, economic, and religious reasons, borne the mark of exception in relation to French state and popular discourses of republicanism.

These examples suggest that the concept of foreigner is an intrinsically political concept and construction, not based ultimately on nationality or race, but on the presumed relation between insiders and outsiders within the body politic of the liberal nation. Birthright is never an a priori determinant of citizenship, but is a subsequent determination of who is in, and who remains outside, the body politic. This leads to a question concerning not only fascist states and regimes, but states and regimes more generally: Are those defined as foreign entitled to the same juridical status as citizens before a court of national law? As we now know, even in the contemporary United States, this is a question with profound implications for matters of nationality, the status of foreigners, and constitutionality, not to mention for citizenship itself.

VIII   Revolt or Revolution

Despite the tumultuous consequences of both characters' desire for revenge, order is restored in each society through the death of the rebellious character. Neither Kohlhaas nor Coalhouse possesses alternative conceptions of the world in which they live. And barring their ability to live comfortably in the existing world, both are willing to upend this world and all who live within it, including their wives and children. For Kohlhaas, if freedom is not grounded in law, then it is found through violence against those who mistreated him. At one point, he responds to his wife Lisbeth's appeal to justice by stating, "If you feel that justice must be done me if I am to continue in my trade, then don't deny me the freedom I need to get it."[31]

Coalhouse's revolt in the second decade of the twentieth century is smaller in scale. The municipal, state, and city authorities invested in his capture and execution in New York City are never in dispute over his eventual execution. Doctorow invests Coalhouse's posse with more revolutionary potentiality than Kleist does Kohlhaas's. The latter figure, after all, could be characterized as happily petit bourgeois, without an expressed contempt for either peasantry or nobility. Content with what would be contemporarily characterized as suburban life, Coalhouse's posse, on the other hand, exhibits no internally discrepant behavior. They behave as one, with Coalhouse serving as their anticharismatic, morally vengeful leader. He is anticharismatic in terms of racial politics because he does not "smile or cakewalk," that is, publicly or privately engage in the sort of performative behavior associated with blacks. In the basement of J. P. Morgan's library, his group "embraced every discipline," including the prohibition of "music in the basement quarters. No instrument of any kind."[32] Again, the distinction between music as vocation and passion and music as an extension of an essential black self is clearly delineated in this scene.

Perhaps the smallness of Coalhouse's posse and the narrowness of their purpose, in contrast with Kohlhaas's incipient army, minimizes the propensity for deviation among the five black men and one white man (Younger Brother) who compose Coalhouse's army. It is Coalhouse who deviates from their plan in the end, in an act of cynical martyrdom. Nevertheless, it is their collective predicament at the end of the book, when they must decide whether to exit the Morgan library as a group or separately, leaving Coalhouse to face the state-sponsored militia alone, that has political implications for rebellious, potentially revolutionary movements at moments of political ambivalence. The final three chapters provide an illustration of the distinction between rebellion and revolution. The implications are evident in the final, intense deliberations among the men after Coalhouse announces his intention to leave through the front door. Doctorow writes:

> All day the followers of Coalhouse had come to him with appeals to change his mind. Their arguments became wilder and wilder. They said they were a nation. He was patient with them. It became apparent they wouldn't know what to do without him. They recognized his decision as suicide. They were forlorn in their abandonment.[33]

The sole white man, Younger Brother, the one with the most experience with positive government, accuses Coalhouse of betrayal: "Either we all ought to go free or we all ought to die. You signed your letter Provisional American Government. Coalhouse nodded. 'It seemed to be the rhetoric we needed for our morale,'" he said. But we meant it! Younger Brother cried. There are enough people in the streets to found an army!"[34]

The limitations of Coalhouse's macro-political vision are thus betrayed. Utilizing guerilla tactics to incite terror and fear, operating in silence, communicating only through cryptic notes, and engaging in behavior sure to get them killed if they are discovered, Coalhouse's posse represents a form of coagulation and aggregation (see chapter 2), keen to redress an injustice but providing no cognitive indication that they know how to function collectively beyond their desire for retribution.

The collective's inability to imagine a life without or after Coalhouse is as much a critique of their leader's aims and objectives as it is an assessment of the limitations of their vision. Like Kohlhaas, Coalhouse's political imaginary produced the *notion* of a provisional government and in so doing *evoked* a sense of macro-political community radically distinct from the one that he inhabited. Yet like Kohlhaas, Coalhouse had no conceptualization, radical or otherwise, of a world different from the one he inhabited. Coalhouse Walker did not and perhaps could not *invoke* a new political community.

Coalhouse's response to Younger Brother reveals the notion of a provisional government to be a rhetorical ploy, nothing more. Perhaps for Coalhouse, such imaginings were futile, with a band of no more than a half-dozen men. An imagined conversation with an imaginary character (Younger Brother) enables us to theoretically traverse the distance between Coalhouse's decision to go it alone and Younger Brother's sense of betrayal. Two general questions, followed by a series of secondary questions, can be posed. The first question, in response to one of the "wild notions" that Coalhouse's posse constituted a nation, is what sort of a nation did the men have in mind? Would they be a nation of men, without a state, in perpetual outlaw status in relation to the U.S. government, residing in Harlem? These are the questions that have haunted black nationalist ideologies and mobilization in the United States for the better part of three centuries. A second question, leading to a series of smaller questions, gets us at the hollowness of Younger Brother's claim of an army in the streets: What would the founded army be fighting in the name of? The Provisional American Army founded to defend the honor of the Model T? A black man's right to property, or even the larger ability of members of the black community to buy and consume commodities as they see fit? Where would black women fit in this provisional army/nation? Where would people like Younger Brother fit within this nation? Would Younger Brother be the fictive equivalent of South Africa's Joe Slovo?[35] All these questions remain unanswerable within the context of the story, but suggest the absence of an ideological substrata to undergird and inform the behavior of Coalhouse's posse. In the absence of their leader and with the return of an automobile, the posse is without purpose. In the end, they simply disperse.

Political radicality in *Ragtime* appears in the form of two white characters. Younger Brother, who escapes from the Morgan library, drives the car to the Mexican border, where he takes up with Pancho Villa in the Mexican Revolution before being killed. The legendary anarchist Emma Goldman is a recurrent ethicopolitical presence in the latter half of the story. At one point she is interviewed by reporters about Coalhouse Walker after she is arrested and charged with conspiracy to overthrow the government of the United States. "The oppressor is wealth, my friends. Wealth is the oppressor. Coalhouse Walker did not need Red Emma to learn that. He needed only to suffer."[36] While Goldman (by way of Doctorow) acknowledges the prospect of autonomous social agency on the part of Coalhouse, there are no clues in the novel of the ideational sources of Coalhouse's convictions. Why couldn't Coalhouse Walker understand, wondered both Father and a black attorney in Harlem that the piano player consulted, that his responsibilities to Sarah were "more important than the need to redress a slight on the part of white folks,"[37] to have a lawyer to "go to Westchester County to plead on a colored man's behalf that someone deposited a bucket of slops in his car."[38] Nor are there any indications of the origins of Sarah's moral intrepidness. As I have discussed in chapter 2, suffering cannot be a recipe for revolution, otherwise revolutions would occur with much greater frequency, variety, and number throughout the world. Although neither Coalhouse nor Sarah are Marxist, anarchosyndicalist activists acting out preformed ideological commitments, must they be the visionless, inchoate agents they are made out to be? In other words, what drives them to behave in the manner they did? One possibility, more suggested by than realized in the text, is that both Coalhouse and Sarah actually *believe* in the possibilities that a liberal democratic polity represent, a normative and administrative bulwark against the idiosyncrasies of processual racial domination.

IX Conclusion

Both the Coalhouse and Kohlhaas characters attempt to forge new social identities and statuses in societies undergoing radical transformation. Kohlhaas's Brandenburg and Saxon tormentors were elites of societies that would, with the creation of Germany, vanish into history. Coalhouse Walker's United States had undergone several transformations, from breakaway colonial ensemble and fledgling democratic experiment for the few to a highly institutionalized society with vast differences in power, status, wealth, and education, and an oligarchy of capital more than making up for the absence of true nobility.

I would classify the Kohlhaas/Coalhouse characters of Kleist and Doctorow as types of status quo rebels, rather than employing Hobsbawm's full characterization of "primitive rebels."[39] Neither Coalhouse nor Kohlhaas would gain political capital or success as a result of their respective revolts. Economic prosperity, invariably tied to political freedoms, would come later for the inheritors of their political and socioeconomic legacies, the middle classes of the Weimar Republic and the black middle-class leadership of the modern civil rights movement in the United States. Their success required the separation or at least distinction between the right to trade and the right to exist as a political subject. This distinction resounds more forcefully in *Ragtime*, I believe, because the Germany that few Saxons (not just Kohlhaas) would live to see extended monarchial rule and had a brief flirtation with republicanism before descending into the most extreme form of fascism.

To the end, Coalhouse remained an apolitical character in the land of democracy, resolutely equating property with freedom. Up until the civil rights movement, the political and legal status of racially or ethnonationally subordinate groups such as U.S. African Americans and Native Americans more closely resembled the status of foreigners, those without voting rights and other privileges befitting citizens, than they resembled whites who had citizenship status. Thus, Coalhouse's status, like that of a foreigner, was the result of political predetermination, not race. Coalhouse, like Kohlhaas, understood the limitations of being an outsider, but little of politics.

Yet in a territory in which a select group of people declared that the pursuit of happiness was part of their declaration of independence from a sovereign, colonial power, empathy must be shown for the figure of Coalhouse Walker. He became, to paraphrase Gunnar Myrdal, an exaggerated American, in part because commodities seemed to be the only bulwark against outright domination and denial. Commodities conveyed the potentiality of respect. Coalhouse envisioned his freedom in the glint of a well-polished Model T— a car, after all, that was the product of a genius whose outlook toward his workers was no different from Kohlhaas's view of his horses, a genius who would have never countenanced a Coalhouse Walker in real life, a black person standing before him as his political equal, regardless of the car he drove. Henry Ford would have never considered the product of a commodity, the child of slaves, worthy of human acknowledgment, much less respect. Freedom indeed.

The first two sections of this book have mostly addressed the individual, disparate and not-quite-collective acts of black politics, evidenced and represented in ideologies, literature, daily life, and popular culture. The two chapters of the third and final section address the transnational dimensions of black politics, which entail some form of collective action. This section returns to the domain of actual histories and politics of black life-worlds in both hemispheric and transnational circumstances. Chapters 7 and 8 provide two seemingly opposite perspectives on race mixture and racial solidarity. Neither race mixture nor racial solidarity are antidotes for the pathologies, coercion, and oppression attributable to racisms, yet many political actors from various positions on the so-called racial divide have assumed one or the other as the cure to racism. These two final chapters will examine the limitations of race-mixture and racial solidarity advocacy and return to the reconceptualization of political community with which this book began.

PART III
Hemispheric Perspectives/ Black Internationalism

CHAPTER 7

Garnet's Dictum, the Color Line, and Mixed Race: Notes on Hybridity and Miscegenation

Introduction

Henry Highland Garnet, the renowned orator and abolitionist, declared in 1848 during a lecture before an attentive suffragist audience in upstate New York that "this Western world is destined to be filled with a mixed race."[1] His lecture emphasized four main points: the abolition of slavery; a social constructionist—rather than a scriptural or biological—explanation for the degradation of black peoples throughout the world; the basic equality of people of African descent as group members of the human family; and the mission and destiny of the colored races of the New World and of the United States in particular to help emancipate their brethren in the African continent from conditions of backwardness, both real and imagined.

Garnet's lecture is worth revisiting. For the purpose of this chapter and book more generally, consider Garnet's prognostication for the fate of the West alongside another, more commonly cited prediction made by W. E. B. Du Bois, who approximately fifty years later in *The Souls of Black Folk*, wrote that the history of the twentieth century would be the history of the color line.[2] Most readers will be more familiar with the latter declaration than the former. Du Bois's oft-quoted, now-weathered prediction concerning "the color line" and Garnet's emphasis on the idea of a "mixed race" for the West create an interesting contrast conceptually and strategically between two thinkers of overlapping generations. Both use the terms "color" and "race" interchangeably in their respective texts. Both were staunch antiracist activists on behalf of African-descended peoples, not just in the United States, but globally. Consequently, their outlooks on the "race" problem, "color" problem, or both were global as well.

Isolated and extracted from more elaborate rhetorical and literary strategies, Du Bois's and Garnet's declarations can be contemporized to suit the rhetorical necessities of arguments relating to color versus racial distinction. As noted by Timothy Mitchell in his powerfully nuanced study of technopolitics and the force of capitalism in Egypt, "Objects of analysis do not occur as natural phenomena, but are partly formed by the discourse that describes them. The more natural the object appears, the less obvious the discursive manufacture will be."[3] The innumerable conference papers that have begun with Du Bois' most well-known statement, and the untold conferences that have used the color line as its organizing, thematic principle testify to its ubiquity. The color line statement, however, is often treated as a truism, rather than using Mitchell's terminology, a discursive manufacture.

Many students of African American studies, Africana, or African diaspora studies have utilized "the century of the color line" phrase to preface arguments that "prove" the truth of Du Bois's claim for the United States. Some have even upheld Du Bois's prediction as an observation about the role of racial formation the world over and consider this incredibly accomplished person a soothsayer. Yet one can agree with his assertion and also acknowledge that the twentieth century had not one color line, but several, and that the twentieth century was also the century of the atomic bomb, the demise of the Soviet Union, and the acknowledgment in many societies that women should have a formal role in political life without fear of sanction.[4] By examining "the color line" as an object of analysis, rather than a discursive formation in need of examination, is to consider the implications of Du Bois's claim for other related objects of analysis, or for what a preoccupation with the color line obscures and neglects.

By contrast, Garnet's dictum has received far less attention, although in many respects it is the more contemporary of the two. The debates over multiculturalism, the presence of nonwhite national minorities in postimperial Europe in particular and the steady transmigration of many former colonial subjects from the Caribbean, Asia, and Africa to Australia, New Zealand, and the United States, signal the reality, worry, and in some cases, celebration of a "mixed race" Western world. Such seeming mixture threatens the organization of the world by phenotype, if not language, culture, geography, and territory. Notwithstanding Stuart Hall's apt characterization of the West as a highly successful fiction,[5] the idea of a racially homogeneous Europe transformed by postcolonial tides of darker-skinned people bringing different cultural and social traditions has affected social and political realities (e.g., social welfare and immigration policies, electoral competition). In societies with much longer postcolonial histories as nation-states, such as the United States and Brazil, multiculturalism and Lusotropicalism have each affected—at different moments—how states and national populations view themselves as a mixed race or multicultural people. The concepts of mixed-race and hybridity, like the related concepts of race and culture, should be assessed well beyond the confines of national territory. Garnet creates a diachronic relationship between hybridity and antiracist practice, an interconnectedness other New World advocates of hybridity barely suggest. Garnet's suggestion has an even more subversive significance, however, if we consider that Garnet envisioned the West's eventual mongrelization in spite of itself.

In this chapter I shall focus on the themes of hybridity and antiracist practice, two critical themes of Garnet's lecture and life work, and a third theme, the race concept's continuing legacy in politics and culture. Both the race concept and the color concept have been utilized in attempts to forge something called, at different times, "African unity," "Black unity," or even "Third World unity." My critique of the limitations of this approach for transnational black politics is outlined in the concluding chapter. Nevertheless, Garnet's global perspective reminds us of the possibility of utilizing a particular population as a unit of analysis to track variation, difference, as well as recurrent patterns across time and space.

For the purpose of this chapter, I will limit my focus to the hemispheric implications of antiblack racisms. Du Bois's preoccupation with mixed race and his attendant concern with a Herderean "conservation of races" did not preclude the anti-essentialist humanism at the core of his political philosophy. Garnet's prediction of total miscegenation in the West did not conflict with his desire to "revindicate" African-descended peoples from a history of oppression and enslavement. What makes Garnet's position unique in relation to Du Bois's is his combined advocacy of formal legal freedoms and prospects of citizenship with one of the West's central taboos—the practice of so-called race mixture—along with a prototypically Pan-Africanist, black transnationalist vision of unity and solidarity. In hemispheric terms, Garnet's position is both like and unlike several other New World intellectuals of the late nineteenth and early twentieth century, most notably Jose Vasconcelos, Jose Martí, and Gilberto Freyre. Each advocated "race mixture" as a means of national development in Mexico, Cuba, and Brazil, yet were also opposed to racially specific political mobilization of any sort.⁶ Du Bois's Herderean view of racial conservation, while not segregationist, accepted the presumed boundaries of racial identification and identity in the United States and the West more generally, despite (or perhaps because of) his own white/nonwhite status within the typology of U.S. apartheid.

Garnet's positioning enables him to catalogue and oppose antiblack racisms and racial hierarchies, advocate political solidarity among African-derived and African peoples, and declare a specific—though not unproblematic—role for U.S. African Americans in elevating the condition of African-descended people.⁷ Garnet's intellectual/activist balancing act was not without its antinomies. It relied on presumptions of the homogeneity of the West, as well as an implicitly polygenesist view of race, evident in the very claim that the West would *become* a mixed race. The political creation of "races" obscured the motley assortment of peoples, cultures, and ethnicities that came to constitute "the European" and the West. Here Garnet, like several commentators I will analyze below, accedes to the scientific racist terminology of the era by arguing that procreation between peoples from different parts of the world will produce new types of humans, while at the same time denying the theory of polygenesis and its hierarchical ordering of human types. Garnet's claim produces a paradox: how can there be mixed races among human beings if there is only one human race? His advocacy of black transnational solidarity and antiracist, social constructivist practice has been the tightrope of "progressive" (center-left) black politics for the entirety of the twentieth and now the twenty-first century.

Ongoing legacies of antiblack racisms in a variety of societies (and not just in the West) makes Garnet's agenda presented in the 1848 lecture as relevant now as it was in the middle of the nineteenth century. One can distinguish, as Garnet did, the phenomenon of "race-mixture" from the phenomenon of racial discrimination and its effect upon the soon-to-be former slaves throughout the hemisphere. The first phenomenon, to the extent that it could be referred to as an actual occurrence, has had varied consequences throughout the world. The second phenomenon influenced the collective ability of former slaves to vote and participate in politics, own land, labor independently, and raise families without interventions by the state or large landowners armed with the rule of law, the whip, and the gun. At the same time, the vast diversity of people, cultures, languages, and idioms that constitute slave and former slave populations, then and now, make the categories of black, Moor, and African ever shifting, malleable, contestable, and frustrating attempts to secure black identity and identification. Blackness, then, is both situated by and helps situate national, local, and transnational contexts of antiblack racism. These three features of Garnet's talk work with and against one another, as they do in real life.

Against the backdrop of ongoing debates about notions of hybridity, multiculturalism, essentialism, and racial and national identities, Garnet's prognostication warrants further examination because of the way it fuses positions often viewed as competing or contradictory in contemporary debates about race, hybridity, and culture. At the very least, it forces us to acknowledge that preoccupation with a notion of human hybridity in the late 1990s might have been new for cultural studies and postmodern critique, but was not new to African diaspora or U.S. African American studies. Garnet's argument is instructive for the manner in which he situated himself among several coordinates: pseudoscience and racist thought, gender equality and women's rights, abolitionism and civil rights, and, finally, a global perspective on black solidarity. Given these four coordinates, one could ask whether Garnet might be considered a "racial essentialist" in contemporary scholarly debate, since he advocates on behalf of a "black people" who, in racial terms, do not exist. Only by understanding race, racism, and, ultimately, racial solidarity as intrinsically political projects, rather than consequences of social construction or biology, can Garnet's position be viewed otherwise. What requires further empirical investigation with greater theoretical and analytic sophistication is how meanings of race are produced, employed, and sustained in societies to name and distinguish communities, undermine distinctions between public and private, and affect many other dimensions of human interaction and identity formation. The concept I shall refer to as racial valuation allows us to focus on hierarchy and conflict, the terrain of politics within the domain of the social. Rather than making the race concept a matter of apprehension of the visual (phenotype), racial valuation focuses on the imposition of differentiated degrees of value upon certain types of people. Races as such don't have to exist in order for certain groups of people to be considered more valuable than others, whether the interpretive schemes utilized to infer and grant value are "racially" or chromatically based.

What I want to offer here is an alternative explanation of racial and cultural construction that supersedes the constructivist as well as the raciological accounts of race by elaborating and developing the concept of valuation. Valuation, rather than phenotype, chromatic, or bipolar classification, is the core of racial and chromatic hierarchies that inform and often (though not always) motivate racist practice.

So Many Cultures, So Few Races: Hybridity in Latin America and Beyond

Garnet's lecture can be viewed as one possible answer to the following question: What is the relationship between politics, culture, race, and hybridity among African-descended populations? As mentioned above, other New World scholars and activists provided their own formulations of the relationship between these four features of modern life. The prospect of racial and cultural mixture was often viewed as an antidote to racial animus as well as the very real prospect of black rebellion and revolution, whether in Bolivar's Gran Colombia, Jefferson's United States, late eighteenth- and early nineteenth-century Haiti, or in Jose Martí's Cuba. The possibility of independent black political mobilization was considered anathema to national political development, a threat to sovereignty, and for outright racists and elites, an inconceivable undertaking among a population deemed intellectually and morally inferior to Europeans as well as to other "races."

Although we certainly occupy a different era with distinct political and socioeconomic realities, the preoccupation with race, culture, and hybridity has remained, and in some ways mutated. What is striking about many late twentieth century and early twenty-first century scholarly discussions about race, culture, and hybridity is the manner in which they resemble their late nineteenth- and early twentieth-century counterparts. In the more contemporary variations on these themes, blatantly racist condemnations of black political mobilization and of African-descended populations are not tolerated in polite circles, as they were in the nineteenth and early twentieth centuries. Commonsense assumptions about the meanings of race and culture from this earlier period have gone largely unexamined, however, even by scholars who claim to want to move beyond the race concept and employ the culture concept as a more accurate description of the interplay,[8] symbiosis, and synthesis of human groupings that have been categorized according to so-called racial distinction. While the highly arbitrary process of racial creation, formation, and distinction has garnered significant scholarly attention and debate, less attention has been given to its significance for politics or for what can be characterized as the metadiscourses of race and culture. This chapter serves as a reminder of the necessity of acknowledging the role of politics, political conflict, and social struggle in the transformation of racial valuation and meaning, in altering the association of specific symbols and symbolic systems with certain types of people, a project that "race mixture" and all that it entails, can never achieve.

The work of Franz Boas and his students did much to debunk the prevailing nineteenth-century view of the race concept as an accurate description of distinct human groups, which almost invariably became the source of hierarchical distinction utilized to justify the domination of one seeming race by another.[9] As is well documented, racial domination assumed many forms, ranging from the organization of economic and political systems to maximize profit at the expense of subordinate groups (not only through the systems of capitalism and slavery) to a celebration of the normative, aesthetic, and overall civilizational superiority of the dominant race.[10]

The writings of Gilberto Freyre, a student of Boas, did much to challenge scientific racist thought in Brazil by chronicling the diverse and indelible contributions of various African and African-descended populations to Brazilian civilization, populations often assumed to be part of the same "African race." Other Franz Boas students such as Melville Herskovits and Zora Neale Hurston developed and utilized critical ethnographies to debunk many of the racial distinctions and hierarchies among human populations in the scholarship of scientific racists. Followed by anthropologists such as Ruth Benedict, the race concept collapsed under the weight of cultural diversity, since none of the variations among Caucasian, Negroid, indigenous, or Asian peoples could be accounted for by racial distinction. Further biological studies at the turn of the twentieth century demonstrated that human diversity could not, for the most part, be accounted for by biology. Scientific proof (based on both "hard" and "soft" evidence), however, did not put an end to racism, nor to the dogged belief in the race concept as a means of human classification.[11] Through apartheid, holocausts, pogroms, and the genocidal horrors of the twentieth century, the application of the race concept in hierarchical categorizations of human beings would persist.

Nonetheless, common to both eras is the belief that "race mixture" and "hybridity" are not only more accurate descriptions of actual human encounters and interchange but also engines to ameliorate conditions of racial inequality and lessen conflict based on racial distinction. Readers unfamiliar with the late nineteenth-century and early twentieth-century debates on these topics should consult texts cited in several footnotes in this chapter. For the purpose of my intervention here, I would like to focus on the mutated versions of this belief in more contemporary scholarship in order to highlight some of the key analytic problems inherent in this perspective, both then and now.

The first problem I will focus on is the conflation of culture and race. Not only does a reified notion of race continue to surface in many "social constructivist," nonpositivist accounts of the race concept, but a static view of culture travels like a stowaway in the interpretive journey from racial to cultural distinction. Evidence of this conflation is found most obviously in the very notion of a mixed race. Both "mixed race" and miscegenation assume that there are indeed distinct races to mix. Thus, race mixture and miscegenation, as conceptual premises, allow the biological/polygenetic mode of racial reasoning to sneak into constructivist accounts of the race concept, which is then linked to the concept of racial miscegenation or hybridity.

For example, a contemporary proponent of the "mixture-centered view of the United States,"[12] David Hollinger, writes the following in a recent *American Historical Review* article as part of a historiography and advocacy of amalgamation. Hollinger claims this is part of the lexical legacy of Wendell Phillips, Frederick Douglass, and Ralph Waldo Emerson,[13] and is contrary both to assimilationist (melting pot) and frontier theses (such as those of Frederick Jackson Turner):

> While there is a danger that the acceptance of mixture will ultimately reinforce white privilege by treating as "white" all but the darkest, who might then be all the more isolated and subject to enduring prejudice, isn't there also a more hopeful prospect? The more that mixture is accepted, the less fear there might be of what is being mixed. Blackness itself might become less stigmatized. If the one-drop rule is an indicator of the depth of anti-black racism, might not the weakening of that rule be an indicator of the diminution of that racism?[14]

I focus here on the slippages between race and culture as symptomatic of a more general elision and seamless passage between concepts of race mixture, hybridity, politics, and culture in Hollinger's argument. If we return to my claim that "race mixture" requires we assume there are indeed races to mix, then one can become immediately suspicious of Hollinger's claim that race mixture can lead to a greater acceptance of blackness and a diminution of antiblack racism.[15] Hollinger suggests two scenarios in this passage—further marginalization or greater acceptance—but the object of acceptance or disapproval remains unclear. The stigmas attached to blackness, which Hollinger acknowledges at several points in his text, produce a peculiar predicament for African-descended subjects in the United States, a predicament improved, as Hollinger readily admits, only by political struggle. Implicit in his argument is the view that antiblack racism is somehow produced by the fear of race mixture. Yet it *must* be the reverse: the fear of race mixture between whites and blacks is a consequence of antiblack racism, otherwise fear of the specific race mixture between so-called whites and blacks would become analytically unintelligible.

Neither side of the argument questions the presumption that "race mixture" and "blackness" share the continuum of racial meaning and valuation, if not a chromatic or bipolar continuum. Amelioration or hardening of racially premised antagonisms between groups is presented as simply generated by the heightened presence or absence of mixed-race people. In Hollinger's and similar arguments, "race mixture" allegedly does the work of politics.[16]

In order to underscore the logical inconsistencies of this mode of argumentation, and the gap between the existence of a "mixed-race" group or individual and the meanings associated with such an individual or group, I will provide a hypothetical situation involving a true hybrid, the tangelo, the outcome of a cross between orange and tangerine seeds. Resemblance to any individual or company in the citrus industry is entirely unintended. In this hypothetical situation, there happens to be a man who detests the taste, appearance, and texture of tangelos, as well as tangerines. He does however, love the taste of oranges. In addition, he happens to be a large-scale orange grower in a very competitive industry, with a sizeable but increasingly challenged market niche, nationally and globally. There is another grower, however, who enjoys the flavor, texture, and appearance of the tangelo, and intends to begin cross-fertilization and production. He intends to enter the same markets as the orange grower, although he operates on a much smaller scale than the orange producer. Given this scenario, there is no reason to believe that the introduction of more tangelos into the produce market will please the orange grower. More personally, as a matter of taste, the presence or absence of tangelos in the market is irrelevant to the orange grower, for he does not like them.

Perhaps if tangelos became a hot commodity in several markets, the orange producer might decide for macroeconomic reasons to actually grow tangelos, without altering his distaste for them. A government subsidy to encourage orange growers to grow fewer oranges and more tangelos might provide an even greater incentive for the orange grower. Yet the decision to grow the tangelo as a commodity is independent of the taste and personal likes and dislikes of the orange grower. If the orange grower continues to dislike the tangelo and there are no economic incentives for him to grow them, why would one think that their increased presence in any market would make him change his mind? Only if the orange producer acquired a taste for tangelos, independent of his economic motivations, would his attitude toward tangelos as an object for consumption change.

I can now draw parallels between this fictitious scenario and several variations on the amalgamation thesis, in the United States as well other parts of the New World. The orange grower in this scenario represents those who have antipathies toward those defined as black. The tangelo growers are the amalgamationists, who are smaller in number and market share. The like or dislike of the tangelo is not intrinsic to the tangelo itself, but the consequence of meanings associated with its existence, in a symbolic field filled with meaningful objects. The tangelo, orange, and the tangerine are only rendered intelligible in relation to the field of objects assigned particular places in a symbolic system. Only within a scheme or regime of taste (valuation) do we discern which fruits are coveted more by consumers and producers. There is nothing inherently valuable about them other than their nutritional virtue. Only with a shift in "disposition" toward the tangelo—the meanings associated with its taste and appearance—would the hybrid fruit generate a more positive response from the orange grower.

Like the tangelo, increased production of "hybrid" peoples will not necessarily shift the meaning and associative symbols attached to blacks and other darker-skinned peoples. Unless there were certain economic and political incentives that would accrue to mixed-race people and their parents, such as government subsidies (as in the case of China for limiting the number of children, or in India, where boys are privileged over girls), it remains unclear how the presence or absence of mixed-race people provides broader societal benefits without a transformation in the society's norms, as well as individual, group, and institutional behaviors and policies toward that group.

The material implications of this scenario, related to the consequences of taste and distaste, should also be clear. Neither "blackness" nor the stigmas emanating from antiblack racism are "products" of race mixture. Racial valuation and meaning do not evolve from racial or color classification. Racial and color classification are themselves symbolic artifacts of racial valuation and meaning. Blackness has both positive and negative associations,[17] while antiblack racism (of which negative attitudes toward blackness are part) is constituted by the incorporation of a prejudicial interpretive scheme into processes of visual apprehension to implement systems of classification that generate and maintain hierarchy.

The epistemological presumptions underlying Hollinger's claim are symptomatic of what can be characterized as the U.S. versions of Brazilian Lusotropical and now neo-Freyrean presumptions that correlate race mixture with increasing societal tolerance of color and phenotypic variation. Despite the exceptionalist tenor of his argument, then, Hollinger's elaboration of the amalgamation thesis shares at least one striking similarity with a key tenet of the race mixture components of Freyre's Lusotropicalism and Vasconcelos's Raza Cosmica: what distinguishes Hollinger's amalgamation formulain from

Freyre's and Vasconcelos's is the absence of a civilizational imperative, critical to Freyre's interpretation of the formation of modern Brazil.

In Freyre's account of the dualism of race and culture, he acknowledges the existence of many miscegenated offspring throughout the world but argues that civilization, rather than biology, accounts for the "maladjustment" of so-called hybrids, providing as an example the case of the Eurasians in colonial India:

> the offspring of Europeans and Hindus, rejected by both English and Hindus, and who today constitute one of the most melancholy population groups in the world. A morbid midway point, less between two races than between two rigid civilizations. It is a unique situation, for neither of the two races, neither the imperial nor the—until recently—subject or dominated, and neither of the two Civilizations—not even the Christian of the conquerors, whose religious doctrines so fervently proclaim humanity and gentleness—will lower itself to absorb them nor make itself elastic enough to tolerate them.[18]

Not so for Brazilian civilization, which according to Freyre not only accepted cultural/racial hybridity, but embraced it as part of its unique national character. Even if we reject—as I do—the bedrock supposition of Freyre's thesis (racial/cultural mixture = antiracist social egalitarianism), at least Freyre treats culture and civilization—not "mixture"—as the critical variables in the acceptance of cultural hybridity as an established norm, rather than a taboo or "illicit union."[19] To use a colloquial expression, Freyre does not put the cart before the horse. Only the nurture of a national culture celebrating miscegenation could transform an illicit union's negative connotation into a positive one.[20] If we accept the Freyrean and now neo-Freyrean thesis, Brazilian civilization would be the deciding factor in determining why mulattoes and especially mulattas in Brazil would be celebrated, and why octoroons and quadroons in the eighteenth- and nineteenth-century United States would serve as the U.S. equivalent of the Anglo-Hindu in India. Similar to Hollinger's thesis, however, Freyre believes culture can do the work of politics in alleviating racist sentiments among human beings, in this case, Brazilians. Freyre's celebration of miscegenation and chromatic/phenotypic variation in Brazilian civilization rests upon the same presumption as Hollinger's amalgamation thesis. Neither account acknowledges or confronts racial valuation, intrinsic to racist hierarchy, apparent in both bipolar and multipolar "multiracial" contexts. The idea of "racial value" lurks behind both bipolar and mulipolar continua. Racial valuation is no less socially constructed than the race concept itself and is the first semiotic ordering of racial hierarchy connected to the visual apprehension and interpretation of human beings as multiracial. When applied by states and economic decision makers, and tied to other social attributes, these hierarchies become racism, evidenced in individual, societal, and state practice. Robin Sherriff's nuanced ethnography of quotidian racism in a Rio de Janeiro slum in Brazil provides great insight into the coexistence of more fluid forms of chromatic self-description with everyday racism. Thus, in spite of the self-classification of *favelados* into various color categories, the inhabitants still found antiblack racism pervasive in their interactions with broader, white *Cariocan* society.[21] Racial valuation means that there is greater social, political, and economic value attached to certain chromatically and phenotypically distinguished groups than others. Bipolar models of racial classification, such as have been operative in the United states, as well as multipolar classifications of racial valuation, as have been historically practiced in Brazil, have interpretive schemes of racial valuation, though these schemes may be distinguished by one's emphasis on color and another's emphasis on origin and phenotype. In the United States, the phenomenon of passing was generally a unidirectional process—black toward white, and not white toward black.[22] Similarly, all the significant "whitening" and Mestizaje theses of the Americas conjoin culture to race, and race to color, as a way of emphasizing hybridity as a feature of nation building, and the lessening of indigenous and African influences in national demography.

Hollinger is no biological determinist, so the most charitable explanation for his use and advocacy of race mixture as "amalgamation" is in the use of the term "race mixture" as a symbolic placeholder for the human bodies who are categorized and hierarchically ordered within the aforementioned classificatory schemes of color or phenotype. The organization of categories of people according to phenotype is the consequence of interpretive schemes, and, ultimately, hierarchies, of beauty and ugliness, safety and danger, dominance and subordination. Bodies categorized in such schemes can neither be the problem nor the solution to the epistemic and interpretive quandaries produced by "race mixture." They are merely cultural artifacts of an interpretive, taxonomic scheme that is itself a form of racial hierarchy, or, at the very least, the reification of the race concept. Only through reification is the race concept given an opportunity to legitimize itself; otherwise, amalgamation, miscegenation, indeed hybridity itself, is impossible. Rather than conceptualize race as something we see, race is presented as something that is seen,[23] already self-evident and inscribed on the bodies of individuals and groups. Only under these conditions is race mixture possible.

Several historians have engaged Hollinger's thesis. Thomas Skidmore, Barbara Fields, and Henry Yu have already highlighted the exceptionalist, U.S.-centric logic and the lack of comparative perspective in Hollinger's attempt to craft a historiographic alternative to assimilationist and frontier paradigms.[24] The Americas, not just the United States, was the first postcolonial site of the modern world. As noted by Thomas Skidmore in his response to Hollinger's thesis, Brazilian society contains many of the same historical variables as the United States, namely, a slave regime, massive immigration, and an indigenous population. Brazil did not develop a law of hypodescent as a means of racial distinction and categorization, but it is nonetheless a society of vast social inequality, much of which can be correlated with racial and color classification. Viewed in a more hemispheric perspective, what links Latin American racial ideologies and categories to their counterparts in most of the New World is that "race-mixture" involving African and indigenous peoples and their descendents was subject to the utmost, almost taxonomic classification while European progeny did not undergo the same level of scrutiny. All of the New World continua of racial and chromatic delineation, move away from blackness and toward whiteness.

The greatest interpretive consequence of the amalgamation thesis as currently formulated is that what actually requires interrogation, the race concept and its material, cultural and political implications, is largely ignored.[25] Barbara Fields, Howard Winant, and other scholars of U.S. history and society have encouraged us to think beyond the now mantralike invocation of race as "a social construction" in order to consider social constructivism as an advance from biologically determinist explanation, but little else. In dialogue with Hollinger, Fields cautions us to remember that "identifying race as a social construction does nothing to solidify the intellectual ground on which it totters. The London Underground and the United States are social constructions, so are the evil eye and the calling of spirits from the vast deep, and so are murder and genocide. All derive from the thoughts, plans, and actions of human beings living in human societies."[26] The largely sociological account under critique assumes the stability of the race concept as a sociological category, without considering its malleability or modes of deployment in social relations or politics.

The implications of the race concept thus appear as self-evident (I'm white, you're black, he's yellow). Gilroy's succinct description of the race concept as a conduit between meaning and social structure[27] allows us to track the race concept's invocations and effects. Utilizing the definitions of micro- and macropolitics developed in chapter 1, issues pertaining to heterosexual domesticity, sexual relations, and marriage are generally classified as "private sphere" issues. Certain qualifications have evolved to socialize or publicize some aspects of the sexual and cohabitational relations between men and women, such as age requirements for marriage in order to protect children, and domestic abuse laws designed to protect people (mostly women) from physical abuse in marriage or common-law relations. The demands of capitalism and bourgeois respectability upon the middle and laboring classes also brought a range of pressures to bear on formal or common-law domestic/family unions (Fordism is one obvious example).[28] Yet for those who either supported or accepted these unions as normative, domesticity could be practiced as a facet of private life.

For those whose activities contravened state and economic norms imposed on domestic unions, whether through homosexual unions,[29] marital infidelity, too many or too few children, relations between minors and adults, or finally, "mixed race" pairings, the state could and often did intervene into the private lives of these individuals and families, since their activities were understood to have the effect of flouting (publicly or privately) state and economic normativity around the institution of the family. In this sense, individual, private matters of sexual desire and preference, when melded with processes of racial hierarchy, are treated as a matter of state. In most socities the ideas and practices associated with race mixture and hybridity are constituted by a combination of macropolitics, norms, and economy.

III Hybridity, Race, and Culture

Garnet's dictum about the West's destiny as a mixed race serves as a reminder that color and race are at root conceptual presuppositions, not ready-made realities we encounter in the world. Color may serve to disrupt the correlation between phenotype and race, but color classification is nonetheless the schematic offspring of racial classification. Color is not a more "accurate" characterization of the human distinctions normally attributed to race, but a variation on a process of cognitive classification of human beings based on interpretive schemes of visual apprehension and perception. The fact that one person's mulatto in Haiti or Brazil would be another person's black in the United States or half-caste in Ghana highlights the arbitrariness of both chromatic and putatively racial classification. Both classification schemes serve as hegemonic ascriptive devices that crowd out other forms of ascription when applied to group dynamics: nation, village, family, neighborhood. Both contain evaluative criteria for associating the "race" or "color" of an individual or group with status and power. Put another way, we can ask why both race and color are preeminent schemes of classification in a world of countless modes of classification.

Having addressed the interpretive and normative limitations of theories of amalgamation, race mixture, and miscegenation that are reliant on a reified application of the race concept, what then of culture and its conceptual possibilities—not only for shifting our interpretive focus to the more "real" or authentic basis of human encounters and syntheses, but also serving as a tool that might aid in the obliteration of racial hierarchy? In the twentieth century, the culture concept supplanted race as the dominant explanatory schema for interpreting and identifying human differentiation. Cultural distinction gained priority and scientific legitimacy over pseudo-ontological mappings of differentiation among human beings according to species and subspecies distinction. Yet the culture concept's rupture with the race concept has not been complete. Many Latin American intellectuals, and the nation-states who championed their visions of mestizaje, cosmic races, and racial democracy, retained the race concept within a theory or cosmology of national culture. This would serve to mutate the culture concept, by attaching the meaning of cultural distinction to specific bodies already categorized by race. The term "hybridity" has subsequently been used to describe both race mixture and cultural synthesis. As a consequence, the very concept of culture has become distorted. Its distortions are apparent in the advocacy of the concept of cultural hybridity as something special and apart from the concept and process of culture itself.

IV Empire and Hybridity

As a concept, hybridity has garnered increasing use in the literatures of postcolonialism, postmodernism, and cultural studies. Yet how modern or recent is the phenomenon of hybridity? There is much historical and archaeological evidence to suggest that hybridity is not a new phenomenon among human beings, and is as ancient as human encounters across territorial and oceanic divides. As my account of the city of Pozzuole below demonstrates, geography, trade and commerce, and technologies of communication and transportation have long been the most important variables in the frequency of cultural contact and synthesis.

The recently unearthed Greek city of Puteolis (now Pozzuole) in what is now Naples, Italy, reminds us of the context in which processes of presumed hybridity and race mixture take place. Port cities have historically provided the greatest opportunity for transoceanic and transterritorial encounters between diverse sectors of the human race, influencing the formation of new modes of cuisine, design, architecture, warfare, and related techniques and technologies, not to mention human beings themselves. By 194 BC, it was a militarily and commercially strategic site to defend Roman control over the western Mediterranean, Puteolis became the most important harbor of the empire, providing the capital with wheat from Egypt and luxury items (fabrics, dyes, perfumes, lotions, fine ceramics) from Arabia and India. Intense commercial activity soon transformed the colony into an international city with merchants, soldiers, sailors, and slaves from Egypt, Syria, Nabataean Arabia, Microasia, Phoenicia, and Cappadoxia. Evidence of this presence is found in many archeological pieces as well as in the writing of distinguished Roman intellectuals such as Cicero and Pliny the Elder. The city's walls bear inscriptions in numerous languages. Its temples contained documents and images of religious cults founded in central Asia, Syria, and Egypt. The *tabernae* of Puteolis (its Latin name) provided hot meals, wine, gambling as well as "musical shows accompanied by female dancers mostly of oriental origins, or by girls usually provided by the owner."[30] The city itself was built on the acropolis, the highest site in the area, as a fortification against a possible invasion by Hannibal's army.

The Roman presence could certainly be characterized as a form of colonization. The cultural and linguistic practices of its inhabitants and visitors helped create new modes of speaking, eating, religious observance, architecture, design, cuisine that would, in turn, inform subsequent generations of Neapolitan society and peoples. With subsequent contact with the Moors, the Spanish, and the French in later years, the city could be said to be both multicultural and hybrid, insofar as it contained several representative clusters of people from distinct parts of the world. The key qualifying question, however, is what brought these populations together? Was it the desire for cultural interface or was cultural contact, incorporation, and transformation a by-product of other processes? This is not to suggest that trade, conquest, enslavement, and commerce are devoid of cross-cultural significance, but that cultural encounters were one set of *outcomes,* not the motivating factors of human synergy, mediated and facilitated by technology (ships and armaments), commerce (trade), and the right doses of brutality. Without these three facets, the cultural encounter described above is historically and anthropologically inconceivable. Pozzuole serves as an important reminder for those who would treat hybridity as a separate phenomenon from the ones that bought hybridity into being.

Anthropologists have worried over the distinction between hybridity and cultural processes[31] in order to remind their colleagues of the contested nature of the culture concept and its interminable elusiveness. Most anthropologists define cultural practice as a process, not a static entity, with multiple influences internal and external to itself. Under this epistemic regime, cultural practice *is* hybridity. If culture is indeed a process of synthesis, accommodation, fusion, and bricolage, then what is so special about the concept of hybridity? Indeed, it is important to remind ourselves that the very term "hybridity" is an anthropological as well as biological concept, not a human activity, which highlights its metadiscursive quality. Its more recent invocation represents another attempt to decouple culture from race, as a means of escaping the dreaded "racial reasoning." Without a prior notion of cultural or racial distinction, the concept of hybridity would be nonsensical. Viewed in this manner, the concept of hybridity serves to mark difference, not obliterate it.

In contemporary discussion of the themes of miscegenation, hybridity, and multiculturalism, there is a tendency to isolate the cultural encounter from the aforementioned factors and subsequently elevate miscegenation and hybridity to the status of independent, stand-alone phenomena. It is assumed that the synergies created by the interface between representative figures of cultural distinction are the engine for economic exchange and growth, improved racial, class, and gender relations, and even "democracy." Culture, treated as a sort of human engine of internal combustion to be turned on and off, is seen as removed from society, rather than itself being constituted by actual social, political, and economic relations. Thus, hybridity can mean any number of things—an antidote, the social and civilizational equivalent of cod liver oil, or, alternatively, a toxin. The Nazis sought to manage racial type through rigid albeit contradictory classification. The Lusotropicalists encouraged miscegenation to create new classifications, and ultimately, a new nation. British colonial projects in India and Africa, for example, forged different elements of Indian and African traditions to create hegemonic modes of symbolic, institutional congruence between British rulers and some indigenous leaders.[32] Hybridity helped mark the borders of difference between colonizer and colonized, and was often utilized by colonial regimes to further fragment colonial societies, creating favored groups based on proximity to power, but claimed on the basis of blood. Distinct colonial trajectories produced different "postcolonial" eras and hybrid forms. So did the imperial demand for cheap, often free colonial labor. The doogla of Trinidad, the product of East Indian and African-descended laborers, and Afro-Chinese Jamaicans are just two of many examples throughout the world of the human contact and variation brought about by the wheels of migration and capture. Like politics, economics brings those together who would not otherwise meet. The necessities of capitalist and imperialist labor produced and preceded transregional cultural contacts and transformations.

Hybridity in substantive content, even if not named as such, has emerged at different times and places roughly correlated with different forms and eras of colonization throughout the world. Latin American debates about the implications of miscegenation for emergent nation-states began as early as the sixteenth century.[33] European debates over the presence of nonwhites in their midst intensified in the 1960s, during their epoch of postcoloniality and long after European nations had been founded. The U.S. preoccupation with hybridity resurfaced after U.S. apartheid and after the United States had been established as the dominant hegemon in the world. This points to the need for situating processes of "mixed raced-ness" within broader landscapes of emergent or decadent imperialisms, monocultural, slave-based, or nominally capitalist economies and culturally homogeneous or plural societies. These factors influence how "hybridity" is defined, since its definition is determined in large part by what a hybrid form is defined against (or in relation to).

Within the crucible of colonial conquest, racial classification and delineation converged with several modes of forced labor, such as Indian and Chinese indentured labor in Trinidad, Jamaica, and Guyana, and various forms of coerced labor regimes imposed upon indigenous peoples. Colonial regimes could be further distinguished in terms of absentee and settler colonies, types of commodities produced, forces of production (the cotton gin, Taylorism, sharecropping), as well as modes of enslavement, and, finally, by different types colonial adminisration. The religious and cultural idiosyncrasies of particular colonizing regimes help to further distinguish colonial schemes of racial and chromatic classification and maintenance.

V Curros versus the Single Origin Thesis: National and Transnational Modes of Racist Hierarchy

As the first postcolonial region of the modern world, the Americas also provide the first opportunity to examine distinctions between colonial and postcolonial forms of phenotypic and chromatic distinction. There would be at least three ways of proceeding to map out a regional examination of these distinctions: by country, colonial spheres of influence (Iberian, Anglophone, Dutch), or by subregion (Andean, Caribbean, North American). Recent historiography of "race relations" and the nexus of racial and national formation in Latin America has emphasized local variation and difference as a means of problematizing models that use chromatic variations to distinguish between bipolar and multipolar racial or chromatically based forms of social distinction. The focus on the national and the local, while certainly in a prima facie sense an obvious way of exploring power relations in national and cross-national perspective, has often obscured what I refer to as the hemispheric template of racial distinction, its origins and variations. A more hemispheric approach to understanding both chromatic and racial distinctions can allow us to trace the relationship between empire and state, and religion and colony, in the formation of ideologies and practices of human classification based on phenotype distinction that local or national approaches cannot. Analyses that focus exclusively on the national dimensions of chromatic and racial hierarchy, often lead to the methodological and interpretive dangers inherent in what I shall call "single origin" theories of racist discourse and practice, wherein a particular phenomenon of racism is associated with the most visible, easily identifiable place that it occurs, rather than with the characteristics, analytic properties, and patterns that allow for abstraction, and, ultimately, assessment and comparison.

The influence of the "single origin" thesis of racialization is evident in Alejandro de la Fuente's *A Nation for All: Race, Inequality and Politics in Twentieth Century Cuba*. A rich book in many ways, de la Fuente's text chronicles the ambiguities of Cuban nationalist discourse on race, the intersections between racial and national formation, and the emergence of an Afro-Cuban petit bourgeoisie whose claims as both an aspirant class and an oppressed population brought forth tensions and contradictions in notions of national and racial allegiance among Cubans. I shall focus on only two particular features of de la Fuente's argument that are germane to my argument: the scope of comparative method and the phenomenon of racial ideological formation in the United States and Cuba. De la Fuente's methodology enables scholars to situate claims of national exceptionalism against a larger regional and genealogical backdrop.

I shall focus primarily on racial ideologies and their implications within nationalist ideologies, because a key element of Cuban nationalism is the articulation of the idea of racial inclusiveness. De la Fuente writes: "The rhetorical exaltation of racial inclusiveness as the very essence of nationhood has made racially defined exclusion considerably more difficult, creating in the process significant opportunities for appropriation and manipulation of dominant racial ideologies by those below by limiting the political options of the elites."[34] Thus, in de la Fuente's view, an ideology of racial inclusion within Cuban nationalist rhetoric does three key things: (1) limits possibilities for racial exclusivity; (2) provides opportunities for contestation by Afro-Cubans; and (3) limits the political opportunities of elites in their use of the language of racial distinction and discrimination.

De la Fuente places great emphasis on the fact that Cuban racial ideologies possess an "ambiguity" that presumably distinguishes them from other national racial ideologies, especially those in the United States. This, according to the author, led to the central ideological and practical political tension between the island's advocates of racial inclusion (whether white, mulatto, or black) and the advocates of racial segregation, Cuban as well as U.S.-based, who were influenced by scientific racisms brought to the island by the "American occupation forces."[35] In de la Fuente's account, like many other accounts of racisms in Latin American nation-states, the United States—not Latin America—is the anomaly.

Given the global and regional character of antiblack and other modes of racist ideologies during the early part of the twentieth century, one could ask if the U.S. occupation forces in Cuba brought the first wave of antiblack prejudice to the island. This is not an insignificant question, for the presumptions of de la Fuente's genealogy of Cuban antiblack racism suggests an almost complete absence of racist ideologies in Cuba prior to the U.S. occupation. If indeed there was a single source of antiblack, anti-African prejudices in Cuban society, particularly among the Cuban upper classes and elite, how does one explain that many of the instances of racial discrimination documented in his and other works[36] were undertaken not only by the Cuban elites, but in popular, nonelite sectors of society? If the rhetorical celebration of racial inclusion made racially defined exclusion considerably more difficult in Cuban society, how does one understand the presence of antiblack *Cuban* racism?

One possible explanation is that Cuban nationalism's popularity waned just before the appearance of U.S. racist ideologies and practices in Cuba, in the form of U.S. corporate and military presence on the island during the first three decades of the twentieth century. In an ideological struggle of sorts, U.S. racist ideologies won out over Cuban antiracist ideologies. But de la Fuente successfully demonstrates that at several critical points, Cuban nationalists of all classes during this period rejected the state-sanctioned racial discrimination of public spaces and institutions advocated by the U.S. government and business interests, and, ambiguities notwithstanding, rejected at least some elements of U.S. racial mores. Another, more plausible explanation, however, is that though distinct in form, certain elements of antiblack racism in Cuba overlapped significantly with some aspects of antiblack ideologies in the United States, through forms of antiblack racism in Cuba that preceded the U.S. occupation. As de la Fuente notes, calls for de-Africanization (the forced shedding of African-influenced religious and cultural practices) of the working-class Afro-Cuban population were prominent among both white and Afro-Cuban elites and middle classes, which would suggest both the rejection of U.S. racial ideologies, and the retention and continuation of antiblack racisms in Cuba, a claim that is consistent with de la Fuente's larger argument.

An "independent" strain of antiblack Cuban racism not attributable to the United States could be employed "on the ground," as it were, rather than at the level of the state, allowing Cuban elites and popular classes who harbored such sentiments to reject state- or corporate-sponsored racism, while harboring and, in certain instances, employing quotidian racism. There is ample evidence to suggest that the legacy of Spanish colonial antiblack racism permeated Cuban society in ways not acknowledged in de la Fuente's account.

Indeed, the one lacuna in his account is the lack of recognition of antiblack racisms in Cuba not attributable to U.S. racism. The Spanish colonial criminal code, which has racially based articles, survived well into the republic.[37] In Fanonian terms, neither scriptural racism, which affected all the Catholic colonies, nor colonial racism is given much attention in de la Fuente's account.

The combined efforts of the Spanish crown and the Catholic Church influenced the development of a distinctly Cuban version of Negrophobia that, though not an obvious component of nationalist rhetoric and ideology in the late nineteenth century, was certainly present and pervasive in national and local culture in Latin America. As Leslie Rout and others have pointed out, anti-Semitism and antiblack racism were conjoined during and after the process of the *reconquista* in images of the African and the Jew as unincorporated, recalcitrant populations that must be expelled from Spain to protect Christianity, and European territory and civilization, *in the name of all of Europe*.[38]

As Étienne Balibar notes, the reconquest was indispensable to the adoption of Catholicism as a state religion. The roots of the preoccupation with purity of blood (*pureza de sangre*) are found in the expulsion of Moors and Jews from Spain, a legacy that "the whole discourse of European and American racism was to inherit: a product of the disavowal of the original interbreeding with the Moors and with the Jews, the hereditary definition of the *raza* serves in effect both to isolate an internal aristocracy and to confer upon the whole of the 'Spanish People' a fictive nobility, to make it 'a people of masters' at a point when, by terror, genocide, slavery and enforced Christianization, it was conquering and dominating the largest of the colonial empires."[39]

Thus, internationalized anti-Jewish and antiblack discourses were first disseminated by imperial and religious rhetoric of Europe before becoming part of national and state rhetoric in Europe and, subsequently, Latin America. The inheritors of this very European legacy in the New World were criollo elites and those who developed national and Pan-American allegiances with them, whether Bolívar, Vasconcelos, Mariátegui, or Martí. National racisms, then, were informed in part by the nation's—and even earlier, the colony's—imperial past. The linkage between race and religion, as a means of distinguishing citizens and subjects, nationals and foreigners, is critical to understanding how racially and religiously chauvinistic discourses assume first imperial, then colonial, transnational, and, ultimately, national form. It would be remarkable if the descendents of the Spanish in Cuba, particularly the first-generation *criollos,* escaped this legacy.

Fernando Ortiz, the Cuban doctor and amateur student of criminology who produced several works concerning the cultural origins of Afro-Cuban cultural practices ranging from Abakuá to Santería, also traced the origins of cultural, social, and ethnic distinction among Afro-Cubans, working back, as it were, from the alleged preponderance of criminality among certain sectors of Afro-Cuban urban dwellers, especially in Havana, in order to understand the triangulation of ethnicity, urbanization, and social behavior among poor Cubans. Even with the tendency to correlate propensities toward aberrant and antisocial behavior with the poor and darker skinned, Ortiz paid a great deal of attention to the confluences and clashes between colonial political culture and national political culture. Though reliant at times on dubious sources, Ortiz's interpretations of Afro-Cubans allow us an opportunity to view Afro-Cubans not only in terms of racial politics but also as the mediating symbols between colonial and national identity, existing symbolically between colonial and national constructions of blackness. Ortiz's *Los Negros Curros*, an unfinished, posthumously published work on a segment of the Afro-Cuban population in La Habana commonly referred to as *curro* or *curra*, provides clues to the iconic role of Afro-Cubans as mediating symbols of colonial and national representation. The origin of the term, as Ortiz details, is Andalucían, referring at once to free blacks and mulattos from Sevilla who were transported to Havana, along with enslaved Africans, in the first three decades of the sixteenth century, as well as Andalucians of any color. The word *curro* was the shortened form of a very common surname in Andalucia, and according to Ortiz's hypothesis, had several equivalences and overlaps with other, adjectival words used to characterize the behaviors of Andalucians in general and *negros curros* in particular.

What concerns me are the particular meanings associated with *negros curros* in Sevilla and La Habana. The distinctions between *cheches*, *ñáñigos*, and *curros* are subtly captured in Ortiz's account. At one point, Ortiz chastises Martín Moruá Delgado, a black Cuban senator, for claiming that *ñáñigo* fraternal associations were supported by criollo Afro-Cubans like *los curros*,[40] highlighting Delgado's ignorance of the distinction between the two. In Sevilla and Havana alike, *negros curros* and *curras* were characterized as ostentatious, loyal, often courageous, and also killers (*matante*), a word introduced in Castillan Spanish by Cervantes, according to Ortiz, and thus distinguished from *curros blancos* as well as other *habaneros*. The words associated and often used to describe *los curros* were *chulo, pícaro, rufián, majo,* and *matante,* among other terms. There were other adjectives used to describe *los curros*: vainglorious, noble, courageous. All were applied to those at the margins of Sevillan and Havana society respectively—a population with a specific material, cultural, and social status—in order to characterize their behavior as a group, internal variation and individual distinction notwithstanding.

The resonance of the category of *curro*, however, and its ambivalent associations, extended beyond Cuba. The term *"curro"* appeared in Haiti, Jamaica, and several other Caribbean locales once colonized by the Spanish. To cite just one example, *curro* was often used in Jamaica at least until the 1960s to refer to unruly, fierce blacks. According to the *Dictionary of Jamaican English*, the term *"kurro"* in Jamaican English may have West African origins. In Brazilian Portuguese, the secondary definition for the term *"curro"* is slave quarters.[41]

Such transfers of racial meaning and signification from empire and nation-state to colony and subsequent republic help to convey a larger point often ignored by Latin Americanists about the presence and permutation of racist categorization in the region. The United States, Jamaica, Trinidad and Tobago, Montserrat, Haiti, and the Dominican Republic, St. Martin/Puerto Rico, among others, had more than one imperial power claiming propriety over their territorial dominion, mostly at different moments in colonial history and competition but, in some instances, simultaneously, as in the case of Haiti, and, briefly, the United States. Thus, it is no mere coincidence that a formally British colony would have Spanish terms in its variations of English, or that in certain parts of the United States French *and* Spanish terminologies for racial and ethnic groups would become part of U.S. English. Viewed in terms of this particular trajectory of racial formation in the New World, the distinctions between nation-states become as blurred as those between colonies and their imperial influences. Ideas about African-descended peoples, the free and the unfree, traveled within and between colonies and nation-states, influencing emergent national cultures.

Once encased in nationalist ideologies professing freedom, liberty, fraternity, rights, and republican ideals, ambivalent or outright racist attitudes toward Afro-Cubans could—and did—persist, even if they did not assume state life in the form of legislated segregation. De la Fuente's emphasis on formal rather than informal modes of racial segregation obscures a more general point about antiblack racisms in Cuba. Racist national-state legislation is not a prerequisite of racism. In the New World, antiblack racisms made their first appearance in colonial regimes and ecclesiastic discourses, not in the civil societies of nation-states. In Cuba as well as in other New World societies, racist taxonomies, chromatic and Manichean, preceded the development of the nationally independent state, structured, in part, by the colonial and religious justifications for racist subordination. The rhetoric of racial egalitarianism present in many nationalist ideologies in Latin America did not eradicate these prior racist meanings and categorizations. Nor did they preclude the creation of nation-specific racisms even as they confronted and refused racist ideologies from other nation-states, such as the United States.

Forms of antiblack racisms under Spanish colonial rule did indeed differ from antiblack racism of Anglo-Saxon colonial rule, but they shared at least one commonality. Due to the legacies of anti-African racisms during the period of Western expansion into the Americas, former colonies that became nation-states have had national and *extra*national racist discourses and practices coexist. The transnational ideological congruence among the vast majority of European nation-states and elites with respect to African-descended peoples (not to mention Asian and indigenous peoples of the New World and Australasia) existed despite differences in religion, modes and philosophies of governance, and direct and indirect rule. There is a book remaining to be written that does for the eighteenth and nineteenth century Western state-generated racist discourses what Anthony Pagden's *Lords of All the World*[42] does for the sixteenth and seventeenth centuries, namely, provide an ethnography of elite and ecclesiastic discourses of the West's transnational imperial powers. The response of Britain, the United States, and other Western powers to the Haitian Revolution, which was seen by the major Western powers as a threat to *their* own forms of colonial domination and ideas about the inherent inferiority of slaves, and not just a catastrophic defeat for the French Empire, provides some indication of the racist dimension of a specifically transnational European identification in the eighteenth and nineteenth centuries.[43]

Unfortunately, the paucity of Cuban slave narratives and autobiographies of former slaves and free Afro-Cubans after abolition limits the documentary record of Afro-Cuban experiences with Cuban and Spanish racisms before the U.S. occupation. Common to the Spanish and Cuban experience is the process of racialization of African subjects: the Muslim Moor became the African, and the African grew into the black, while aforementioned Africans of various nationalities became *negros* and Afro-Cubanos. The negation of variation and difference is one of the consequences of racial characterization.[44]

Novels as well as newspaper accounts in the Afro-Cuban press (amply used by de la Fuente) provide some evidence of quotidian racism. The distance between, on the one hand, the ambivalent characterizations of *curros* and the more blatantly negative depictions of *ñáñigos* and *mambises* in the nineteenth century, and, on the other, the real-life scenarios of everyday racism in twentieth-century Cuba does not take a significant leap of imagination. The *curro* who is assumed to be a ruffian and is denied work by a *criollo* shopkeeper, the *curra* who is perceived to be a woman of easy virtue, and the young *curro* male who is deemed potentially violent by an early twentieth-century Havana police officer are the endpoints of discriminatory logics that arise from the convergence of colonial, imperial, and national racist stereotype. The very malleability of putatively racial categories allows for many different populations to be fitted with the thorned crown of racist association, symbolism, and iconography. The normative matrix of racism becomes inscribed in the cultural, as well as legal-juridical, spatial, social, and economic features of postcolonial existence, and becomes part of a larger legacy of antiblack racism.

It is not surprising, then, to find "residual" elements of de-Africanization tendencies among the revolutionary elite well after 1959, the year of the revolution. Afro-Cuban religious and cultural practices such as Abakuá and various cleansing and initiation rituals associated with Santería were denounced as the "focus of criminality and juvenile delinquency" by Afro-Cubans. (I once witnessed in Santiago, during the weeklong celebration of Afro-Cuban culture in 1988, a local governmental official decry the bloodletting of a goat in preparation for cooking: "The next step for *these* people are human beings.")[45] From the state-sponsored to the individually idiosyncratic, attitudes of revulsion toward certain Afro-Cuban cultural forms and practitioners cannot automatically be attributed to U.S. state intervention, especially when the opinions and policies expressed do not advocate formal segregation of any sort, but rather cultural repression. This particular genealogy of racial meaning traverses Spanish, Cuban colonial and republican, and Cuban Marxist models of societal organization, thereby limiting the explanatory power of an analysis of racism solely based on the presence or absence of state intervention. This particular genealogy reveals what is distinctly Cuban about certain forms of cultural antipathy toward specific Afro-Cuban populations and against Afro-Cubans as a group.

This leads more broadly to matters of ideology, and de la Fuente's claims about the role of nationalist rhetoric in limiting the impact and pervasiveness of institutionalized racism in twentieth-century Cuba. My difficulty with this assertion is not only based upon an interpretation of historical evidence of different, noninstitutionalized forms of antiblack prejudice throughout the period but also on a more complicated account of how ideologies emanate from and feed back into daily social, political, and cultural practices. The idea that ideologies of any form "work" in society in an unmediated fashion, as asserted by de la Fuente, runs counter to the overwhelming majority of studies of ideologies and their effects on mass populations in a host of societies.[46]

Ideological formations utilized by various regime types *justify, explain, and influence certain political and cultural behaviors, but do not determine them* (for a more elaborate discussion of ideology, see chapter 3). In terms of racial politics, apartheid, segregationist regimes, and their attendant ideological justifications did not preclude the development of antisegregationist and antiapartheid movements in the United States and South Africa. Rarely are nationalist ideologies accurate, objectively informed accounts of societal practices; they are instead idealized versions of what a national society could or should resemble. De la Fuente's argument effectively *congratulates* Cuban national ideology for providing limits to its own articulation, as if ideologies, whether by design or unwitting consequence, ever create their own limitations.

I raise this point and the accompanying examples to guide readers to the unintended consequences of de la Fuente's assertions concerning the comparative benefits of the racially egalitarian components of Cuban nationalist rhetoric. De la Fuente credits Cuban nationalist ideologies with providing collective political and economic opportunities, which they did not, on their own, provide. For example, Joséí Martí's pronouncements concerning a multiracial ideal in Cuba are a projection of an individual ideal that became, through propaganda, nationalized, without ever being implemented in the economy and polity. Vera Kutzninski writes that Martí's "high minded, well-intentioned words, designed to soften the racial differences that threatened to divide Cuba and other budding Hispanic American nations at a crucial stage in their respective histories"[47] constitute a series of "evasive maneuvers his writings perform particularly around racial issues."[48]

Cuba's seemingly paradoxical history of the acceptance of symbols of Afro-Cubana in cultural practice, combined with the denial and repression of Afro-Cubans in politics, economics, and society in the pre- and postrevolutionary periods provides an opportunity for comparativists to consider the hemispheric implications of racial ideologies in Latin America, particularly in their sometimes tempestuous, otherwise pacific, marriage to nationalist discourses. The constant comparison with the United States, in my view, reinforces the preoccupation with the "colossus of the north." The comparison of antiblack, anti-indigenous and other forms of racism within the region will undoubtedly yield both similarities and distinctions in the forms and modes of antiblack sentiments and violence.

VI Hybridity, Mestizaje, and the Politics of Pluralism

In an essay entitled, "Racial Histories and Their Regimes of Truth,"[49] Ann Laura Stoler suggests that hybridization may not be the sort of trenchant postmodern critique of modernity many of its advocates make it out to be. If we disabuse the term of its eugenicist, biologically rooted connotations, it can perhaps be claimed that hybridity, the joining of distinct parts to create new forms, can be found in most phases of human interaction.[50] What I would like to emphasize here are the interrelated forms, phenomena, and processes that lead to multiple hybridities, and not just of the "racial" or "cultural" varieties. Colonialism, conquest, and trade helped generate what Mary Louise Pratt has termed "contact zones," sites where populations of distinct economic, social, and cultural status are compelled to interact.[51] This is as true of Europe's imperial expansion into the Americas, Asia, and Africa, as it is true for the imperial incursions of the Oyo, Tsarist, and Ottoman empires into the territories and spaces of people who were eventually made subordinate to imperial aims. As suggested above with the Pozzuole example, contact zones provide multiple opportunities for interaction, not always positive and certainly not unilinear.

Melting pot and hybridity models share at least one common feature, however—a unilinear trajectory of human interaction from initial conflict to harmony, which distinguish them from miscegenation taboos and prohibitions.[52] Thus, miscegenation and related concepts of hybridity and multiculturalism are actually metadiscourses (forms of discursive manufacture that, as I have noted at the outset of the chapter, require examination). These categorizations name what is a fairly common occurrence across civilizations, regions, cultures, and histories—the sharing and absorption of patterns of behavior, customs, traditions, artifacts, and technologies among distinct human populations. As I argued in chapter 4, even under the most seemingly constrained circumstances—slavery and segregation—assimilation of difference is a feature and outcome of human social interaction. What is important about miscegenation, hybridity, and multiculturalism, then, is not the fact of their occurrence, but the context in which they emerge: Do these processes occur within dynamics of inequality or equality?

The concept of pluralism has broad implications for considering politics and culture as distinct but invariably related modalities of human social and normative/ideational fluidity. In its political denotation, pluralism implies the multiplicity and coexistence of competing political beliefs and interests, the opposite of totalitarianism; open, transparent competition among ideologies, political parties, and other organizational sources of belief systems. Political pluralism has been seen as fundamental to the formation and maintenance of a liberal democratic polity.

In the realm of culture, a societal condition of pluralism is characterized by the existence of culturally discrete groups whose distinctions, over time, are mediated (though not necessarily overcome) by the common meanings that are produced from their interactions. These new meanings serve to undermine the idea of cultural practice and form that are bounded, sealed off within the categories of race, class, religion, or ethnicity. Differences can only be maintained through their institutionalization, whether by the state, the economy, or organizations designed to preserve and protect what have been deemed "sacred" cultural practices. John Furnivall, the father of the idea of pluralism, posited that plural societies are marked by the absence of cultural commonality, wherein the only commonality among the differentiated groups is the marketplace, the site of commodities, trade, consumers, and producers. Otherwise, groups in plural societies practice a form of aversion (see chapter 4), which Ivar Oxaal, in his classic study of Trinidad, referred to as selective affinity or disassociation.[53]

Ironically, the cultural denotation of pluralism is thus less normatively tainted than the political denotation of pluralism. Cultural pluralism, unlike political pluralism, is not considered inherently democratic. Most applications of the concept of cultural pluralism focus on colonial and postcolonial societies as prehybrid or protohybrid societies, places of multiple distinctions without cultural mixture.[54] Part of the normative underpinning of political pluralism is the assumption that a political culture of democratic pluralism will lead to a national cultural pluralism. Unfortunately, there have been few instances of societies where cultural pluralism begat democratic pluralism, or vice versa. A highly restrictive form of democratic political culture emerged in the thirteen colonies that became the United States without any immediate consequences for the prospect of incorporation of non-Europeans into mainstream political culture for nearly two centuries. In Brazil, ideologies of cultural pluralism and *mestiçagem* long preceded liberal or popular democratic rule.

Political pluralism and democratic participation has been conflated with the definition of cultural pluralism, called multiculturalism, in debates in the United States and now in many other nation-states of the Americas. As a consequence, many advocates of multiculturalism, in their desire to banish once and for all the concept of race, ignore politics. In this sense, the two distinct meanings of pluralism have been fused, without, however, interrogating the macropolitical implications of this fusion.[55]

The distinction between cultural and political pluralism can enable us to avoid some of the blurred, conflated explanations for what are essentially two distinct phenomena. Indonesia, for example, with its ethnonational groups such as Javanese, Sundanese, Madurese, and many others, as well as religious adherents such as practicing Muslims, Protestants, Roman Catholics, Hindus, and Buddhists could not be said to be more egalitarian or democratically plural because of its myriad forms of human diversity.[56] Similarly, India and Nigeria, to take two very different cases, have very complicated overlays of ethnic and phenotypic categorization. The presence of multiple ethnic categories in both societies could not be positively correlated with democratic or democratizing rule. If this were true, then these polities would have been more democratic quite a while ago. The point here is that there are culturally plural societies that are not politically plural.

Racial differentiation, hierarchy, and solidarity are interrelated yet distinct processes for identifying and mobilizing human and institutional resources. Plural societies with multiple ethnic, religious, and racial groups typically make distinctions involving forms of differentiation, hierarchy, and solidarity without necessarily succumbing to racism. This is not to suggest that members of minority groups in such societies cannot exhibit racist behavior, but that analytically it is important to distinguish groups and individuals who engage in activities designed to impugn, injure, and restrict the movement and access of certain groups in society from those who engage in activities, often defensive and reactive, to limit the injuries and restrictions imposed upon them by dominant groups and institutions. If we are to understand valuation within a process of racial and chromatic distinction, we must examine the multiple, varied, and unstable dispositions among political and cultural actors and organizations represented, at least in part, by racial description and designation.

What are the attributes associated with various groups? What are the meanings attributed to their body types and practices?[57]

Nevertheless, the examination of racial and chromatic differentiation provide an opportunity to consider the tensions between cultural and political pluralism. In the case of the United States, or Brazil, or France, for example, contradictions between commitments to republicanism and liberal democracy, on the one hand, and apartheid and racial inequality on the other are manifested in racial valuation. In this sense, civil rights struggles and movements can be interpreted as a struggle for the symmetry of cultural and political pluralism.

It is not coincidental that national societies such as those of Cuba, Brazil, and France, each with very specific national configurations of racial, chromatic or ethnonational hierarchies, have not had, until recently, state-mandated legislation and policies to address racial discrimination. In each national society, cultural pluralism, and in the French case, republicanism, made juridical normative sanctions against racism appear redundant and unnecessary, at least according to national elites and the majority of national populations. Cultural pluralism thus was assumed to precede and inaugurate racial equality. Yet in each of these cases, as well as many others, political struggles for recognition by national minority or disempowered groups challenged the normative assumptions of the nation-state. In Cuba, short-lived Black Power and civil rights movements[58] and their repression by the Cuban state challenged Cuban exceptionalist ideologies. In Brazil, the black movement and other antiracist social movements have helped usher in an era of state-mandated antiracist practices. In France, white French racism toward North Africans, particularly Algerians, and many other African and nonwhite populations has prompted national debate about racial discrimination and inequality. In many national examples, neither cultural pluralism nor political pluralism has ensured nonhierarchical relations between phenotypically categorized groups. Only antiracist macropolitics that have sought to overturn racist meaning and practices at the level of the state, and society more generally, have produced changes in attitudes, behaviors, and law. Cultural and political pluralism, on their own, have not eradicated enmities and disassociation based on racial meaning.[59]

As distinctions between settler, colonial, and postcolonial societies become increasingly blurred, the literature on citizenship in diverse societies has increasing relevance for debates about hybridity, multiculturalism, and miscegenation. There should be an increasing dialogue between scholars in anthropology and political science concerning the cultural and political implications of pluralism, or the fact of difference in societies throughout the world.[60] A nation-state's decision to define a society as plural, multicultural, or hybrid is a description and categorization of human difference amidst extant hierarchies in a given social order. Scholars who study these states must first acknowledge the attendant political realities of racial valuation before proceeding to invoke hybridity as a cause for celebration.

VII Templates of Race and Lessons from Political Economy

A major aim of this chapter is to foreground the respective roles of material conditions and politics in the assessment of culture, hybridity, and miscegenation. Rather than viewing cultural processes and their subsets—creolization and hybridization—as either absolutely autonomous or wholly subsidiary phenomena, I have suggested that we designations of racial and cultural hybridity in a wider context.

This chapter also emphasizes the importance of a hemispheric perspective in the comparison of national ideologies of racial and chromatic variation. Such an approach admittedly tends toward what is often referred to as "grand theorizing." Among the valid criticisms of large-scale comparison is its tendency to diminish internal variation, contradiction, and anomalous cases, that complicate if not confound cross-spatial comparison. One of the consequences of the move away from grand theorizing, however, is the neglect of the interconnectedness between forms of racial valuation and racist ideologies across multiple sites.

There is actually little scholarship focusing on the global effects of antiblack racism. The challenge posed by Garnet's exhortations for present-day scholars is to attempt to comprehend the continuing, transnational implications of antiblack racisms. Most scholarship focuses on single nation-states, regions, or even towns, and then attempts (or not) to situate a particular site of racial politics within the context of a larger whole. One of the consequences of these "midrange" or small-scale approaches, however, is the methodological tendency to move from seemingly endogenous forms (town, region, or nation) to exogenous forms (two or three country comparisons). With this methodological proclivity, the congruence of racial ideologies and formations across regions and nation-states is obscured or neglected outright, as nation-states are compared to one another as relatively isolated, discrete entities. The almost obsessive focus on the national and local to underscore the difference and distinction between one national context and another minimizes the important—and prior—transnational reach of colonial racisms.

Claims of interdisciplinarity notwithstanding, much contemporary writing on racial politics tends to treat national-state distinction as *determinant* and causal in its relation to a particular country's national culture and history, rendering certain comparisons untenable. The more hemispheric approaches of Peter Wade and Charles Hale[61] in the examination of ideologies of race mixture and mestizaje have encouraged cross-national comparison that debunks one of the shibboleths of Pan-Americanist Latin American discourses, namely, that race mixture and mestizaje lead to more egalitarian social orders. More exhaustive forms of comparative analysis could potentially yield cross-national parallels within the region by first acknowledging the hemispheric legacies of colonial racisms.

Few contemporary scholars have taken up or addressed a theme first posed by Rout in *The African Experience in Spanish America*: "The equation of dark skin with debased labor may be the greatest crime committed upon African peoples."[62] The methodological and interpretive implications of Rout's assertion are manifold, yet few scholars have undertaken the significance of Rout's declaration for African-descended peoples hemispherically. In addition to the equation between phenotype and debased labor, what are some of the other legacies of antiblack racisms? How should scholars compare the legacies of antiblack racisms cross-nationally?

One antidote to this tendency is to return to some of the positive and clarifying aspects of large-scale comparison, especially those approaches that enable us to track the distinction and variation of specific material or ideological phenomena and their interrelationship with various political systems, institutions, cultures, and civilizations. Studies of plantation economies, for example, provide an opportunity to understand the idiosyncrasies and distinguishing characteristics of specific plantation economies, while at the same time remaining mindful of a larger imperial political economy and its imperatives of profit and enslaved labor across different colonial spaces. For example, a student of plantation economies would not be deterred from cross-spatial comparison because the United States' political economy of sugar and cotton production was distinct from Colombia's, or Guyana's from Cuba's. Certainly the processing of sugar on the banks of the Demerara River[63] was distinct from sugar production in Cuba, but what were their commonalities? Despite distinctions in modalities of enslavement among the major Western powers, slavery under *any* colonial regime inhibited the range of movement and exercise of something called "individual rights" among slaves in *every* European colony.[64]

What all plantation economies held in common was the intention and practice of commodity production, utilizing slave labor. I am not suggesting that a return to the methodologies of cross-spatial political economy will provide answers to questions concerning the ongoing political and material legacies of racial valuation. What I am suggesting is that scholars might be better able to comprehend both the distinctive and intertwined ideologies of racial formation and signification by obtaining greater clarity in the identification of what is and is not purely or peculiarly *national* about racial and racist ideologies.

One challenge for students of racial politics, racist ideology, and ideologies emphasizing race mixture is to comprehend racial ideologies at the level of *meaning*, and relate the production of racial meaning to daily life. This understanding will enable scholars to trace racial meanings from ideas (stereotypes) to institutionalization in state bureaucracies, popular culture, mass media, and labor markets, thus treating racial meaning as a conduit between meaning (ideas and their definitions) and social structure. Racial ideologies provide the parameters of social structure that, when enacted in bureaucracies and social relations, limit certain forms of social and cultural interaction. Which communities require more intense policing and surveillance? What people are depicted as being more prone or susceptible to violence? Which women and men are perceived as more promiscuous? These are not abstract questions in many societies, but queries informed by racial valuation and meaning in countries as diverse as Cuba, Venezuela, Argentina, Colombia, Mexico, and the United States. Responses to these questions according to racist logics inform the role of the police and army, social mores, expectations and sanctions, and employment patterns and prospects, as well as public policy and social services.

Renewed attention to racial meanings can remind us of the influence and diffusion of racist ideologies in ways that more institutionalist, materialist, and nation-based analyses of race and ethnicity cannot. Racial categories on their own only provide part of the story. Categories neither "prove" nor "disprove" the existence of inequalities and prejudices according to racial ascription, nor do they provide any sense of how societies have shifted in their attitudes about specific groups. For example, antiblack prejudice can thrive even in national contexts where so-called blacks were either minimal or nonexistent, such as eighteenth- and nineteenth-century Ireland, or Germany under the Third Reich. The meanings attached to the Irish by English colonizers and to Jews by the Nazis and their sympathizers point to the ultimately secondary quality of skin color as a requisite for racial classification. The differences between racial classification in the Anglophone world from Hispanophone, Dutch, Francophone, and Lusophone New World societies, does not, as in the Cuban case, obliterate similarities between antiblack racisms across these same colonial/postcolonial sites.

Garnet's prescription for curing the ills of the black world was premised not on a single colony, nation-state, or even empire as the unit of analysis, but was focused on the idea of racial difference itself, its symbolic and material orders, and its effect on African-descended populations in various parts of the New World. There are methodological implications for investigation into the interplay between colonial/imperial legacies and subsequent national histories of racial valuation. The study of republicanism or political economy (to give just two examples) requires comprehension of the interrelationship between institutions, ideas, norms, markets, regions, territories, and states, as well as an understanding of international and supranational elements in a nation-state's economic, political, and even cultural policies. What I am emphasizing here is how a nation-state's ideologies, institutions, and political cultures do not emanate primarily or solely from the nation-state itself.

The so-called racial categories of white, black, and even mulatto have their origins in the emergent discourses of racial hierarchy in Western Europe. Since at least the sixteenth century, national elites in Spain, Britain, and, subsequently, France, the Netherlands, and other Western European nation-states utilized these categorizations to distinguish the "European" from the "African," and to classify those who fell somewhere in between or did not seem to fit anywhere. From Code Noir of the French in the seventeenth century to the very invention of the term "black" in the English language, the category of blackness and the modes of being ascribed to the bodies of those identified as black existed well before the United States existed as a nation-state, much less one with imperial designs and hegemonic possibilities.

Common to all national societies, with some semblance of citizenship categories in the state apparatus has been the specter of difference within a national society. Regardless of the type of regime, state consideration of the specter of difference in national society has emanated from the following questions: should we eradicated difference (through genocide or assimilation) or celebrate difference (through miscegenation and hybridity)? Whether in Brazil, Germany, the United States, Australia, New Zealand, Ghana, Indonesia, China, or Sri Lanka, states and regimes have answered these questions, with divergent consequences for those populations whose fate was determined by a states' response to the questions above.

One possible objection to my interpretation could be the essentializing potential of treating African-descended populations as a unit of analysis. At various points from the sixteenth century onward, the Irish, Jewish,

Maori, Australian indigenous, Polish, and Slavic peoples have been referred to as black by European colonizers and other racist pontificates. The absence of superficially common phenotypic attributes does not make these forms of antiblack chauvinism any less racist. Their commonality is neither phenotype nor national origin, but an association with blackness, itself a cluster of negative meanings involving debased labor, licentiousness, timidity, cowardice, and the most antimodern term of them all, backwardness.

Racial valuation does not rely on phenotypic congruence, but the recurrence of symbolic associations across time and space to organize certain people under derogatory categories. These people can then be ordered and situated into a political economy of unequal access, opportunities, and outcomes. What is needed is a template of sorts to track and chart forms of racial valuation (symbolic, material, coercive) in order to compare and contrast these modes within the region. This begins the work of developing a more comprehensive view of the particular modes of prejudice and discrimination against those defined as black, brown, and mulatto. Similar projects could be undertaken for other minority populations within the region (such as indigenous populations), but also cross-regionally. One benefit of such an approach would be to complement the more theoretical thrust of scholarship by George Fredrickson, and Étienne Balibar and Immanuel Wallerstein, which provides conceptual tools to begin theorizing about the transnational features of racist behavior. The second benefit of such an approach is its potential ability to replace the nation-centric cast of much scholarship on race. The scholarship of Thomas Skidmore, Patrick Wolffe, Paul Johnson, and Ann Laura Stoler, among others, situates nationally specific dynamics and their structuring processes (the role of states and institutions, market forces) within broader ideologies created and adapted to local circumstances and populations.

Most multiethnic and multiracial polities with ongoing histories of racial tensions involving one or more minority populations have practices of "borrowing" certain norms, labor regimes, and state and societal mechanisms to construct and maintain racial and ethnic hierarchies. Nineteenth-century Cuban racism and Cuban nationalism, for example, were both profoundly influenced by dominant racial attitudes and behaviors in the United States, which found their way into Cuba through military intervention and U.S corporate subsidiaries setting up industry on the island. Nazi racial theories were influenced by anti-Jewish, antiblack, and a host of other bigoted beliefs that predated the German nation-state, though they were given new form by the Nazi regime. French racisms did not remain in France, but were circulated by French colonial administrations in many parts of the world. There are many other examples I could cite, but these suffice to underscore the ways in which national ideologies of race in one nation-state seep into other national ideological formations, proving once again that territorial demarcations between nations are often not matched by normative ones.

In his discussion of methods for the comparative historical analysis of race, racism, and social mobilization, George Fredrickson reminds us that:

> . . . variability and change in the salience of ethnic status and consciousness depend to a considerable extent, it would appear, on variations or changes in the power relationship among ethnic groups. To the degree that an oppressed and stigmatized group can somehow gain in physical resources, political power, and cultural recognition or prestige, it can induce or force a dominant group to share some of its rights and privileges.[65]

In his discussion of a cross-spatial comparative method, Fredrickson utilizes a Weberian interpretation of the terms "ethnic" and "ethnic status" to encompass racial and ethnic modes of social and political domination. What is important for Fredrickson are the means and processes utilized by members and institutions of dominant groups to create and maintain these hierarchies, independent of the means (whether "scientific" or "cultural") used to define terms such as "race" and "ethnicity."

Stephan Palmié, however, reminds us of the limitations of the nation-centered approach to studying racisms and black social movements. His work on the movements of Afro-Cuban and even white members of African-derived secret societies demonstrates how transnational movements across several nation-states and regions of the world complicate our understanding of national, racial, and cultural identities.[66] A comparative tracking of antiblack racial, racialist, and racist meanings could be undertaken cross-nationally in relation to popular, state, private, and corporate documentation. Visual, corporeal, artistic, and other symbolic mediums evidence interpretive schemes reliant on the hierarchical ordering of members of the "national" population based upon phenotypical and somatic traits. Consider the following three examples of color/class/status correlations in the United States, Cuba, and Brazil, culled by some of the best students of national folklore in these countries:

> Brazil
> The white man drinks champagne,
> The caboclo, Port Wine,

The mulatto drinks rum,
And the Negro, pig piss.[67]

Cuba
The mulatto eats yucca
And the creoles cassava,
The Spaniards eat white bread
And the poor blacks ñame[68]

United States
I don't want no jet black woman for my regular,
O give me brown, and oh my Lord, give me brown.
For black is evil, evil, yella so low down,
When you git in trouble, and oh my Lord, yella can't be found.[69]

Although the third refrain from the United States focuses on consumption patterns of a more carnal kind, the themes of status hierarchy, color, and phenotype, and the derogation of blackness occur in all three ditties. Blacks are at the bottom of the status hierarchy. Interestingly, the United States example extols the virtues of a brown-skinned woman who, in Latin, Lusophone, and Francophone terms, is a *mulata*. Each makes an inverse correlation between social status and skin color. Moreover, this correlation is quite consistent *across* the three examples, national idiosyncrasies and phenotypic distinction among and within categories notwithstanding. Although mulatto-ness in New Orleans, for example, should certainly be differentiated from its categorical counterpart in Venezuela, Cuba, Brazil, or Haiti, the mulatto and mulatta categorization within the U.S. symbolic economy of racial valuation is nevertheless similar to the "in-between" status of other "mixed-race" categorizations. The darkest skinned people in each case are correlated with the bottom of the social, political, and cultural order, independent of the distinctions *across* phenotypic categories (i.e., regardless of the possibility that a Venezuelan negro is distinct phenotypically from her Brazilian or Haitian counterpart).

The "success" of racist ideologies is based on their ability to *re-present* individuals, groups, and their social, cultural, and institutional practices in a manner that *represses* internal variation and individual distinction. Thus, Jews, for example, are depicted as good with money, despite the many Jews who could not care less about money and the Talmudic prohibitions against many practices of monetary exchange. African-descended peoples are thought of as talented in singing and dancing, even though there are both Black New World and African peoples who are not, or who frown upon certain forms of bodily expression. One way of engaging the cross-national aspects of antiblack racisms is to move outside the confines of racial categorization and investigate phenomena seemingly devoid of racist implications. Some of this has already been undertaken in national studies in the region on criminalization, disease, marriage, and cohabitation.[70] The next step in the evolution of this important, emergent literature is to chart the regional, transnational, and global implications of these discourses and the practices.

Frantz Fanon's writing on the relationship between racism and form does some of the conceptual work of racial valuation. Fanon's typology in "Racism and Culture" delineates five different types of racism: biological, scriptural, scientific, cultural, and colonial.[71] Fanon's typology corresponds to Western colonialism and imperialism in rather chronological terms; each matches up with a distinct phase of Western European expansion into Africa, Asia, and Latin America and the means that were utilized to justify the enslavement, discrimination, and subjugated status of a majority of the world's population. This typology has its uses, for it helps chart and characterize racial logics that are inextricably linked to distinct regimes (the Catholic Church, Dutch versus French versus British colonialisms) yet operate within a multinational-territorial theater. The epochal and ideational features implicit in such typologies help ground and situate ideological formations—racial or otherwise—a world-historical context.

Fanon's typology, however, is framed in a unilinear fashion wherein certain forms of racist practices are attributed exclusively to a particular era. No single justification for racial hierarchy (scientific, religious, scriptural) has ever been completely banished from popular or elite discourse. As students of the "new" racism have pointed out, the substitution of culture for biology in late twentieth-century racist rhetoric in North America and Western Europe underscores the malleability, flexibility, and multitemporal character of racial ideologies.

Garnet, like many advocates for African-descended populations during the past two centuries, retained what can be characterized as a strategic notion of race, a mode of racial reasoning that is neither static nor biologically rooted, but based on existing relations between African-descended populations and other populations in the world, structured by the experiences of enslavement and colonialism. He juxtaposed the West's destiny of miscegenation with what Fanon referred to as "the fact of blackness," the internally differentiated but transnational semiotics that equates not only African-descended populations with a degraded status, but also deems populations "black" in order to justify their subordinate status.[72]

Neither scientific, philosophical, nor explicitly polemical arguments could eradicate the conditions of subordinate status. The relegation of the idea of race to the dustbin of archaic language does not on its own alter conditions of slavery or servitude. There were no guarantees, but certainly a call to action among like-minded individuals, groups, and organizations (in this specific instance, abolitionists and suffragists) could increase prospects among a wider, popular audience, not only for the eradication of conditions of inequality among members of the human family but also of the very assignations of blackness correlated with negativity. Despite the scientific dubiousness of the term "race" and its attendant categorizations, it mattered less what the term meant in scientific terms than what it meant in political and normative terms. In short, the rhetorical work that the term "race" performed in interactions between people was far more significant than its scholarly, scientific verity.

Garnet's predication of a mixed-race Western civilization can be read as the identification of a very insidious process: attempts at Western racial purity would be undermined by the West itself, through its encounters with non-Western peoples. For the student of race and racism, culture and hybridity, Garnet's predication also represents a starting point different from Du Bois' pronouncement of the color line separating darker peoples from lighter ones. At this stage in the disciplines of African American studies, Africana studies, and, to a lesser extent, the social sciences, Garnet's distinctive starting point provides an opportunity to consider scholarly paths not taken or given less emphasis, to identify and investigate what was missed when one began from the premise of the color line, rather than that of mixed race. In historiographic and analytic terms, Garnet's starting point allows scholars to have a longer view of debates about miscegenation and hybridity and to discover that none of the more contemporary critical enterprises associated with mixed-raceness and hybridity (cultural studies, critical race theory, postmodern critique) has a monopoly on these concepts, or on the presumptions of their potential value.

Garnet's call for a global solidarity amongst African-descended peoples was also a call for political community. Many black political actors and organizations responded to Garnet's call during the course of the nineteenth and twentieth centuries, advocating racial rather than racist solidarity. Many of their political parties and social movements aimed at fusing racial and political solidarities, however, failed more often then not. Ironically, advocates of positive racial solidarity, or what Sartre termed antiracist racism, share certain assumptions with advocates of race-mixture. The concluding chapter 8 will examine some of the reasons for these failures within the context of transnational black politics during the post–World War II period.

CHAPTER 8

Conclusion: Which Community?

> *It once occurred to me that while socialism claims to be internationalist, there is something which is even more internationalist: the bourgeoisie. The bourgeois are absolutely identical in every country in the world. A German bourgeois recognizes his French or Uruguayan counterpart more quickly than the socialists manage to recognize each other.*[1]

Abolition and emancipation provided Henry Highland Garnet and others with the first organizing principles of transnational black politics; causes around which black macropolitical actors could mobilize resources and create networks that traversed national-territorial boundaries, colonies, and in some instances, state sovereignty. There would be other organizing principles of black political actors across national territorial boundaries during the nineteenth and twentieth centuries: anti-colonialism, nationalism, civil rights, apartheid, and more recently, reparations.

These organizing principles, when combined with very specific notions of justice, equality, citizenship, provide the macropolitical ideas of black transnationalism, what could be characterized as the imaginaries of transnational black politics. At the same time, however, the organizing principles, ideals and imaginaries of black transnationalism that bring together individuals and organizations from distinct black life-worlds also, as a consequence, make it difficult, if not impossible, to assert that "black consciousness," "black solidarity," or "black culture" can be reduced to one constellation of beliefs, organizations, or people. These imaginaries, and the communities of people they help bring together, often obscure disagreement, dissent, and outright conflict over the goals of a particular transnational black community as well as the means by which to bring those goals about. This chapter focuses on the specifically macropolitical forms of black transnationalism, the varied and often divergent responses of multiple black life-worlds to the conditions and circumstances of the modern age (colonialism, racial slavery, capitalism, and the nation-state system among them).

This concluding chapter can be read as a retrospective assessment of black politics in various parts of the world in the period roughly between 1945 to the end of the twentieth century. Here, as in the previous chapter, readers can consider the epistemic and interpretive shifts in historical interpretation and political analysis beginning from a distinct starting point, the course of black transnationalism in the latter half of the twentieth century. What I offer here is an initial attempt to make sense of the ethicopolitical and tactical dilemmas of transnational black politics at the outset of the twenty-first century, at a moment when twentieth-century visions of black emancipation have been increasingly obscured by the spectre of globalization, postmodernist claims of increasingly fragmented identities, and the death, in some circles, of race, if not racism. Thus, I return to concepts of politics, the political, and political community with which this book began. I am particularly interested in the acts of will and imagination that help instantiate political communities, and the forms of politics that flow from them.

To borrow from Jean Luc-Nancy's *The Inoperative Community*, "The first task in understanding what is at stake here consists in focusing on the horizon *behind* us."[2] Viewed more comprehensively, the various black social and political movements of the twentieth century provide an opportunity to examine the forms of transnational black political imaginery that relate most directly to macropolitics.

One of the functions of black political thought, like all political and social theory, is to contend with the death of the political imaginaries associated with an era, project, or people, just as seriously as the more empirically driven historian, political scientist, or sociologist strives to explain the success or failure of a particular social movement, political party, or project in achieving its aims. If there is such as thing as black political thought and theory, then it must both chart and provide opportunities for imagining political community, both past and present.

There is little within the literature on the African diaspora or black transnationalism that engages the contemporary political challenges—both conceptual and practical—posed by new modes of globalization, new or "postmodern" social movements, and the emergence of nonstate, nongovernmental actors. There is even less scholarship within the Euro-American debates about modernity and postmodernity that addresses the multiple, varied forms of black subjectivity and politics, aside from a handful of black intellectuals such as Ronald Judy, Fred Moten, Wahneema Lubiano, David Scott, Cathy Cohen, and Tejumola Olaniyan (though this list is by no means exhaustive). How, for example, does discussion and debate about reparations throughout the black world, from the Americas to the African continent, resonate with theories of justice and fairness, as well as tensions between capitalism and morality (a favorite subject of early Marxism and of contemporary political theory)? In chapter 6 I pursue the question, To what extent do the cases of blacks—as subjects—attempting to engage federal and national courts concerning the right of movement (Dred Scott), education (*Brown v. Board of Education*), or escape from enslavement (*Amistad*, the Haitian Revolution, Paul Bogle's revolt) prefigure the conditions of statelessness and human sacrifice in the modern world that many political theorists attribute to either postmodernity or fascism, or both? These are questions to be taken up not just by historians, philosophers, practitioners of critical legal studies and African American or American studies, but by students of political and social theory. While the questions I have posed may be peculiar to the history of black transnationalism, the answers certainly will not be, and can bring political and social theorists into greater dialogue with the themes and issues of transnational black politics.[3]

Students of feminism and international labor organizations, and social movement scholars have traced the history and contours of international feminisms, labor movements, and crises, as well as Green parties, antinuclear, and other forms of international environmentalism. The interactions between these movements and world historical events, shifts in the international political economy, and the technological advances of the late twentieth century have fundamentally transformed how politics will be (and is being) conducted in the twenty-first century. Mass media, the breakup of the Soviet Union, increasing economic, territorial, and technological cooperation among nation-states in various regions of the world have together, without coordinated effort, challenged the notion of a territorially discrete, nation-state–based ethical and political community. At the same time, this challenge has not, as some would suggest, completely transformed extant notions of ethical and political community premised on categories and concepts of race, nation, territory, and the innumerable other ideational axes people use as symbols of community.

Along with many other interested spectators of and participants in late modernity, feminists, Marxists, modernists and postmodernists, and liberal and conservative philosophers have their own versions of the reconfiguration of the modern world, West and non-West alike, atop the rubble of the cold war. Africanist scholars have thought about the relevance of the cataclysmic events of the period roughly between the end of the cold war and the present moment for notions of political community on the African continent itself, and other black life-worlds.[4]

Acknowledging fragmentation in contemporary black transnationalism is an important part of reimagining black politics nationally and transnationally. I would like to emphasize the importance of macropolitics for reimagining the egalitarian possibilities of transnational black politics and distinguishing political community from racial community. As will be apparent by this chapter's end, advocates as well as opponents of racial essentialism tend to forget that politics and power, not society or biology, helps forge political communities. The limitations of race-first politics lie not only in the fetishization of race, but in the equation of the race concept with politics itself. Actual politics can provide lessons about the limitations of the race concept not only as an organizing principle or epistemological category but also as the basis and foundation of something more complicated—a political community. Racial community and political community are not one and the same. We thus arrive at the impasse of racial reasoning on the terrain of actual politics but from a direction other than the routes of the largely sociological account of race as a social construction. The terrain of politics—coalitions, alliances, ideologies, beliefs, and mobilizations—belies the race concept's limited utility in implementing and practicing political community.

Aside from several Caribbean nation-states, there are no communities of people in the black world except on the continent of Africa itself who constitute a demographic and political majority. In most nation-states where African-descended populations are in the numerical minority, these populations lack political power, have relatively few institutions either within their communities or in the society at large to address concerns of equal access, full citizenship, or human rights. To the extent that there are organizations, individuals and social movements in various parts of the globe that consider themselves part of a community of people, with artifacts, cultural practices, and ideas that help constitute "blackness" beyond the boundaries of any single nation-state, we must attempt to come to terms with shifts in modalities of political mobilization when the predominant rallying cries from a previous era sound archaic (to some at least).

The fall of apartheid in Rhodesia, and later South Africa, constituted the black world's historical and epochal parallel to the end of the cold war and the fall of the Berlin wall. Though there are many forms of ongoing social and political struggle, as well as the institutionalization of antiracist measures affecting African-descended peoples in various parts of the world, these events effectively ended a specific set of strategic alliances of the period roughly between the end of World War II and 1989. The cessation of state-mandated racial segregation, exploitation, and oppression required a shift on the part of political actors to new terrains of antiracist struggle. From SOS Racisme in France to TransAfrica in the United States, the fall of apartheid brought with it a distinct agenda for antiracist organizations that were also committed to black internationalism. Within South Africa itself, the politics of former anti-apartheid leaders in the "new" South Africa are radically different from anti-apartheid politics. The governments of Nelson Mandela and Tabo Mbeki have had to assure international investors that capitalist enterprise in South Africa would not be dismantled with apartheid.

As is the case with most social movement actors and organizations that achieve their aims, political actors who become part of the states they once contested represent not only the culmination of specific political aims but also the increased fragmentation of movement organizations. Examples abound, from the antiauthoritarian ensemble of environmentalists, Trotskyists, liberals, feminists, indigenous and black movement actors in Brazil, civil rights activists and sympathizers in the United States, to prodemocracy advocates in Poland; a unified front against a common foe becomes harder to sustain after the immediate aims of mobilization are achieved. In each of the examples, positions adopted and affirmed during phases of contestation with status quo power have been radically transformed, if not reversed. Former outsiders become insiders, movement activists become heads of state, and key leaders of movements ranging from democratization and civil rights to trade unions become cabinet members.

The Overview

The postapartheid era of transnational black politics designates not only an epochal shift in transnational and national black politics but also marks the exhaustion of certain utopic narratives of freedom, progress, and autonomy premised on statehood, nationalism, citizenship, and sovereignty. The attainment of political sovereignty by former colonies in Africa and the Caribbean in the 1960s did not lead to economic sovereignty or even, in some cases, to the expansion of civil rights or a more egalitarian social order. Haiti, Nigeria, Kenya, and Congo, though each with its distinct political history, evidence the crash of utopic visions against the hard wall of realpolitik. Africa's "first world war" produced by the second Congo crisis (the first, CIA induced, brought down Lumumba) and involving Congo, Uganda, Rwanda, Ghana, Nigeria, Zimbabwe, and Angola provided a counterpoint to claims that the end of colonialism and apartheid would produce African unity. The assassination of Joseph Kabila in 2001, a former guerrilla-turned-statesman who, along with Che Guevara, huddled in the Congo jungle during the Argentine revolutionary's ill-fated foray into African revolution, further punctured the bubble of Pan-Africanist solidarity in the postindependence era. This holds true for the politics of black life-worlds outside of Africa as well.

How do we make sense of transnational black politics in light of this shift? As noted in chapter 1, one of the central tensions in black political thought concerns the relationship between politics and culture, and their respective instrumentality as means to power or at least equality. This tension, as I have suggested in various ways throughout this book, is one of the central and perhaps most consistent themes of transnational black politics that recurs in multiple national cultures and local communities. A cursory examination of several key voices in national and transnational dialogue reveals how central this tension is to interpretations and practices of black politics.

Paul Gilroy's classic *There Ain't No Black in the Union Jack* engages themes of racism, nationalism, and antiracist politics in Britain in the 1980s without addressing black politics itself, the role and location of black political actors in formal political parties, and electoral competition. In this book, Gilroy examines the cultural politics of race and nation and underscores some of the limitations of formal party politics for addressing racism in contemporary Britain when neither of the two dominant political parties aggressively addressed the problems of quotidian racism. The nonrecognition of racial discrimination by the state contributed not only to escalation of racist violence in many forms but also to high levels of unemployment and underemployment among black and Asian youth.[5] The "Rock Against Racism" project, which received the most attention in this book as an antiracist cultural and political formation, was highlighted as one of the key normative and coalitional bulwarks against Thatcherism's authoritarian and neoliberal remapping of British economy and polity.

Although Gilroy's working definition of politics encompasses both micro- and macropolitics, his more expansive view of politics largely ignores formal party politics as a site for the articulation not only of a black transnational political identification but also political expression of any sort. For Gilroy, party politics of the formal sort is the least hopeful route toward true freedom. Given the state of representative democracies in the West these days, he may be right. Although by his own admission black politics was not the focus of his study, the question of political community for black British social and cultural actors remains a topic of debate in contemporary Britain, as these actors try to navigate the contours of racism, nationalism, and the state in daily life in ways that are meaningful and productive. I believe the question of political community for black social and cultural actors remains an underexplored topic in many parts of the black world, not just Britain.

Adolph Reed, on the other hand, has neither patience nor sympathy for the late twentieth- and twenty-first-century preoccupation with popular culture in U.S. African American politics, referring to the present generation's preoccupation with the cultural politics of contemporary black nationalism as a form of political evasion: "In defining participation in popular culture as political action, this stance merges the avant-garde in fashion and ideological radicalism, thus vesting fad with strategic political significance."[6] Consequently, the characteristics associated with capitalist popular culture—consumption, commodity fetishism, and reification—become equated with true political engagement, and "work to reduce politics to the purely affective and symbolic endeavor. And that is a construction of politics in which the appeal to icons readily takes the place of careful argument and critical analysis."[7] Reed's assessment does not necessarily preclude a role for culture and symbols in either political engagement or analysis, but it does strongly caution against equating any form of cultural practice with macropolitical forms of engagement with dominant political or economic orders. Cathy Cohen, Robin D. G. Kelley, and Richard Iton, on the other hand, search for and find subversive and deviant behaviors within more subterranean modes of popular culture and intracommunal expression, in black gay and queer publics, music cultures such as house music, and a limited number of hip-hop and rap artists, which perhaps bear greater possibilities for radical political practice than those associated with either mass-oriented consumer culture or even participation in political parties.[8]

What makes the tension between these divergent perspectives on the relationship between cultural and political articulation in black public spheres intellectually productive is that they help me, and hopefully readers, to consider several questions posed below that I believe are central to understanding the role of culture in black politics transnationally.

If we step outside the categorical determinations of what constitutes culture or politics, however, and pose the following questions, we may be able to arrive at a more nuanced examination of the diversity and interplay of political and cultural forms in black public spheres. Have political parties or states operating under the banner of black, African-descended, or African peoples liberated and emancipated black citizens and subjects of the black world, and if not, why not? To what extent have visions of cultural expression and emancipated black people the world over, and if not, why not? In the course of attempting to provide my own answers to these questions, I shall focus on the trope of unity in black transnationalism, and the concept of intention as the common basis of black political and cultural articulation aimed at liberation.

II. After the Election: Party Politics and Black Political Representation

Whether in postsegregation United States, postcolonial politics in the former European colonies, or social democratic politics in former empires, African-descended minority groups in nation-states outside of Africa have experienced *some* incorporation and recognition of their citizenship rights and cultural practices. Even in polities with large or majority African-descended populations such as Brazil, and in African countries such as South Africa and Zimbabwe, the emergence of black and African-descended political actors in positions of state leadership and cabinet-level positions is a recent development in national politics.[9]

Yet these unprecedented levels of political power, influence, and authority have not necessarily followed the projected paths to political development, consolidation, and democratic participation prescribed by many transnational black political actors and Third Worldists of the 1950s, 1960s, and 1970s. With few exceptions, the black radical political imaginaries that projected democratic socialism or at least liberal democratic practices in places as diverse as Grenada, Guyana, Haiti, Jamaica, Brazil, and Britain have faltered, often due to external and internal constraints outside the control of black political actors. The republic of Haiti, with the recent ouster of Jean-Betrand Aristide from the presidency of this long-beleaguered nation-state, is in some ways paradigmatic of the frustrated quests for black, African-descended autonomy globally. Neither territory, statehood, nor sovereignty has guaranteed political stability, social and economic welfare, or relief from violence.

Racial commonality as the interpretive lens through which to view the complicated alliances, betrayals, and strategies in Africa, the Caribbean, and other parts of the New World is of little use in making sense of these examples. The legacy of "firsts" in black public spheres outside of Africa displays the recurrent frequency of this pattern. In Brazil, Celso Pitta, the first Afro-Brazilian—and now former—mayor of São Paulo, conducted a campaign from a center-right party based on "competence," not racial solidarity.[10] The Conservative Party in Britain, responding to years of neglect of black and Indo-Pakistani communities that have overwhelmingly voted Labour, has promoted its own Indo-Pakistani, Caribbean, and African-descended candidates for elected office since the early 1990s. Although black voters in the United States have not, for the most part, accepted the invitation, the Republican Party has proclaimed a place for increasing numbers of U.S. African American voters, in part, based on the prominence of two U.S. African Americans in the first administration of U.S. President George W. Bush. Rabella de Faria, a black woman of Surinamese descent, running on the ticket of the late right-wing populist Pim Fortuyn in the Netherlands, became the first black mayor of the Rotterdam city government in 2002.[11]

The pattern I am identifying here is one of initial political incorporation and integration into existing political parties and institutions, accompanied by increased diversification along the ideological spectrum in public discourse, policy, and electoral competition. This has occurred during a period when the Western world has undergone a rightward shift in its politics. Countries once considered relatively immune to the prospect of right-wing governance, such as Norway, Sweden, Denmark, and the Netherlands, have all shifted rightward.

It would appear as if the price of black political incorporation has been decreased participation in more radical politics. As black political actors enter into parties and institutions of formal power, accusations of their abandonment of "community concerns" in each case are evident, as are countercharges concerning the need for political efficacy, compromise, and negotiation—not protest—within formal institutions and processes of power. In each of these cases, black political actors have come to occupy unprecedented, nonracially designated positions within political parties and institutions in postcolonial, post-segregation polities. These unprecedented advances mark the inclusion of African-descended political actors into status quo modes of political participation and competition as well as the increased ideological complexity of racial politics. Tracking the "race" of any of the political actors in these parties would provide few clues as to their actual ideological dispositions.

There has also been an alternative path to political party incorporation, participation, and mobilization, evidenced in attempts to create all-black political parties. Afro-Colombian, Afro-Caribbean, U.S. African American, Black British, Afro-Guyanese, and Afro-Brazilian politics each have their histories of deliberation concerning the tactical advantages of becoming part of a dominant political party during the latter half of the twentieth century, creating an independent "race-first" political party, or seeking alternative means to political engagement altogether.[12] All of the attempts, under varying circumstances, to create and sustain "race first" political parties, were short lived. By the first two decades of the twentieth century, independent organizations and political parties of African-descended populations were created in Britain, Cuba, the United States, Argentina, and Brazil. Participation in dominant-group, status quo political parties occurred in Venezuela, Jamaica, and other locales with former slave populations during this period as well. The first independent black party in the Americas was the Partido Independiente de Color in Cuba. Marcus Garvey's political party of the 1940s, ran candidates in Jamaica and the United States. In Brazil, there was the Frente Negra Brasileira of 1931–37 and, more recently, the PPPM, the Partido Popular Pela Maioría, founded in 2001.[13] The United States has been the site for several all-black political parties and, most notably Richard Hatcher's tenure as mayor of Gary, Indiana, and the rise of the Black Panther Party in the 1970s. Trinidad and Columbia had their own versions of all-black political parties in the 1970s during the period of Black Power.[14]

Part of the appeal of racially exclusive political parties and other forms of independent political mobilization is the prospect of political and popular autonomy from the political organization and domination by other groups. These quests for organizational political autonomy are also responses and reactions to prior and ongoing modes of political exclusion and segregation. What makes the idea and practice of an independent political party a recurrent dream in black life-worlds is that such parties are conceived, almost deductively, as the outgrowth of subtle and outright exclusion in national public spheres dominated by white and white creole elites and the relative absence of organizations within black public spheres to engage in dominant elite politics. Once a black identity is fixed, a political identity could be successfully mapped onto it.

During the early phase of African independence movements,[15] Negritude, Pan-Africanist, and Afro-Marxist regimes emphasizing "African" (not necessarily racial) solidarities sought to utilize African Unity as an overarching principle, superseding ideological, personal, regional, and political-economic diversity. In all of these instances, political parties were forged out of frustration with an existing political order, based on the belief that the political party would prove a more efficacious way of promoting political unity and discipline and, barring that, would at least provide a vehicle through which the concerns of a formerly colonial population could be addressed.

Pan-Africanism, Black Consciousness, and Black Power movements, Negritude, and the Nation of Islam all prescribed racial unity in some form as both goal and barrier of "black progress," and in some cases, national territorial sovereignty. A brief examination of their respective ideational formulations and "philosophies of the future" reveals that their paths toward racial unity are distinct. In these movements and many others, the call for racial unity has invariably been accompanied by ideological divergence: Negritudeans versus black Marxists, cultural nationalists versus Pan-African Socialists, Black Power advocates versus integrationists, Black Democrats versus Republicans, Brazzaville Pan-Africanists versus Cairo Pan-Africanists, or the Grupo Negro do PT versus the Grupo Negro do PSDB in Brazil. Inevitably, one had to be more than black or vaguely committed to black liberation. There were—and are—political, economic, and cultural agendas to contend with, fight for, and argue over, which invariably helped produce new friends as well as enemies. The premise, indeed promise, of racial unity has led its advocates throughout Africa and the African diaspora down very discrete, divergent paths.

Independent political parties have not been viable as minority voice positions within white elite dominant public spheres in many countries for two reasons. The first is quantitative; most "race first" political parties (with the exception of those in Jamaica, Trinidad, Barbados, and Guyana to a lesser extent) seek to represent minority populations whose numbers are too small within the broader population to achieve national significance. The second reason is qualitative; given the ideological diversity within minority and majority populations in plural and multiracial societies, most "race first" parties ultimately attract people who, for ideological rather than purely "racial" reasons, adopt the platforms of parties claiming to work on behalf of the entire black race. The idea of unity appears as a Lazarus-like icon within black ideological systems according to the following logic:

Conditions of Subordination: Racial Consciousness ⟶ *Racial Unity* ⟶

Collective Action (Macropolitics) ⟶ *Agency* ⟶ *Victory*

Figure 8.1

With some qualification, throughout the black world, this has been the general modern formula for political emancipation evoked by political actors, organized around presumptions of unified consciousness and agency. This logic can be found in discourses ranging fron black nationalism, black liberation theology, civil rights, anti-colonialism, and even some independence movements. Closer to reality, however, is the following trajectory:

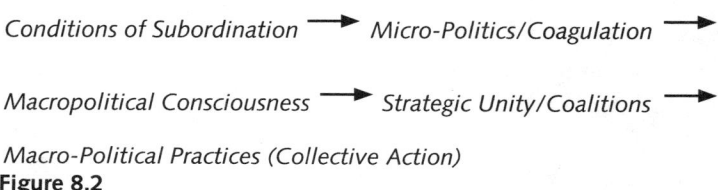

Macro-Political Practices (Collective Action)
Figure 8.2

I believe the trajectory above more closely resembles the intersection of micro- and macropolitics, daily and spectacular life, and better approximates the range of action and inaction occurring in most communities under forms of racial domination. We know from various studies of social mobilization, from the U.S. civil rights movement to Palestinians living in the occupied territories, that even under the most extreme circumstances macropolitical actors within subordinated groups often have competing ideas about the best path toward liberation.

As developed in chapter 2, political parties and social movements, as well as the crowds associated with revolt, riot, and rebellion, produce spectacle—and spectators—in ways that more isolated modes such as coagulation and aggregation do not. The spectacular also lends itself to historiography in the way that the quotidian usually does not. Yet politics in spectacular form, ranging from the overthrow and assassination of Patrice Lumumba, Martin Luther King's assassination, or Jean-Bertrand Aristide's ouster from power in Haiti can often seduce spectators in ways that give the illusion of coherent, holistic historical narratives. The spectacle, more often than not, might itself be the product or consequence of a disparate act or event that requires its own investigation. Quotidian politics is, after all, formed and structured by the combination of state power (or lack thereof), the economy, and social actors who, intentionally or not, become macropolitical actors. How these actors make meaning places their creation of a political community into some cultural context. Thus, quotidian politics often informs the most explicit modes of protest and formal political mobilization, just as state power (or its absence), political economy, and dominant norms and values inform the politics of daily life.

My discussion of "quotidian politics" in chapter 2 first raised the theoretical possibility that many forms of political behavior and thought in daily life do not fit under extant rubrics of left or right, progressive or reactionary, even during periods in the history of black struggles with clearly established lines of political conflict and allegiance. The advantage of individuated action, particularly coagulate politics, lies in its lack of a need for broader communal adherence to strategies of resistance. The dreamers (theorists, really) of a new order, however, seek to go beyond coagulate politics and embrace an even larger community of people already named or identified as members of the same community, in this instance, people of African descent. Coagulate politics will persist as long as there are forms of conflict that neither elite representation, state intervention, nor ideas of a common cause can immediately address.[16] The distance between any political party's projection of its interests—in the name of political community—and the daily lives of its adherents reveals different conceptions of the political as well as the limits of the political party's ability to represent and cohere an entire social or racial community. Further attempts to do so eventually undermine a political party's efficacy.

The era of African and Caribbean anticolonial and independence movements provides innumerable examples of what I suggest here. From Bernard Coard's dispute with Maurice Bishop in Grenada, which led to Bishop's murder, to Walter Rodney's disagreements with Forbes Burnham, which led to Rodney's assassination, from Lumumba's undoing by Mobutu and Tshombe to Malcolm X's killing in broad daylight by the right wing of the Nation of Islam—these events are merely the most violent representation of the principle of irreconcilability in politics, which no group of people, subaltern or not, can avoid.

"Proper" responses by a subordinated population to domination are hardly uniform. What must be acknowledged by practitioners and scholars alike is the persistence of ideological diversity and distinction as the first principle of politics. The desire for political community is not a vague enterprise but an attempt to enact a very specific set of principles and themes that come to constitute the aspirations—as well as the ills—of daily life. Political communities simultaneously define insiders and outsiders, distinctions that not even racial or cultural unity can resolve. There are moments in any social community, whether defined by class, gender, nation, sexuality, or any other potential organizing principle, when political differences become irreconcilable. At these moments, the "splinters" or "fissures" of one presumption of community (the social or the racial) lead to other modes of community—political communities distinguished by their break with the first seemingly nonpolitical community.

There will be black nationalists and Pan-Africanists who after reading the above passage, will retort with phrases like "if only the CIA and the United States were not involved in the foreign affairs of Africa and the Caribbean," "There is always a Judas among us," or "Nkrumah and Boigny would have been united if there weren't so many different colonial rulers" seek to displace politics, to place the blame of political disunity upon "external" factors, rather than on the irreconcilability that is intrinsic to macropolitics. The political differences between these individuals and the organizations they represented at different periods in black internationalist history constitute the political communities of black internationalism. To erase the differences among these various communities is to erase the politics of black internationalism itself. It is for this reason, if no other, that all-black political parties could not last under the banner of black unity, for there are multiple banners.[17] Unity is not a prerequisite of politics, just one of its many possible outcomes.

III Cultural Unity

There have been many calls for unity in the black world. Perhaps the most recurrent plea has been in the form of cultural unity, particularly after World War II, on the African continent and throughout other locales of the black world. A majority of political actors, thinkers, and everyday folk have conceived of cultural practice, production, and artifacts as antidotes to the disparate nature of black political articulation in national and transnational spheres. Alioune Diop, one of the founders of *Presence Africaine* and an important theoretician for cultural autonomy during the nationalist phase of the African continent, highlighted the importance of cultural unity and coherence. In his address to the Second Pan-African Youth Seminar at Dar-es-Salaam in 1961, Diop outlined three distinct though overlapping spheres of struggle for Africa's general emancipation from the clutches of the dominant nation-states of the West. In "African Culture and Its Place in Work for African Unity," Diop provides a broad, macrolevel analysis of the tensions between African cultures, peoples, and nation-states attempting to negotiate cold war politics and Western imperialism during the transition from colonialism to independence.

Diop distinguishes clearly between the three types of independence—economic, political and cultural. For Diop, full emancipation from the West could only come about through cultural unity following economic and political independence. Diop also makes clear that the sort of cultural unity to which he refers has an explicitly political dimension, in that it is concerned with the distribution of resources and questions of power as well as matters of identity formation and reproduction.

> Unity and independence can only be achieved with cultural unity, cultural unity can only be sustained if we are not involved in the cold war. We are subject to the influences of foreign powers, who, not only exert economic pressure, as Africa abounds in riches, but also political and ideological pressures. Our populations are, however, not yet fully prepared to weigh and appreciate the value of these cultural and ideological influences.[18]

Further on, Diop discusses the role of culture as a glue of sorts to cohere and connect political parties to religious organizations "to take care that the activities of political parties on the one hand and the religious movements on the other be coordinated and harmonized according to the true aspirations of the people."[19] Here Diop is concerned with the continental implications of religious pluralism, specifically Christian, Muslim, and indigenous religions whose struggles for dominance and, in the case of certain animist traditions, survival, were exacerbated in the postindependence period, leading in several tragic instances to genocidal religious intolerance masquerading as civil war.

Diop's view of a distinctly African cultural politics was also profoundly Afro-modern, in terms of the role that culture was presumed to play in freeing African territory and consciousness from the gaze and preoccupation of the West. For Diop, African culture contained diversity rather than contradictions[20] and could be juxtaposed against Western humanism and aesthetics to emancipate African and African-descended peoples from the clutches of Western imperialism and cultural depravities. Interestingly enough, Diop called for cultural unity, not racial unity. Racial unity could perhaps address matters of white supremacy but not the ethnonational conflicts that have survived colonial rule. As Clifford Geertz suggested in the wake of the nationalist independence movements on the African continent, the inability of newly independent states to make nations and national citizen/subjects out of colonial subjects meant that the state, as a symbol of unification for the continent's diverse peoples, brought neither independence, autonomy, nor unity, much less competence and honesty. The attribution of state mismanagement, kleptocracy, expropriation, and exploitation to the legacies of colonial rule rings increasingly hollow in the canyon of postcolonial history.

Variations of this tension between autonomist cultural politics and state- and party-driven political culture would emerge in Angola, Jamaica, Grenada, Ghana, Guinea, and other parts of the black world in the aftermath of the independence period, as black nations became black states. The transition from independence movement to the consolidation of state power and territorial sovereignty revealed existing internal fissures (ethnicity, regionalism, religion) that could no longer be deterred or repressed in the absence of a common foe (colonialism, imperialism, apartheid). If culture could possibly have served to unite, for example, the distinct and divergent visions of Gamal Adel Nasser, Kwame Nkrumah, Sekou Toure, Felix Houphouét Boigny, Nnamdi Azikiwe, Leopold Senghor, and others, what specific set of values and norms could have been utilized to bring about unity? Which tools or implements of culture could resolve conflicts such as the Biafran War, apartheid, or, more recently, the crisis of the Republic of the Congo or AIDS? In each of these instances, political and cultural actors need to utilize means or tools outside the realm of culture to resolve the crisis.

Diop's claim that cultural unity could only be achieved in the absence of the cold war expresses one of the ironies of postcolonial history in the African context—that calls for African unity were strongest and most widespread in the era preceding national independence. But even then, there was no single transcontinental directive that the assortment of colonies, movements, and leaders adhered to or followed. Thus, unity, as in the diasporic context, was more of an ideal than a clear objective.

In the United States, calls for black cultural unity in the post–World War II period bore many similarities with their African counterparts. Harold Cruse's *The Crisis of the Negro Intellectual* made a dual claim, first asserting that U.S. African American intellectuals did not, as a group, have a comprehensive understanding of the relationship between politics, materialism, and authentic cultural production.[21] Second, he argued that the crisis of the Negro intellectual in the United States, particularly in the U.S. African American left, was symptomatic of the under-theorized role of culture in black emancipation. Cruse detested what he characterized as reductionist Marxist perspectives that treated U.S. African American communities as real or potential "proletarians," part of some "black belt" of the U.S. south. Given the practical political limitations of either a territorial black nationalism or Marxism on U.S. soil, Cruse saw cultural transformation as the sole prospect for the radical transformation of U.S. African Americans and, ultimately, the United States itself. Cruse saw the integrationist techniques of the U.S. civil rights movement, the myopia of both the American Communist Party and the black left, and the celebration and exaggeration of black "folk" traditions by white and black intelligentsia alike as stifling the true revolutionary character of black arts and aesthetics. Thus, Cruse wrote:

> As long as the Negro's cultural identity is in question, or open to self-doubts, then there can be no positive identification with the real demands of his political and economic existence. Further than that, without a cultural identity that adequately defines *himself* (emphasis in original), the Negro cannot even identify with the American nation as a whole.[22]

Running throughout Cruse's impassioned, often embittered prose is a consistent claim about the fundamental importance of cultural politics and its relationship to material and political autonomy. In his critique of the dominant tendency of the civil rights movement, Cruse wrote:

> The civil rights movement cannot really give cultural leadership in any effective way—it is too suffused with the compulsion to legitimize its social aims with American standards. The leaders of the civil rights movement, along with all the "civil writers," subordinate themselves to the very cultural values of the white world that are used either to negate, or deny the Negro cultural equality, and to exploit his cultural ingredients and use them against him. This is one of the great traps of racial integrationism.[23]

Another example can be found in the eloquent, urgent voice of black transnationalist Larry Neal, one of the most important writers and polemicists of the Black Arts Movement in the United States in the 1970s. Neal argued for a contrapuntal ethics to contest the political culture of liberal integrationists, seeking instead the creation, nurturing, inculcation, and institutionalization of a new black aesthetic that sought to dissolve the distinction between art and political practice.[24] In response to the Pulitzer Prize's ultimate rejection of Duke Ellington's nomination for the award, Neal urged U.S. African American audiences to comprehend

> the necessity of establishing our own norms, our own values, and if there must be standards, let them be our own. Recognition of Duke Ellington's genius lies not with the white society that has exploited

him and his fellow musicians. It lies with us, the black public, black musicians and artists. Essentially, recognition of that sort, from a society that hates us and has no real way of evaluating our artistic accomplishments, is the meanest kind of intrusion upon the territory of black people.[25]

Such arguments have recurred in U.S. African American critical discourses, most recently in debates involving August Wilson, Robert Brustein, Spike Lee, and many other artists and critics of the U.S. African American and U.S. American experience.[26] The "territory of black people" that Neal referred to is not literal firmament but a constellation of ethicopolitical and aesthetic judgments that help constitute some notion of black identity in contradistinction to a more hegemonically situated white, Western subject whose overall sense of art and the artist's place in the world was seemingly divorced from politics. Neal's retort does more than support Ellington's genius. It implies that the evaluative criteria utilized to exclude Ellington from consideration fail to appreciate not only Ellington's music but U.S. African American cultural production more generally. Neal's counternarrative suggests an epistemic chasm between white and black, a chasm filled with racism and ignorance that renders committees (and the people who serve upon them), such as the Pulitzer Prize committee, incapable of objectively critical judgment of U.S. African American cultural production.

The metaphor of territory is significant, suggesting stability, constancy, and tangibility. The territory of black culture warrants jealous protection for it is the terrain on which race, community, art, and politics are mediated. But as I will explore below, the implicit definition of culture as both territory and occupant requires that a particular cultural complex remain constant, if not stagnant, for both white and black alike. How do we make sense of the fact that Neal's claims made against the Pulitzer Prize nomination committee bear striking similarities to Dadaist and surrealist critiques of the role of the artist in Western bourgeois culture, German social realism, and the attempts of Austro-Marxists to forge an aesthetic political tradition that some on the Austrian left in the 1880s referred to as "metapolitics," or politics in a new key,[27] calling for an aesthetic revolution to accompany the transformation of national politics and economy in Austrian society?

This is not to suggest that the conditions of oppression and the strategies of U.S. African American radical political actors in response are indistinguishable from the struggles, circumstances, and fate of Marxist movements in the Western world (or anywhere else). What I am suggesting, however, is that black nationalist and transnationalist responses to Western bourgeois norms, national chauvinisms, and racisms share normative similarities with *some* critiques of these ills from within the West itself. My point here is that conditions of inequality of the modern world, and the imagined solutions to those conditions, are far less varied than the people who experience them. While singular, Neal's call to action, the people for whom he wrote, are not alone in their singularity.

IV Laboratories and Scientists of Revolution: Black Political Thought and Its Parallels with Marxism

Neal's call for an alternative value system to counteract the influence of Euro-American values upon black peoples bears two features important for rethinking black transnationalism. First, his emphasis on values takes us into the domain of culture and norms that, for many marginalized political positions, is one of the few areas of political disputation in the United States (and now most nation-states) where anticapitalist, antiracist projects have been able to make the case for other, more humane ways of being in the world. Neal's emphasis on values is a starting point for distinguishing political community from racial community, as those U.S. African Americans who share Neal's ideals could be distinguished from those who do not and, more pointedly, from those who accept status quo norms. Here we can begin to draw parallels between black nationalist and transnationalist attempts to create and conserve a counterculture and political and cultural projects almost wholly unrelated to black politics and culture. As will soon become evident, Marxism, black left internationalism, and some variants of black nationalism share the telos of modern politics, believing that a singular organizing principle can mobilize and transform a people, if not a society.

Marxist thought, particularly in its preoccupation with matters of political culture and organization, offers rich empirical examples and theorizations of strategy that are especially relevant for comprehending modern left political and cultural practices in various parts of the black world. Political actors and theoreticians of twentieth-century Marxist traditions attempted to form political parties and cultural organizations, and unions, to serve as sites for the institutionalization of countercultural practices in relation to the capitalist world.

Unlike conservative political organizations, states, and intellectuals, Marxist intellectuals sought a fundamental reordering of values that would not only challenge bourgeois norms but also ultimately transform capitalist societies. There are few parallels in modern transnational social movements to this dimension of Marxism and Marxist-influenced projects, from the horrific Khmer Rouge to Kwame Nkrumah's Consciencism. One of the ironies of the precipitous decline of "actually existing socialism" and the subsequent implosion of the Soviet experiment is that the Soviet state and its satellites were never really in any position to challenge Western cultural, political, and economic dominance, two key points to bear in mind when considering the parallels between African diaspora and Marxist politics and culture.

The Russian Revolution of 1917 provided Marxists and other factions of an internationalist European left with glimmers of hope for the prospect of a poor, relatively underdeveloped society actually overthrowing centuries of monarchal rule and implementing a socialist state. Debates among the Bolsheviks over the role of culture not only for fomenting revolution but also in helping to create an ethos capable of sustaining a revolution after the seizure of state power were waged intensely during the first decade of Bolshevik rule. Leon Trotsky, Joseph Stalin, Nikolai Bukharin, Vladimir Lenin, and Aleksandrovich Malinovskii (Bogdanov) as well as key artists and intellectuals, struggled over the meaning of culture in a revolutionary society. Russian Communist intellectuals such as Bogdanov sought to institutionalize new norms and values amongst a populace that had only known the pomp, pageantry, vast suffering and inequities of a feudal order; capitalism had not yet arrived in Tsarist Russia.[28] Prolekult, the Marxist literary society that spawned thousands of cultural educational institutions in the years immediately following the overthrow of Czar Nicholas II, provides one example of the complicated relation between states, social movements, cultural politics, and attempts at the institutionalization of new norms. Bogdanov's efforts to institutionalize a cultural politics geared toward the education of peasants and proletarians through Prolekult enraged Lenin, who was opposed to the idea of an institution operating independent of party dictates. Lenin eventually succeeded in having Prolekult shut down as an independent organization.[29]

The years 1918 to 1919 were pivotal in Western politics and in the international mobilization of various forms of wage labor in response to what was perceived as a global crisis of capitalism. The Third International was founded in 1919. The armistice of World War I, economic recession, the breakup of several empires, geopolitical realignment of several regions of the world, and a reconfiguration of East-West relations led many nationalist, Marxist, Communist, anarchist, and anarcho-syndicalist movements to perceive a complete breakdown of capitalism and the nation-state system.[30] Many commentators have already noted the inability of much of the European left to distinguish between a significant crisis and the thoroughgoing dissolution of capitalist, imperial hegemonies.[31]

The year 1919 posed at least two major quandaries for Marxist interpretation: first, correctly ascertaining the severity of crises that befell the major powers; and second, determining the means by which the International could effectively replace the political economy and nation-state rubic of Western capitalism with their own template and vision of a world order. For those who predicted the fall of the West, 1919 proved to be a year of grave miscalculation. A more fundamental and prior interpretive problem haunted the internationalist European left and its adherents in various parts of the world—the challenge of actually organizing and mobilizing the vastly divergent and heterogeneous masses of people referred to as the proletariat. Even if the capitalist world was, as some prognosticators indicated, in its death throes, how would the left organize Latin American and Russian peasants, African American sharecroppers, Indian Dalits and East Indian serfs in Trinidad and Guyana—among other peoples and places—to overthrow capitalist states, financial institutions, armies, and industries in the total reformulation of the world order? This question was never successfully answered, not for lack of effort, but due rather to the enormity and impracticality of the presumptions inherent in the question itself.

The sheer impossibility of organizing entire populations whose linguistic, material, and cultural conditions do not render them neatly contained within the category of the "world proletariat," populations of multiple, often conflicting, allegiances, identities, and subject positions reveals the conceit of historical materialism's engine—class conflict. There are those who have posed the "what if" counterfactual to suggest that the organization of coalitions between laboring groups in various national and international contexts would have produced the desired effect of global revolution.

To paraphrase Kenneth Burke, however, the devil is in the details. The view of 1919 as a "lost opportunity" in the history of left internationalism avoids the logistic, strategic and epistemological limitations of the totalized view of the laboring classes and their potential for revolution. Many dispossessed, laboring populations in the world were not among the proletariat. Even if they labored to produce commodities for capital markets, many people throughout the world were (and are) engaged in conditions of labor that could not be described as capitalist (serfdom, servitude, caste, and outright enslavement). The relatively large numbers of the industrial proletariat in the developed First World represented only a portion of millions of people engaged in forms of labor that were even more exploitive than capitalist wage labor. The vision of a world revolution led by European revolutionaries and their accompanying, wage-laboring masses carries with it leftist Eurocentrism that assumed that what was good for the European industrial proletariat was automatically good for laborers of all sorts in the rest of the world.

Robert Young has characterized the conflict between Western capitalist and socialist advocates as a form of sibling rivalry inasmuch as there is ample evidence to suggest that neither Marx, Engels, Adam Smith, nor David Ricardo believed that the non-Western world, with all of its variation, was culturally capable of producing technologies or economic and political systems to match what bourgeois culture achieved in the West.[32] Leninist and Maoist interpretations of Marxism can also be viewed as responses to the cultural-normative gap between a vision of revolution hatched in Berlin and one forged in St. Petersburg or Beijing in the attempt to adopt a theory of revolution imagined for the first world to the realities of the second and third world.

Few Marxist intellectuals acknowledged the practical impossibilities of the Second International's position of a united front. Georg Lukács and Antonio Gramsci were among the few to address the limitations of Euro-left internationalism. In his essay, "Towards a Methodology of the Problem of Organization," Lukács considers the problem of party organization as "one of the most important intellectual questions of the revolution."[33] Specifically, Lukács is concerned with the ever-elusive proletarian revolution that was already late in coming. For Lukács, too many political parties of the left conceived of affecting revolution "in a theoretical way rather than as something that informed all the actions of daily life."[34] He characterized the Second International as replete with "attempts to synthesize the most disparate, the most sharply divergent and incompatible views in the 'unity' of a decision, of a resolution that would do justice to them all. Inevitably these resolutions could not provide any guidance for concrete action and remained ambivalent and open to the most divergent interpretations."[35]

Lukács's critique of the Second International's vague, pluralist strategy of organization was followed by the explication of a less ambitious (and admittedly more sectarian) vision of Communist social and political mobilization, less broad in scope but perhaps more politically viable and feasible. Lukács underscored the distinction between grand histories (the spectacular) and the everyday in macropolitics. To underscore the distinction he drew, Lukács unpacked the dual meaning of "party" to elaborate on two, competing definitions: party as festivity, and party as discipline. *Festum* is the Latin word for *feast*, or, conversely, feast and activities relating to festivity. For Lukács, *post festum* meant the "merely contemplative,"[36] the celebration of resolutions drafted at the party conference and the subsequent euphoria among its participants, not goals attained in actual political engagement with contending political parties, governments, and populations either opposed to or indifferent to the Communist Party's aims, which he described as the "interaction of spontaneity and conscious control."[37] Lukács describes goal orientation in the following way: "As long as an objective still lies beyond reach, observers with particularly acute insight will be able to a certain extent envisage the goal itself, its nature and its social necessity. They will be unable, however, to discern clearly either the concrete steps that would lead to that goal."[38] Thus, for Lukács, the relation between goal and movement is nothing more than the relationship between theory and practice. The chasm between how the Second International represented itself and the reality of its political incoherence and ineffectiveness could only be bridged, according to Lukács, by a more thoroughgoing critique of existing practices and the development of more precise policies capable of implementation.

Gramsci, a contemporary of Lukács, theorized about the relationship between vanguard and mass, between an ideologically based political and popular culture. In his writings after 1919, Gramsci acknowledged that the political opportunities for the left created by the events of 1919 were no longer present. Although he certainly critiqued (in sloganeering jargon at times) the forces of international capital, nationalism, and the emergent fascist movement in Italy, he also offered a very sobering assessment of the internal failures of Italian Communist and trade union movements as well as the internationalist left of continental Europe.

In the essay "Predictions," Gramsci argues that many third and second international advocates sounded much like their capitalist adversaries when their vague and indiscriminate use of messianic, utopian visions of a new world order. Left organizations

> had not succeeded in expelling from itself its petit-bourgeois and intellectual slag. . . . One finds the same element of boundless vanity (The proletariat is the greatest force! The proletariat is invincible! Nothing can halt the inexorable forward march!) and the same element of international ambition, without any precise understanding of the historical forces which dominate the life of the world: without the ability to discover one's own place and function in the world system.

> ... The Third International, just like the League of Nations, is only a crude myth, not an organization of the real wills and actions that can transform the world equilibrium.[39]

Embedded within this passage and made explicit elsewhere in Gramsci's writings is a critique of history and political mobilization as a linear process leading ultimately to mass advance and victory over "the dominant social group." For Gramsci, subaltern movement histories were "fragmented and episodic" and thus resistant to the neat formulations of "the world proletariat" popularized by many of his contemporaries on the left. Modes of subaltern resistance were—and are—nonlinear, disjunctive in their temporalities, and often spontaneous. For Gramsci and Lukács, utopianism and a formulaic certitude about the proletariat's historical mission led to strategic and practical disasters, producing not only disorganization and incoherent agendas but also an inability to envision the very possibilities of death, imprisonment, and outright eradication. These errors were not only strategic gaffes but also lapses in political imagination, an inability to comprehend the left's cultural mission to create imaginaries that did not simply reverse or upend the imaginaries of the powerful. For Gramsci and Lucas, the left needed to acknowledge their own relative powerlessness as part of their political imaginaries.[40] Gramsci's writings provide some evidence of this sensibility, rare among Euro-Marxists:

> It was through a critique of capitalist civilization that the unified consciousness of the proletariat was or is still being formed, and a critique implies culture, not simply a spontaneous and naturalistic evolution ... we cannot be successful in this unless we also know others, their history, the successive efforts they have made to be what they are, to create the civilization they have created and that we seek to replace with our own.[41]

Linking but also distinguishing the term "culture" from its more agricultural origins, Gramsci's definition of culture as critique also implies cultivation, the creating and nurturing of practices and ideas that emerge in oppositional relation to dominant values of bourgeois society. Gramsci assumed culture to provide normative if not actual space and critical distance from dominant institutions and norms. This assessment led Gramsci and other Italian Marxists to try to create organizational conditions within the framework of daily life, such as the Turin workers councils, for example, to protect working-class political culture from the ravages and intrusions of fascist ideologies, bourgeois norms, and daily habits, and not just the nightsticks, guns, clubs, and fists of Mussolini's minions. Gramsci's "war of position" strategy could be viewed as a last best hope for rallying counterfascist movements, a tactical maneuver, a concession to the relative powerlessness of the Italian left. Through war metaphors and analogies, Gramsci nearly always situated cultural politics within the entirety of the social terrain; trench warfare is but one form of warfare. Cultural struggle, the battle of ideas, was both the first and last terrain in the struggle against the fascists, before he himself, and others like him were apprehended, imprisoned, or killed. Therein lies a key strategic quandary of cultural politics that informs not merely Gramscian Marxism, but cultural politics of many forms in the modern era. Laboratories of political culture and cultural politics, while perhaps the last best hope for movements without armies, guerillas, and captains of industry at their disposal, did not represent the mobilization of the left at its most vital, but at its weakest.

The black postnationalist era shares certain common paradoxes with the period of the international left after 1919. When placed alongside Lukács and Gramsci, Diop's harmonious view of culture considered above elides basic questions. Diop's cultural politics avoids internal conflict. Even if we were to accept Diop's claim that culture can serve as a unifying principal for the distinct economic, political, and cultural spheres of properly African existence, how would cultural politics reconcile tensions between economic and political spheres? Lukács's critique of the vast pluralism of the Second International, which banished sectarianism in the embrace of broad coalition, enables us to view the central role—and lack thereof—of ideological formation, articulation, and clarity in the various black world movements. The forward march of black transnationalism, Third Worldism, anticolonialism leading eventually, no matter what cost, catastrophe, or detour, to black emancipation, was not to be.

The breakup of colonial empires did not spell the end of imperialism, the demise of Western powers, or the socialization of the political economy of capital. In moments of so-called global crisis, as in 1898, 1919, 1945, 1968, and 1989, capital regrouped, as did the states, markets, industries, and financial institutions that profited most from it.

The prospects of not merely transnational solidarity, but the complete overthrow of conditions of inequality and domination, ebbed like a wave hurling itself from shore to sea. As part of the *festum* aspect of party politics, Third Worldist, Second Internationalist, and Third Internationalist expressions of solidarity allowed for congregation and mobilization, but were baby steps toward a world of greater possibilities and practices of freedom. The global conditions that conjured up imagery of "the wretched of the earth" and the political possibility of coalitions and strategies among the poor and dispossessed against the world's dominant powers and peoples were not coterminus with the means to bring about mass revolt and transformation on a global scale.[42] What provided the sense of transnational solidarity among African-descended populations, expressed in the work of people like Franz Fanon, Albert Memmi, Angelas Davis and Gilliam, and Malcolm X toward the end of his life, was the larger idea of "Third Worldism," which provided the paradoxical opportunity for transregional, transcolonial political coalitions between third-world peoples as well as their allies in the first and second worlds. The Bandung Conference of Non-Aligned Peoples and the New World Information Order and New World Economic Orders of the 1970s represented instantiations of an alternative world charter generated by these alliances. By the 1970s, however, the theoretical premises of the Bandung era were jolted by the realpolitik of OPEC, as well as the atrocities committed by leaders and regimes of newly minted nation-states.

What links black transnational and the Second and Third Internationalist visions of a liberated future is the commonly shared imaginary of popular unity and progress without the political, technological, or ideological means to bring it about. Although the fall of the Berlin wall, the implosion of the Soviet Union, and the fall of apartheid bear different dates, each bears the mark of an era with dreams seemingly betrayed, frustrated not only by stronger foes but also the impracticality of the dreams themselves. The communities imagined in each instance, a unified black, third-world, or unified proletariat, could only come about with the abolition of the constitutive differences across several national and local communities. The abolition of internal distinction, differentiation, and contradiction could only be achieved with the abolition of the communities themselves.

V. Retreat, Reorganization, and Response

Diop's implicit suggestion that African peoples were not yet ready to comprehend, critically assess, and finally respond to Western impositions hints at a common occurrence—the need felt by African and African American political and cultural actors to retreat from a normative matrix of Western values and create an alternative scheme of cultural material and political valuation. These systems were the black world's analogue to the Socialist world's institutes of socialization—schools, committees for the defense of the revolution, centers and institutes—designed to further and deepen a commitment to Socialist values. From the mosques of the Nation of Islam to self-styled quilombos of 1970s Brazil to Kwame Nkrumah's Ideological Institutes to the centers of the New Jewel Movement in Grenada, centers for retreat and reflection across the black world aimed to develop critical capacities with which to confront the ongoing legacies of colonialism and racial discrimination and to develop popular, critical capacities.

The urge among political actors to create a new society is generated by frustration with an existing social order and the activation of political and social imagination, the desire to experience in daily life what one dreams. Yet the forging of a new society requires more than just imagination. It is not enough for an organization to harbor beliefs and dreams of an alternative world. The imaginative process in politics involves an impulse to nurture an alternative world in private, to seal off a particular formation as a bulwark against the incursions of other, more dominant norms and values. This impulse I shall refer to as the laboratory of political culture. Marxism has had its own variant of the cultural laboratory—organizations designed to create new cultural forms in response to ongoing, repressive conditions. Seeking to constitute cultural forms, commodities, artifacts, and aesthetic and artistic trends, several Marxist regimes imposed productivist models wherein painters, poets, sculptors, and other artists were encouraged or forced to produce art that closely corresponded to the state's ideal of the new man or woman. The Chinese and Russian cultural revolutions, several African and Caribbean nationalist movements of the 1960s and 1970s, and African nationalist mobilization such as Sekou Toure's revolution in Guinea adhered to the productivist model of national culture.[43] Negritude, the Black Consciousness Movement, and the Black Arts Movement each had its own laboratories of political culture for a cultural politics that was both distinctive and oppositional.

A key distinction between the Pan-Africanist, black internationalist, and Negritude projects, on the one hand, and Euro-Marxist political cultures that helped create and nurture oppositional cultural and political strategies, on the other, is that the projects of the Second and Third Internationals were undertaken at a moment in global history when it became increasingly clear that neither capitalism, liberal democracy, nor fascism was about to succumb to proletarian unity or an international socialist political economy. Cultural politics were emphasized in radical European visions at a moment in Western history when leftist political culture represented one of the few political possibilities available to those opposed to both fascism and capitalism, when political dissent was met with repression.

Pan-Africanist nationalism and black internationalism's ascent occurred at a period in world history when the formal demise of Western colonialism and imperialism that led to political independence seemed to almost automatically lead to political, cultural, and economic liberation for much of the world. Cultural emancipation, as Diop, Toure, Neale, Amiri Baraka, Amilcar Cabral, Archie Shepp, Efua Sutherland, Tom Feelings, Odetta, and so many others believed, would provide the lyrics and rhythms to enable African-descended and Third World–people to move within a more egalitarian reality. Cultural struggles were thus part of a larger project of emancipation and liberation.

Like the race concept, the culture concept bears its own set of complications when utilized for political aims. Cultural forms cannot be cordoned off by their producers to serve the intentions and purposes of community members exclusively. Whether it is tango in Argentina, Santería in Cuba, blues in the United States, ska or reggae in Jamaica or Britain, or soca in Guadeloupe, cultural phenomena that have emerged from different corners of the black world have seeped into the national consciousness of many countries without emancipating the peoples from which these practices sprang. Culture, as we've come to know through the work of many anthropologists, is hardly the discrete, self-sustaining, and hermetically sealed entity it is often made out to be. Attempts to designate a cultural form for one purpose, and one purpose only, are often undermined either by groups or individuals who seek to transform the meaning of a cultural form or practice for divergent purposes. Whether it is *capoeira* in Brazil, Martin Luther King's "I Have a Dream" speech, Santeria or son in Cuba, or dub poetry in Brixton, the more militant uses of cultural politics often end up being domesticated and consumed by the very people, societies, and states they were initially designed to decry. There are temporal components here as well, as described in chapter 2 in my conceptualization of parallel politics, as forms of music lyrics or poetry that are considered radical in one generation are rendered tame in the next.

As with presumptions of racial totality, cultural totality also assumes internal stability and the absence of fissures. Yet cultural practices are processes of contestation over meaning, intention, and usage. They are conflicted, never entirely pure, authentic, or unadulterated. This more fluid view of culture forces us to view culture not as a rallying cry, nor simply as another place where politics takes place, but as a process in constant flux, where notions of tradition and community are recast, discarded, upheld, and invented not only in the spheres of cultural practice and articulation deemed as innovative but also in the realms of cultural practice considered traditional. If culture is everything that human beings do, in some sense, to make meaning, then culture is everywhere, and is not the sole province of any specific group, people, or place.

Based on my earlier work on Afro-Brazilian mobilization and cultural politics and the present work, some readers might conclude that I have a particular disdain for the more discourse-centered, symbolic, expressive, and artifact-laden dimensions of resistance by subordinate groups in power relations. The suspicions I hold about cultural politics do not relate to their validity as a form of macropolitical expressions, nor their effectivity in certain spheres and instances, as outlined in chapter 1. My suspicions about cultural practices concern their position in critical interpretations that privilege cultural politics without contextualizing the temporal and contextual circumstances under which cultural practices "become" political. Sorely missing in the study of black politics are efforts to reconsider the relations between political, cultural, and economic practices at a moment in history when commodification has overshadowed most organic forms of black popular culture. Popular culture has become indistinguishable from mass culture in many black public spheres in the United States (although it is not so in Brazil, for example) and radical, organic modes of cultural politics, along with their practitioners, are assessed in terms of popularity, sales, and celebrity, not political and cultural effect. Mass culture and its commodity forms and fetishes are treated in terms of "freedom of expression" and considered paradigmatic of a politics of the downtrodden, poor, and oppressed. What is often considered political expression through cultural practice under these circumstances results in what Adolph Reed has called political concessions.

Cultural politics are thus treated as a compensatory device for the limitations of formal electoral politics and the absence of mass mobilization. Similar to advocates of a resolutely practical, bourgeois politics of elite representation and the economism of advocates of a class-based politics, advocates of cultural practices also exhibit at times a political naïveté. As compensatory politics, cultural politics' relation to macroeconomic and macropolitical phenomena is analogous to the understudy who gets the opportunity to assume the starring role when the marquee actor falls ill. The only drawback however, is that the understudy (cultural politics) assumes the lead role in a hapless production of short duration.[44]

If allegedly countercultural, radical, or alternative cultural actors have the same political imaginaries as their establishmentarian counterparts, then there is little hope for radical black political imaginaries capable of projecting a vision of any society that is distinct from the status quo. If the members of SNCC, SCLC, the Black Panthers, FRELIMO, the ANC, the early Convention People's Party of Ghana, and many more disparate examples in the black world, could not imagine a more just future, then what sense would it have made to risk one's life in the present? If the examination of black popular culture is reduced to the study, celebration, or condemnation of hip-hop culture and rap music, then how distinct really are black political and cultural imaginaries when black intellectuals tend to mine the same, hypercommodified cultural forms that so fascinate white and other commentators? Part of Larry Neal's vision was to provide the critical intellectual means to distinguish cultural forms valued and useful to black emancipation from those that simply enriched entertainment and mass media industries.

This leads to the most critical consideration of the politics/culture nexus. In my view, a political imaginary that encapsulates a vision of what a particular society or community *should* be or become must precede any determination of how cultural practices are created or transformed into instruments of macropolitics. Derrideans and students of Paul Ricoeuer notwithstanding, cultural practices become political thanks to the intentions of their producers. Artifacts, music, and lyrics assume macropolitical meaning on an already contested political terrain. Political community is, after all, the cognitive disposition to distinguish, on the basis of perceived or actual modes of behavior, expression or worldview or both, one individual or group of people from another. This is necessarily distinguished from ethnonational or racial distinction, since neither race, ethnicity, nor nation actually "speaks," makes decisions, or provides a set of dispositions to organize people. Racism, ethnic chauvinism, and nationalism are altogether different matters, since they usually come with a specific set of recommendations about whom to consider inside or outside of a particular community.

The recommendations of the racist or the ethnonational chauvinist are invariably articulated in terms that exceed their bigotry. Neither Hitler, George Wallace, nor Joerg Haider of Austria became politically popular by mere mention of their hatreds. Otherwise, every bigot would be and could be a successful politician. Most justifications of racial inequality and hierarchy, whether in the form of anti-immigration speeches or the advocacy of spatial/racial segregation, are implicit negations of one political community and the affirmation of another. In such invocations of community, ethnonational or racial communities are conflated with political communities.

Let me provide one more example to illustrate the necessity of conceptualizing cultural politics as an outcome of extant political perspectives. James Brown (the Godfather of Soul) was scheduled to give a concert in Boston on Friday, April 5, 1968, a day after Martin Luther King's assassination in Memphis, Tennessee. Brown, a personal friend of King's, was at first asked by the mayor of the city of Boston to cancel the concert, for fear of rioting, particularly in Roxbury and Dorchester, the predominantly black neighborhoods of that city. After much deliberation and negotiation between city officials and Brown's management, the show proceeded. Brown worked with city officials to help keep the crowd calm. He urged the audience, particularly its black members, to respond peacefully, rather than violently, to King's assassination.[45] There were riots in many urban centers of the United States in the days following King's assassination, but Boston was one of the few cities spared the tumult.

Brown's next show was to be held in the nation's capital, Washington, D.C., the day after his show in Boston. Washington, D.C., was one of the many cities torn up by rioting in the aftermath of the assassination. In order to spare the city further structural damage and a higher casualty and injury toll, Brown went on local television and said the following:

> I know how everybody feels . . . I feel the same way. But you can't accomplish anything by blowing up, burning up, stealing and looting. Don't terrorize. Organize. Don't burn. Give kids a chance to learn. Go home. Look at TV. Listen to the radio. Listen to some James Brown records. The real answer to race problems in this country is education. Not burning and killing. Be ready. Be qualified. Own something. Be somebody. That's Black Power.[46]

Lyndon Baines Johnson and public officials in the city of Boston knew what we all know about James Brown: for one thing, he can move a crowd. The question is, Where? We can only wonder what kind of message Pablo Neruda, Oscar Brown Jr., Odetta, or Victor Hara from Chile would have delivered under those circumstances. Neruda might have told the crowd to march toward the capitol and seize it, Odetta, Nina Simone (Mr. Backlash), or Oscar Brown Jr. might have told the audience to engage in civil disobedience. The two points I am making here are as follows: (1) we cannot deduce the form or content of an artist's creativity from his or her politics; and (2) the political perspective of a cultural actor influences, if not determines, the explicit and implicit political content of the actor's form of artistic production.

When cultural practices and forms are utilized to articulate macro- or micropolitical aims, the politics, not the cultural forms, require our attention first. It is not that a realm referred to as "culture" does not, or could not, give rise to practices and principles that oppose a particular macropolitical community. Rather, the exercise of macropolitical imagination within a form or sphere defined as cultural must first be conditioned to the macropolitical imagination of the practitioners. It would be nonsensical, in my view, to declare an artifact or practice defined as cultural to be macropolitical simply because it is a cultural practice. As already outlined in chapter 1, if cultural practices are mere instruments of politics or, at best, only modes of political articulation, then culture itself would not exist as an entity distinct from politics. The "culture is politics" argument is thus flawed because it relies on an equivalence that conflates distinction. We could not explain why Aimí Cesaire, for example, was a surrealist and Negritude artist and not a social realist poet. Pablo Neruda happened to be a brilliant poet, independent of his tirade against the overthrow of Allende, but he was also a Communist. Rather than engage in sterile and ultimately futile worry over whether he was a poet or a Communist first, I believe it is safe to assert that his poetic attack of Nixon is not among his best verse. Nevertheless, Neruda's condemnation of Nixon would be absolutely nonsensical if Neruda were a facist. Neruda's poem then only makes macropolitical sense if we acknowledge first that he was after all, on the left.

The third problem with the culture-is-politics formulation is the transideological dimensions of cultural politics. There are innumerable examples of modern nation-states, particularly authoritarian and totalitarian regimes, utilizing ideas, artifacts, and practices to conserve and to project ideals about the nuclear family, race, gender, and regional and national identity and render them religiously or politically sacred. The Third Reich is the most obvious case, but there are many others, particularly in the histories of nationalism. Examples range from James Brown's appeal to D.C. blacks to go home and watch television to "Papa Doc" Duvalier's use of Voudun iconography and practices to develop popular support for his populist and ultimately ruthlessly authoritarian regime to J. K. Tuffour's assumption of multiple vestiges during the presidential campaigns in Ghana to appeal to different regional and ethnic constituencies.[47] The U.S. state has consistently utilized a full array of cultural practices for global dissemination whenever there has been a perceived crisis at the level of state, during wars cold and hot. The flooding of Italy with U.S. films after World War II, the use of jazz musicians such as Dizzy Gillespie to travel throughout the world during the cold war[48], and most recently, George W. Bush's regime's use of novelists and poets (including "Arab-American" writers sent to many countries in the Middle East) after September 11, 2001, to project an image of internal cultural diversity and variation, all point to the ways in which cultural articulation, often viewed as divorced from politics proper, is utilized to service particular ideologies, regimes, and states.

Anthropologists such as Victor Turner and Renato Rosaldo have shown us how[49] states and dominant groups often assume more conciliatory and accommodating stances toward militant groups and their iconographies of protest once those marginalized political actors have been defeated, killed, or made to exist in a sort of symbolic détente. Time blunts, softens, or erodes cultural politics of protest, allowing the norms of emergent subordinate groups to become incorporated into dominant strains of thought and action. The dialectic of cultural preservation and erosion characterizes cultural politics among the oppressed and its incorporation or repression by states and dominant groups, as evidenced in transnational black public spheres. In the United States, Ida B. Wells, Malcolm X, and A. Philip Randolph are all now on U.S. postage stamps (first-class!). Marcus Garvey, now a national hero in Jamaica, also has his own postage stamp long after he was considered a buffoon by much of the Creole elite. In Congo and Ghana, Patrice Lumumba and Kwame Nkrumah are acknowledged as national heroes by political actors and regimes that sought to—and did—oust them from formal political power. In Brazil, Anastasia, Ganga Zumba, and Zumbi are now part of the national iconography, achieving status recognition and honor in death that they did not come close to achieving in life. Each of these examples provide evidence of how states come to incorporate once recalcitrant political figures into an iconography of national inclusion.

It is important to acknowledge that many transnational black imaginaries are incorporated into the extant disjuncture and inequalities separating the largely well-off, overdeveloped world from what used to be referred to as the undeveloped. In Brazil and, even more starkly, in Cuba, African-derived music, dance, and other modes of artistry are means for states and industries to obtain tourist dollars. African states such as Ghana, Togo, Burkina Faso, and Guinea now generate tourist dollars by projecting imagery of trans-African and diaspora continuities to African-descended peoples all over the world in search of their roots, or at least a reasonable facsimile.[50] Thus, freedom and emancipation from slavery, colonialism, and neocolonialism have now been packaged as travel excursions, transforming African-descended peoples into a cadre of Pan-Africanist consumers. In the global marketplace, kente cloth can coexist with the iconic imagery of black lawn jockeys that still grace front lawns and storefronts in various parts of Europe and the Americas. The disjuncture between political and cultural representation is ubiquitous enough throughout the black world to at least cause us to question the claim that culture is the sole or even the appropriate means to collective empowerment.

Black cultural practitioners nevertheless serve as an important barometer of formal political participation in the institutions and public spaces of Western societies. Black cultural practices have often preceded formal, contestatory political participation in white-dominated public spheres. Black public festivity in white society has often foreshadowed black macropolitics, by making congregation and open association between African-descended subjects possible. In Britain and the United States, West Indian immigrant celebrations of carnival were themselves macropolitical struggles over the ability of community members to engage in public discourse and cultural events and organizations outside of their relegated spheres in segregated societies.[51] In Brazil, Getulio Vargas's approval and recognition of *capoerista* performances as a national treasure helped carve out space for the proliferation of *capoeira* academies as well as other cultural and religious institutions of the *comunidade negra*,[52] institutions that, in turn, engaged in various forms of cultural and political struggle over racial discrimination. In these and many other examples, black cultural practitioners in many black life-worlds have done important macropolitical work in blurring the formal and informal markers between non-white and white spaces. Sometimes it is cultural actors with their own macropolitical visions who make black congregation and macropolitics in white public spheres possible.

VI Conclusion: Communities and Politics Imagined

The course of this book moved from the more implicit, disparate, and elusive forms of political life to the most explicit mode of macropolitical articulation, social movements, political parties, nationalist and anticolonial struggles. Political parties, their related sites of disputation and discourse, and social movements are where most studies of black political phenomena begin. Ending rather than beginning with the most obvious forms of political community and struggle might allow readers to trace the gestation of political community in the discrete and disparate practices of daily life, the isolated acts of individuals, which are then transformed into groups of people who decide to create common cause. Quest for unity through both forms of party have proven elusive in black life-worlds, as a means of conclusion, for now, I will elaborate on this elusiveness.

Vanderlei Jose Maria's hybrid vision of utopia and pragmatism was rooted firmly in the belief that a single organizational entity could encompass the political aspirations, will, and forms of Afro-Brazilian politics. This part of his vision remains utopic. The political histories of modern national and extranational movements, transnational black politics among them, have never been encompassed by a single political party. No single party or organism could possibly contain and organize all the political tendencies of a community that itself has been characterized in racial or chromatic terms not ideological terms. Given the synergies and mediations between micro- and macropolitics, political parties cannot always anticipate the political phenomena in a society that will force the party's platforms, aims, and agendas to change, expand, or narrow. Whether in the United States, with the civil rights movement and the change in allegiance from the Republican to Democratic Party in the 1930s; the shift in Brazil from monarchy to republic; authoritarian to democratic regimes; or in Tanzania and Trinidad, where anticolonial movements transformed into nationalist political parties and, ultimately, regimes, political parties with initial aims of total representation ultimately narrow their focus and, consequently, their base of popular support.[53]

Political parties and social movements invariably represent interests, not races. One of the recurrent silences in the study of African diaspora culture and politics is an exploration into the tensions between calls for racial unity and the realities of political interests, and the need to distinguish between the social and political subjectivities of African and African-descended populations. As socially constituted subjects, there are individuals and populations whose constellation of cultural identifications, forms and artifacts, and worldviews (in addition to phenotype) would be characterized as black. Not all of those people, however, process, create, and reproduce micro- and macropolitics in identical ways. Political distinctions between black transnationalists on matters of women's rights or the rights of homosexuals and bisexuals to participate in black politics provide two of many examples that suggest that the very category and practice of black transnationalism is unstable and open, rather than closed. The political subjectivities of black transnationalism are necessarily distinct from its social subjectivities. Transnational mobilization against African and U.S. apartheid, the U.S. invasion of Grenada, or the capital murder of Ken-Saro Wiwa in Nigeria brought about alliances among political actors and organizations who were defined more by their opposition to specific state activities—and perhaps ideology—than by racial or cultural symmetry.

I would like to return now to Gramsci's critique of the Third International, specifically his charge that the sloganeering adherents to the popular front internationalism of the epoch failed to comprehend "the historical forces that dominate the life of the world" and were, as a result, unable "to discover one's own place and function in the world system." The African diaspora, is incomprehensible apart from the phenomena of racial slavery and the formation of global capitalism that preceded it. The cultural continuities and discontinuities among African and African-descended populations, as well as their social movements for freedom, are structured by the historical, political, and economic processes that have unfolded from these two macrophenomena. Political agency, then, has been moored to the legacies of slavery and colonialism. The attainment of freedom, first from bondage, then from colonialism, nonsovereignty, and noncitizenship became the next stage in the evolution of transnational black politics and in the political maturity of nation-states with majority or near-majority African and African-descended populations. The coalitions that helped bring about the end of various forms of state and nonstate oppression among African and African-descended populations, however, are not timeless. The fissures and ruptures of strategic alliances are constituted by and constitutive of politics. Political communities, and the political identities and identifications associated with them, are activated and maintained through acts of will and imagination in response to constraints and limitations, as well as possibilities.

The next phase, however, of political agency in transnational black politics is more difficult to chart, precisely because its moorings are anchored in specific rather than general phenomena. Will black immigrants and long-time residents of EU countries adopt aversive strategies in relation to their white EU counterparts? What black ideologies, if any, might be utilized to mobilize black citizens and subjects in these countries? In the absence of explicit antiracist mobilization, will coagulation and aggregation occur with greater frequency than before? Distinction and fragmentation, rather than black or Third World solidarity, might come to characterize contemporary forms of black diaspora micro- and macropolitics more consistently than movements emphasizing complete solidarity and unity.

The discontinuities of transnational black politics are evidenced in the first decade of the twenty-first century by the divergent trajectories of racially conscious political mobilization in several of the aforementioned countries, with perhaps the starkest contrasts among the United States, Brazil, and South Africa. In South Africa, the "residual" effect of apartheid racism has wended its way into present-day political institutions and practices. The demands made by the ANC and other organizations for black South Africans to abandon racialism of all forms has not eradicated racism itself.

In the United States, retrenchment and reformulation of the New Right has led to even further narrowing of the spectrum of considered public opinion and discourse. With the continued dismantling of affirmative action and a society that increasingly resembles the dysfunctional companies upheld by public funds during the Bush I, Reagan, and Bush II regimes, vast segments of white labor, Mexican Americans, U.S. African Americans, and immigrant groups work and live under conditions of existential nakedness, uncovered by health insurance and lacking legal redress for conditions of racial violence and discrimination. In this respect at least, U.S. government domestic policies toward its poor and vulnerable are perhaps synchronized with the neoliberal globalization, as the distinction between domestic and foreign policy decreases. States and industries collude to protect their respective corporate interests, leaving people to rely on trumped-up individualism and voluntarism as a means to mere subsistence. From airline bailouts after 9/11 to the continued privatization of Medicare, increasing numbers of the U.S. populace are now more, to use the polite Brazilian expression, "*desbunda*." With respect to Brazil, one of the ironies of the insurgence of the Black Movement and its allies with regard to placing issues of affirmative action on the national policy agenda is that the Brazilian government has begun to implement institutional practices that are currently being abandoned in the United States—at least for now.

Taken as part of a black transnational whole, these three national struggles for human rights, state-sanctioned protections, and political participation do not point to a single or singular "forward march" of black mobilization and enfranchisement but rather to the disparate, jagged, and sometimes regressive features of the movement toward the actual emancipation of African diaspora subjects from legacies of slavery and ongoing practices of racial discrimination. In each case, however, institutional racism, social mobilization, and state policy are critical variables in the dynamics of racism and anti-racism and in the quest for justice and equality.

Part of a new understanding of contemporary racisms and racial solidarities, racism should be distinguished from racial construct. Even if we do accept the social constructivist stance and distinguish between race and racism, the social constructivist account of the race concept tells us little about how the race concept is deployed in actual power relations, within societies, between and among individuals and groups, and by or against states. Viewed as ideological forms or rhetorical utterances (see chapter 3), iterations of the race concept and racism are but two utterances upon a wider discursive and rhetorical field of racial politics. (See fig. 8.3.)

Upon this wider field, there are *many* utterances (constructs) related to race and racism. These utterances are not necessarily related to one another. Nor are they coded or imbued with the dynamics of dominance and subor-

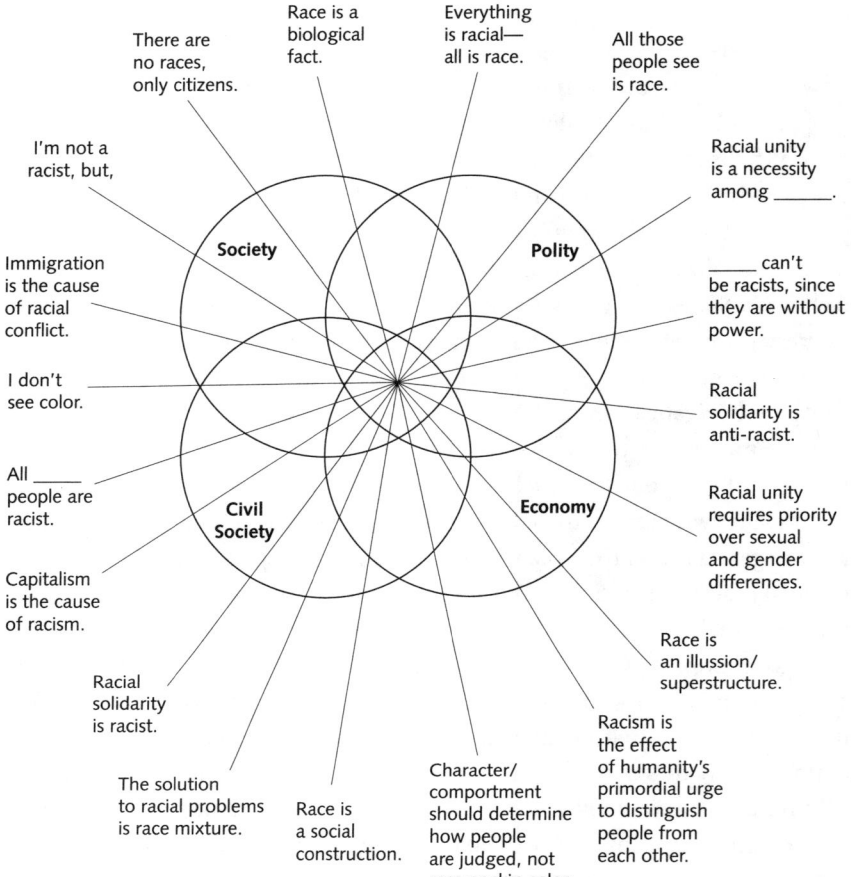

Figure 8.3
The Discursive Field of Racial Politics

dination, resistance and acquiescence, in identical fashion. Nationalism, yet another social construct no matter how many times nationalist leaders and imposters evoke imageries of blood, earth, and skin has led many, willingly and unwillingly, to their deaths. The political importance of nationalism as a thoroughly modern ideal cannot be grasped by identifying its artificial—as opposed to its supposedly organic, inherently human—character, but by recognizing that it is cloaked in ideals that matter to people: ideals of family, community, dignity, freedom, oppression, and fear, which impel them to engage in death-defying, often dastardly acts. Race's instrumentality, rather than its essence, is what requires more attention.

Neither the race concept nor racism operates outside or separate from other ideas, concepts, or social dynamics. They are usually bound up with or implicated in other political, material, and cultural phenomena, even if they are not reducible to those phenomena. This leads to a second limitation of the social constructivist's resolutely philosophical, analytic, and somewhat apolitical understanding of the race concept and racism's relation to politics and political communities. On its own, the social constructivist definition of the race concept does not address a key concern/question for politically and economically subordinate groups and their members: How do minority-group members build and maintain affective—not to mention, macropolitical—relationships in a racist environment? The social constructivist denial of the existence of multiple races within the human family may provide a more appropriate answer to a question on an advanced undergraduate or graduate student examination about the race concept than will the answer given by a student educated and socialized to believe in inherently biological differences to account for racial distinctions among humanity, but it will not stop racially motivated attacks against minority group members, institutional racism in police departments, or a preference for lighter skinned beauty pageant contestants in India, Brazil, or Jamaica. The social constructivist account does not provide minority groups seeking to counter racisms within and against their communities with answers to the existential and communitarian challenges racisms pose for those who have no choice but to live in their midst.

Thus, the community organizer who uses the idea of blackness, even Afrocentric ideals, to promote "racial solidarity" in an impoverished black community in Los Angeles, Rio de Janeiro, or Johannesburg does not necessarily employ the same rhetoric as the white supremacist who exhorts potential and actual followers to kill all Jews and blacks. Nor do they necessarily share the same macropolitics because of their deployment of race constructs. Both actors may operate within the same discursive, rhetorical field of national, even transnational racial politics, but from different subject positions and perhaps most important, with different *reasons* for employing the race concept and the notion of racial hierarchy. Merely attributing the deployment of these concepts to identical or similar origins does not get us very far in explaining the motivations for or the consequences of their actions.

Part of the problem in equating certain, not all forms of racial solidarity, with racial essentialism is that advocates as well as detractors of "racial unity" neglect the existential and ontological challenges posed by a notion of a single black community, whether domestic or transnational.[54] Advocates of "racial unity" often conflate political and racial identifications. Detractors who oppose racial solidarity (antiessentialists among them) rarely provide an alternative scenario for black political actors to draw on in creating political and cultural communities.

The problem lies, as outlined in chapters 4 and 7, in identifying black communities and individuals as victims of or respondents to racism, rather than as community makers in their own right. The social constructivist who responds to the so-called racial essentialist with the admonition that "race is a social construction" neglects to account for the fact that victims and respondents of racism live in communities with preoccupations and aspirations that extend beyond racism's clutches. Even within the seemingly most essentialized forms of black politics and identity claims, decidedly nonracial judgments and qualifications are operative in deliberation and discourse. These people and their communities are not *defined* by racism but by a multiplicity of experiences of which racism is a part. Although Gilroy's *There Ain't No Black in the Union Jack* does not address black British politics, his identification of the need to distinguish between antiracist strategies and black politics and community identifications is useful here.

> The concrete settings in which racial subordination is experienced may shape the patterns of discontent which precede protest so that they do not progress beyond the immediate circumstances in which spontaneous resistance or accommodation are the most likely responses. People do not encounter racism in general or in the abstract, they feel the effects of its particular expressions; poor housing, unemployment, repatriation, violence or aggressive indifference.[55]

The "concrete settings" to which Gilroy refers, are also the places and spaces where community is made and remade. They are the locales and circumstances in which people embrace or avoid interaction with members of other groups. The coagulate politics of chapter 2 and the aversive strategies outlined in chapter 4 occur in such settings. Questions such as "How do I live with racism?" "How am I going to pay next month's rent?" "How do I forge bonds with members of my immediate community, as well as with those outside of my (spatial, religious, racial, national) community?" and "Where can I find affordable childcare?" are the sorts of questions—by no means exhaustive—that take precedence over whether race is "real" or imagined. Other questions, posed in chapter 7, concern matters of hybridity, such as interracial adoption of black children in Canada, the United States, and the United Kingdom. How one lives and conducts oneself in such communities is a separate question, though not unrelated, from whether one believes in a biological, political, or social constructivist understanding of race. A notion and practice of political community, short of ideas of racial, cultural, or national unity could aid in the reconstitution of national and transnational modes of black politics.

A materially based humanism aimed specifically at the amelioration of conditions of poverty, homelessness, land evictions, and the provision of health care, in addition to the elimination of racisms, could become part of nationally specific and transnational agendas for black activism. A transnational black humanism, in the form of a radical communitarianism, could remind many within as well as outside of black communities of the need, as Sylvia Wynter wrote in an important article, to enter the ceremony of the human.[56] At the same time however, the humanism to which I refer, is not a fetishization of the human or the black at the expense of the ecology and a larger world in which we live. The black humanism I am suggesting here is not a celebration of fictive racial essences but of actually existing communities in places as distinct as Johannesburg, Detroit, São Paulo, Veracruz, Berlin, Brussels, Kingston, and Georgetown. Rather than run from the notion of community, as in the work of Jean Luc Nancy and Michel Foucault, the politics of racial segregation and the ensuing bonds formed by cultural practice make black communities in the Caribbean, Europe, the Americas, as well as Africa, inescapable.

The search for political community necessarily leads people to unfamiliar places, away from families, neighbors, nations, and states, toward convergences that are, in some cases, yet to be mapped, convergences that do not correspond to extant political orders. In the case of black political communities and political thought, we should keep in mind that the search for political community must be distinguished from a quest for perfection and sameness, while it is also distinct from "the way things are." Somewhere in between reality and utopia are operative quests for a better world, or at least, communities better than the ones in which people find themselves. This is the stuff of which politics, people, and community are made and remade.

NOTES

1. Introduction

1. Octavio Paz in Rita Guibert's *Seven Voices: Seven Latin American Writers Talk to Rita Guibert* (New York: Knopf, 1973), 181–276.
2. That is, with the exception, of course, of the literature on social movements.
3. The term "black public sphere" came into prominence with the publication of the edited volume *The Black Public Sphere*, the result of a special issue of the journal *Public Culture*, concerning the spaces of deliberation available to black populations in multiple societies, the articulation and enunciation of various black life-worlds, as well as the interaction between black public spheres and other spaces and forms of public discourse and deliberation. Readers would be best served consulting these texts for further elaboration on this topic.
4. See Alfred Schutz and Thomas Luckman, *Structures of the Life-World, Volumes 1 and 2*, trans. Richard M. Zaner and H. Tristram Engelhardt Jr. (Evanston, Ill.: Northwestern University Press, 1973; 1975).
5. See, for example, Percy Hintzen and Jean Muteba Rahier, eds. *Problematizing Blackness* (New York: Routledge, 2003).
6. See Sheldon Wolin, "Political Theory as a Vocation," *American Political Science Review* 63, no. 4 (December 1969): 1062–1082.
7. See Robert Bates, "Comparative Politics and Rational Choice: A Review Essay" *American Political Science Review* 91, no. 3 (September 1997): 699–704.
8. See Raymond Williams, *The Long Revolution* (New York: Columbia University Press, 1961); Raymond Williams, *The Year 2000* (New York: Pantheon, 1983); Aaron Wildavsky, *Federalism and Political Culture*, eds. David Schleicher and Brendon Swedlow (New Brunswick, N.J.: Transaction Publishers, 1998); Marvin Harris, *Cultural Materialism: The Struggle for a Science of Culture* (New York: Random House, 1979); and Lloyd and Susanne Hoeber Rudolph, *The Modernity of Tradition Political Development in India* (Chicago: University of Chicago Press, 1967). See also Alan Ryan, *Philosophy of the Social Sciences* (London: Macmillan, 1976); and Anthony M. Messina, *Race and Party Competition in Britain* (Oxford: Clarendon Press, 1989).
9. Carl Schmitt, *The Concept of the Political* (New Brunswick, N.J.: Rutgers University Press, 1976). Schmitt argues, "In contrast to the various relatively indepen-

dent endeavors of human thought and action, particularly the moral, aesthetic, and economic, the political has its own criteria which express themselves in a characteristic way. The political must therefore rest on its own ultimate distinctions, to which all action with a specifically political meaning can be traced. Let us assume that in the realm of morality the final distinctions are between good and evil, in aesthetics beautiful and ugly, in economics profitable and unprofitable. The question is then whether there is also a special distinction which can serve as a simple criterion of the political and what it consists" (26).

10. Ibid., 23.
11. Ibid., 30.
12. Ibid., 22.
13. Ibid., 38.
14. Ibid., 32.
15. See Leo Strauss, "Comments on Carl Schmitt's Der Bergriff des Politischen" in *The Concept of the Political by Carl Schmitt* (New Brunswick, N.J.: Rutgers University Press, 1976), 82–87.
16. There are limitations, however, to the distinction between micro- and macropolitics and its application to nonliberal societies and states. Antonio Gramsci understood that in authoritarian societies the distinction between politics and culture becomes insoluble due to the repression of relatively free and spontaneous association in the public sphere. Yet the realm of culture can become a sphere of political deliberation and resistance under conditions that prohibit or severely limit deliberation within the state and in civil society.
17. Schmitt, 1976, 26.
18. The Los Angeles riots are an example of a site where the chasm between micro- and macropolitics is bridged. The acquittal of the police officers who brutally beat Rodney King in Los Angeles in 1992 provided the opportunity for many black and brown residents of the city to respond, at times collectively, other times indiscriminately, to long-simmering tensions in the form of violent rebellion. See Robert Gooding-Williams, ed., *Reading Rodney King, Reading Urban Uprising* (New York: Routledge, 1993). For a distinct though in some ways related conceptualization of micro- and macropolitics, see William E. Connolly, *Why I Am Not a Secularist* (Minneapolis: University of Minnesota Press, 1999). See, particularly, chapter 6, "An Ethos of Engagement."
19. For a description of Wittgenstein's introspection and self-examination after concealing his Jewish heritage to gain membership into an Aryan-only gymnasium, see Ray Monk, *Ludwig Wittgenstein: the Duty of Genius* (New York: Free Press, 1990); W. E. B. Du Bois, *The Souls of Black Folk* (New York: Vintage, 1986); and Frantz Fanon, "Racism and Culture" in *Black Skin, White Masks*, trans. Charles Lam Markmann (New York: Grove, 1967).

Chapter 2

1. Henri Lefebvre, *Critique of Everyday Life, Vol. 1*, trans. John Moore (London: Verso, 1991), 14–15.

2. Ray Charles, "You Don't Know Me." Written by Cindy Walker and Eddy Arnold (New York: ABC Paramount Records, 1962). Ray Charles's rendition of this particular song conveyed its dual meaning, as a love song and as a reminder to whites in the United States of the incipient but still not fully articulated protest to conditions of racial domination. Its dual meaning then, is in keeping with a long line of stories and songs in many forms of black New World cultures that emphasize indirection. For discussions of this broader practice in Afrodiasporic cultural practices, see Lawrence W. Levine, *Black Culture and Black Consciousness* (New York: Oxford University Press, 1978); David Scott, *Refashioning Futures: Criticism after Postcoloniality* (Princeton, N.J.: Princeton University Press, 1999); Robert Farris Thompson, *Flash of the Spirit: African and Afro-American Art and Philosophy* (New York: Vintage, 1984); and Henry Louis Gates, *The Signifying Monkey: A Theory of African American Literary Criticism* (New York: Oxford University Press, 1988).
3. See Kamal Sadiq, "When States Prefer Non-Citizens over Citizens: Conflict over Illegal Immigration into Malaysia," *International Studies Quarterly* 49 (March 2005): 101–122; and "Have Documents, Will Travel: The Challenge of Illegal Citizenship in Developing Countries," under review, February 2006.
4. C. L. R. James interview in *Visions of History*, eds. Henry Abelove, Betsey Blackmar, Peter Dimock, and Jonathan Schneer (New York: Pantheon, 1983), 274.
5. See Doug McAdam, Sidney Tarrow, and Charles Tilly, *Dynamics of Contention* (New York: Cambridge University Press, 2001).
6. My reading of these incidents could be perceived by some as precluding the possibility that solidarity among black males motivated the responses of the two clerks to my plights, rather than any "racial" motivation. My interpretation of quotidian racism does not preclude the simultaneous examination of gender discrimination. My purpose here is to develop a theory of quotidian politics that is defined by its explication, not by the empirical or even fictional examples utilized to illustrate the theory and its constituent concepts. A theory's utility and endurance lies in its explanatory capacity beyond the immediate conditions and objects of its explanation. Thus, Newton's understanding of gravitational pull could be demonstrated with an object other than an apple, and the top of someone's head other than Newton's own. Similarly, a theory of quotidian politics and more specifically, coagulation, could be applied to instances of intergender conflict (as could Williams's structure of feeling) involving women and men, or the moment in Tony Kushner's play *Angels in America* when the male nurse attending Roy Cohn's character provides the latter character with information about the deleterious effects of a particular treatment for HIV/AIDS. When the character of Roy Cohn asks the male nurse character for an explanation of his almost conspiratorial provision of information, the nurse character replies, "from one faggot to another." It is a remarkable moment in the play, particularly since it is followed by the Cohn character's rejection of the male nurse's attempt at solidarity, and preceded by the male nurse's barely contained expressions of contempt and suspicion of

the Roy Cohn character and what he (Cohn) stands for, his hatreds and self-hatreds. This is an ideal moment of coagulation as Cohn makes clear that he wants nothing to do with the black male nurse's politics or the communities—racial, sexual, and spatial—which the nurse inhabits. There is no prospect of coalition between them. Yet a third opportunity to extend and apply the concept of coagulation outside the immediate examples I have provided comes from the very real example of librarians and librarian associations across the United States reacting to the Department of Homeland Security's attempts to monitor the reading habits of documented library patrons by allowing patrons to access books and other media without recording their usage histories in formal library records that would detail a patron's loan history. In these instances, a second, nonformal transcript is thus produced as a means of circumventing a nation-state policy to engage in surveillance of library patrons in the attempt to discern reading habits that might reveal familiarity with "terrorist" literature. This collective act to limit the state's reach into reading and media consumption habits of individuals within U.S. society was not part of a movement to gain more federal funding for libraries or to engender a movement against the Bush government's policies in Iraq or Afghanistan. It is not clear if either the librarians or patrons would share macropolitical affinities on issues other than the right to privacy in the selection and consumption of reading and other materials available at a public library. See Raymond Williams, *Marxism and Literature* (Oxford: Oxford University Press, 1977); and Tony Kushner, *Angels in America* (New York: Theatre Communications Group, 1993).

7. For a discussion of minimalist and maximalist approaches to the study of domination and resistance in peasant studies, see David Hunt, "From the Millennial to the Everyday: James Scott's Search for the Essence of Peasant Politics," *Radical History Review* 42 (Fall 1988): 156–172.
8. Michel De Certeau, *The Practice of Everyday Life* (Berkeley and Los Angeles: University of California Press, 2002).
9. See James Scott, *Weapons of the Weak: Everyday Forms of Peasant Resistance* (New Haven, Conn.: Yale University Press, 1985), especially, chapter 7, "Beyond the War of Words: Cautious Resistance and Calculated Conformity," 241–304.
10. See Elias Canetti, *Crowds and Power* (London: Gollancz, 1962).
11. Timothy Mitchell, *Rule of Experts: Egypt, Techno-Politics, Modernity* (Berkeley and Los Angeles: University of California Press, 2002).
12. For a review of this literature and incidents, see Michael Hanchard and Erin Chung, "From Race Relations to Comparative Racial Politics: A Survey of Cross-National Scholarship on Race in the Sociaal Sciences" *Du Bois Review*, vol. 1, no. 2 (September 2004): 319–343.
13. See Hannah Arendt, *On Violence* (New York: Harcourt, Brace and World, 1969). For example, Arendt makes the following claim about the emergence of violent protest during the student movements of the 1960s: "Serious violence entered the scene only with the appearance of the Black Power movement on the campuses. Negro students, the majority of them admitted without aca-

demic qualification, regarded and organized themselves as an interest group, the representatives of the black community" (18).
14. Ibid.
15. Franz Fanon, *The Wretched of the Earth* (New York: Grove Press, 1968), 37.
16. Arendt, 1969, 21.
17. Anne McClintock, *Imperial Leather: Race, Gender and Sex in the Colonial Contest* (New York: Routledge, 1995).
18. A more benign reading of Arendt on the topic of racist violence is offered in Danielle Allen, *Talking to Strangers* (Chicago: University of Chicago Press, 2004).
19. Frederick Douglass, *Narrative of the Life of Frederick Douglass, An American Slave* (New York: Anchor, 1963), 74.
20. Michel Foucault, "*Society Must Be Defended: Lectures at the Collèges de France, 1975–1976*" (New York: Picador Books, 2003), 28.
21. Thomas Hobbes, *Leviathan* (New York: Penguin, 1968), 394.
22. Australian outlaw and national hero Ned Kelly. See John Phillips, *The Trial of Ned Kelly* (Sydney: Law Book Co., 1987).
23. Guiliani was subsequently knighted by the British monarchy for his expressions of empathy to the citizens of New York City after the 9/11 attacks.
24. Terry Callier, "Lament for the Late AD" on *Terry Callier Alive* [audio recording], Mr. Bongo 2001 (permission granted by Terry Callier and Bongo Records).
25. See Levine, *Black Culture and Black Consciousness*; Gates, *The Signifying Monkey*; and Thompson, *Flash of the Spirit*.
26. For a sample discussion of spatial racial segregation in urban cities, see Teresa Caldiera, *City of Walls: Crime, Segregation, and Citizenship in São Paulo* (Berkeley: University of California Press, 2000); Nancy Denton and Douglas Massey, *American Apartheid: Segregation and the Making of the Underclass* (Cambridge, Mass.: Harvard University Press, 1998); Mike Davis, *City of Quartz* (London and New York: Verso, 1990); and George Reid Andrews, *The Afro-Argentines of Buenos Aires, 1800–1900* (Madison: University of Wisconsin Press, 1980).
27. Pablo Neruda, *Incitación Al Nixonicidio Y Alabanza de La Revolución Chilena* (Lima, Perú: Edición Causachún, 1973), 11–12; © Fundación Pablo Neruda, 1973. Used by permission.
28. English translation by Emma Cervone.
29. For example, see my exchange with the late Pierre Bourdieu and Loic Wacquant concerning the specter of U.S. cultural imperialism. See also Michael Hanchard, "Afro-Modernity: Temporality, Politics, and the African Diaspora" in *Alternative Modernities*, ed., D. P. Gaonkar (Durham, N.C.: Duke University Press, 2001) 272–298; and Pierre Bourdieu and Loic Wacquant, "On the Cunning of Imperialist Reason," *Theory, Culture, and Society* 16, no. 1 (1999): 41–58.
30. James Scott, *Domination and the Arts of Resistance: Hidden Transcripts* (New Haven, Conn.: Yale University Press, 1990), x.
31. Ibid, xi.
32. Ibid., xvii.

33. Ibid., 111.
34. Criticisms of Scott's work, principally by historians, sociologists, and, less so, political scientists, can be organized into three broad areas. Although Scott's account of power is nonpositivist, one commentator has argued that Scott's representation of peasant politics in the mythical village shares at least one methodological affinity with models that posit politics as a series of rational actions. In political science, Timothy Mitchell has teased out the ways in which Scott's distinction between thought and practice is symptomatic of mind-body distinctions in Western thought. The third area of critique places Scott in a long line of romanticists who describe essentially good, almost prepolitical subjects in their accounts of class conflict in Britain, slave culture and revolt in the New World, and scholarship that is loosely encompassed by the term "subaltern studies." As Charles Tilly writes, the "populist turn" in U.S. sociology and history in the 1960s led a generation of scholars and their successors to emphasize "history from below," "empowerment," and "agency." See Charles Tilly, "Domination, Resistance, Compliance…Discourse," *Sociological Forum* 6, no. 3 (September 1991): 593–602; Timothy Mitchell, "Everyday Metaphors of Power," *Theory and Society* 19, no. 5 (October 1990): 545–577; David Hunt, "From the Millennial to the Everyday."
35. See Richard Iton, *Solidarity Blues: Race, Culture and the American Left* (Chapel Hill: University of North Carolina Press, 2000); and Adolph Reed, *Stirrings in the Jug: Black Politics in the Post-Segregation Era* (Minneapolis: University of Minnesota Press, 1999).
36. Robin D. G. Kelley, *Race Rebels: Culture, Politics, and the Black Working Class* (New York: The Free Press, 1994), 8.
37. Ibid., 8.
38. Ibid., 9.
39. Ibid., 3–4.
40. Ibid., 8.
41. See Aline Helg, *Our Rightful Share: The Afro-Cuban Struggle for Equality* (Chapel Hill: University of North Carolina Press, 1995). See also W. E. B. Du Bois's view of Sam Hose's knuckles in Atlanta in Du Bois *The Souls of Black Folk* (New York: Vintage, 1986).
42. See my discussion of Agamben in chapter 6.
43. Richard Bensel, *The American Ballot Box in the Mid-Nineteenth Century* (New York: Cambridge University Press, 2004).
44. Kelley, *Race Rebels*, 59.
45. See Timothy Tyson, *Radio Free Dixie: Robert F. Williams and the Roots of Black Power* (Chapel Hill: University of North Carolina Press, 1999).
46. Linda M. G. Zerilli, *Feminism and the Abyss of Freedom* (Chicago and London: University of Chicago Press, 2005).

Chapter 3

1. Karl Mannheim, *Ideology and Utopia* (New York: Harcourt Brace Jovanovich, 1936), 89.

2. Ibid., 89n26.
3. In his famous essay on mass beliefs, Philip Converse eschewed use of the term "ideology" largely in accordance with this assumption. As a consequence, the more Durkheimian, Hegelian, and Gramscian understandings of ideology (lower case ideologies that have their influence upon daily life), were ignored by students of American political culture in political science. In European circles, however, thinkers ranging from Louis Althusser and Henri Lefebvre to Cornelius Castoriadis have provided alternative theorizations and examinations of ideology in daily life that are not inevitably bound up with a state- or elite-generated ideological form. See Philip Converse, "The Nature of Belief Systems in Mass Publics" in *Ideology and Discontent,* ed., David Apter (New York: Free Press, 1964), 206–261; John Zaller, *The Nature and Origins of Mass Opinion* (Cambridge: Cambridge University Press, 1992).
4. Highlighting the paucity of APSR articles between 1958 to 1967 on issues of racial conflict, poverty, civil disobedience, and violence in the United States during this period, David Easton writes "There can be little doubt that political science as an enterprise has failed to anticipate the crises that are upon us... we have also worn collective blinders that have prevented us from recognizing other major problems in our discipline" ("The New Revolution in Political Science" *APSR* 63, no. 4 [December 1969], 1051–1061); 1057.
5. As Fogg-Davis's careful review of the state of recent books on race-focused research in the discipline of political science highlights (correctly, in our view), there is very little scholarship produced by Western political theorists on the politics of race. See Hawley Fogg-Davis, "The Racial Retreat of Contemporary Political Science," *Perpectives on Politics* 1 (2003), 555–64.
6. For one of the few accounts of the ideological context in which the study of American politics has been situated as related to the neglect of the study of ideology itself, see William E. Connolly, *Political Science and Ideology* (New York: Atherton Press, 1967).
7. This is also true for formal political participation in New World and African polities, though this is not the focus of this chapter.
8. Debates over the relevance of quantitative methods in political science are too vast to enjoin here.
9. See Alvin Gouldner, *The Dialectic of Ideology and Technology* (London: Macmillan Press, 1976).
10. See Taeku Lee, *Mobilizing Public Opinion: Black Insurgency and Racial Attitudes in the Civil Rights Era* (Chicago: University of Chicago Press, 2002); and Doug McAdam, *Political Process and the Development of Black Insurgency, 1930–1970* (Chicago: University of Chicago Press, 1982).
11. Eddie Glaude, *Exodus! Religion, Race and Nation in Early 19th Century Black America* (Chicago: University of Chicago Press, 2000); Cornel West, *Prophetic Fragments: Illumination of the Crisis in American Relations and Culture* (Grand Rapids, Mich.: William B. Eerdmans, 1993); and Cornel West, *Prophecy Deliverance: An African American Revolutionary Christianity* (Louisville, Ky.: Westminster John Knox Press, 2002).

12. See Alexander Weheliye, "'I Am I Be': The Subject of Sonic Afro Modernity," *Boundary 2*, 30, no. 2 (2003), 97–114; Fred Moten, *In the Break: The Aesthetics of the Black Radical Tradition* (Minneapolis: University of Minnesota Press, 2003).
13. Robert E. Lane, *Political Thinking and Consciousness: The Private Life of the Political Mind* (Chicago: Markham Publishing Company, 1969), 324.
14. Ibid.
15. Robert E. Lane, *Political Ideology: Why the American Common Man Believes What He Does* (New York: The Free Press, 1962), 324.
16. I use the term "pragmatism" here with some qualification, acknowledging the difference between a tactical form of pragmatism that Lane may have glimpsed in the responses of his informants to moral dilemmas in daily life and the more philosophical treatment of pragmatism as a strategic component of reflective and quotidian life in the work of William James and John Dewey. For both James and Dewey, there was no distinction between the pragmatic and the moral in deliberation and consideration of practical dilemmas of daily life. See John Dewey and James Hayden Tufts, *Ethics* (New York: Henry Holt, 1908); John Dewey, *Context and Thought* (Berkeley and Los Angeles: University of California Press, 1931); William James, *Essays in Philosophy* (Cambridge, Mass.: Harvard University Press, 1978). For a more nuanced treatment of the relation between ideological forms and public opinion in U.S. political culture, see David Truman, *The Governmental Process: Political Interests and Public Opinion* (New York: Knopf, 1971).
17. Henry Highland Garnet, "An Address to the Slaves of the United States of America" (1843), in *Black Nationalism in America*, ed. John H. Bracey Jr., August Meier, and Elliot Rudwick (Indianapolis, Ind.: Bobbs-Merrill, 1970), 71. Emphasis in original.
18. Ibid., 75.
19. See Taylor Branch, *Parting the Waters: America in the King Years, 1954–1963* (New York: Simon & Schuster, 1998).
20. James Baldwin, "The Black Boy Looks at the White Boy," in *Nobody Knows My Name* (New York: Vintage International, 1993), 216–241.
21. Ibid, xii.
22. James Baldwin, *Tell Me How the Long the Train's Been Gone* (New York: Dell, 1968), 12–13.
23. Sander Gilman, *Jewish Self-Hatred: Anti-Semitism and the Hidden Language of the Jews* (Baltimore, Md.: Johns Hopkins University Press, 1986), 2.
24. Ibid., 1.
25. Ibid., 2.
26. The controversies surrounding Spike Lee's film *Bamboozled*, the paintings of Michael Ray Charles, and the art of Lorna Simpson and Kara Walker attest to the fact that self-hatred remains a relevant theme in contemporary black public and critical discourses. Self-hatred can be characterized as a black ideological form. It is not material in an objective sense; self-hatred won't be found in any job description for which a black person is sought. People as varied as Louis Armstrong, Clarence Thomas, Sammy Davis Jr., Chris Tucker, Butter-

fly McQueen, and Halle Berry have been accused of self-hatred. Minstrelsy, blackface, and other exaggerations and mutilations of the self to conform to an image of blacks—as distinct from their social, political, and cultural realities—can be encompassed by Gilman's definition of the forms of self-abnegation employed to render derogatory imagery of blacks simultaneously natural, reasonable, and plausible, but no less objectionable, to vast segments of black populations. For examples, see Donald Bogle, *Toms, Coons, Mulattoes, Mammies and Bucks: An Interpretive History of Blacks in American Films*, 4th ed. (New York: Continuum, 2001); and Saidiya V. Hartman, *Scenes of Subjection: Terror, Slavery and Self-Making in Nineteenth Century America* (New York: Oxford University Press, 1997).

27. Eldridge Cleaver, *Soul on Ice* (New York: Dell, 1992), 26–27.
28. Robyn Wiegman, *American Anatomies: Theorizing Race and Gender* (Durham, N.C.: Duke University Press, 1995).
29. Cleaver, 1992, 101.
30. Robert E. Lane, *Political Thinking and Consciousness*, 89.
31. Karl Mannheim, *Ideology and Utopia*, 58. Mannheim concludes this particular passage with a discussion of the implications of the very disparate quality of working-class consciousness and sociality in relation to its bourgeois counterparts in the modern age: "The individual members of the working-class for instance, do not experience all the elements of an outlook which could be called the proletarian *Weltanschauung*. Every individual participates only in certain fragments of this thought-system, the totality of which is not in the least a mere sum of these fragmentary individual experiences." This point echoes in some ways my discussion of the diversity of responses to racial domination in chapter 3.
32. Ibid., 59.
33. Ibid., 55.
34. Ibid., 56.
35. This fragmentation and reduction of more comprehensive perspectives on politics is one of the many pitiful consequences of the political spectacle in U.S. political culture since the latter half of the twentieth century, and has affected black critical public discourse as well. The world of sound bites has little time for context or the elaboration of a larger worldview, other than on specialized talk shows. Black macropolitical discourse is affected by this as well.
36. See Franklin Frazier, *Black Bourgeoisie: The Book That Brought the Shock of Self-Revelation to Middle-Class Blacks in America* (New York: The Free Press, 1997).
37. See Philip Foner. *American Socialism and Black Americans: From the Age of Jackson to WWII*. (Westport, Conn: Greenport Press, 1977).
38. W. Jeffrey Bolster, *Black Jacks: African American Seamen in the Age of Sail* (Cambridge, Mass.: Harvard University Press, 1997).
39. See Paul Gilroy, *Against Race: Imagining Political Culture beyond the Color Line* (Cambridge, Mass.: Harvard University Press, 2000).
40. See Winston James, *Holding Aloft the Banner of Ethiopia* (New York: Verso, 1998); and Huey P. Newton's discussion of "pork chop nationalism" to charac-

terize the culturalist tendencies of Karenga's organization US in his 1968 publication *Huey Newton Talks to the Movement: About the Black Panther Party, Cultural Nationalism, SNCC, Liberals and White Revolutionaries* (Chicago: SDS).

41. See George Padmore, *Pan-Africanism or Communism* (New York: Doubleday, 1971).

42. As noted by Miroslav Hroch, *Social Proclamations of National Revival in Europe: A Comparative Analysis of the Social Composition of Patriotic Groups among the Smaller European Nations* (New York: Cambridge University Press, 1985), Eric Hobsbawm, *Nations and Nationalism Since 1780* (Cambridge: Cambridge Univeristy Press, 1990), and Benedict Anderson, *Imagined Communities: Reflections on the Origin and Spread of Nationalism* (London: Verson, 1983), among other students of nationalism, nationalist leaders most often emerge from what could be characterized as petit bourgeois strata of societies. There are many parallels and sociological similarities among black nationalists and transnationalists. A political sociology of black transnationalist figures is a project sorely needed.

43. See Stephen Thernstrom and Abigail Thernstrom, *America in Black and White* (New York: Simon and & Schuster, 1999); Michael C. Dawson, *Black Visions: The Roots of Contemporary African-American Political Ideology* (Chicago: University of Chicago Press, 2001); Tali Mendelberg, *The Race Card: Campaign Strategy, Implicit Messages, and the Norm of Equality* (Princeton, N.J.: Princeton University Press, 2001).

44. Raymond Williams, *Marxism and Literature* (Oxford: Oxford University Press, 1977); Terry Eagleton, *Ideology: An Introduction* (New York: Verso, 1991).

45. The lead author on this chapter, by his own admission, is in no position to assess the quantitative dimensions of their survey research design.

46. The disciplines of sociology and anthropology, as well as many literatures of the humanities, have a much more comprehensive literature on the topic of self-hatred than political science, as a means of elaborating and distinguishing exogenous and endogenous forms of racism among racial and ethnic groups in the United States, Europe, and various postcolonial settlements.

47. Paul Sniderman and Thomas Piazza, *Black Pride and Black Prejudice* (Princeton, N.J.: Princeton University Press, 2002), 27–29.

48. Ibid., 22.

49. Ibid.

50. Molefi Asante, who is most often associated with Afrocentrism, has actually developed a theory of Afrocentricity that, like most theories, can be distinguished from other theories of Afrocentrism by its internal components and mode of argumentation.

51. Mary Lefkowitz, *Not Out of Africa: How Afrocentrism Became an Excuse to Teach Myth as History* (New York: Basic Books, 1996); Stephen Howe, *Afrocentrism: Mythical Pasts and Imagined Homes* (London: Verso 1998).

52. See for example, Molefi Asante, *The Painful Demise of Euro-Centrism* (Trenton, N.J.: Africa New World Press, Inc, 1999), 199n2.

53. The question of whether Afrocentrism is coherent as either philosophy or theory is a separate consideration, and is not the object of our evaluation.
54. Sniderman and Piazza, *Black Pride and Black Prejudice*, 22.
55. Philip Curtin, "Recent Trends in African Historiography and Their Contribution to History in General" in *General History of Africa, Volume 6* (Berkeley and Los Angeles: University of California Press, 1989), 54–71.
56. See Curtin, "Ghettoizing African History" in *The Chronicle of Higher Education*, March 3, 1995.
57. Basil Davidson, ed., *The African Past: Chronicles from Antiquity to Modern Times* (Boston: Little, Brown, 1964), 3–4.
58. Curtin certainly has distinguished himself in polemical exchanges by proclaiming the alleged politicization of the study of Africa by U.S. African Americans that has, in his view, lowered standards of scholarship in the teaching, hiring, and written scholarship on Africa in the United States. Davidson, a self-described African, friend, and comrade to many African leaders including the legendary Amilcar Cabral of Guinea-Bissau, sought to demystify African history against those who would either glorify a precolonial African past or make Africa out to be a receptacle for European penetration.
59. Edward Said's *Orientalism* (New York: Vintage, 1979), for example, has been a simultaneously polarizing and galvanizing text for scholars and activists in various parts of the world on the subject of Eurocentrism. Bitter polemics around the "truths" and "falsehoods" of Said's argument were and are a form of ideological struggle between adherents to causes, movements, and positions who view their arguments in political terms as having stakes and implications that exceed the realm of the literary. So too with Afrocentrism and its variants. See Lucius Outlaw, *On Race and Philosophy* (New York: Routledge, 1996); Mia Bay, *The White Image in the Black Mind: African American Ideas about White People, 1830–1925* (New York: Oxford University Press, 2000).
60. Gouldner characterizes the proliferation of ideology as the consequence of the battle between religion and science. Those who utilized specious reasoning to formulate arguments were thus cast in the role of ideologues, people who willfully provided misinformation, often in very skillful ways, to deceive the uneducated and the unfamiliar. By the mid-nineteenth century, Kant would declare that he, along with other Europeans, lived in "the age of criticism," a characterization of an era when the grudging decline of religious and monarchial monopolies upon knowledge led to the proliferation of independent scholars, pundits, novelists, poets, and writers of dramatic verse who used literature to both celebrate and denounce the transformation of societies in the process of capitalist development and the destruction of feudal, monarchial orders. See Gouldner, *The Dialectic of Ideology and Technology* and *The Two Marxisms: Contradictions and Anomalies in the Development of Theory* (New York: Seabury Press, 1980); Immanuel Kant, *Critique of Pure Reason* (London: Macmillan, 1973).
61. See Cecil Conteen Gray, *Afrocentric Thought and Praxis: An Intellectual History* (Trenton, N.J.: Africa World Press, 2001).

62. For example, Marcus Garvey, considered by many to be the prototypical black nationalist of the twentieth century, drew much of the inspiration for his political and economic agenda and theory from classical and then contemporary Western sources ranging from Plato to Lenin, from Mussolini to Henry Ford. A similar claim could be made about contemporary Afrocentrists, many of whose ideologies rely heavily on certain ideas about human evolution that spring directly from Western racist theories of hierarchically ordered human development—polygenesis, to be precise. Thus, even the most opposed examples of black cognition and behaviors contain evidence of assimilation, even if only minimally— of certain elements of Western (U.S.- and non-U.S.-based) mores, technologies, tastes, habits, and ideologies into their "black" belief systems, and cultural-political and ideological practices.
63. See Padmore, *Pan-Africanism or Communism*.
64. Sniderman and Piazza, *Black Pride and Black Prejudice*, 69–71.
65. In their view, any skepticism about canonical accounts of Africa's relation to the West or claims attesting to the presence of African philosophy in European philosophical systems are evidence enough of Afrocentrism's paranoic elements among educated, middle-class blacks. One need not ascribe to Afrocentric principles, or agree with the totality of Martin Bernal's claims about African intellectual contributions to European philosophy to doubt previous generations' accounts of Africa's contributions to world civilizations. In distinguishing revisionist historiography from imperial history, there are a number of accounts that document extensive trade, travel, and intellectual exchanges between those known as Africans and Europeans well before the two slave trades. Thus, it is quite plausible that at least some blacks who are familiar with this historiography would at least question several dominant accounts of Africa's relation to the West.
66. See Sniderman and Piazza, *Black Pride and Black Prejudice*, 24.
67. Ibid., 46.
68. Ibid., 24.
69. Ibid., 47.
70. See Richard Hofstadter, *The Paranoid Style in American Politics and Other Essays* (New York: Knopf, 1965).
71. See Ronld Fryer and Matthew O. Jackson, "Categorical Cognition: A Psychological Model of Categories and Identification in Decision Making," American Bar Foundation working paper no. 2115 (2002), 9.
72. See Robert L. Allen, *The Port Chicago Mutiny* (New York: Amistad, 1993).
73. See Sniderman and Piazza, *Black Pride and Black Prejudice*, 24.
74. For Wolin, the antitheoretical thrust of the behavioral revolution was a reflection of the pragmatic dimension of American political culture and its preoccupation with technique and technology rather than ideology.
75. See Sheldon Wolin, "Political Theory as a Vocation," *American Political Science Review* 63, no. 4 (December 1969): 1071.
76. Dawson, *Black Visions*.

77. Carl G. Hempel, "Typological Methods in the Natural and Social Sciences," in *Science, Language and Human Rights* (Philadelphia: American Philosophical Association, 1952), 71.
78. The sense of harmony, of wholeness, in Taylor is what critics of hermeneutical approaches and communitarianism in general complain about. They claim that Taylor and other adherents to these means of interpreting human agency ignore internal hierarchies and tensions in communal life. Power and inequality are overlooked in the search for community.
79. Charles Taylor, "Interpretation and the Sciences of Man," in *Understanding and Social Inquiry*, ed. Fred Dallmayr and Thomas McCarthy (Notre Dame, Ind.: University of Notre Dame Press, 1977), 101–131.
80. Glaude, *Exodus!*; West, *Prophetic Fragments*; West, *Prophecy Deliverance*; Outlaw, *On Race and Philosophy*; Evelyn Brooks Higginbotham, *Righteous Discontent: The Women's Movement in Black Baptist Churches, 1880–1920* (Cambridge, Mass.: Harvard University Press, 1993); P. Sterling Stuckey, *Going through the Storm: The Influence of African American Art in History* (Oxford: Oxford University Press, 1994); James H. Cone, *A Black Theology of Liberation* (Philadelphia: Lippincott, 1970).

Chapter 4

1. C. L. R. James, *American Civilization* (Cambridge, Mass.: Blackwell, 1992), 200.
2. See Ellis Cose, *The Rage of a Privileged Class* (New York: HarperCollins, 1993); and Joe R. Feagin and Melvin P. Sikes, *Living with Racism: The Black Middle Class Experience* (Boston: Beacon Press, 1994).
3. See Nicole J. Shelton, "A Reconceptualization of How We Study Issues of Racial Prejudice," *Personality and Psychology Review* 4, no.4 (2000): 4374–4390.
4. See Kristin Myers, "Race Talk: The Perpetuation of Racism through Private Discourse," *Race and Society* 4 (2001): 3–26; Eduardo Bonilla-Silva and Tyrone Forman, "'I Am Not a Racist but...' Mapping White College Students' Racial Ideology in the USA," *Discourse and Society* 11, no. (1) (2000): 50–85.
5. For Britain, see Barnor Hesse and S. Sayyid, "Narrating the Postcolonial Political and the Immigrant Imaginary" in *A Post-Colonial People: South Asians in Britain*, eds. N. Ali, V. Kai, and S. Sayyid (London: Hurst, forthcoming 2006); Paul Gilroy, *There Ain't No Black in the Union Jack: The Cultural Politics of Race and Nation* (Chicago: University of Chicago Press, 1991). For France, see Nonna Mayer, "Is France Racist?" *Contemporary European History* 5 (1996): 119–127; Ariane Chebel d'Appollonia, *Les Racismes ordinaires* (Paris: Presses de Sciences Po, 1998).
6. See William Smith, "Black Faculty Coping with Racial Battle Fatigue: The Campus Racial Climate in a Post-Civil Rights Era" in *A Long Way to Go: Conversations about Race with African American Faculty and Graduate Students*, ed. Darren Cleaveland (New York: Peter Lang Publishers, 2004); Chester Pierce, "Offensive Mechanisms" in *The Black Seventies*, ed. Floyd B. Barbour (Boston: Porter Sargent, 1969), 265–282.

7. See Robert Miles, *Racism after "Race Relations"* (New York: Routledge, 1993); Paul Gilroy, *Against Race: Imagining Political Culture Beyond the Culture Line* (Cambridge, Mass.: Harvard University Press, 2000).
8. See David Theo Goldberg, *The Racial State* (Malden, Mass.: Blackwell, 2002); Kwame Anthony Appiah, *In My Father's House: Africa in the Philosophy of Culture* (New York: Oxford University Press, 1992).
9. Michael Hanchard and Erin Chung, "From Race Relations to Comparative Racial Politics: A Survey of Cross-National Scholarship on Race in the Social Sciences," *Du Bois Review* 1, no. 2 (September 2004): 319–343.
10. Owen Flanagan and Amelie Rorty, *Identity, Character, and Morality* (Cambridge, Mass.: MIT Press, 1990).
11. In the case of Brazil, the work of Robin E. Sheriff provides one comparative possibility. In *Dreaming Equality: Color, Race and Racism in Urban Brazil* (New Brunswick, N.J.: Rutgers University Press, 2001), 72, she writes about the role of silence in *favela* (slum) communities in response to racist slights. This ethnography of the Morro do Sangue Bom (not its true name) describes *favelados* (*favela* residents) and provides description and linguistic analysis of conversations as well as silences about experiences of racial discrimination. Silence may be a form of avoidance of feeling "defenseless and dependent. If my informants' narratives of racism sometimes seemed to be articulated in a confessional register, what was being confessed was not only vulnerability but the demoralizing and humiliating failure to defend oneself."
12. This helps to distinguish my use of the term "aversion" from the more restrictive use of the term in clinical and experimental psychology, wherein "aversion" refers specifically to techniques designed and employed to modify behavior in institutionally controlled populations (electric shocks producing certain predictable outcomes for example). Unlike controlled settings, where the experimenter well understands the effects of his implementation of a technique or technology designed to modify behavior, racism's practice and its effects are often not well understood by those who unwittingly engage in racist or prejudicial behavior toward another group member. Depending upon the institutional context and the controlled population under consideration, the recipient of a behavior-modification practice may not be fully aware of the effect of an aversive strategy (such as the mentally ill or developmentally disabled). In actual encounters in the public sphere, however, it is my contention that practitioners of aversive strategies comprehend the effects of racially discriminatory attitudes, practice, and behaviors, particularly given their previous experience with the racially or ethnonationally dominant population and the patterns of behavior exhibited and observed among them. Aversion is thus the sociological equivalent of a withdrawal or recoil after a sudden "shock." The shock is associated with context, the person or persons who initiated the shock in the first instance, which greatly influences subsequent interactions with members of the dominant group. Unlike controlled settings, there are instances when those social/contextual "shocks" can be avoided.
13. See Rogers Smith, *Civic Ideals* (New Haven, Conn.: Yale University Press, 1999).

14. My formulation of secondary discrimination is distinct from Adrian M. S. Piper's conceptualization of "higher-order discrimination" (also called second-order discrimination) to explain the more nuanced forms of racial bigotry experienced and exhibited by members of dominant racial groups in the United States, whose harboring of racially prejudicial attitudes toward blacks and other minorities is distinct from more blatant forms of discrimination, but also leads to moral crisis or self-denial. See Adrian M. S. Piper, "Higher Order Discrimination" in *Identity, Character and Morality,* Owen Flanagan and Amelie Oksenberg Rorty, eds. (Cambridge, Mass.: MIT Press, 1990), 12.
15. See, for example, Jennifer Hochschild, *Facing Up to the American Dream* (Princeton, N.J.: Princeton University Press, 1996).
16. See Saul Axelrod and Jack Apsche, *The Effects of Punishment on Human Behavior* (New York: Academic Press, 1983).
17. Joseph Carens, *Culture, Citizenship and Community* (Cambridge: Oxford University Press, 2000), 98.
18. Ibid., 99.
19. See Jon Elster, *Sour Grapes: Studies in the Subversion of Rationality* (Cambridge: Cambridge University Press, 1983).
20. See Stephen Lukes, *Power: A Radical View* (London: Macmillan, 1974); John Gaventa, *Power and Powerlessness: Quiescence and Rebellion in an Appalachian Valley* (Champaign: University of Illinois Press, 1982); Robert Dahl, *Who Governs? Democracy and Power in an American City* (New Haven, Conn.: Yale University Press, 1961).
21. Anticipating charges of essentialism because of the use of such phrases as "black life" or "black behavior," the more phenomenological term "life-world" is utilized to convey the sense of interaction between individuals and ideas within a particular community, the interaction of individuals as group members with those "outside" the self-defined group, and the multiple variation, cross-cutting cleavages within racial- or ethnic-minority communities as well as between these communities, their individual members and segments, and other communities. Black life or black life-worlds are *already* plural, constituted by various external and internal mechanisms and phenomena that are both peculiar to a particular group as well as symptomatic of the society in which the group finds itself.
22. John Langston Gwaltney, *Drylongso: A Self Portrait of Black America* (New York: Random House, 1980).
23. Ibid., 38.
24. Ibid., 102.
25. Ibid., 130.
26. Frederick Harris, "Collective Memory, Collective Action, and Black Activism in the 1960's" in *Breaking the Cycles of Hatred: Memory, Law, and Repair,* ed. Martha Minow (Princeton, N.J.: Princeton University Press, 2002).
27. Amelie Oksenberg Rorty and David Wong, "Aspects of Identity and Agency" in *Identity, Character and Morality,* Owen Flanagan and Amelie Oksenberg Rorty, eds. (Cambridge, Mass.: MIT Press, 1990), 21.

28. Piper, *Identity, Character and Morality*, 286.
29. See Donald Bogle, *Toms, Coons, Mulattoes, Mammies and Bucks: An Interpretive Story of Blacks in American Films* (New York: Continuum, 2001); Michael Rogin, *Blackface, White Noise: Jewish Immigrants in the Hollywood Melting Pot* (Berkeley and Los Angeles: University of California Press, 1998); Saidiya V. Hartman, *Scenes of Subjection: Terror, Slavery and Self-Making in Nineteenth Century America* (New York: Oxford University Press, 1997); and Eric Lott, *Love and Theft: Blackface Minstrelsy and the American Working Class* (New York: Oxford University Press, 1995), 27.
30. See "Fight Grows over a Stamp U.S. Sees as Racist and Mexico Adores," Elisabeth Malkin, *New York Times*, July 2, 2005.
31. See Ronald G. Fryer and Matthew O. Jackson, "Categorical Cognition: A Psychological Model of Categories and Identification in Decision Making." ABF working paper no. 12115 (Chicago: American Bar Foundation, 2002), 9.
32. See Michael C. Dawson, "A Black Counterpublic? Economic Earthquakes, Racial Agendas and Black Politics" in *The Black Public Sphere*, ed. The Black Public Sphere Collective (Chicago: University of Chicago Press, 1995), 199–228.
33. See Reuel Rogers, *Afro-Caribbean Immigrants and the Politics of Incorporation: Ethnicity, Exception, or Exit* (Cambridge: Cambridge University Press, 2006).
34. For a critique of the politics of recognition position from the vantage point of political theory, see Patchen Markell, *Bound by Recognition* (Princeton, N.J.: Princeton University Press, 2004).
35. G. W. Allport, *The Nature of Prejudice* (Reading, Mass.: Addison-Wesley, 1954); Thomas Pettigrew, "Inter-group Contact Theory," *Annual Review of Psychology* 49 (1998): 65–85.
36. For a similar argument see Mary Jackman and Marie Crane, "'Some of My Best Friends Are Black' . . . Interracial Friendship and Whites' Racial Attitudes," *Public Opinion Quarterly* 50 (1986): 459–486.
37. Michael Dawson, "The Widening Racial Divide in American Public Opinion: War, Protest, and Support for the President." Presented at Bellagio Center, Rockefeller Foundation, Lake Como, Italy, July 17, 2004.
38. See Craig Calhoun, ed., *Habermas and the Public Sphere* (Cambridge, Mass.: MIT Press, 1993).

Chapter 5

1. Belated articles by Eduardo Mendieta and Eddie Glaude address some of the modular and comparative implications of the debate about black public intellectuals for thinking about Latino intellectuals. See Eduardo Mendieta, "What Can Latinas/os Learn from Cornel West? The Latino Postcolonial Intellectual in the Age of the Exhaustion of Public Spheres," *Neplanta*, Vol. 4, No. 2 (2003): 213–235; and Eddie Glaude, "On Mendieta's Latino Public Intellectual," *Nepalta: Views from the South* 4, no. 2 (2003): 257–261.
2. See Michael Berube, "The New Black Intellectuals," *The New Yorker* (January 1995), pp. 73–80.

3. Robert Boynton, "The New Intellectuals" in *Atlantic Monthly* 275 no. 3 (March 1995): 53–70.
4. Adolph Reed, "What Are the Drums Saying, Booker?: The Current Crisis of the Black Intellectual," *Village Voice* (April 11, 1995): 31–36.
5. Ibid.
6. Martha Biondi, *To Stand and Fight* (Cambridge, Mass.: Harvard University Press, 2003).
7. See Robin D. G. Kelley, *Race Rebels: Culture, Politics, and the Black Working Class* (New York: The Free Press, 1994).
8. See Cornel West, "The Dilemma of the Black Intellectual" in *The Journal of Blacks in Higher Education*, No. 2 (Winter 1993–94): 59–67; Michael Foucault, *Politics, Philosophy, Culture: Interviews and Other Writings, 1977–1984*, trans. Alan Sheridan, ed. L. D. Kritzman (New York: Routledge, 1988).
9. Reed, "What Are the Drums Saying, Booker?" 36.
10. Ibid., 36.
11. Rigoberta Menchu, *I Rigoberta Menchu*, ed. Elizabeth Burgos-Debray, trans. Ann Wright (London: Verso, 1984).
12. Tom Ling, Kevin Bonnet, Simon Bromley, and Bob Jessop, "Thatcherism and the Politics of Hegemony: A Reply to Stuart Hall," *New Left Review* 153, no. 1 (September–October 1985): 87–101.
13. Edward Said, *Representations of the Intellectual* (New York: Pantheon, 1994).

Chapter 6

1. Henri Lefebvre, *Critique of Everyday Life, Vol. 1*, trans. John Moore (London: Verso, 1991), 146.
2. One of the enduring ironies of the role of literature as a mode of political articulation in republican societies (where rule of law and codes of conduct presumably govern the market and the polity) is literature's capacity to reveal the processes of privilege and powerlessness—rather than the text of constitutions, laws, and edicts—that actually govern daily life. When the powerful are brought down by misdeeds, whether Martha Stewart, Helmut Kohl, Alberto Fujimori, or Richard M. Nixon, details about their hubris are often cited as cautionary morality tales in a society presumed to be just and egalitarian overall. As many of the less privileged have discerned, however, the occasionally scandalized powerful are merely those who get caught.
3. Giorgio Agamben, *Homo Sacer: Sovereign Power and Bare Life*, trans. Daniel Heller-Roazen (Stanford, Calif.: Stanford University Press, 1998).
4. See John M. Ellis, *Heinrich Von Kleist: Studies in the Character and Meaning of His Writings* (Chapel Hill: University of North Carolina Press, 1979); and Jay Hillis Miller, "Laying Down the Law in Literature: The Example of Kleist," *The Cardozo Law Review* (July–August 1990), 11: 1491–1514. Ellis's critical interpretation of Kohlhaas treats the story as if it were two stories, with the first portion focusing on the details of the swindle, the nepotistic machinations that frustrated justice, and Kohlhaas's enactment of vengeance. The second

portion is treated in terms of an increasingly mystical turn in the narrative, and the seemingly inexplicable role of gypsies in the latter half of the story is considered a symbol of this turn. Ellis explains this turn as Kleist's way of conveying Kohlhaas's irrationality, his rigidity, and his own attempt to curry favor with the Elector of Saxony, who is not an evil administrator but, actually, a rather weak and feeble man with vaguely amorous connections to one of the noble families involved in this shady affair. Thus, a character flaw, rather than a strongly immoral state and administrator, is at the source of Kohlhaas's problems. Yet the specter of racial alterity is hardly mentioned in Ellis's account or in much of the Kleist criticism. The specter of alterity, I am suggesting, is clearly a preoccupation for Kleist, as evidenced in another Kleist story, "The Betrothal in Santo Domingo." This story focuses on the Haitian Revolution, a mestizo girl (mulatta would have been the more appropriate translation), and a former slave from the Gold Coast who kills his kindly master during the uprising that produced the Haitian Revolution. Given these two stories, there is at least a plausible hypothesis for Kleist's preoccupation with the idea of so-called race mixture, violence, and rebellion, more than the critical literature gives credit for. See Heinrich Von Kleist, "Michael Kohlhaas" and "The Betrothal in Santo Domingo," in *The Marquise of O and Other Stories*, trans. Martin Greenberg (New York: New American Library, 1960).

5. Kleist, *The Marquise of O and Other Stories*, 87.
6. Ibid..
7. Ibid., 104.
8. Ibid., 107.
9. E. L. Doctorow, *Ragtime* (New York: Fawcett Crest, 1974), 133.
10. Ibid.
11. See Edward Berlin, *King of Ragtime: Scott Joplin and His Era* (New York: Oxford University Press, 1994).
12. Doctorow, *Ragtime*, 158.
13. Ibid., 199.
14. Ibid., 156.
15. Kleist, *The Marquise of O and Other Stories*, 125.
16. Ibid.
17. Ibid., 129.
18. Ibid.
19. Martin Luther's admonitions to the German people against Jews and Turks can be gleaned in his writings on Turks and his open letter to the German people. See J. M. Porter, ed., *Luther: Selected Political Writings* (Philadelphia: Fortress, 1974); Gerhard Falk, *The Jew in Christian Theology: Martin Luther's Anti-Jewish Vom Schem Hamphoras* (Jefferson, N.C.: McFarland, 1992).
20. Rogers Brubaker, *Citizenship and Nationhood in France and Germany* (Cambridge, Mass.: Harvard University Press, 1992).
21. Doctorow, *Ragtime*, 237. The silent character acting as a characterological backdrop to Coalhouse Walker and Booker T. Washington is Jack Johnson, the first black heavyweight champion of the world and the one black man during

the epoch in which *Ragtime* is set who actually lived as if he were a reckless white man—and paid dearly for it. For Johnson, freedom was not simply a textual, constitutional reference, but a practice. The opposition between Walker and Washington is illuminating in this way, because Doctorow does not juxtapose Washington against W. E. B. Du Bois or Monroe Trotter or Ida B. Wells, but against a dandified, self-actualized everyman who is a practitioner and purveyor of an emergent, distinctive musical form that itself is denigrated by whites as well as some blacks. Walker is closer in character in some respects to Johnson than he is to either Du Bois or Washington.

22. See David Levering Lewis, *W. E. B. Du Bois: Biography of a Race 1868–1919*, vol. 1 (New York: Henry Holt, 1994).
23. Kleist, *The Marquise of O and Other Stories*, 175–177.
24. Ibid., 176.
25. Thanks to Professor Irene Kacandes of Dartmouth University for leading me to this particular insight.
26. Doctorow, *Ragtime*, 231.
27. Ibid., 197.
28. Ibid., 242.
29. Ibid., 151.
30. Agamben, *Homo Sacer*, 168.
31. Kleist, *The Marquise of O and Other Stories*, 108.
32. Doctorow, *Ragtime*, 206.
33. Ibid., 249.
34. Ibid., 245–246.
35. See Joe Slovo, *Slovo: The Unfinished Autobiography*, with an introduction by Helena Dolny (London: Hodder & Stoughton, 1996).
36. Doctorow, *Ragtime*, 233.
37. Ibid., 191–192.
38. Ibid., 192.
39. See Eric Hobsbawm, *Primitive Rebels: Studies in Archaic Forms of Social Movements in the 19th and 20th Centuries* (New York: Norton, 1965).

Chapter 7

1. Henry Highland Garnet, "The Past and The Present Condition, and the Destiny of the Colored Race: A Discourse Delivered at the Fifteenth Anniversary of the Female Benevolent Society of Troy, N.Y. February 14, 1848" (Miami: Mnemosyne Publishing, 1969), 26.
2. This was not the first time Du Bois made this assertion, only the most cited textual reference. See Brent Hayes Edwards, *The Practice of Diaspora* (Cambridge, Mass.: Harvard University Press, 2003).
3. Timothy Mitchell, *Rule of Experts: Egypt, Techno-Politics, Modernity* (Berkeley and Los Angeles: University of California Press, 2002), 210.
4. Oracy Nogueira's distinction between "mark of blood" and "mark of origin" has often been utilized to distinguish the preoccupations of color in Brazil and other Latin American nations from the Anglo-Saxon tendency to emphasize hypo-

descent for racial classification and distinction. Yet as many students of racial and ethnic relations in comparative perspective have pointed out, "color" and "race" often have distinct meanings and applications in actual social relations. This introduces a tension in more contemporary interpretations of both Du Bois's and Garnet's often interchangeable use of the two terms. It was quite common in nineteenth-century and early twentieth-century language about human distinction to correlate color with race (the "yellow," "black," and "white" races, for example). Many scholars of race and ethnicity, particularly students of Latin and South America, have focused on the distinction between race and color as a way of distinguishing between racial and ethnic relations patterns of North and South America, particularly the United States.

5. See Stuart Hall, "Europe's Other Self," *Marxism Today* 35 (August 1991): 18–19.
6. See Alan Knight, *The Mexican Revolution* (New York: Cambridge University Press, 1986); José Martí, "My Race" in *Our America: Writings on Latin America and the Struggle for Cuban Independence*, ed. Philip Foner (New York: Monthly Review Press, 1977), 311–314; José Vasconcelos, *La Raza Cósmica: Misión de la Raza Iberoamericana, Argentina y Brazil* (Mexico City: Espase Calpe Mexicana, 1948); Michael Hanchard, *Orpheus and Power: The Movimiento Negro of Rio de Janeiro and São Paulo, Brazil 1945–1988* (Princeton, N.J.: Princeton University Press, 1994); Gilberto Freyre, *The Masters and the Slaves (Casa Grande e Sensala): A Study in the Development of Brazilian Civilization* (New York: Knopf: 1956).
7. There are two significant aspects of Garnet's political thought that will not be engaged here. First, Garnet's specification of the role of U.S. African Americans as singularly responsible for uplifting African and African-descended people has been discussed elsewhere, and is not the focus of my assessment here. The second is Garnet's strategic and seemingly heartfelt desire to locate U.S. African Americans within the territorial, state, and cultural logos of the United States. This is paradigmatic of a generation of Africana-centered U.S. African American intellectuals who fought desperately to occupy the categories of citizenship. The nearly Faustian aspects of this pact with U.S. culture and domestic and foreign policies have led some scholars to criticize Garnet and other "salvationist" Africana intellectuals of this generation for succumbing to dominant, assimilationalist ideologies of the United States. Garnet's zeal for becoming "American" is in several important respects a prototype of the Ellisonian vision of U.S. African Americans' contributions and relation to "American" culture and society.
8. The anthropological warriors in the battle to attribute differences in "race" to cultural distinction were Ashley Montagu, George Mosse, Frantz Boaz, and Ruth Benedict. There is a certain "noble naivete" in the notion that in abandoning the race concept, scholars, and societies were somehow abandoning racism or that employing the race concept as a means of identifying and classifying people, even in promoting racialist solidarities among oppressed groups, was tantamount to racism. Without going into much detail here, the first problem inherent in these claims is that concepts such as race end up outside of

any rhetorical context or symbolic field, and we thus end up attributing racist intent to those who use the term in a nonracist manner. "Nation" and "nationalism," two terms that often end up in conversation and scholarly treatment of the race concept and the phenomena of racism, have some sordid histories attached to them. Not everyone, however, who has used them is a nationalist, even if many people who use the term are themselves national subjects.

9. See Troy Duster, *Backdoor to Eugenics* (New York: Routledge, 2003); Charles Mills, *Blackness Visible: Essays on Philosophy and Race* (Ithaca, N.Y.: Cornell University Press, 1998); and Nancy Leys Stepan, *The Hour of Eugenics: Race, Gender and Nation in Latin America* (Ithaca, N.Y.: Cornell University Press, 1991).

10. For an account of the role of aesthetics in the formation of ideologies and practices of racial domination, see Clyde R. Taylor, *The Mask of Art: Breaking the Aesthetic Contract* (Bloomington: Indiana University Press, 1998).

11. See Troy Duster, "Enhanced: Race and Reification in Science," *Science Magazine* 307 (2005): 1050–1051.

12. David Hollinger, "Amalgamation and Hypodescent: The Question of Ethnoracial Mixture in the History of the United States," in *American Historical Review* 108 (December 2003): 1363–1390.

13. Ibid., 1386. He might have added Ralph Ellison to this list, as well as a number of Ellisonian accounts of the role of U.S. African American culture in creolizing U.S. society and culture more generally. See also Kenneth Warren, *So Black and Blue: Ralph Ellison and the Occasion of Criticism* (Chicago: University of Chicago Press, 2003); and Jerry Watts, *Heroism and the Black Intellectual: Ralph Ellison, Politics, and Afro-American Intellectual Life* (Chapel Hill: University of North Carolina Press, 1994).

14. Hollinger, "Amalgamation and Hypodescent," 1370.

15. The Americanist historian Gary Nash has made a similar argument in "The Hidden History of Mestizo America," *Journal of American History* 82:3 (1995): 941–964. For a nuanced critique, see Peter Wade, "Images of Latin American Mestizaje and the Politics of Comparison" in *Bulletin of Latin American Research* 23 3 (2004): 355–366.

16. In plural societies such as Brazil, for example, racial categories are inextricably bound up with macropolitics (the state), and thus are politically constituted. See Melissa Nobles, *Shades of Citizenship: Race and the Census in Modern Politics* (Stanford, Calif.: Stanford University Press, 2000).

17. See Gilroy, *There Ain't No Black in the Union Jack* (London: Hutchinson, 1987); Edmund Gordon, *Disparate Diasporas: Identities and Politics in an African Nicaraguan Community* (Austin: University of Texas Press, 1998); and Livio Sansone, *Blackness without Ethnicity: Constructing Race in Brazil* (New York: Palgrave MacMillan, 2003).

18. Gilberto Freyre, "Reflections on Miscegenation," in *The Mansions and the Shanties (Sobrados e Mucambos): The Making of Modern Brazil* (New York: Knopf, 1963), 404.

19. Ibid., 403.

20. There are many other examples of "maladjusted" hybrids, such as the Mau Mau of Kenya whose political aspirations during the period of independence were attributed to their "hybrid" nature that fit into neither indigenous nor colonial culture.
21. Robin E. Sheriff, *Dreaming Equality: Color, Race and Racism in Urban Brazil* (New Brunswick, N.J.: Rutgers University Press, 2001),
22. The obverse, whether it is the colloquially understood "slumming" of negrophiles in various parts of the New and Western worlds, or the well-known colloquial and sexually connotative expression in Brazil, "navinegreiro," "passing in reverse" generally has not had cache outside academic and artistic circles. See Matthew Jacobson, *Whiteness of a Different Color: European Immigrants and the Alchemy of Race* (Cambridge, Mass.: Harvard University Press, 1999).
23. See Clifford Geertz, *The Interpretation of Cultures* (New York: Basic, 1973). Thanks to Paul Johnson for suggesting this.
24. See "Amalgamation and the Historical Distinctiveness of the United States," *The American Historical Review* 108, no. 5, AHR Forum (December 2003).
25. See David Theo Goldberg, *The Racial State* (Malden, Mass.: Blackwell Publishers, 2002).
26. See Barbara Fields, "Of Rogues and Geldings" in *The American Historical Review* 108 (December 2003), 1400. Fields's distinction between race and racism, however, is less convincing. She is certainly correct in her distinction between race and racism: "racism, unlike race, is not a fiction, an illusion, a superstition, or a hoax." Nevertheless, the race concept originated in racist theory, even though commonsense employment of the race concept in many Western and non-Western societies has altered the meaning of the race concept in many instances, so that racial categorization can be applied in nonhierarchical contexts (that black woman over there, that white man over here) as a mode of description. I am referring to situations that are not part of a project of surveillance. For a discussion of the race concept and its relation to racism, see Étienne Balibar and Immanuel Wallerstein, *Race, Nation, and Class: Ambiguous Identities* (London and New York: Verso, 1994).
27. See Gilroy, *There Ain't No Black in the Union Jack*.
28. See, for example, Michael J. Shapiro, *For Moral Ambiguity: National Culture and the Politics of the Family* (Minneapolis: University of Minnesota Press, 2001).
29. Formal gay marriage and even civic unions between members of the same sex are perhaps the best examples of the state's ability to render micropolitical practices macropolitical, and vice versa. Several students of queer theory and gender studies have examined the implications of formal gay marriage for gay sexual politics in relation to state and societal normativity. While there are certain material benefits to civic unions and marriage for gay couples, several scholars and activists worry that the desire among certain gay activists and organizations for formal recognition by the state implicitly and explicitly reproduces the chase for respectability, and a politics of recognition à la Charles Taylor, consequently undermining the radical potentialities of queer

politics and gay sexualities. How could a gay union be viewed as "radical" or "alternative" when positively sanctioned by the state? See Michael Warner, *The Trouble with Normal: Sex, Politics, and the Ethics of Queer Life* (Cambridge, Mass.: Harvard University Press, 1999); and Cathy Cohen, "Deviance as Resistance: A New Research Agenda for the Study of Black Politics" in *Du Bois Review* 1:1 (Spring 2004): 27–46.

30. See Luigi Crimaco, "La Taverna di via Ripa in Rione Terra," in *Percorso Archeologico*, trans. Emma Cervone (Naples: Ministerio per Beni e le Attivata Culturali, Sopraintendenza per I Beni Archeologici delle provincza di Napoli e Caserta, n/d), 36.

31. See Nicholas Dirks, "History as a Sign of the Modern" *Public Culture* 2, no. 2 (Spring 1990): 25–33; Antonio Benítez Rojo, *The Magic Dog and Other Stories* (Hanover, N.H.: Ediciones Del Norte, 1990); Néstor García Canclini, *Hybrid Cultures: Strategies for Entering and Leaving Modernity,* trans. Christopher Chiappari and Silvia López (Minneapolis: University of Minnesota Press, 1995).

32. See Eric J. Hobsbawm and Terence O. Ranger, *The Invention of Tradition* (Cambridge: Cambridge University Press, 1983).

33. R. Douglas Cope, *The Limits of Racial Domination: Plebeian Society in Colonial Mexico City, 1660–1720* (Madison: University of Wisconsin Press, 1994); and Mark Turner, *From Two Republics to One Divided: Considerations of Postcolonial Nationmaking in Andean Peru* (Durham, N.C.: Duke University Press, 1999).

34. Alejandro de la Fuente, *A Nation for All: Race, Inequality and Politics in Twentieth Century Cuba* (Chapel Hill: University of North Carolina Press, 2001), 8.

35. Ibid., 40.

36. Aline Helg, *Our Rightful Share: The Afro-Cuban Struggle for Equality* (Chapel Hill: University of North Carolina Press, 1995).

37. Ibid., 25–54.

38. Irene Silverblatt, *Modern Inquisitions: Peru and the Colonial Origins of the Civilized World* (Durham, N.C.: Duke University Press, 2004).

39. Balibar and Wallerstein, *Race, Nation, and Class*.

40. Fernando Ortiz, *Los Negros Curros* (Havana: Editorial de Ciencias Sociales, 1944), 8.

41. *Novo Michaelis Dicionário*, ed. 43 (São Paulo: Melhoramentos, 1986), 377.

42. Anthony Pagden, *Lords of All the World: Ideologies of Empire in Spain, Britain, and France c. 1500—c. 1800* (New Haven, Conn.: Yale University Press, 1995).

43. See David Barry Gaspar and David Patrick Geggus, *A Turbulent Time: The French Revolution and the Greater Caribbean* (Bloomington: Indiana University Press, 1997); Michel-Rolph Trouillot, *Silencing the Past: Power and the Production of History* (Boston: Beacon Press, 1995).

44. All national ideologies, not just Cuban ones, produce ambiguity when held up against the mirror of a competing ideal or someone else's vision of reality. Nationalist or other ideologies never simply provide opportunities for contestation. Opportunities, such as they are, are assumed by individuals, organizations, and groups.

45. Ironically, 1988 was the same year in which Fidel Castro acknowledged at the Third Party Congress of the Cuban Communist Party that racism and sexism were the two social maladies the Cuban Revolution had yet to conquer. Yet Castro made this declaration without suggesting any state-sponsored policies to address Cuban racism. His statement also highlighted the increasingly inadequate reductionist explanation of racism's origins in capitalist exploitation.
46. See for example, Thomas Holt, "Marking: Race, Race-Making and the Writing of History," *American Historical Review* 100:1 (February 1995): 1–20; or Holt, *The Problem of Freedom* (Cambridge, Mass.: Harvard University Press, 2001).
47. Vera Kutzinski, *Sugar's Secrets* (Charlottesville and London: University of Virginia Press, 1993), 6.
48. Ibid.
49. Ann Laura Stoler, "Racial Histories and Their Regimes of Truth," in *Political Power and Social Theory* 11 (London: JAI, 1997): 183–206.
50. Michael Hardt and Antonio Negri, *Empire* (Cambridge, Mass.: Harvard University Press, 2000).
51. Mary Louise Pratt, *Imperial Eyes: Travel Writing and Transculturation* (New York: Routledge, 1992).
52. Walter Rodney, *How Europe Underdeveloped Africa* (Washington, D.C.: Howard University Press), 181.
53. See John Furnivall, *Colonial Policy and Practice: A Comparative Study of Burma and Netherlands India* (Oxford: Oxford University Press, 1948); Ivar Oxaal, *Black Intellectuals and the Dilemmas of Race and Class in Trinidad* (Cambridge, Mass.: Schenkman Publishing, 1982).
54. From a vast literature, see M. G. Smith, "Social and Cultural Pluralism," in *Social and Cultural Pluralism in the Caribbean*, ed. Vera Rubin. Annals of the American Academy of Sciences 83 (January 1960): 763–777; Stuart Hall, "Ethnicity: Identity and Difference," *Radical America* 23, no. 4 (1989): 9–20; "Cultural Identity and Diaspora," in *Identity: Community, Culture, Difference*, ed. Jonathan Rutherford (London: Lawrence and Wishart, 1990): 222–237; Crawford Young, *The Politics of Cultural Pluralism* (Madison: University of Wisconsin Press, 1976); and John S. Furnivall, *Colonial Policy and Practice*.
55. In the United States, as well as in many nation-states of Western Europe during the post–World War II years, pluralism has meant political variation in the form of multiple political parties, societies that allow for coalitions encompassing multiple political and ideological tendencies. Pluralism has a particular resonance among liberal theorists and politicians. Nevertheless, Lionel Trilling, pluralism's most sophisticated defender in the United States, worried over the possibility that pluralism would become dominant and hegemonic, its advocates lazy and self-satisfied, thereby undermining the pursuit of individual freedoms and happiness. Liberalism, Trilling feared, would become just another dominant ideology. Lionel Trilling, *The Liberal Imagination: Essays on Literature and Society* (New York: Doubleday Anchor Books, 1957).

56. John Pemberton, *On the Subject of Java* (Ithaca, N.Y.: Cornell University Press, 1994).
57. In this regard, Gilberto Freyre is particularly helpful for his recognition of the various forms of anti–Afro-Brazilian sentiment prevalent during his lifetime. *Casa Grande e Senzala* provides numerous examples of antiblack racism, as well as commentary on the number of mulattos and pardos in Brazil who were virulently antiblack as part of a more comprehensive racist ideology. See, especially, Gilberto Freyre, "Reflections on Miscegenation."
58. See Mark Q. Sawyer, *Racial Politics in Post-Revolutionary Cuba* (Cambridge: Cambridge University Press, 2005).
59. Demographers, anthropologists, and historians of Latin America have led the way in avoiding dichotomized comparisons between nation-states. Demographic data on life expectancy, residential segregation, police violence and arrest, historical accounts of regional and local patterns of interaction that appear atypical in relation to national historiography, as well as ethnographic accounts of interactions between groups defined in terms of racial distinction, provide evidence to suggest that many plural societies have "hard" and "soft" zones of intergroup relations. Demographic analysis has been particularly helpful in comparing national societies such as those of the United States and Brazil and in problematizing the neat distinctions and generalizations made about supposedly opposite race relations paradigms. Both societies have spaces in which conflicts premised on racism are less operative (whether through repression or actual instances of cooperation) and parts that are more conflict ridden. Issues, neighborhood segregation, state practice, and many other factors contribute to the absence or presence of conflict.
60. See Ruud Koopmans and Paul Statham, *Challenging Immigration and Ethnic Relations Politics: Comparative European Perspectives* (New York: Oxford University Press, 2001).
61. Peter Wade, *Race and Ethnicity in Latin America* (Chicago: Pluto Press, 1997); Peter Wade, *Music, Race, and Nation: Música Tropical in Colombia* (Chicago: University of Chicago Press, 2000); Charles Hale, "Neoliberal Multiculturalism: The Remaking of Cultural Rights and Racial Dominance in Central America," *Polar*, vol. 28(1) (2005): 10–28; "Cultural Politics of Identity in Latin America," *Annual Review of Anthropology*, vol. 26 (1994): 67–90.
62. Leslie Rout, *The African Experience in Spanish America, 1502 to the Present Day* (Cambridge: Cambridge University Press, 1976), 79.
63. Emilia Viotti da Costa, *Crowns of Glory, Tears of Blood: The Demerara Slave Rebellion of 1823* (New York: Oxford University Press, 1997).
64. Sidney Mintz, *Sweetness and Power: The Place of Sugar in Modern History* (New York: Penguin Books, 1985).
65. George Fredrickson, *Race and Racism in Comparative Perspective* (Berkeley and Los Angeles: University of California Press, 1997), 87–88.
66. Stephan Palmié, "Against Syncretism: 'Africanizing' and 'Cubanizing' Discourses in North American òrisà Worship" in *Counterworks: Managing Diverse Knowledge*, ed. Richard Fardon (London: Routledge, 1995), 73–104.

See also J. Lorand Matory, "The English Professors of Brazil: On the Diasporic Roots of the Yorùbá Nation," *Comparative Studies in Society and History* 41, no. 1 (January 1999): 72–103; Winston James, *Holding Aloft the Banner of Ethiopia: Caribbean Radicalism in Early 20th Century America* (New York: Verso, 1998); Brent Hayes Edwards, *The Practice of Diaspora* (Cambridge, Mass.: Harvard University Press, 2003).

67. Gilberto Freyre, "Reflections on Miscegenation," 410. What is so fascinating about this section is Freyre's comparative focus, which situates miscegenation in Brazil against the backdrop of "mixed-race" populations in various parts of the world and examines the institutional, normative, governmental, cultural, and socioeconomic factors contributing to the relative access or limits to social mobility and the elevation of prestige.

68. Samuel Feijoo, ed., "El Negro en la Quarteta Cubana," in *Negro en la Literatura Folklórica Cubana* (Havana: Editorial Letras Cubanas, 1987), 40.

69. Lawrence W. Levine, *Black Culture and Black Consciousness* (New York: Oxford University Press, 1978), 286.

70. See Sidney Chaloub, "Febre amarela e ideologia racial no Rio de Janeiro," *Estudos Afro-Asiaticos*, no. 27 (Rio de Janeiro: Centro de Estudos Afro-Asiaticos, 1995); and Julio Ramos, *Divergent Modernities: Culture and Politics in 19th Century Latin America* (Durham, N.C.: Duke University Press), 2001.

71. Frantz Fanon, "Racism and Culture," in *Black Skin, White Masks,* trans. Charles Lam Markmann (New York: Grove Press, 1967), 32–33.

72. Fanon, "Racism and Culture"; Howard Winant, *The World Is a Ghetto: Race and Democracy since World War II* (New York: Basic Books, 2001).

Chapter 8

1. Julio Cortázar, *Nicaraguan Sketches,* trans. Kathleen Weaver (New York: Norton, 1989), 71.

2. Jean-Luc Nancy, *The Inoperative Community*, trans. Peter Connor, Lisa Garbus, Michael Holland, and Simona Sawhney (Minneapolis: University of Minnesota Press, 1990), 9; italics in the original.

3. See Michael Hanchard, "Afro-Modernity: Temporality, Politics, and the African Diaspora," in *Alternative Modernities*, ed. D. P. Gaonkar (Durham, N.C.: Duke University Press, 2001): 272–298.

4. See Femi Taiwo, "Of Citizens and Citizenship," *Tempo* (September/October 1996) (Lagos, Nigeria: 1996); Achille Mbembe, *On the Postcolony* (Berkeley and Los Angeles: University of California Press, 2001); Cornel West, *Race Matters* (New York: Vintage Books, 1994); Wahneema Lubiano, *Messing with the Machine: Politics, Form, and African American Fiction* (New York: Verso, forthcoming); Eddie Glaude, *Exodus! Religion, Race and Nation in Early 19th Century Black America* (Chicago: University of Chicago Press, 2000); Alexander Weheliye, "'I Am I Be': The Subject of Sonic Afro Modernity," *Boundary 2* 30, no. 2 (2003); Fred Moten, *In the Break: The Aesthetics of the Black Radical Tradition* (Minneapolis: University of Minnesota Press, 2003); Ronald Judy, "Introduction: On W. E. B. Du Bois and Hyberbolic Thinking," *Boundary 2* 27,

no. 3 (Fall 2000): 1–35; Robin D. G. Kelley, *Freedom Dreams: The Black Radical Imagination* (Boston: Beacon, 2002).

5. Paul Gilroy, *There Ain't No Black in the Union Jack: The Cultural Politics of Race and Nation* (Chicago: University of Chicago Press, 1991).
6. Adolph Reed, *Stirrings in the Jug: Black Politics in the Post-Segregation Era* (Minneapolis: University of Minnesota Press, 1999), 219.
7. Ibid.
8. See Cathy Cohen, "Deviance as Resistance: A New Research Agenda for the Study of Black Politics" in *Du Bois Review* 1, no. 1 (Spring 2004): 27–46; Richard Iton, *In Search of the Black Fantastic: Politics and Popular Culture in the Post-Civil Rights Era* (New York: Oxford University Press, forthcoming); and Robin Kelley, *Race Rebels: Culture, Politics, and the Black Working Class* (New York: Free Press, 1994).
9. See Anthony M. Messina, *Race and Party Competition in Britain* (Oxford: Clarendon, 1989); Stephen Small, *Racialised Barriers: The Black Experience in the United States and England in the 1980's* (London: Routledge, 1994); John Solomos, *Race and Racism in Contemporary Britain* (Houndmills: Macmillan, 1989); Erik Bleich, *Race Politics in Britain and France* (Cambridge: Cambridge University Press, 2003).
10. See Seth Racusen, "Making the 'Impossible' Determination: Flexible Identity and Targeted Opportunity" in *Contemporary Brazil* 36 Conn. L. Rev. 787 (2004): 803–808.
11. Philomena Essed, *Everyday Racism: Reports from Women of Two Cultures* (Claremont, Calif.: Hunter House, 1990).
12. See Manning Marable, *How Capitalism Underdeveloped Black America* (Cambridge, Mass.: South End Press, 2000); Brian Meeks, *Narratives of Resistance: Jamaica, Trinidad, The Caribbean* (Barbados: University of the West Indies Press, 2000); Lloyd Best, *Black Power and National Reconstruction: Proposals Following the February Revolution* (Santo Domingo, Trinidad: Tapia House, 1970); Richard Hatcher and Lee Sloan, *Blacks and Metro Politics* (Washington, D.C.: Joint Center for Political Studies, 1973).
13. See Kim D. Butler, *Freedoms Given, Freedoms Won: Afro-Brazilians in Post-Abolition Sao Paulo and Salvador* (New Brunswick, N.J.: Rutgers University Press, 1998); George Reid Andrews, *Slavery and Race Relations in Brazil* (Albuquerque, N.M.: Latin American Institute University of New Mexico, 1997).
14. See Selwyn D. Ryan, *Race and Nationalism in Trinidad and Tobago: A Study of Decolonization in a Multiracial Society* (Toronto, Buffalo: University of Toronto Press, 1972); and Brackette Williams, *Stains on My Name, War in My Veins: Guyana and the Politics of Struggle* (Durham, N.C.: Duke University Press, 1991).
15. See Anthony Marx, *Making Race and Nation: A Comparison of the United States, South Africa and Brazil* (Cambridge: Cambridge University Press, 1998); Harold Wolpe, *Race, Class, and the Apartheid State* (London: Currey, 1988); George Fredrickson, *The Comparative Imagination: On the History of Racism, Nationalism and Social Movements* (Berkeley and Los Angeles: University of California Press, 2000).

16. In the United States, for example, the Million Man March of U.S. African American males, the Million Woman March, and the Million Latino Woman's March each exemplify popular mobilization along the lines of a "united front" perspective. Although these marches carry a certain symbolic importance, they give very little indication of how these people will behave politically in subsequent daily life. Ever since the inauguration of the nuclear age and mutually assured destruction, popular unity provides no guarantee of social and political change. It's time that black politics, domestic and transnational, catches up to this reality.
17. Examples of such calls to unity abound in black political thought. Malcolm X's famous speech in which he distinguishes the house slave from the field slave is a classic example. In his speech, the house slave is presented as the more pampered of the two, and, consequently, more influenced by the values of the slave owner and the plantation economy. The field slave, on the other hand, is presented as the more authentic black subject, one who is capable of greater violence toward the systems of domination that white supremacy and plantocracies jointly pose. This greater propensity to buck the system is premised, we are led to assume, by the spatial and normative distance the field slave has from "the big house." Yet there are many studies of slave resistance that complicate the neat distinction between field slave resistance and house slave compliance, in the examples of house slaves poisoning or otherwise harming their masters. See Sidney Mintz, *Sweetness and Power: The Place of Sugar in Modern History* (New York: Penguin, 1985); and C. L. R. James, *The Black Jacobins: Toussaint L'Ouverture and the San Domingo Revolution* (New York: Vintage, 1989). The house slave/field slave has obvious class correlations that Malcolm sought to make at the time. Though rhetorically powerful, the correlations actually simplify the histories of slave resistance as well as the greater difficulties of coalitional politics across class and status positions in black communities.
18. Alioune Diop, "African Culture and Its Place in Work for African Unity" in *The Second Pan-African Youth Seminar, August 5–14, 1961, Dar-es-Salaam, Tanganyika*, 28–39 (Brussels: World Assembly of Youth, 1961), 30.
19. Ibid., 32.
20. Hanchard, "Afro-Modernity."
21. It is not coincidental that most commentators on black politics in the United States, ranging from Martin Kilson and Adolph Reed in contemporary black political thought to Thurgood Marshall, Monroe Trotter, W. E. B. Du Bois, Ida B. Wells, Marvel Cooke, and Ella Baker in the past, have all at some point analyzed the relative virtue of the first or second form of politics. Conservative commentators like Thomas Sowell, Carol Swain, and Shelby Steele have disparaged and dismissed informal politics as the politics of victimization. See Thomas Sowell, *Civil Rights: Rhetoric or Reality?* (New York: William Morrow, 1984); Carole Swain, *The New White Nationalism in America: Its Challenge to Integration* (Cambridge: Cambridge University Press, 2002); and

Shelby Steele, *The Content of Our Character: A New Vision of Race in America* (New York: St. Martin's Press, 1990). Sowell argues that the contestatory politics of the civil rights movement have little utility in the post–civil rights era and have largely served to contribute to white backlash and limited black achievement. Political actors who have engaged in type-two politics are often criticized for participating in forms of politics marginal to the status quo, thereby limiting the prospects for enmeshment in the fabric of conventional U.S. political culture.

22. Harold Cruse, *The Crisis of the Negro Intellectual* (New York: William Morrow, 1967), 13.
23. Ibid., 100.
24. For a discussion of the black arts movement in relation to black aesthetics, see Clyde R. Taylor, *The Mask of Art: Breaking the Aesthetic Contract* (Bloomington: Indiana University Press), 1998).
25. Larry Neal, "The Genius and the Prize" in *Visions of a Liberated Future: Black Arts Movement Writings*, ed. Larry Neal (New York: Thunder's Mouth, 1989), 79–80.
26. The debates involving Robert Brustein and August Wilson are instructive in this regard. Amidst Brustein's claim that Wilson plays amounted to no more than "ethnic" (nonuniversal) theatre and Wilson's calls for an autonomous black theatre, particularly in light of the continued dearth of plays and theatre companies that cultivate and nurture black playwrights, theatre production and actors, are ethicopolitical and material considerations for black cultural politics. If predominately white companies continue to neglect black actors, plays, and dramatic themes, and if there are no black theatre companies to stage black plays, and employ black playwrights and actors, who will? One of the enduring legacies of the black arts movement was the attempt of black artists to answer this question. For example, see Elizabeth Alexander, *The Black Interior: Essays* (Saint Paul, Minn.: Graywolf, 2004).
27. See William J. McGrath, "Cultural Politics in Austria: From Empire to Republic" in *The Austrian Socialist Experiment: Social Democracy and Austromarxism, 1918–1934,* ed. Anson Rabinbach (Boulder, Colo.: Westview, 1985).
28. See Zenovia A. Sochor, *Revolution and Culture: The Bogdanov-Lenin Controversy* (Ithaca, N.Y.: Cornell University Press, 1988).
29. Ibid.
30. The years 1918–19 have a certain resonance in the history of transnational social movements, much as the more recent years 1968 and 2000 have in contemporary history and politics. There are monographs that trace the significance of 1918–19 in individual countries but offer surprisingly little engagement with the transnational implications of the moment. See, for example, ed. Anson Rabinbach, *The Austrian Social Experiment: Social Democracy and Austo-Marxism, 1918–1934* (Boulder, Colo.: Westview, 1985); Charles S. Maier, *Recasting Bourgeois Europe* (Princeton, N.J.: Princeton University Press, 1975); Barbara Foley, *Spectres of 1919: Class and Nation in*

the Making of the New Negro (Urbana: University of Illinois Press, 2003); and Larry Ceplair, *Under the Shadow of War* (New York: Columbia University Press, 1987).

31. For a brief account of the left's miscalculations of the crisis of capitalism during this period, see "Introduction" in Antonio Gramsci, *Selections from the Prison Notebook* (New York: International Publishers, 1985).
32. See Robert Young, *White Mythologies: Writing, History, and the West* (London: Routledge, 1990).
33. Georg Lukács, "Towards a Methodology of the Problem of Organization," in *History and Class Consciousness* (Cambridge, Mass.: MIT Press, 1971), 295.
34. Ibid., 297.
35. Ibid., 301.
36. Ibid., 317.
37. Ibid.
38. Ibid., 296.
39. Antonio Gramsci, "Predictions" in *Selections from Political Writings, 1910–1920*, ed. Quintin Hoare, trans. John Matthews (Minneapolis: University of Minnesota Press, 1977a), 356–359.
40. In his essay "Socialism and Culture," in *Selections from Political Writings*, 12, Gramsci wrote, "Every revolution has been preceded by an intense labour of criticism, by the diffusion of culture and the spread of ideas amongst the masses of men who are at first resistant, and think only of solving their own immediate economic and political problems for themselves, who have no ties of solidarities with others in the same condition."
41. Ibid., 13.
42. See Franz Fanon, *The Wretched of the Earth* (New York: Grove, 1968) and David Macey, *Frantz Fanon: A Biography* (New York: Picador, 2000).
43. See Manthia Diawara, "Malcolm X and the Black Public Sphere: Conversionists vs. Culturalists," in *Public Culture* 7 (Fall 1994): 39–52; and Lansiné Kaba, "The Cultural Revolution, Artistic Creativity, and Freedom of Expression in Guinea," *The Journal of Modern African Studies* 14, 2 (1976): 201–218.
44. See Huey Newton's critique of cultural nationalism, what he famously referred to as "pork chop nationalism," which certainly has certain resonances with Leninist and Trotskyist critiques of reformist, bread-and-butter trade unionism. See Huey P. Newton, *Huey Newton Talks to the Movement: About the Black Panther Party, Cultural Nationalism, SNCC, Liberals and White Revolutionaries* (Chicago: SDS, 1968).
45. James Brown and Bruce Tucker, *James Brown, The Godfather of Soul* (New York: Thunder's Mouth Press, 1990), 183–189.
46. Ibid, 189.
47. See Jean Allman, *The Quills of the Porcupine: Asante Nationalism in an Emergent Ghana* (Madison: University of Wisconsin Press, 1993).
48. See Penny Von Eschen, *Satchmo Blows Up the World: Jazz, Race and Empire During the Cold War* (Cambridge, Mass.: Harvard University Press, 2004).

49. See Renato Rosaldo, *Ilongot Headhunting 1883–1974: A Study in Society and History* (Stanford, Calif.: Stanford University Press, 1980); Victor Turner and Edward Bruner, eds. *Anthropology of Experience* (Champaign: University of Illinois Press, 1986).
50. See Sandra Richards, "Cultural Travel to Ghana's Slave Castles: A Commentary" in *International Research in Geographical and Environmental Education* 11 no. 4 (2002): 372–375.
51. See Richard Iton, *Solidarity Blues: Race, Culture and the American Left* (Chapel Hill: University of North Carolina Press, 2000).
52. See Julio Cesar Tavares, *Dança da guerra: arguiro-arma. Dissertação de mestrado* (Barsília: Departamento de Ciências Sociais, Universidade de Brasília, 1984).
53. As Walter Dean Burnham has suggested, the process of critical realignment generally entails the reformulation of values, which in turn helps reconstitute the ideational and practical dimensions of political institutions, actors, and cultures. See Walter Dean Burnham, "Pattern Recognition and 'Doing' Political History: Art, Science, or Bootless Enterprise?" in *The Dynamics of American Politics: Approaches and Interpretations*, eds. Lawrence C. Dodd and Calvin Jillson (Boulder, Colo.: Westview, 1994): 59–82.
54. The use of the term "Africans" by many black scholars and activists to denote people of African descent, regardless of their current national status, typifies the transnational dimensions of this assumption of a unified or totalized African identity, which, presumably, neither includes nor refers to *white* Africans. This exclusion thereby makes the continental signifier simultaneously and not-so-implicitly a racial signifier.
55. Gilroy, *There Ain't No Black in the Union Jack*, 116.
56. Sylvia Wynter, "The Ceremony Must Be Found: After Humanism," *Boundary 2* (Spring/Fall 1994): 19–70.

REFERENCES

Abelove, Henry, Betsey Blackmar, Peter Dimock, and Jonathan Schneer, eds. 1983. *Visions of History*. New York: Pantheon.
Agamben, Giorgio. 1998. *Homo Sacer: Sovereign Power and Bare Life*. Trans. Daniel Heller-Roazen. Palo Alto, Calif.: Stanford University Press.
Akyeampong, Emmanuel. 2000. "Africans in the Diaspora: The Diaspora and Africa." *African Affairs* 99 (April): 183–215.
Alexander, Elizabeth 2004. *The Black Interior: Essays*. St. Paul, Minn.: Graywolf.
Allen, Danielle S. 2004. *Talking to Strangers*. Chicago: University of Chicago Press.
Allen, Robert L. 1993. *The Port Chicago Mutiny*. New York: Amistad.
Allman, Jean. 1993. *The Quills of the Porcupine: Asante Nationalism in an Emergent Ghana*. Madison: University of Wisconsin Press.
Allport, G. W. 1954. *The Nature of Prejudice*. Reading, Mass.: Addison-Wesley.
Althusser, Louis. 1971. "Ideology and Ideological State Apparatus." In *Lenin and Philosophy, and Other Essays*, 127–186. London: New Left Books.
"Amalgamation and the Historical Distinctiveness of the United States." *The American Historical Review*, 108, no. 5, Forum. December 2003.
Anderson, Benedict. 1983. *Imagined Communities: Reflections on the Origin and Spread of Nationalism*. London: Verso.
Andre, Gunder Frank. 1969. *Latin America: Underdevelopment or Revolution: Essays on the Development of Underdevelopment and the Immediate Enemy*. New York: Monthly Review Press.
Andrews, George Reid. 1980. *The Afro-Argentines of Buenos Aires, 1800–1900*. Madison: University of Wisconsin Press.
———. 1997. *Slavery and Race Relations in Brazil*. Albuquerque, N.M: Latin American Institute University of New Mexico.
Appiah, K. Anthony. 1992. *In My Father's House: Africa in the Philosophy of Culture*. New York: Oxford University Press.
Arendt, Hannah. 1969. *On Violence*. New York: Harcourt, Brace and World.
Asante, Molefi. 1980. *Afrocentricity, A Theory of Social Change*. Buffalo, N.Y.: Amulefi Publishing.
———. 1999. *The Painful Demise of Euro-Centrism*. Trenton, N.J.: Africa New World Press.

Axelrod, Saul, and Jack Apsche. 1983. *The Effects of Punishment on Human Behavior*. New York: Academic Press.

Baldwin, James. 1968. *Tell Me How Long the Train's Been Gone*. New York: Dell.

———. 1993. "The Black Boy Looks at the White Boy." In *Nobody Knows My Name*, 216–241. New York: Vintage International.

Balibar, Étienne, and Immanuel Wallerstein. 1994. *Race, Nation, Class: Ambiguous Identities*. London and New York: Verso.

Bates, Robert. 1997. "Comparative Politics and Rational Choice: A Review Essay." *American Political Science Review* 91 no. 3 (September): 699–704.

Bay, Mia. 2000. *The White Image in the Black Mind: African American Ideas about White People, 1830–1925*. New York: Oxford University Press.

Benítez Rojo, Antonio. 1990. *The Magic Dog and Other Stories*. Hanover, N.H.: Ediciones Del Norte.

Benjamin, Walter. 1968. "The Work of Art in the Age of Mechanical Reproduction." In *Illuminations*, ed. Hannah Arendt, 217–254. New York: Schocken.

Bensel, Richard. 2004. *The American Ballot Box in the Mid-Nineteenth Century*. New York: Cambridge University Press.

Berlant, Lauren. 1997. *The Queen of America Goes to Washington City: Essays on Sex and Citizenship*. Durham, N.C.: Duke University Press.

———, ed. 2004. *Compassion: The Culture and Politics of an Emotion*. London: Routledge.

Berlin, Edward A. 1994. *King of Ragtime: Scott Joplin and His Era*. New York: Oxford University Press.

Bernal, Martin. 1987. *Black Athena: The Afroasiatic Roots of Classical Civilization*. New Brunswick, N.J.: Rutgers University Press.

Berube, Michael. 1995. "The New Black Intellectuals." *The New Yorker* (January 9): 73–80.

Best, Lloyd. 1970. *Black Power and National Reconstruction: Proposals Following the February Revolution*. Santo Domingo, Trinidad: Tapia House.

Biondi, Martha. 2003. *To Stand and Fight*. Cambridge, Mass.: Harvard University Press.

Bleich, Erik. 2003. *Race Politics in Britain and France*. Cambridge: Cambridge University Press.

Boas, Franz. 1940. *Race, Language and Culture*. New York: Macmillan.

Bobo, Lawrence. 1994. "Review of Paul M. Sniderman and Thomas Piazza, The Scar of Race." *American Political Science Review* 88: 488–489.

Bogle, Donald. 2001. *Toms, Coons, Mulattoes, Mammies and Bucks: An Interpretive History of Blacks in American Films*. 4th ed. New York: Continuum.

Bolívar, Simón. 1951. *Selected Writings*. Comp. Vicente Lecuna, ed. Harold A. Bierck Jr., and trans. Lewis Bertrand. New York: Colonial.

Bolster, W. Jeffrey. 1997. *Black Jacks: African American Seamen in the Age of Sail*. Cambridge, Mass.: Harvard University Press.

Bonilla-Silva, Eduardo, and Tyrone Forman. 2000. " 'I Am Not a Racist but . . . ' Mapping White College Students' Racial Ideology in the USA." *Discourse and Society* 11 (1): 50–85.

Boynton, Robert. 1995. "The New Intellectuals." *Atlantic Monthly* vol. 275, no. 3 (March): 53–70.
Bourdieu, Pierre and Loic Waquant. 1999. "On the Cunning of Imperialist Reason," *Theory, Culture, and Society* 16 (1): 41–58.
Branch, Taylor. 1988. *Parting the Waters: America in the King Years, 1954–63*. New York: Simon & Schuster.
Brown, Elaine. 1992. *A Taste of Power*. New York: Pantheon.
Brown, Elsa Barkely. 1995. "Negotiating and Transforming the Public Sphere: African American Political Life in the Transition from Slavery to Freedom." In *The Black Public Sphere*, ed. Black Public Sphere Collective, 111–150. Chicago: University of Chicago Press.
Brown, James, and Bruce Tucker. 1990. *James Brown, The Godfather of Soul*. New York: Thunder's Mouth.
Brubaker, Rogers. 1992. *Citizenship and Nationhood in France and Germany*. Cambridge, Mass.: Harvard University Press.
Burnham, Walter Dean. 1994. "Pattern Recognition and 'Doing' Political History: Art, Science, or Bootless Enterprise?" In *The Dynamics of American Politics: Approaches and Interpretations*, eds. Lawrence C. Dodd and Calvin Jillson, 59–82. Boulder, Colo.: Westview.
Butler, Kim. 1998. *Freedoms Given, Freedoms Won: Afro-Brazilians in Post-Abolition São Paulo and Salvador*. New Brunswick, N.J: Rutgers University Press.
Caldiera, Teresa P. R. 2000. *City of Walls: Crime, Segregation, and Citizenship in São Paulo*. Berkeley and Los Angeles: University of California Press.
Calhoun, Craig. 1993. *Habermas and the Public Sphere*. Boston: MIT Press.
Callier, Terry. 2001. "Lament for the late AD" on *Terry Callier Alive*. [audio recording]. Mr. Bongo. Permission granted by Terry Callier and Bongo Records.
Calvino, Italo. 1978. *Invisible Cities*. Trans. William Weaver. New York: Harcourt Brace Jovanovich.
Campbell, James. 1995. *Songs of Zion: The African Methodist Episcopal Church in the United States and South Africa*. New York: Oxford University Press.
Canclini, Néstor García. 1995. *Hybrid Cultures: Strategies for Entering and Leaving Modernity*. Trans. Christopher Chiappari and Silvia López. Minneapolis: University of Minnesota Press.
Canetti, Elias. 1962. *Crowds and Power*. London: Gollancz.
Carens, Joseph. 2000. *Culture, Citizenship and Community*. Cambridge: Oxford University Press.
Carter, Stephen. 1991. *Reflections of an Affirmative Action Baby*. New York: Basic.
Castaneda, Jorge. 1993. *Utopia Unarmed: The Latin American Left After the Cold War*. New York: Knopf.
Cavell, Stanley. 1979. *The Claim of Reason: Wittgenstein, Skepticism, Morality and Tragedy*. Oxford: Clarendon.
Ceplair, Larry. 1987. *Under the Shadow of War*. New York: Columbia University Press.
Chaloub, Sidney. 1995. "Febre amarela e ideologia racial no Rio de Janeiro." *Estudos Afro-Asiaticos* (27): 87–110. Rio de Janeiro: Centro de Estudos Afro-Asiaticos.

Charles, Ray. 1962. "You Don't Know Me." Written by Cindy Walker, and Eddy Arnold. New York: ABC Paramount Records.
Chatterjee, Partha. 1993. *The Nation and Its Fragments*. Princeton, N.J.: Princeton University Press.
Chebel, D'Appollonia, Ariane. 1998. *Les Racismes Ordinaires*. Paris: Presses de Sciences Po.
Cleaver, Eldridge. 1992. *Soul on Ice*. New York: Dell.
Cohen, Cathy. 1999. *The Boundaries of Blackness: AIDS and the Breakdown of Black Politics*. Chicago: University of Chicago Press.
———. 2004. "Deviance as Resistance: A New Research Agenda for the Study of Black Politics." *Du Bois Review* 1 (Spring): 27–46.
Cone, James H. 1970. *A Black Theology of Liberation*. Philadelphia: Lippincott.
Connolly, William E. 1967. *Political Science and Ideology*. New York: Atherton.
———. 1999. *Why I Am Not a Secularist*. Minneapolis: University of Minnesota Press.
Converse, Philip. 1964. "The Nature of Belief Systems in Mass Publics." In *Ideology and Discontent*, ed. David Apter, 206–261. New York: Free Press.
Cope, R. Douglas. 1994. *The Limits of Racial Domination: Plebeian Society in Colonial Mexico City, 1660–1720*. Madison: University of Wisconsin Press.
Cortázar, Julio. 1989. *Nicaraguan Sketches*, trans. Kathleen Weaver. New York: Norton.
Cose, Ellis. 1993. *The Rage of a Privileged Class*. New York: HarperCollins.
Crimaco, Luigi. n.d. "La Taverna di via Ripa in Rione Terra." In *Percorso Archeologico*. Naples: Ministerio per Beni e le Attivata Culturali, Sopraintendenza per I Beni Archeologici delle provincza di Napoli e Caserta 36. Unofficial translation by Emma Cervone.
Cruse, Harold. 1967. *The Crisis of the Negro Intellectual*. New York: William Morrow.
Curtin, Philip. 1989. "Recent Trends in African Historiography and Their Contribution to History in General." In *General History of Africa, Volume 6*, 54–71. Berkeley and Los Angeles: University of California Press.
———. 1995. "Ghettoizing African History." *Chronicle of Higher Education*. March 3.
Dahl, Robert. 1961. *Who Governs? Democracy and Power in an American City*. New Haven, Conn.: Yale University Press.
Das, Veena, ed. 2000. *Violence and Subjectivity*. Berkeley and Los Angeles: University of California Press.
Davidson, Basil, ed. 1964. *The African Past: Chronicles from Antiquity to Modern Times*. Boston: Little, Brown.
Davis, Mike. 1990. *City of Quartz*. London and New York: Verso.
Dawson, Michael C. 1995. "A Black Counterpublic? Economic Earthquakes, Racial Agendas and Black Politics." In *The Black Public Sphere*. The Black Public Sphere Collective, ed., 199–228. Chicago: University of Chicago Press.
———. 2001. *Black Visions: The Roots of Contemporary African-American Political Ideology*. Chicago: University of Chicago Press.
———. 2004. "The Widening Racial Divide in American Public Opinion: War, Protest, and Support for the President." Presentation at Bellagio Center, Rockefeller Foundation, Lake Como, Italy, July 17.

De Certeau, Michel. 2002. *The Practice of Everyday Life*. Berkeley and Los Angeles: University of California Press.

De lacroix, Perú. 1912. *Diario de Bucaramanga o Vida Pública y Privada del Libertador Simón Bolívar*. Paris: Onlendorff.

De la Fuente, Alejandro. 2001. *A Nation for All: Race, Inequality and Politics in Twentieth Century Cuba*. Chapel Hill: The University of North Carolina Press.

Debord, Guy. 1995. *The Society of the Spectacle*. New York: Zone Books.

Dent, Gina, and Michele Wallace. 1992. *Black Popular Culture*. Seattle: Bay Press.

Denton, Nancy and Douglass Massey. 1998. *American Apartheid: Segregation and the Making of the Underclass*. Cambridge, Mass.; Harvard University Press.

Dewey, John. 1931. *Context and Thought*. Berkeley and Los Angeles: University of California Press.

Dewey, John, and James Hayden Tufts. 1908. *Ethics*. New York: Henry Holt.

Diawara, Manthia. 1994. "Malcolm X and the Black Public Sphere: Conversionists vs. Culturalists." *Public Culture* 7 (Fall): 39–52.

———. 1998. *In Search of Africa*. Cambridge, Mass.; Harvard University Press.

Diop, Alioune. 1961. "African Culture and Its Place in Work for African Unity." In *The Second Pan-African Youth Seminar, August 5–14, 1961, Dar-es-Salaam, Tanganyika*, 28–39. Brussels: World Assembly of Youth.

Dirks, Nicholas. 1990. "History as a Sign of the Modern." *Public Culture* 2 (Spring): vol. 2, issue 2: 25–33.

Doctorow, E. L. 1974. *Ragtime*. New York: Fawcett Crest.

Douglass, Frederick. 1963. *Narrative of the Life of Frederick Douglass, An American Slave*. New York: Anchor.

Du Bois, W. E. B. 1986. *The Souls of Black Folk*. New York: Vintage.

Durkheim, Émile. 1965. *The Elementary Forms of the Religious Life*, trans. Joseph Ward Swain. New York: Free Press.

Duster, Troy. 2003. *Backdoor to Eugenics*. New York: Routledge.

———. 2005. "Enhanced: Race and Reification in Science." *Science Magazine* 307: 1050–1051.

Eagleton, Terry. 1991. *Ideology: An Introduction*. New York: Verso.

Easton, David. 1969. "The New Revolution in Political Science." *APSR* 63 (December) (4)1051–1061.

Echevarría, Roberto González. 1990. *The Voice of the Masters: Writing and Authority in Modern Latin American Literature*. Austin: University of Texas Press.

Edelman, Murray. 1985. *The Symbolic Uses of Politics*. Champaign: University of Illinois Press.

———. 1988. *Constructing the Political Spectacle*. Chicago: University of Chicago Press.

Edwards, Brent Hayes. 2003. *The Practice of Diaspora*. Cambridge, Mass.: Harvard University Press.

Ellis, John M. 1979. *Heinrich Von Kleist: Studies in the Character and Meaning of His Writings*. Chapel Hill: The University of North Carolina Press.

Ellison, Ralph. 1995a. *Going to the Territory*. New York: Vintage.

———. 1995b. *Shadow and Act*. New York: Vintage.
Elster, Jon. 1983. *Sour Grapes: Studies in the Subversion of Rationality*. Cambridge: Cambridge University Press.
Essed, Philomena. 1990. *Everyday Racism: Reports from Women of Two Cultures*. Claremont, Calif.: Hunter House.
European Monitoring Centre on Racism and Xenophobia. (2001). *Attitudes Towards Minority Groups in the European Union*. Vienna: European Monitoring Centre on Racism and Xenophobia.
Falk, Gerhard. 1992. *The Jew in Christian Theology: Martin Luther's Anti-Jewish Vom Schem Hamphoras*. Jefferson, N.C.: McFarland.
Fanon, Frantz. 1967. *Black Skin, White Masks*, trans. Charles Lam Markmann. New York: Grove.
———. 1968. *The Wretched of the Earth*. New York: Grove.
Feagin, Joe R., and Melvin P. Sikes. 1994. *Living with Racism: The Black Middle Class Experience*. Boston: Beacon.
Feijoo, Samuel, ed. 1987. "El Negro en la Quarteta Cubana." In *Negro en la Literatura Folklórica Cubana*, 40–45. Havana: Editorial Letras Cubanas.
Ferreira da Silva, Denise. 1998. "Facts of Blackness: Brazil Is Not (Quite) the United States . . . and Racial Politics in Brazil." *Social Identities* 4 (March): 201–234.
———. 2001. "Towards a Critique of the Socio-logics of Justice: The Analytics of Raciality and the Production of Universality." *Social Identities* 7 (3): 421–453.
Fields, Barbara. 1990. "Slavery, Race and Ideology in the United States of America." *New Left Review* vol. 181 (May/June): 95–118.
———. 2003. "Of Rogues and Geldings." In *The American Historical Review* 108 (December): 1397–1405.
Flanagan, Owen, and Amelie Rorty. 1990. *Identity, Character, and Morality*. Cambridge, Mass.: MIT Press.
Fogg-Davis, Hawley. 2002. *The Ethics of Transracial Adoption*. Ithaca, N.Y.: Cornell University Press.
———. 2003. "The Racial Retreat of Contemporary Political Science." *Perspectives on Politics* 1: 555–564.
Foley, Barbara. 2003. *Spectres of 1919: Class and Nation in the Making of the New Negro*. Urbana: University of Illinois Press.
Foner, Philip. 1977. *American Socialism and Black Americans: From the Age of Jackson to WWII*. Westport, Conn.: Greenport Press.
Foucault, Michel. 1979. *Discipline and Punish: The Birth of the Prison*. Trans. Alan Sheridan. New York: Vintage.
———. 1988. *Politics, Philosophy, Culture: Interviews and Other Writings 1977–1984*. L. D. Kritzman, ed. Alan Sheridan, trans. New York: Routledge.
———. 2003. "Society Must Be Defended": Lectures at the Collège de France, 1975–1976. New York: Picador Books.
Frazier, Franklin. 1997. *Black Bourgeoisie: The Book That Bought the Shock of Self-Revelation to Middle-Class Black in America*. New York: The Free Press.
Fredrickson, George. 1997. *Race and Racism in Comparative Perspective*. Berkeley and Los Angeles: University of California Press.

———. 2000. *The Comparative Imagination: On the History of Racism, Nationalism and Social Movements*. Berkeley and Los Angeles: University of California Press.
Freyre, Gilberto. 1956. *The Masters and the Slaves (Casa Grande e Sensala): A Study in the Development of Brazilian Civilization*. New York: Knopf.
———. 1963. "Reflections on Miscegenation." In *The Mansions and the Shanties (Sobrados e Mucambos): The Making of Modern Brazil*. New York: Knopf.
Fryer, Ronald G., and Matthew O. Jackson. 2002. "Categorical Cognition: A Psychological Model of Categories and Identification in Decision Making." American Bar Foundation working paper # 2115. Chicago: American Bar Foundation.
Fukuyama, Francis. 1992. *The End of History and the Last Man*. New York: Free Press.
Furnivall, John S. 1948. *Colonial Policy and Practice: A Comparative Study of Burma and Netherlands India*. Oxford: Oxford University Press.
Garnet, Henry Highland. 1969. "The Past and The Present Condition, and the Destiny of the Colored Race: A Discourse Delivered at the Fifteenth Anniversary of the Female Benevolent Society of Troy, N.Y. February 14, 1848." Miami: Mnemosyne Publishing.
———. 1970. "An Address to the Slaves of the United States of America (1843)." In *Black Nationalism in America*, eds. John H. Bracey Jr., August Meier, and Elliot Rudwick, 67–73. Indianapolis: Bobbs-Merrill.
Gaspar, David Barry and David Patrick Geggus, eds. 1997. *A Turbulent Time: The French Revolution and the Greater Caribbean*. Bloomington: Indiana University Press.
Gates, Henry Louis. 1988. *The Signifying Monkey: A Theory of African American Literary Criticism*. New York: Oxford University Press.
Gaventa, John. 1982. *Power and Powerlessness: Quiescence and Rebellion in an Appalachian Valley*. Champaign: University of Illinois Press.
Geddes, Barbara. 1994. *Politician's Dilemma: Building State Capacity in Latin America*. California Series on Social Choice and Political Economy. Berkeley: University of California Press.
Geertz, Clifford. 1973. *The Interpretation of Cultures*. New York: Basic.
Gilman, Sander. 1986. *Jewish Self-Hatred: Anti-Semitism and the Hidden Language of the Jews*. Baltimore: Johns Hopkins University Press.
———. 1991. *The Jew's Body*. New York: Routledge.
Gilroy, Paul. 1991. *There Ain't No Black in the Union Jack: The Cultural Politics of Race and Nation*. Chicago: University of Chicago Press.
———. 1992. *The Black Atlantic: Modernity and Double Consciousness*. Cambridge, Mass.: Harvard University Press.
———. 2000. *Against Race: Imagining Political Culture beyond the Color Line*. Cambridge, Mass.: Harvard University Press.
Glaude, Eddie. 2000. *Exodus! Religion, Race and Nation in Early 19th Century Black America*. Chicago: University of Chicago Press.
———. 2003. "On Mendieta's Latino Public Intellectual." In *Nepalta: Views from the South* 4 (2): 257–261.

Goldberg, David Theo, ed. 1990. *The Anatomy of Racism*. Minneapolis: University of Minnesota Press.

———. 2002. *The Racial State*. Malden, Mass.: Blackwell Publishers.

Gooding-Williams, Robert, ed. 1993. *Reading Rodney King, Reading Urban Uprising*. New York: Routledge.

———. 1998. "Race, Multiculturalism and Democracy." *Constellations* 5 (Spring): 18–41.

Gordon, Edmund. 1998. *Disparate Diasporas: Identities and Politics in an African Nicaraguan Community*. Austin: University of Texas Press.

Gordon, Lewis. 1997. *Existence in Black: An Anthology of Black Existence*. New York: Routledge.

Gouldner, Alvin. 1976. *The Dialectic of Ideology and Technology*. London: Macmillan.

———. 1980. *The Two Marxisms: Contradictions and Anomalies in the Development of Theory*. New York: Seabury Press.

Graham, Sandra Lauderdale. 1992. *House and Street: The Domestic World of Servants and Masters in Nineteenth Century Rio de Janiero*. Austin: University of Texas Press.

Gramsci, Antonio. 1977a. "Predictions." In *Selections from Political Writings, 1910–1920*. Quintin Hoare, ed., trans. John Matthews, 356–359. Minneapolis: University of Minnesota Press.

———. 1977b. "Socialism and Culture." In *Selections from Political Writings, 1910–1920*. Quintin Hoare, ed., trans. John Matthews, 10–13. Minneapolis: University of Minnesota Press.

———. 1985. *Selections from the Prison Notebooks*. New York: International Publishers.

Gray, Cecil Conteen. 2001. *Afrocentric Thought and Praxis: An Intellectual History*. Trenton, N.J.: Africa World Press.

Grossberg, Lawrence, ed. 1986. "On Postmodernism and Articulation: An Interview with Stuart Hall." *Journal of Communication Inquiry* 10 (2): 45–60.

Guss, David M. 2000. *The Festive State: Race, Ethnicity and Nationalism as Cultural Performance*. Berkeley and Los Angeles: University of California Press.

Guzmán, Patricio, director. 1975. *The Battle of Chile*. New York: Tricontinental Film Center.

———. 1997. *Chile: The Obstinate Memory*. Brooklyn, N.Y.: First Run/Icarus Films.

Gwaltney, John Langston. 1980. *Drylongso: A Self Portrait of Black America*. New York: Random House.

Hale, Charles. 1994. "Cultural Politics of Identity in Latin America." *Annual Review of Anthropology* vol. 26: 67–90.

———. 2005. "Neoliberal Multiculturalism: The Remaking of Cultural rights and Racial Dominance in Central America." *Polar* vol. 28 (1): 10–28.

Hall, Stuart. 1988. "Race, Articulation, and Societies Structured in Dominance." In *Marxism and the Interpretation of Culture*. Cary Nelson and Lawrence Grossberg, eds. Champaign: University of Illinois Press.

———. 1989. "Ethnicity: Identity and Difference." *Radical America* 23 (4): (December): 9–20.

———. 1990. "Cultural Identity and Diaspora." In *Identity: Community, Culture, Difference*. Jonathan Rutherford, ed., 222–237. London: Lawrence and Wishart.

———. 1991. "Europe's Other Self." *Marxism Today* 35 (August): 18–19.

———. 1997. "The Local and the Global: Globalization and Ethnicity." *Dangerous Liaisons: Gender, Nation and Postcolonial Perspectives*. Anne McClintock, Aamir Mufti, and Ella Shohat, eds., 173–187. Minneapolis: University of Minnesota Press.

Hampton, Fred 1969. *You've Got to Make a Commitment*. Chicago: People's Information Center.

Hanchard, Michael. 1994. *Orpheus and Power: The Movimiento Negro of Rio de Janeiro and São Paulo, Brazil 1945–1988*. Princeton, N.J.: Princeton University Press.

———. 1997. "Identity, Meaning, and the African American." In *Dangerous Liaisons: Gender, Nation and Postcolonial Perspectives*. Anne McClintock, Aamir Mufti, and Ella Shohat, eds., 230–239. Minneapolis: University of Minnesota Press.

———. 2001. "Afro-Modernity: Temporality, Politics, and the African Diaspora." In *Alternative Modernities*. D. P. Gaonkar, ed., 272–298. Durham, N.C.: Duke University Press.

Hanchard, Michael, and Erin Chung. 2004. "From Race Relations to Comparative Racial Politics: A Survey of Cross-National Scholarship on Race in the Social Sciences." *Du Bois Review* 1 (2): (September): 319–343.

Hanzell, Perry, director. 1973. *The Harder They Come*. Santa Monica, Calif.: Xenon Entertainment.

Hardt, Michael, and Antonio Negri. 2000. *Empire*. Cambridge, Mass.: Harvard University Press.

Harris, Frederick. 2002. "Collective Memory, Collective Action, and Black Activism in the 1960's." In *Breaking the Cycles of Hatred: Memory, Law, and Repair*. Martha Minow, ed. Princeton, N.J.: Princeton University Press.

Harris, Marvin. 1979. *Cultural Materialism: The Struggle for a Science of Culture*. New York: Random House.

Hartman, Saidiya V. 1997. *Scenes of Subjection: Terror, Slavery and Self-Making in Nineteenth Century America*. New York: Oxford University Press.

Hatcher, Richard, and Lee Sloan. 1973. *Blacks and Metro Politics*. Washington, D.C.: Joint Center for Political Studies.

Harvey, David. 1989. *The Condition of Postmodernity: An Enquiry into the Origins of Cultural Change*. Cambridge, Mass.: Blackwell Publishers.

Heer, Rolf de, director. 2002. *The Tracker*. New York: ArtMattan Productions.

Hegel, Georg Friedrich. 1956. *The Philosophy of History*. New York: Dover.

Helg, Aline. 1995. *Our Rightful Share: The Afro-Cuban Struggle for Equality*. Chapel Hill: The University of North Carolina Press.

———. 1999. "La Mejorana y la independencia cubana: un choque de ideas y liderazgo entre José Martí y Antonio Maceo." *Cudadernos de Historia Contemporánea* (21): 227–257.

Hempel, Carl G. 1952. "Typological Methods in the Natural and Social Sciences." In *Science, Language and Human Rights,* 65–86. Philadelphia: American Philosophical Association.

Hesse, Barnor, ed. 2001. *Un/Settled Multiculturalisms: Diasporas, Entanglements, Transruptions.* London: Zed.

Hesse, Barnor and S. Sayyid, 2006. "Narrative Postcolonial Political and the Immigrant Imaginery." N. Ali, V. Kalra, and S. Sayyid, eds. *A Postcolonial People: South Asians in Britain.* London: Hurst.

Higginbotham, Evelyn Brooks. 1993. *Righteous Discontent: The Women's Movement in the Black Baptist Church, 1880–1920.* Cambridge, Mass.: Harvard University Press.

Hintzen, Percy, and Jean Muteba Rahier, eds. 2003. *Problematizing Blackness.* New York: Routledge.

Hobbes, Thomas. 1968. *Leviathan.* New York: Penguin.

Hobsbawm, Eric J. 1965. *Primitive Rebels: Studies in Archaic Forms of Social Movements in the 19th and 20th Centuries.* New York: Norton.

———. 1990. *Nations and Nationalism Since 1780.* Cambridge: Cambridge University Press.

Hobsbawm, Eric J., and Terence O. Ranger. 1983. *The Invention of Tradition.* Cambridge: Cambridge University Press.

Hochschild, Jennifer. 1996. *Facing Up to the American Dream.* Princeton, N.J.: Princeton University Press.

Hofstadter, Richard. 1965. *The Paranoid Style in American Politics and Other Essays.* New York: Knopf.

Hollinger, David. 2003. "Amalgamation and Hypodescent: The Question of Ethnoracial Mixture in the History of the United States." *American Historical Review* 108 (December): 1363–1390.

Holston, James. 1989. *The Modernist City.* Chicago: University of Chicago Press.

Holt, Thomas. 1995. "Marking: Race, Race-Making and the Writing of History." *American Historical Review* 100 no. 1 (February): 1–20.

———. 2001. *The Problem of Freedom.* Cambridge, Mass.: Harvard University Press.

hooks, bell. 1995. Performance Practice as a Site of Opposition. In *Let's Get It On: The Politics of Black Performance,* Catherine Ugwa, ed., 210–221. London: Institute of Contemporary Arts.

Horne, Gerald. 1994. *Black Liberation/Red Scare: Ben Davis and the Communist Party.* Newark: University of Delaware Press.

Howe, Stephen. 1998. *Afrocentrism: Mythical Pasts and Imagined Homes.* London: Verso.

Hroch, Miroslav. 1985. *Social Proclamations of National Revival in Europe: A Comparative Analysis of the Social Composition of Patriotic Groups among the Smaller European Nations.* New York: Cambridge University Press.

Hunt, David. 1988. "From the Millennial to the Everyday: James Scott's Search for the Essence of Peasant Politics." *Radical History Review* 42 (Fall): 156–172.

Hunter, Floyd. 1969. *Community Power Structure: A Study of Decision Makers.* Chapel Hill: The University of North Carolina Press.

Iton, Richard. 2000. *Solidarity Blues: Race, Culture and the American Left*. Chapel Hill: The University of North Carolina Press.
———. Forthcoming. *In Search of the Black Fantastic: Politics and Popular culture in the Post-Civil Rights Era*. New York: Oxford University Press.
Jackman, Mary, and Marie Crane. 1986. "Some of My Best Friends Are Black… Interracial Friendship and Whites' Racial Attitudes." *Public Opinion Quarterly* 50: 459–486.
Jacobson, Matthew. 1999. *Whiteness of a Different Color: European Immigrants and the Alchemy of Race*. Cambridge, Mass.: Harvard University Press.
James, C. L. R. 1989. *The Black Jacobins: Toussaint L'Ouverture and the San Domingo Revolution*. New York: Vintage.
———. 1993a. *American Civilization*. Cambridge, Mass.: Blackwell.
———. 1993b. *Beyond Boundary*. Durham, N.C.: Duke University Press.
James, William. 1978. *Essays in Philosophy*. Cambridge, Mass.: Harvard University Press.
James, Winston. 1998. *Holding Aloft the Banner of Ethiopia: Caribbean Radicalism in Early 20th Century America*. New York: Verso.
Judy, Ronald. 2000. "Introduction: On W. E. B. Du Bois and Hyberbolic Thinking." *Boundary 2* 27 (Fall): 1–35.
Kaba, Lasiné. 1976. "The Cultural Revolution, Artistic Creativity, and Freedom of Expression in Guinea." *The Journal of Modern Africa Studies*, 14 (2): 201–218.
Kant, Immanuel. 1973. *Critique of Pure Reason*. London: Macmillan.
Katz, Friedrich. 1981. *The Secret War in Mexico: Europe, the United States, and the Mexican Revolution*. Chicago: University of Chicago Press.
Katznelson, Ira. 1994. *Marxism and the City*. Oxford: Oxford University Press.
Kelley, Robin D. G. 1994. *Race Rebels: Culture, Politics, and the Black Working Class*. New York: Free Press.
———. 1997. *Yo' Mama's Disfunctional? Fighting the Culture Wars in Urban America*. Boston: Beacon Press.
———. 1999. "But a Local Phase of a World Problem: Black History's Global Vision, 1883–1950." *Journal of American History* 86 (December): 1045–1077.
———. 2002. *Freedom Dreams: The Black Radical Imagination*. Boston: Beacon.
Kemp, Amanda. 1998. "This Black Body in Question." In *The Ends of Performance*. Peggy Phelan and Jill Lane, eds., 116–130. New York: New York University Press.
Kierkegaard, Søren. 1954. *Fear and Trembling, and the Sickness unto Death*. Garden City, N.Y.: Doubleday.
Kleist, Heinrich Von. 1960. "Michael Kohlhaas" and "The Betrothal in Santo Domingo." In *The Marquise of O and Other Stories*, trans. Martin Greenberg. New York: New American Library.
Klinkner, Philip A., and Rogers M. Smith. 2002. *The Unsteady March: The Rise and Decline of Racial Equality in America*. Chicago: University of Chicago Press.
Knight, Alan. 1986. *The Mexican Revolution*. New York: Cambridge University Press.
Koopmans, Ruud and Paul Statham. 2001. *Challenging Immigration and Ethnic Relations Politics: Comparative European Perspectives*. New York: Oxford University Press.

Kushner, Tony. 1993. *Angels in America*. New York: Theatre Communications Group.
Kutzinski, Vera. 1993. *Sugar's Secrets*. Charlottesville: University Press of Virginia.
Lane, Robert E. 1962. *Political Ideology: Why the American Common Man Believes What He Does*. New York: Free Press.
———. 1969. *Political Thinking and Consciousness: The Private Life of the Political Mind*. Chicago: Markham.
Lee, Taeku. 2002. *Mobilizing Public Opinion: Black Insurgency and Racial Attitudes in the Civil Rights Era*. Chicago: University of Chicago Press.
Lefebvre, Henri. 1991. *Critique of Everyday Life, Vol. 1*. Trans. John Moore. London: Verso.
Lefkowitz, Mary. 1996. *Not Out of Africa: How Afrocentrism Became an Excuse to Teach Myth as History*. New York: Basic.
Lenin, Vladimir Il'ich. 1995. "The Two Tasks of Political Parties." In *The Lenin Anthology*. Robert C. Tucker, ed., 120–147. New York: Norton.
Levine, Lawrence W. 1978. *Black Culture and Black Consciousness*. New York: Oxford University Press.
Lewin, Linda. 1979. "The Oligarchical Limitations of Social Banditry in Brazil: The Case of the 'Good' Thief Antonio Silvino." In *Past and Present*. Richard W. Slatta, ed., 82 (February), 116–146.
Lewis, David Levering. 1994. *W. E. B. Du Bois: Biography of a Race 1868–1919*, vol. 1. New York: Henry Holt.
Leys Stepan, Nancy. 1991. *The Hour of Eugenics: Race, Gender and Nation in Latin America*. Ithaca, N.Y.: Cornell University Press.
Ling, Tom, Kevin Bonnett, Simon Bromley, and Bob Jessop. 1985. "Thatcherism and the Politics of Hegemony: A Reply to Stuart Hall." *New Left Review* 1:153 September–October: 87–101.
Locke, Alain, ed. 1999. *The New Negro: Voices of the Harlem Renaissance*. New York: Touchstone.
Lott, Eric. 1995. *Love and Theft: Blackface Minstrelsy and the American Working Class*. New York: Oxford University Press.
Lubiano, Wahneema. Forthcoming. *Messing with the Machine: Politics, Form, and African American Fiction*. New York: Verso.
Lukács, Georg. 1971. "Towards a Methodology of the Problem of Organization." In *History and Class Consciousness*, 295–342. Cambridge, Mass.: MIT Press.
Lukes, Stephen. 1974. *Power: A Radical View*. London: Macmillan.
Macey, David. 2000. *Frantz Fanon: A Biography*. New York: Picador.
Maier, Charles S. 1975. *Recasting Bourgeois Europe*. Princeton, N.J.: Princeton University Press.
Malcolm X. 1965. *The Autobiography of Malcolm X*. New York: Grove.
Malik, Kenan. 1996. *The Meaning of Race: Race, History and Culture in Western Society*. Washington Square, N.Y.: New York University Press.
Malkin, Elisabeth. July 2, 2005. "Fight Grows over a Stamp U.S. Sees as Racist and Mexico Adores." *New York Times*.

Mannheim, Karl. 1936. *Ideology and Utopia*. New York: Harcourt Brace Jovanovich.
Marable, Manning. 1998. *Black Leadership*. New York: Columbia University Press.
———. 2000. *How Capitalism Underdeveloped Black America*. Cambridge, Mass.: South End Press.
Markell, Patchen. 2004. *Bound by Recognition*. Princeton, N.J.: Princeton University Press.
Márquez, Gabriel García. 2000. *Chronicle of a Death Foretold*. New York: Vintage.
Martí, José. 1959. *La Cuestión Racial*. Havana: Lex.
———. 1975. *Inside the Monster: Writings United States and American Imperialism*. Philip Foner, ed. New York: Monthly Review Press.
———. 1977. "My Race." In *Our America: Writings on the Latin America and the Struggle for Cuban Independence*. Philip Foner, ed., 311–314. New York: Monthly Review Press.
Marx, Anthony. 1998. *Making Race and Nation: A Comparison of the United States, South Africa and Brazil*. Cambridge: Cambridge University Press.
Matory, J. Lorand. 1999. "The English Professors of Brazil: On the Diasporic Roots of the Yorùbá Nation." *Comparative Studies in Society and History* 41, 1 (January): 72–103
Mattiace, Shannan L. 2003. *To See with Two Eyes: Peasant Activism and Indian Autonomy in Chiapas Mexico*. Albuquerque: University of New Mexico Press.
Mayer, Nonna. 1996. "Is France Racist?" In *Contemporary European History* 5 I: 119–127.
Mbembe, Achille. 2001. *On the Postcolony*. Berkeley and Los Angeles: University of California Press.
McAdam, Doug. 1982. *Political Process and the Development of Black Insurgency, 1930–1970*. Chicago: University of Chicago Press.
McAdam, Doug, Sidney Tarrow, Charles Tilley. 2001. *Dynamics of Contention*. New York: Cambridge University Press.
McClintock, Anne. 1995. *Imperial Leather: Race, Gender and Sex in the Colonial Contest*. New York: Routledge.
McGrath, William J. 1985. "Cultural Politics in Austria: From Empire to Republic." In *The Austrian Socialist Experiment: Social Democracy and Austromarxism, 1918–1934*, Anson Rabinbach, ed. Boulder, Colo.: Westview.
McWhorter, John. 2003. *Authentically Black: Essays for the Black Silent Majority*. New York: Gotham.
Meeks, Brian. 2000. *Narratives of Resistance: Jamaica, Trinidad, The Caribbean*. Barbados: University of the West Indies Press.
Mehta, Uday. 1999. *Liberalism and Empire: A Study in 19th Century British Legal Thought*. Chicago: University of Chicago Press.
Menchú, Rigoberta. 1984. *I Rigoberta Menchú*. Elizabeth Burgos-Debray, ed., trans. Ann Wright. London: Verso.
Mendelberg, Tali. 2001. *The Race Card: Campaign Strategy, Implicit Messages, and the Norm of Equality*. Princeton, N.J.: Princeton University Press.

Mendieta, Eduardo. 2003. "What Can Latinas/os Learn from Cornel West? The Latino Postcolonial Intellectual in the Age of the Exhaustion of Public Spheres." *Neplanta* 4 (2): 213–235.

Meriweather, James Hunter. 2002. *Proudly We Can Be Africans: Black Americans and Africa, 1935–1961*. Chapel Hill: The University of North Carolina Press.

Messina, Anthony M. 1989. *Race and Party Competition in Britain*. Oxford: Clarendon.

Miles, Robert. 1993. *Racism after "Race Relations."* New York: Routledge.

Miller, Jay Hillis. 1990. "Laying Down the Law in Literature: The Example of Kleist." *The Cardozo Law Review* (July–August), 11: 1491–1514.

Mills, Charles. 1997. *The Racial Contract*. Ithaca, N.Y.: Cornell University Press.

———. 1998. *Blackness Visible: Essays on Philosophy and Race*. Ithaca, N.Y.: Cornell University Press.

———. 1999. *The Racial Contract*. Ithaca, N.Y.: Cornell University Press.

Mintz, Sidney. 1985. *Sweetness and Power: The Place of Sugar in Modern History*. New York: Penguin.

Mitchell, Michael. 1977. "Racial Consciousness and the Political Attitudes and Behavior of Blacks in São Paulo, Brazil." Ph.D. thesis, University of Michigan Microfilms.

Mitchell, Timothy. 1990. "Everyday Metaphors of Power." *Theory and Society* 19:5 (October), 545–577.

———. 2002. *Rule of Experts: Egypt, Techno-Politics, Modernity*. Berkeley and Los Angeles: University of California Press.

Monk, Ray. 1990. *Ludwig Wittgenstein: The Duty of Genius*. New York: Free Press.

Moore, Donald. 1999. "The Crucible of Cultural Politics: Reworking 'Development" in Zimbabwe's Eastern Highlands." *American Ethnologist* 26 (3): 654–689.

Moten, Fred. 2003. *In the Break: The Aesthetics of the Black Radical Tradition*. Minneapolis: University of Minnesota Press.

Murray, Albert. 1990. *The Omni-Americans: Some Alternatives to the Folklore of White Supremacy*. Cambridge, Mass.: Da Capo.

Myers, Kristin. 2001. "Race Talk: The Perpetuation of Racism through Private Discourse." *Race and Society* 4: 3–26.

Nairn, Tom. 1977. *The Break-up of Britain: Crisis and Neo-nationalism*. London: New Left Books.

Nancy, Jean-Luc. 1990. Peter Connor, Lisa Garbus, Michael Holland and Simona Sawhney, trans. *The Inoperative Community*. Minneapolis: University of Minnesota Press.

Nash, Gary. 1995. "The Hidden History of Mestizo America." *Journal of American History* 82 (3): 941–964.

Neal, Larry. 1989a. "Black Power in the International Context." In *Visions of a Liberated Future: Black Arts Movement Writings*, Larry Neal, ed., 133–146. New York: Thunder's Mouth.

———. 1989b. "The Genius and the Prize." In *Visions of a Liberated Future: Black Arts Movement Writings*. Larry Neal, ed., 79–80. New York: Thunder's Mouth.

Neruda, Pablo. 1973. *Incitación Al Nixonicidio Y Alabanza de La Revolución Chilena*. Lima, Perú: Edición Causachún.
Newton, Huey P. 1968. *Huey Newton Talks to the Movement: About the Black Panther Party, Cultural Nationalism, SNCC, Liberals and White Revolutionaries*. Chicago: SDS.
Nobles, Melissa. 2000. *Shades of Citizenship: Race and the Census in Modern Politics*. Stanford, Calif.: Stanford University Press.
Novo Michaelis Diccionário, ed. *Michaelis*, 43. 1986. São Paulo: Melhoramentos.
Olson, Mancur. 1971. *The Logic of Collective Action: Public Goods and the Theory of Groups*. Cambridge, Mass.: Harvard University Press.
Ortiz, Fernando. 1944. *Los Negros Curros*. Havana: Editorial de Ciencias Sociales.
Outlaw, Lucius. 1996. *On Race and Philosophy*. New York: Routledge.
Oxaal, Ivar. 1982. *Black Intellectuals and the Dilemmas of Race and Class in Trinidad*. Cambridge, Mass.: Schenkman.
Padmore, George. 1971. *Pan-Africanism or Communism*. New York: Doubleday.
Padgen, Anthony. 1995. *Lords of All the World: Ideologies of Empire in Spain, Britain, and France c. 1500–1800*. New Haven, Conn.: Yale University Press.
Painter, Nell Irvin. 1977. *Exodusters: Black Migration to Kansas after Reconstruction*. New York: Norton.
———. 1989. "Martin Delaney, a Black Nationalist in Two Kinds of Time." *New England Journal of Black Studies* 8 (November).
Palmié, Stephan. 1995a. "African Frontiers in the Americas?" In *Born Out of Resistance? On Caribbean Cultural Creativity*. Wim Hoogbergen, ed., 286–300. Utrecht, Netherlands: ISOR Publications.
———. 1995b. "Against Syncretism: 'Africanizing' and 'Cubanizing' Discourses in North American òrìsà Worship." In *Counterworks: Managing Diverse Knowledge*, ed. Richard Fardon, 73–104. London: Routledge.
Patterson, Tiffany, and Robin Kelley. 2000. "Unfinished Migrations: Reflections on the African Diaspora and the Making of the Modern World." *African Studies Review* 43 (1) 11–46.
Paz, Octavio. 1973. In Rita Guibert. *Seven Voices: Seven Latin American Writers Talk to Rita Guibea*. New York: Knopf.
Pemberton, John. 1994. *On the Subject of Java*. Ithaca, N.Y.: Cornell University Press.
Pettigrew, Thomas. 1998. "Inter-group Contact Theory." *Annual Review of Psychology* 49: 65–85.
Pettit, Philip. 1997. *Republicanism: A Theory of Freedom and Government*. New York: Oxford University Press.
Phillips, John. 1987. *The Trail of Ned Kelly*. Sidney: Law Book Co.
Pierce, Chester. 1969. "Offensive Mechanisms." In *The Black Seventies*. Floyd B. Barbour, ed. 265–282. Boston: Porter Sargent.
Piper, Adrian M. S. 1990. "Higher Order Discrimination." In *Identity, Character and Morality*. Owen Flanagan and Amelie Oksenberg Rorty, eds., 285–307. Cambridge, Mass.: MIT Press.
Pollock, Della. 1998. "Performing Writing." In *The Ends of Performance*. Peggy Thelan and Jill Lane, eds., 73–103. New York: New York University Press.

Porter, J. M., ed. 1974. *Luther: Selected Political Writings*. Philadelphia: Fortress.

Prandi, Reginaldo J. 1991. *Os Candomblés de São Paulo: a vehla magia na metrópole nova*. São Paulo: Editora de Universidade de São Paulo.

Pratt, Mary Louise. 1992. *Imperial Eyes: Travel Writing and Transculturation*. New York: Routledge.

Rabinbach, Anson, ed. 1985. *The Austrian Social Experiment: Social Democracy and Austromarxism, 1918–1934*. Boulder, Colo.: Westview.

Raboteau, Albert. 1995. *A Fire in the Bones: Reflections on African-American Religious History*. Boston: Beacon.

Racusen, Seth. 2004. "Making the 'Impossible' Determination: Flexible Identity and Targeted Opportunity." In *Contemporary Brazil* 36 Conn. L. Rev. 787, 803–808.

Ramos, Julio. 2001. *Divergent Modernities: Culture and Politics in 19th Century Latin America*. Durham, N.C.: Duke University Press.

Reed, Adolph. 1995. "What Are the Drums Saying, Booker?: The Current Crisis of the Black Intellectual." *Village Voice* (April 11): 31–36.

———. 1999. *Stirrings in the Jug: Black Politics in the Post-Segregation Era*. Minneapolis: University of Minnesota Press.

Richards, Sandra. 2002. Cultural Travel to Ghana's Slave Castles: A Commentary in International Research in Geographical and Environmental Education 11(4): 372–375.

———. Forthcoming. *Who Is This Ancestor? Performing Memory in Ghana's Slave Castles*. In *Horror and Human Tragedy Revisited: The Management of Sites of Atrocities for Tourism*. Gregory Ashworth and Rudi Hartmann, eds. New York: Cognizant Communication Corporation.

Roberts, Dorothy. 1997. *Killing the Black Body: Race, Reproduction, and the Meaning of Liberalism*. New York: Pantheon.

Robinson, Cedric J. 1983. *Black Marxism: The Making of the Black Radical Tradition*. London: Zed.

Rodney, Walter. 1981a. *A History of the Guyanese Working People*. Baltimore, Md.: Johns Hopkins University Press.

———. 1981b. *How Europe Underdeveloped Africa*. Washington, D.C.: Howard University Press.

Rogers, Revel. 2006. *Afro-Caribbean Immigrants and the Politics of Incorporation: Ethnicity, Exception, or Exit*. Cambridge: Cambridge University Press.

Rogin, Michael. 1998. *Blackface, White Noise: Jewish Immigrants in the Hollywood Melting Pot*. Berkeley and Los Angeles: University of California Press.

Roodt, Darrell, director. *Serafina!* 1992. Burbank, Calif.: Buena Vista Pictures.

Rorty, Amelie Oksenberg, and David Wong. 1990. "Aspects of Identity and Agency." In *Identity, Character and Morality*. Owen Flanagan and Amelie Oksenberg Rorty, eds. 19–37. Cambridge, Mass.: MIT Press.

Rosaldo, Renato. 1980. *Ilongot Headhunting 1883–1974: A Study in Society and History*. Stanford, Calif.: Stanford University Press.

Rose, Jacqueline. 1986. *Sexuality in the Field of Vision*. London: Verso.

Ross, Andrew, ed. 1988. *Universal Abandon? The Politics of Postmodernism.* Minneapolis: University of Minnesota Press.
Rout, Leslie. 1976. *The African Experience in Spanish America, 1502 to the Present Day.* Cambridge; New York: Cambridge University Press.
Rudolph, Lloyd I., and Susanne Hoeber Rudolph. 1967. *The Modernity of Tradition: Political Development in India.* Chicago: University of Chicago Press.
Rudolph, Susanne Hoeber, and Lloyd I. Rudolph, eds. 1972. *Education and Politics in India: Studies in Organization, Society, and Policy.* Cambridge, Mass.: Harvard University Press.
———. 1984. *Essays on Rajputana: Reflections on History, Culture and Administration.* New Delhi: Concept.
Ryan, Alan. 1976. *Philosophy of the Social Sciences.* London: Macmillan.
Ryan, Selwyn, D. 1972. *Race and Nationalism in Trinidad and Tobago: A Study of Decolonization in a Multiracial Society.* Toronto and Buffalo: University of Toronto Press.
Sadiq, Kamal. 2005. "When States Prefer Non-Citizens Over Citizens: Conflict over Illegal Immigration into Malaysia," *International Studies Quarterly* 49 (March): 101–122.
———. 2006. "Have Documents Will Travel: Illegal 'Citizenship' in Developing Countries," Article manuscript under review. February.
Said, Edward. 1979. *Orientalism.* New York: Vintage.
———. 1994. *Representations of the Intellectual.* New York: Pantheon.
Sánchez, George. 1993. *Becoming Mexican American: Ethnicity, Culture, and Identity in Chicano Los Angeles, 1900–1945.* New York: Oxford University Press.
Sansone, Livio. 2003. *Blackness without Ethnicity: Constructing Race in Brazil.* New York: Palgrave MacMillan.
Savigliano, Marta E. 1995. *Tango and the Political Economy of Passion.* Boulder, Colo.: Westview.
Sawyer, Mark Q. 2005. *Racial Politics in Post-Revolutionary Cuba.* Cambridge: Cambridge University Press.
Schepisi, Fred, director. 1978. *The Chant of Jimmy Blacksmith.* New York: New Yorker Films.
Schmitt, Carl. 1976. *The Concept of the Political.* New Brunswick, N.J.: Rutgers University Press.
Schmitter, Philippe. 1974. "Still the Century of Corporatism?" *Review of Politics* 36 (January): 85–131.
Schutz, Alfred. 1970. *On Phenomenology and Social Relations: Selected Writings.* Chicago: University of Chicago Press.
Schutz, Alfred, and Thomas Luckmann. 1973–75. *Structures of the Life-World, Volumes 1 and 2,* trans. Richard M. Zaner and H. Tristram Engelhardt Jr. Evanston, Ill.: Northwestern University Press.
Scott, David. 1999. *Refashioning Futures: Criticism after Postcoloniality.* Princeton, N.J.: Princeton University Press.
———. 2004. *Conscripts of Modernity: The Tragedy of Colonial Enlightenment.* Durham, N.C.: Duke University Press.

Scott, James. 1977. *The Moral Economy of the Peasant: Rebellion and Subsistence in Southeast Asia*. New Haven, Conn.: Yale University Press.

———. 1985. *Weapons of the Weak: Everyday Forms of Peasant Resistance*. New Haven, Conn.: Yale University Press.

———. 1990. *Domination and the Arts of Resistance: Hidden Transcripts*. New Haven, Conn.: Yale University Press.

———. 1999. *Seeing Like a State: How Certain Schemes to Improve the Human Condition Have Failed*. New Haven, Conn.: Yale University Press.

Scott, Rebecca. 1985. *Slave Emancipation in Cuba*. Princeton, N.J.: Princeton University Press.

Sears, David, and Jim Sidanius. 2000. *Racialized Politics: The Debate about Politics in America*. Chicago: Chicago University Press.

Shakur, Assata. 1987. *Assata*. Westport, Conn.: Lawrence Hill and Company.

Shapiro, Michael J. 2001. *For Moral Ambiguity: National Culture and the Politics of the Family*. Minneapolis: University of Minnesota Press.

Shelton, J. Nicole. 2000. "A Reconceptualization of How We Study Issues of Racial Prejudice." *Personality and Psychology Review* 4 (4): 4374–4390.

Sheriff, Robin E. 2001. *Dreaming Equality: Color, Race and Racism in Urban Brazil*. New Brunswick, N.J.: Rutgers University Press.

Silverblatt, Irene. 2004. *Modern Inquisitions: Peru and the Colonial Origins of the Civilized World*. Durham, N.C.: Duke University Press.

Singelmann, Peter. 1975. "Political Structure and Social Banditry in Northeast Brazil." *Journal of Latin American Studies* 7 (1): 59–83.

Skidmore, Thomas. 2003. "Racial Mixture and Affirmative Action: The Cases of Brazil and the United States." *The American Historical Review* 108 (5): 1391–1396.

Slovo, Joe. 1996. *Slovo: The Unfinished Autobiography, with an Introduction by Helena Dolny*. London: Hodder and Stoughton.

Small, Stephen. 1994. *Racialised Barriers: The Black Experience in the United States and England in the 1980's*. London: Routledge.

Smith, M. G. 1960. "Social and Cultural Pluralism." In *Social and Cultural Pluralism in the Caribbean*, ed. Vera Rubin. Annals of the American Academy of Sciences (83): 763–777.

Smith, Rogers. 1999. *Civic Ideals*. New Haven, Conn.: Yale University Press.

Smith, William. 2004. "Black Faculty Coping with Racial Battle Fatigue: The Campus Racial Climate in a Post-Civil Rights Era." In *A Long Way to Go: Conversations about Race with African American Faculty and Graduate Students*. Darrell Cleaveland, ed. New York: Peter Lang Publishers.

Sniderman, Paul, and Thomas Piazza. 2002. *Black Pride and Black Prejudice*. Princeton, N.J.: Princeton University Press.

Sochor, Zenovia A. 1988. *Revolution and Culture: The Bogdanov-Lenin Controversy*. Ithaca, N.Y.: Cornell University Press.

Solomos, John. 1989. *Race and Racism in Contemporary Britain*. Houndmills: Macmillan.

Sowell, Thomas. 1984. *Civil Rights: Rhetoric or Reality?* New York: William Morrow.

Spillers, Hortense. 1987. "Mama's Baby, Papa's Maybe: An American Grammar Book." *Diacritics* 17 (Summer): 65–81.

———. 1994. "The Crisis of the Negro Intellectual: A Post-Date." *Boundary 2* 21 (3): 65–116.

Stavenhagen, Rodolfo. 1996. *Ethnic Conflicts and the Nation-State*. New York: St. Martin's.

Steele, Shelby. 1990. *The Content of Our Character: A New Vision of Race in America*. New York: St. Martin's.

Stoler, Ann Laura. 1997. "Racial Histories and Their Regimes of Truth." In *Political Power and Social Theory* 11, 183–206. London: JAI.

Strauss, Leo. 1976. Comments on Carl Schmitt's Der Bergriff des Politischen. In *The Concept of the Political* Carl Schmitt, 82–87. New Brunswick, N.J.: Rutgers University Press.

Stuckey, P. Sterling. 1994. *Going through the Storm: The Influence of African American Art in History*. Oxford: Oxford University Press.

Swain, Carole. 2002. *The New White Nationalism in America: Its Challenge to Integration*. Cambridge: Cambridge University Press.

Taiwo, Femi. 1996. "Of Citizens and Citizenship." *Tempo* (September/October): Lagos, Nigeria.

Tamahori, Lee, director. 1995. *Once Were Warriors*. Los Angeles: Fine Line Features.

Tavares, Julio Cesar, Dança da Guerra: Arquivo-Arma. (Dissertaçao de Mestrado) Brasília: Departmento de Ciências Socias, Universidade de Brasília.

Taylor, Charles. 1977. "Interpretation and the Sciences of Man." In *Understanding and Social Inquiry*, ed. Fred Dallmayr and Thomas McCarthy, 101–131. Notre Dame, Ind.: University of Notre Dame Press.

Taylor, Clyde R. 1998. *The Mask of Art: Breaking the Aesthetic Contract*. Bloomington: Indiana University Press.

The Black Public Sphere Collective. 1995. *The Black Public Sphere: A Public Culture Book*. Edited by The Black Public Sphere Collective. Chicago: University of Chicago Press.

Thernstrom, Stephen, and Abigail Thernstrom. 1999. *America in Black and White*. New York: Simon & Schuster.

Thompson, E. P. 1971. The Moral Economy of the English Crowd in the Eighteenth Century. *Past & Present* 50: 76–136.

Thompson, Robert Farris. 1984. *Flash of the Spirit: African and Afro-American Art and Philosophy*. New York: Vintage.

Thorne, Eva. 2004. Land Rights and Garifuna Identity. *NACLA Report on the Americas* (September/October): 21–25.

Thornton, John. 1992. *Africans and Africa in the Making of the Atlantic World, 1400–1680*. Cambridge: Cambridge University Press.

Tilly, Charles. 1991. "Domination, Resistance, Compliance . . . Discourse." *Sociological Forum* 6 no. 3 (September): 593–602.

Todorov, Tzvetan. 1984. *The Conquest of America: The Question of the Other*. New York: Harper & Row.

Trilling, Lionel. 1957. *The Liberal Imagination: Essays on Literature and Society*. New York: Doubleday Anchor.
Trouillot, Michel-Rolph. 1995. *Silencing the Past: Power and the Production of History*. Boston: Beacon Press.
Truman, David. 1971. *The Governmental Process: Political Interests and Public Opinion*. New York: Knopf.
Turner, Mark. 1999. *From Two Republics to One Divided: Considerations of Postcolonial Nationmaking in Andean Peru*. Durham, N.C.: Duke University Press.
Turner, Victor, and Edward Bruner, eds. 1986. *Anthropology of Experience*. Champaign: University of Illinois Press.
Tyson, Timothy. 1999. *Radio Free Dixie: Robert F. Williams and the Roots of Black Power*. Chapel Hill: The University of North Carolina Press.
Van Peebles, Melvin, director. 1971. *Sweet Sweetback's Badasssss Song*. Magnum Entertainment.
Varga, Joao Costa. 2003. The Inner City and the Favela: Transnational Black Politics. *Race and Class* 44 (4): 19–40.
Vasconcelos, José. 1948. *La Raza Cósmica: Misión de la Raza Iberoamericana, Argentina y Brasil*. México City: Espasa-Calpe Mexicana.
Veloso, Caetano. 2000. Orpheus, Rising from Caricature. *New York Times*. August 20.
Viotti da Costa, Emilia. 1997. *Crowns of Glory, Tears of Blood: The Demerara Slave Rebellion of 1823*. New York: Oxford University Press.
Von Eschen, Penny. 1997. *Race against Empire: Black Americans and Anticolonialism 1937–1957*. Ithaca, N.Y.: Cornell University Press.
———. 2004. *Satchmo Blows Up the World: Jazz, Race and Empire During the Cold War*. Cambridge, Mass.: Harvard University Press.
Wade, Peter. 1993. *Blackness and Race Mixture: The Dynamics of Racial Identity in Colombia*. Baltimore, Md.: Johns Hopkins University Press.
———. 1997. *Race and Ethnicity in Latin America*. Chicago: Pluto.
———.2000. *Music, Race, and Nation: Música Tropical in Columbia*. Chicago: University of Chicago Press.
———.2004. "Images of Latin American *Mestizaje* and the Politics of Comparison." *Bulletin of Latin American Research* 23 (3): 355–366.
Walker, David. 2000. *David Walker's Appeal to the Coloured Citizens of the World*. Peter Hinks, ed. University Park: Pennsylvania State University Press.
Walzer, Michael. 1988. *The Company of Critics: Social Criticism and Political Communication in the Twentieth Century*. New York: Basic.
Warner, Michael. 1999. *The Trouble with Normal: Sex, Politics, and the Ethics of Queer Life*. Cambridge, Mass.: Harvard University Press.
Warren, Kenneth. 2003. *So Black and Blue: Ralph Ellison and the Occasion of Criticism*. Chicago: University of Chicago Press.
Watts, Jerry. 1994. *Heroism and the Black Intellectual: Ralph Ellison, Politics, and Afro-American Intellectual Life*. Chapel Hill: The University of North Carolina Press.
Weheliye, Alexander. 2003. "I Am I Be: The Subject of Sonic Afro Modernity." *Boundary 2* 30 (2): 97–114.

West, Cornel. 1989. *The American Evasion of Philosophy: A Genealogy of Pragmatism*. Madison: University of Wisconsin Press.

———. 1993. *Prophetic Fragments: Illumination of the Crisis in American Relations and Culture*. Grand Rapids, Mich.: William B. Eerdmans.

———. 1993–94. "The Dilemma of the Black Intellectual." *The Journal of Blacks in Higher Education*, no. 2/Winter, 59–67.

———. 1994. *Race Matters*. New York: Vintage.

———. 2002. *Prophecy Deliverance: An African American Revolutionary Christianity*. Louisville, Ky.: Westminster John Knox.

Wiegman, Robyn. 1995. *American Anatomies: Theorizing Race and Gender*. Durham, N.C.: Duke University Press.

Wildavsky, Aaron. 1998. *Federalism and Political Culture*. David Schleicher and Brendon Swedlow, eds. New Brunswick, N.J.: Transaction.

———. 1998. *Culture and Social Theory*. Sun-Ki Chai and Brendon Swedlow, eds. New Brunswick, N.J.: Transaction.

Winant, Howard. 2001. *The World Is a Ghetto: Race and Democracy since World War II*. New York: Basic Books.

Wolfe, Patrick. 2001. "Land, Labor, and Difference: Elementary Structures of Race." *The American Historical Review* 106 (June): 866–905.

Williams, Brackette. 1991. *Stains on My Name, War in My Veins: Guyana and the Politics of Cultural Struggle*. Durham, N.C.: Duke University Press.

Williams, Raymond. 1961. *The Long Revolution*. New York: Columbia University Press.

———. 1977. *Marxism and Literature*. Oxford: Oxford University Press.

———. 1983. *The Year 2000*. New York: Pantheon.

Wolin, Sheldon. 1969. "Political Theory as a Vocation." *American Political Science Review* 63, no. 4 (December): 1062–1082.

Wolpe, Harold. 1988. *Race, Class, and the Apartheid State*. London: Currey.

Womack, John. 1969. *Zapata and the Mexican Revolution*. New York: Knopf.

Wood, Davida. 1993. "Politics of Identity in a Palestinian Village in Israel." In *The Violence Within: Cultural and Political Opposition in Divided Nations*. Kay B. Warren, ed., 87–122. Boulder, Colo.: Westview.

Wood, Joe, ed. 1992. *Malcolm X: In Our Own Image*. New York: St. Martin's.

Wynter, Sylvia. 1994. "The Ceremony Must Be Found: After Humanism." *Boundary 2* (Spring/Fall): 19–70.

Young, Crawford. 1976. *The Politics of Cultural Pluralism*. Madison: University of Wisconsin Press.

Young, Robert. 1990. *White Mythologies: Writing History and the West*. London: Routledge.

Zaller, John. 1992. *The Nature and Origins of Mass Opinion*. Cambridge: Cambridge University Press.

Zerilli, Linda. 2005. *Feminism and the Abyss of Freedom*. Chicago: University of Chicago Press.

INDEX

Africology, 89–96, 226
Afro-Centrism, 18, 74, 80, 85–96, 119
Agamben, Giorgio, 49, 157–58, 173 (*see also* exception, state of)
aggregation. See coagulate politics
AIDS, 4, 21, 96, 238
Ali, Muhammad, 136, 147
Allen, Robert, 73
Althusser, Louis, 26
anti-Semitism, 92, 94–95, 165, 203–4
Appiah, K. Anthony, 109
Apt, John, 137
Aptheker, Herbert, 32, 59, 137
Arendt, Hannah, 26, 45–47
Argentina, 60, 78, 144, 215
Aristide, Jean-Bertrand, 230, 234
Aristotle, 101
Asante, Molefi, 88–89, 94
Australia, 49, 59
Austro-Marxism, 240–49 (*see also* Marxism)
aversion, 34, 88, 101–2, 105–30, 210

Baca, Susannah, 146
Baker, Ella, 135
Baldwin, James, 78–83
Balibar, Étienne, 203, 217
Bataille, Georges, 26
Beckford, George, 149
Beissinger, Mark, 66
Benedict, Ruth, 189
Berube, Michael, 136–38, 142–45, 148

Biondi, Martha, 137
biopower. See Foucault, Michel
Birmingham, Alabama, 48–50, 62–63
black ideologies 17–18, 69–75, 83–102, 106, 233 (*see also* black life-worlds)
black internationalism
    and activism, 19–21, 145, 247–48
    and cultural identity, 71–72, 213, 238–41
    and macropolitics, 218, 222–30, 249–61
    and miscegenation, 185–86, 220
black life-worlds, 6–8, 69, 223–24, 228–32, 256
Black Panthers, 31, 82, 84, 86
Black Power movement, 7–9, 46–47, 143, 212
black public intellectuals, 19, 133–53, 225, 238–40
black public opinion, 74–78, 87–89, 97–99, 102
Boas, Franz, 189
Bobbio, Noberto, 26
Bogle, Paul, 225
Boston, 62, 85
boycotts, 12, 62, 121, 128 (*see also* Birmingham, Alabama)
Boynton, Robert, 136–37
Brazil
    and macropolitics, 255–61
    mixed-races in, 185, 189, 192–96, 218–19

319

Brazil (*continued*)
  and pluralism, 211–12
  political mobilization in, 3–7, 71–72, 227, 230–32
  racial violence in, 15, 49
Brechtian resistance, 33–34, 38–43, 57–58, 65 (*see also* quotidian politics)
Briggs, Asa, 86
Britain, 71–72, 216
Brown, H. Rap, 50
Brown, James, 252–54
Brown, John, 111, 113
Brubaker, Rogers, 165, 174
Burke, Kenneth, 243
Bush, George W., 129, 231, 254

Calhoun, John, 111, 113
Callier, Terry, 50–52
Canada, 7, 66
Canetti, Elias, 42
Cardoso, Fernando Henrique, 5
Carens, Joseph, 66, 117
Carpentier, Alejo, 144, 155
Casswell, Harold, 75
Castoriadis, Cornelius, 26
Certeau, Michel de, 34, 39–43
Cervantes, 205
Charles, Ray, 28
Chesinard, Joanne, 63
Chile, 52–54, 60, 78
China, 15, 192
Chung, Erin, 109
Cleaver, Eldridge, 28, 50, 78–83
coagulation (coagulate politics)
  and literature, 155–58
  and quotidian resistance, 57–60, 64–67, 234–35
  as related to aggregation, 33–44
  and violence, 44–50
Cohen, Cathy, 225, 229
Colombia, 214–15
Converse, Philip, 69, 74–75, 84–85
Cooke, Marvel, 135, 137–38
Cose, Ellis, 113
Crouch, Stanley, 137

Cruse, Harold, 238–39
Cuba, 144–146, 154, 185, 202–9, 212–19
Curtin, Philip, 90–92, 94

Dadaism, 240
Dahl, Robert, 62, 118
Dalton, Roque, 144, 149
Davidson, Basil, 91–92, 94
Davis, Angela, 84, 248
Davis, Ben, 137
Dawson, Michael, 18, 98
Debord, Guy, 152
Debray, Regis, 45
Delaney, Martin, 138
Delgado, Martín Morúa, 205
Diallo, Amadou, 51
Diop, Alioune, 236–38, 247–48, 250
displacement. *See* parallel politics
Doctorow, E. L., 19, 155–58, 160–63, 166–79
Douglass, Frederick, 46–48, 73, 100–1, 138, 190
Du Bois, W. E. B., 8, 84–86, 138, 146, 183–87
Drake, St. Clair, 94
Drylongso, 120–21
Durkheim, Emile, 84

Ecuador, 144
Ellison, Ralph, 144, 168
Elster, Jon, 117
Emerson, Ralph Waldo, 190
ethico-political, 18, 21, 108, 118–21 (see also Gramsci, Antonio)
evil, concept of, 76–78, 81
exception, state of, 19, 49, 157, 173

Fanon, Franz, 22, 45–50, 145, 203, 248
Faria, Rabella de, 231,
Fields, Barbara, 195
Ford, Henry, 179
Foucault, Michel, 45–48, 122, 141, 174, 263
France, 108, 112, 174–75, 212, 216–17
Fraser, Nancy, 151

Frazier, E. Franklin, 84
Fredrickson, George, 44, 217–18
Freudianism, 76, 81
Freyre, Gilberto, 185, 189, 192–93
Fryer, Roland, 125
de la Fuente, Alejandro, 201–3, 206, 208
Furnivall, John, 210 (*see also* pluralism)

Garnet, Henry Highland
   and hermeneutics, 100–1
   and hybridity, 109, 183–88, 196, 220–23
   and ideologies of racial egalitarianism, 20, 77
Garvey, Marcus (Garveyism), 9, 66, 84–86, 138, 232
Gates Jr., Henry Louis, 137
Geertz, Clifford, 56, 237
Germany, 49, 71, 108, 174–75, 215–17
Ghana, 196
Gilman, Sander, 80
Gilroy, Paul, 228–29, 262
Girvan, Norman, 149
Glaude, Eddie, 74
Goldberg, David Theo, 109
Gouldner, Alvin, 72
Gramsci, Antonio, 16–17, 84, 244–47, 257
Greene, Graham, 155
Guatemala, 144
Guevara, Che, 228
Guiliani, Rudolph, 51

Habermas, Jürgen, 129
Haiti, 147, 188, 196, 205, 219
Hale, Charles, 214
half-breed. *See* mulatto
half-caste. *See* mulatto
Hall, Stuart, 26, 150, 184
Hamer, Fannie Lou, 135
Harris, Frederick, 122
Harris, Marvin, 12
Hatcher, Richard, 232
Hayek, Friedrich, 26
Hegelianism, 13, 32, 84, 145, 164

hermeneutics, 18, 99–102
Herskovits, Melville, 189
Hobbes, Thomas, 147, 163
Hofstadter, Richard, 96
Hollinger, David, 190–95
hooks, bell, 133, 137, 145, 149
Horne, Gerald, 137
Howe, Stephen, 89
Hunter, Floyd, 118
Hurston, Zora Neale, 189
hybridity
   and antiracist practice, 185–87, 200
   and ideology, 214–20 (*see also* miscegenation)
   in Latin America, 188–95
   and pluralism, 209–13

ideology, 72–84, 87–111, 201–19, 257–61 (*see also* Nkrumah, Kwame)
India, 66, 192–93, 211
Indonesia, 211
infrapolitics. *See* Scott, James
intention, 230
Ireland, 215
Israel, 94
issue publics. *See* Converse, Philip
Iton, Richard, 229

Jackson, Matthew, 125
Jackson, Sr., Jesse, 138
Jacoby, Russell, 137, 152
Jamaica, 44, 66, 85–86, 144, 205
James, C. L. R., 16, 32, 59–60, 103, 144–46
Japan, 112
Jefferson, Thomas, 15, 188
Jessop, Bob, 150
Jewish intellectuals, 134, 136–39, 146, 149
Johnson, Paul, 217
Judy, Ronald, 225

Kabila, Joseph, 228
Kafka, Franz, 155
Kantianism, 32, 41, 164
Kantorowicz, Ernst, 157

Karenga, Malauna, 85–86, 93
Kelley, Robin, 16, 44, 55–66, 140, 229
Kelly, Ned, 49
Kenyatta, Jomo, 50
Kerry, John, 134
King, Martin Luther, 73, 135, 167, 234, 250–53
Kirkpatrick, Jeanne, 142
Kilson, Martin, 139
Kitt, Eartha, 136
Klu Klux Klan, 78
Kohlhaas, Michael. *See* Von Kleist, Heinrich
Kutzninski, Vera, 208
Kwame Nkrumah Ideologial Institutes. *See* Nkrumah, Kwame
Kwanzaa, 73, 84–85, 87, 93
Kymlicka, Will, 66, 127

Laclau, Ernesto, 39
Lane, Robert, 74–78, 81–83, 85
Lee, Spike, 240
Lefebvre, Henri, 16, 26, 28
Lefkowitz, Mary, 89
Leninism, 4–5, 26, 242
Lindblom, Charles, 26
Little Rock, Arkansas, 76
Locke, Alain, 146
Loury, Glenn, 140
Lubiano, Wahneema, 225
Lukács, Georg, 244–47
Luther, Martin, 165–67

macropolitics,
  and black public intellectuals, 135, 139, 144–48, 152–53
  and black transnationalism, 17, 21, 223–30, 255–58, 261
  and coagulation, 34–38, 55–62, 65–67, 234–36
  and cultural practice, 15, 50–55, 229, 251–56
  and literature, 19, 51–52, 154–57, 174–80
Malcom X, 48, 77, 135, 167, 235

Mali, 7
Mandela, Nelson, 9, 227
Manley, Michael, 86
Manley, Norman, 86
Mannheim, Karl, 32, 69, 82–84, 87
Márquez, Gabriel García, 169
Martí, José, 185, 188, 204, 208
Marxism, 25–26, 98–99, 225–26 (*see also* Austro-Marxism)
Mayfield, Julian, 63
McAdam, Doug, 35
McClintock, Anne, 46
Memmi, Albert, 50, 248
Menchú, Rigoberta, 149, 151
Mendes, Chico, 149
metapolitics, 240–48
Methodism. *See* Wolin, Sheldon.
Metis. *See* Scott, James.
México, 122, 185, 215
micropolitics, 16–22, 31–35, 56–59, 65–67, 234
Mill, John Stuart, 99, 145
Minh, Ho Chi, 46, 50
miscegenation, 183–90, 197–200, 209, 213
Mitchell, Timothy, 44, 184
Morejón, Nancy, 146
Moten, Fred, 225
Moynihan, Daniel Patrick, 142
Muhammad, Elijah, 73
mulatto, 139, 196, 204, 216–19 (*see also* miscegenation)

Nancy, Jean Luc, 263
Nation of Islam, 61, 77–78, 82–83
Nazis, 78, 173, 199, 217
Neal, Larry, 239–41, 250–53
Negritude, 92, 232–33, 249
Neruda, Pablo, 50–55, 253–54
Netherlands, the, 15, 49, 216, 231
New World, the
  anti-black racism and, 204–6
  expressions of dissent in, 50–55
  hybridity in, 191, 195, 215–16
  intelligentsia of, 145–50, 185–87

New York City, 51–52, 136–39, 152
New Zealand, 49, 59, 112
Nietzsche, Friedrich, 101
Nigeria, 60, 154, 211
Nixon, Richard, 52–55
Nkrumah, Kwame, 93, 242, 249

Obama, Barack, 138
Olaniyan, Tejumola, 225
Ortiz, Fernando, 204–05
Outlaw, Lucius, 89
Oxaal, Ivar, 210

Pagden, Anthony, 206
Padmore, George, 93
Palmié, Stephan, 218
Pan-Africanism and Pan Africanist, 9, 84–86, 232–33, 236–41, 249–50 (*see also* Garvey, Marcus)
parallel politics, 50–54, 57–59, 155 (*see also* quotidian politics)
Pasternak, Boris, 155
Payne, Charles, 63
Paz, Octavio, 21, 149
Pelé, 147
Penn, Sean, 142
Perú, 55, 71
Pettit, Phillip, 27
Phillips, Wendell, 190
Piazza, Thomas, 87–97, 118
Pinochet, Augusto, 54
Piper, Adrian M. S., 122
pluralism, 110, 210–13, 247
poaching. *See* Certeau, Michel de
political community, 6–12, 18–22, 103–26, 224–30, 235–63
Pozzuole, 197–99, 209
Pratt, Mary Louise, 209

quilombos (quilombismo), 49 (*see also* Brazil, political mobilization in)
quotidian politics
 and aversion, 102–14, 127
 and coagulation, 33–44, 65–67
 and displacement, 50–55, 58–60
 and nonviolent resistance 31–32, 36–44, 49–50, 55–67
 the theorization of, 16, 28–68, 235
 and violence, 44–50

racial valuation, 187, 192, 211–213, 217, 220
Randolph, A. Phillip, 84, 86
Reed, Adolph, 137, 139–45, 229, 251
Ricardo, David, 244
Ricoeur, Paul, 252
Rivers, Eugene, 140
Robeson, Paul, 136–37
Robinson, Cedric, 145
Rodney, Walter, 146, 148–49, 235
Roemer, John, 63
Rogin, Michael Paul, 152
Rorty, Amelie Oksenberg, 122
Rosaldo, Renato, 255
Rousseau, Jean-Jacques, 145
Rout, Leslie, 203, 214
Rudolph, Lloyd, 12
Rudolph, Suzanne, 12
Rushdie, Salman, 154

Sadiq, Kamal, 30
Said, Edward, 151
Sartre, Jean-Paul, 45–46, 222
Schmitt, Carl, 13–15, 32, 157, 173–74 (*see also* exception, state of)
Schutz, Alfred. *See* black life-worlds
Scott, David, 225
Scott, Dred, 225
Scott, James, 16, 33, 41, 55–66, 102
self-hatred, concept of, 80–82, 88
Senghor, Leopold, 94
sensibilities, 21–24
Sharpton, Al, 135, 148
Shelton, Nicole, 104
Sherriff, Robin, 194
Silva, Luis Ignacio Lula da, 3–4
Simpson, O. J., 102
Skidmore, Thomas, 195, 217
Smith, Adam, 99, 244
Sniderman, Paul, 87–97, 118

social realism, German, 240
Solzhenitsyn, Alexandr, 155
South Africa, 44–46, 108, 173, 208, 258
Southern Christian Leadership Conference, 9, 78
Soviet Union, 66, 154, 184, 225, 248 (*see also* Marxism)
Sowell, Thomas, 137
Stoler, Ann Laura, 209, 217
Strauss, Leo, 14
surrealism, 240

tacit political knowledge, 126–28
Tarrow, Sidney, 35
Taylor, Charles, 56, 66, 99–100, 127–28
temporality, 75
Third Reich, 15, 215
Thomas, Clarence, 15
Thompson, E. P., 57, 59
Thurmond, Strom, 15
Touré, Sékou, 93, 249–51
transnationalism. *See* black internationalism
Trinidad, 144, 146, 205, 210
Truth, Sojourner, 100, 138
Tully, James, 127–28
Turner, Frederick Jackson, 190
Turner, Nat, 101
Turner, Victor, 255
Tuskegee experiments, 97, 109

Underground Railroad, 100
United Nations Security Council, 30
Unknown Slaves (US), 31, 86

Vanderlei, José María, 3, 5, 7, 256
Vasconcelos, José, 185, 192–93, 204

Venezuela, 20, 144, 215, 219
Von Kleist, Heinrich, 19, 155–61, 163–69, 172–79

Wade, Peter, 214
Walker, Coalhouse. *See* Doctorow, E. L.
Walker, David, 101
Wallerstein, Immanuel, 217
Walzer, Michael, 152
Washington, Booker T., 166
Wells Barnet, Ida B., 73, 101
West, Cornel, 74, 133, 140, 145, 149
Wheatley, Phillis, 140
Whitman, Walt, 53–54
Wildavsky, Aaron, 12
Wilkerson, Doxie, 137
Williams, Eric, 149
Williams, Raymond, 12, 26
Williams, Robert, 50, 63
Wilson, August, 240
Winant, Howard, 195
Wittgenstein, Ludwig, 21
Wolffe, Patrick, 217
Wolin, Sheldon, 56, 97–98
Wong, David, 122
Workers' Party, 3–5, 31
World War II, 108, 236
Wright, Richard, 145
Wynter, Sylvia, 263

Young, Robert, 244
Yu, Henry, 195

Zaller, John, 69
Zerilli, Linda, 64
Zimbabwe, 17, 173, 230
Zoot Suit Riots, 48, 61